CONSTITUTIONAL RIGHTS AND POWERS
OF THE PEOPLE

CONSTITUTIONAL RIGHTS AND POWERS OF THE PEOPLE

Wayne D. Moore

PRINCETON UNIVERSITY PRESS   PRINCETON, NEW JERSEY

Copyright © 1996 by Princeton University Press
Published by Princeton University Press, 41 William Street,
Princeton, New Jersey 08540
In the United Kingdom: Princeton University Press,
Chichester, West Sussex
All Rights Reserved

Library of Congress Cataloging-in-Publication Data

Moore, Wayne D.
Constitutional rights and powers of the people / Wayne D. Moore.
p. cm.
Includes bibliographical references and index.
ISBN 0-691-01111-7
ISBN 0-691-00244-4 (pbk.)
1. United States—Constitutional law—Interpretation and
construction.   2. People (Constitutional law)—United States.
3. United States—Constitutional history   4. Political rights—
United States.   I. Title
KF4552.M66   1996
323'.0973—dc20   95-52897
CIP

This book has been composed in Sabon

Princeton University Press books are printed on acid-free paper
and meet the guidelines for permanence and durability of the
Committee on Production Guidelines for Book Longevity of the
Council on Library Resources

Second printing, and first paperback printing, 1998

http://pup.princeton.edu

Printed in the United States of America

3   5   7   9   10   8   6   4   2

To Mary

Contents

Figures

_____ *Preface* _____

THIS BOOK has moved far from its origins. Although I have continued to pursue my original objectives, my efforts to achieve those objectives have led me in directions I could not have foreseen when I started. My hope is that this work will lead its readers through similar transformations. It is appropriate to place this challenge at the outset: Like the Constitution, this book invites its readers to see new things, and to see familiar things in new ways.

Much of the analysis is relatively abstract. In addition, the rhetoric is distinctive, the reasoning complex. Gaining access requires active engagement. These are peculiar demands of constitutional interpretation, not just this book. It is possible to avoid these demands, along with the opportunities they offer. But they are worth confronting.

I have come to understand that writing this book has been an exercise in constitutional citizenship, not only professional scholarship. I have learned the importance of commitment to principles of American constitutionalism by citizens as well as government officials. Many who read this book will probably do so primarily for scholarly and professional reasons. These are good reasons, but there are others of equal importance. This study offers insights into roles that various persons— members of "the people" and those who presume to act on their behalf— may play in creating and re-creating the law of the Constitution.

Contexts are important. The ones surrounding me as I have worked on this project have doubtless influenced the finished product. It would not have been possible without much support—scholarly, financial, personal, spiritual.

I am not the first to acknowledge Walter F. Murphy's role in creating and sustaining unique conditions for the study of public law at Princeton University. It has been a blessing to be mentored by such a gracious man and exemplary scholar. Alas, his retirement leaves voids that cannot be filled.

I have also been profoundly affected by William F. Harris II, Sotirios Barber, Robert George, Amy Gutmann, Dennis Thompson, Sheldon Wolin, and others who guided and enriched my graduate studies. Harris in particular has given me valuable encouragement at crucial stages, offered constructive criticism, and challenged me to deepen my theoretical insights. My intellectual debts to him are unmistakable.

I presented early versions of my analysis at the 1989 annual meeting of the American Political Science Association, and chapters were presented at the 1993 and 1994 meetings and a 1995 conference on constitutional politics at Princeton University. I appreciate the questions and comments of discussants, fellow panelists, and other participants. In addition to serving these roles, Mark Brandon, Judy Failer, and Sue Hemberger have otherwise exemplified virtues of scholarly citizenship by commenting on my work, suggesting research leads, and sharing in the life of the mind. Noah Pickus and Phil Jordon have also provided me with welcome opportunities to explore problems of political theory and American constitutionalism.

Christopher L. Eisgruber, Paul Finkelman, Karen M. Hult, Sanford Levinson, Stephen K. White, and an anonymous reviewer for Princeton University Press have asked probing questions at various stages, pressed me to be clearer, challenged me to make the analysis better cohere, and otherwise offered valuable assistance. I have been made acutely aware of how much remains to be done, even as I seek some measure of closure for a project that fundamentally defies it.

I doubtless approach the Constitution (and the world more generally) differently as a result of my undergraduate studies and legal training. Thanks to Henry Abraham and Dick Howard in particular for nurturing my formative interests in constitutional law and politics and for their continuing support.

As the University of Virginia and Princeton University have offered stimulating learning environments, the University of Vermont and Virginia Tech have provided hospitable teaching and research environments and other forms of assistance. My students have given me fresh perspectives toward constitutional politics, helped me to understand problems with my analysis, and reinforced my commitment to liberal education.

A number of persons at Princeton University Press—including Malcolm DeBevoise, Beth Gianfagna, Malcolm Litchfield, and Heidi Sheehan—have provided excellent editorial and production assistance, as has Roy Thomas. I also appreciate Gordon Miller's help in preparing the five figures that appear in this book.

My father did not live to see this book's publication. But without his support, along with my mother's, it would never have been started, much less completed. May this book honor both my parents, along with the God of forgiveness.

Mary Irwin Moore has shared in my many joys and struggles, supporting my aspirations and helping me to confront the challenges. In her art and her faith, she exemplifies a life of commitment. I dedicate this book to her.

CONSTITUTIONAL RIGHTS AND POWERS
OF THE PEOPLE

Reconceiving Constitutional Politics

We the People of the United States . . . do ordain and
establish this Constitution for the United States of
America.[1]

PREDOMINANT MODELS of American constitutionalism are blind to many
of its distinctive attributes. Constitutional politics in the United States
extends beyond the practice of judges enforcing fundamental norms made
in the past or creating new ones to deal with changed circumstances. It is
also a function of commitments and actions within the polity at large.
Creating and maintaining constitutional meaning and authority are ongoing and normal processes, not periodic or extraordinary. American
constitutionalism is fundamentally organic, not inert. The law of the land
is richly textured, not capable of being reduced to either-or propositions
of the sort that drive constitutional litigation.

One may compare conventional models of constitutionalism in the
United States to viewing aerial photographs. The pictures identify boundaries between land and sea. In the case of the Constitution, the boundaries are between rights of the people and governmental powers. Constitutional decision-making consists of judges interpreting the snapshots
and making sure those engaged in "politics" do not cross normative
boundaries established during periodic bursts of higher lawmaking.

The pictures fail to capture incremental changes, layers, height, and
depth. As soil holds water and there is land beneath the sea, governmental
powers and popular rights overlap and mix together—often in a mutually
sustaining manner. Events on the surface of constitutional rhetoric obscure underlying elements of law. Dichotomies are inadequate to account
for the land's rich texture: gradations of constitutional meaning and authority, with complex configurations of political power. As riverbanks
direct the course of water to the sea, constitutional structures channel
popular choices. These movements both cause erosion and leave behind
deposits. As water comes from and returns to the sea, activities of American constitutionalism are ongoing and cyclical processes which intersect
variously and at different stages with choices by "the people" and their

---

[1] U.S. Constitution, preamble.

representatives. There are elements of continuity as the more solid structures gain reinforcement and resist change. Yet much of the constitutional landscape is dynamic. Waves, currents, strata, and fissures may not be perceptible from a distance, but they are powerful forces.

There have been substantial costs associated with narrowness of vision. As constitutional interpretation has been filtered through forms of adjudication, broader dimensions of American constitutionalism have remained largely unexplored. False distinctions between "law" and "politics" have blocked awareness of how constitutional meaning and authority have evolved through ordinary processes. Efforts to defend particular conceptions of constitutional meaning have obscured understanding of how America's fundamental law depends on large measures of openness and tentativeness rather than closure or rigidity. Excessive preoccupation with the roles of judges within the constitutional system has distorted analysis of actions taken and options available to other governmental officials and to citizens.

More is at stake than the adequacy of academic scholarship. The rhetoric of constitutional law forms a prominent component of political practices in the United States. Insofar as those practices are distorted by artificially narrow conceptions of constitutional politics, a broader vision may direct attention toward options available in practice. At issue is not simply how judges exercise their powers but also how other governmental officials and the people at large deliberate and act with reference to the law of the Constitution.

Continuing the analogy just suggested, constitutional scholars need to do more than probe the surface and take pictures from additional angles. They need to radically rethink the character of American constitutionalism and their roles within the polity. They may do more than serve the judges who are trying to describe the landscape. They should start addressing those who are creating, maintaining, and eroding the law of the land through the disparate practices that shape its terrain.

Judges alone cannot sustain the conditions of constitutional government. It is imperative that others understand options available to them, along with constraints they may encounter. In this connection, the past may offer examples of practices to emulate or avoid. But the Constitution's continuing viability depends on choices by the people at large and those who represent them in various capacities. Constitutional politics involves more than taking and interpreting snapshots. Reorientations in thinking are necessary.

I

American constitutionalism rests on premises of popular sovereignty. According to its preamble, the United States Constitution depends on the foundational political authority of "the people of the United States." They are its purported authors. In addition, one of the Constitution's self-proclaimed objectives is to secure the "blessings of liberty" to "the people" and their "posterity." The text establishes governmental institutions and empowers them to act on behalf of "the people." It also enumerates rights of "the people" and prohibits the denial or disparagement of other rights "retained by the people." The tenth amendment refers to "powers" reserved to "the people." Article V's mechanisms for constitutional amending may be understood as endorsing participation by "the people" and their immediate representatives in constitutional revision.

But despite the centrality of the concept of popular sovereignty within the rhetoric of American constitutionalism, there remain serious questions about how "the people" and their "rights" and "powers" fit within the constitutional design. Judges, legislative and executive officials, scholars, and other individuals continue to disagree, for example, about who is included among "the people," how they are politically configured, and what characterizes their identity or identities. Competing positions on these issues complement distinctive approaches to analyzing how "the people" may act through constitutional forms and independently of them—including to support, challenge, or revise the Constitution and institutions established or affirmed by it.

In order to clarify these issues and their implications for studying foundational attributes of American constitutionalism and problems of practical politics, this book examines competing conceptions of "the people" and their "rights" and "powers." My objectives extend beyond interpreting particular parts of the Constitution or reaching definitive conclusions of legal validity or invalidity.[2] Instead, my analysis underscores the open-ended and richly textured character of American constitutionalism.

I confront four main sets of problems surrounding the concept of popular sovereignty. First, who is included among "the people"? This question is important to identifying the political body or bodies upon whose authority the United States Constitution purports to rest. Dealing with this

---

[2] This work began as a study of the ninth and tenth amendments' references to unspecified "rights" and "powers" of "the people." The ninth amendment provides: "The enumeration in the Constitution of certain rights, shall not be construed to deny or disparage others retained by the people." The tenth declares: "The powers not delegated to the United States by the Constitution, nor prohibited to it by the States, are reserved to the States respectively, or to the people."
My primary concern has been to study general problems of constitutional meaning, authority, and structure raised by these open-ended provisions, not to focus on the amendments as such. My research has led me further away from examining these two parts of the constitutional text, but this book continues to deal with interpretive problems linked to them. In addition, I draw on these two amendments and materials relating to them insofar as they contribute to analyzing the problems at issue. But this book emphatically is *not* a narrow exercise in specific textual interpretation.

question is also integral to analyzing who holds the "rights" and "powers" established and secured by constitutional forms.

Second, how are "the people" politically configured? Various parts of the Constitution and a range of interpretive precedents support four main positions. One may reasonably conceive of "the people" as forming one nation, as members of the respective states, as parts of other communities and associations, and as having separate constitutional identities as individuals. These organizing principles correspond to distinctive conceptions of popular sovereignty and support complementary conceptions of constitutional prerogatives.

Third, how may "the people" act? Leading candidates for principles of action include unanimity, super-majoritarianism, simple-majoritarianism, by groups or other associations, and on an individual basis. There are crosscutting distinctions between deliberative choices and expressions of more momentary inclinations, along with problems of normative coherence. At issue are ideals of equality, principles of representation, problems of political feasibility, and relationships between the Constitution and extrinsic norms (such as moral principles).

Fourth, how do "the people" and their constitutional prerogatives relate to governmental institutions and other representative structures? Parts of the constitutional design reflect a premise that "the people" have an identity or identities antecedent to and independent of constitutional norms. Other parts of the Constitution support a position that "the people" gain new identities—are reconstituted—by the creation and maintenance of fundamental law. Overlapping these positions are questions about whether "the people" may act through representative structures and/or independently of them, and there are further questions about whether governmental institutions limit and/or provide security for rights and powers of the people. At issue are the character and scope of constitutional norms and the structures they create and sustain. Combinations and permutations of the competing positions have profound normative and practical implications.

Several parts of the constitutional text and a number of interpretive precedents contribute distinctively to analyzing these four sets of problems. The preamble and articles V and VII inform analysis of how "the people" may act to establish and change constitutional norms. These parts of the constitutional text, along with the ninth and tenth amendments, also offer bridges for exploring connections between norms intrinsic and extrinsic to the constitutional enterprise. These two amendments also provide lenses for analyzing relationships among constitutional rights and powers of the people and their respective relationships to federal and state governmental powers. In addition, the fourteenth amendment and the other provisions just cited offer further insights into who is included among "the people," how they are politically organized, and how their constitutional rights and powers both limit and depend for their security upon representative structures.

These parts of the text have historic pedigrees and remain at the center of ongoing interpretive practices. Accordingly, it is necessary to analyze issues of constitutional character and structure with reference to actual political developments that have shaped the constitutional landscape. Among other things, precedents set in various contexts confirm the text's ability to accommodate a range of interpretive frameworks. Competing conceptions of the constitutional design have been mutually reinforcing in some respects but have supported radically diverging positions in others. Relationships of complementarity and opposition have each affected the constitutional terrain, yielding multilayered findings.

In addition to shedding light on the Constitution's historic attributes, interpretive precedents identify current options and offer critical perspectives for analyzing and evaluating existing practices. For example, arguments from the founding period that some rights would be beyond the reach of federal powers offer models for thinking about relationships between state powers and rights of reproductive autonomy. Competing conceptions of economic liberties suggest alternative conceptions of relationships between popular rights and governmental powers. Examples of constitutional interpretation by members of Congress, presidents, state officials, and citizens at large are reminders that various persons may play pivotal roles in ongoing constitutional debates. Materials that exemplify distinctive conceptions of constitutional structures reinforce some contemporary arguments and provide vantage points for opposing others.

Acting in pursuance of such objectives, chapters 1 and 2 of this book examine precedents from the antebellum period dealing with questions about who was included among "the people." Chief Justice Roger B. Taney, writing for a fractured majority in *Dred Scott v. Sandford*, presumed that "the people" and "the citizenry" were coextensive. He also argued that blacks were not among "the people," did not have any rights as constitutional "citizens," and thus had no standing to sue in federal courts. Justice Benjamin R. Curtis, dissenting, also conflated citizenship and popular sovereignty. But he argued that the states had authority to treat some but not all black persons as among "the people" or "citizens" whose rights the Constitution secured. These opinions provide access to competing conceptions of formal and participatory citizenship, offer analogous conceptions of "the people," and direct attention toward enduring tensions within the constitutional order.

Frederick Douglass's writings and speeches provide additional points of departure for examining problems of citizenship and popular sovereignty that erupted during the antebellum period. The former slave satisfied neither Taney's nor Curtis's criteria for citizenship—not even after he obtained formal freedom. Yet Douglass made persuasive arguments that he was a "citizen" and a member of "the people" for whom the Constitution had been ordained and established. In addition, he exhibited numerous attributes of active citizenship: He *exercised* many of the "rights" and "powers" that the Constitution affirms as fundamental prerogatives of "the people." Furthermore, he ironically created and re-created constitutional norms through such practices. His example thus underscores a need to account for unofficial along with official creation and interpretation of supreme law. Doing so further emphasizes historic tensions within American constitutionalism and practices it has reinforced or accommodated. Equally important, his assumption of new identities as constitutional author and subject demonstrates extralegal attributes of American constitutionalism.

Materials from the founding period also contribute distinctively to analyzing fundamental elements of the constitutional design. As explained in chapters 3 and 4, debates over the Constitution's ratification and initial amending brought to the surface competing positions on how "the people" may act independently of government and through representative structures. Problems of normative theory overlapped issues of practical politics. Instead of being single-dimensional, the available sources underscore the complexity of relationships among the people at large and institutions of federal and state governance.

Several models of the constitutional order emerge. Of particular importance are four recurring conceptions of relationships among federal and state governmental powers and the people's rights and powers. In various contexts members of the founding generation conceived of such prerogatives as horizontally divided into coordinate spheres, as vertically arrayed into hierarchical relationships, as overlapping and ordered into relationships of preemption and subordination, or as overlapping but not prioritized. I diagram these main interpretive postures in chapter 4, along with corresponding schemes of constitutional relations that portray additional features of the constitutional landscape and problems of constitutional continuity and change.

Subsequent controversies provide further contexts for exploring relationships among basic categories of constitutional discourse: citizens, the people, rights, powers, norms, practices, continuity, change, delegations, reservations, enumerations, implications, and residuals. Accordingly, chapters 5, 6, and 7 examine precedents set during prominent controversies involving the establishment of a national bank, regulations of the economy, and efforts to limit sexual and reproductive choices. Legislative and executive officials, along with judges, took positions reflecting variations of the relational premises offered as models by sources from the founding period. The later precedents also underscore the need to move beyond excessive preoccupation with the Constitution's *judicial* interpretation and enforcement.

Chapter 8 builds on this insight by returning to sources from the founding period that deal with relationships among federal and state interpretive powers. In response to the national government's making and enforcing the Alien and Sedition Acts of 1798, the Virginia and Kentucky legislatures approved resolutions declaring the federal enactments unconstitutional. Significantly, these resolutions offer models of governmental interposition: public officials expressing commitment to constitutional norms on behalf of the people at large. The two dissenting state legislatures also exemplified forms of interpretive autonomy that citizens and other governmental officials may emulate.

The conclusion explores intersections among competing interpretive premises and corresponding positions on issues of practical politics. Drawing on sources from throughout the book, I describe the major features of "unitary" and "pluralistic" models of constitutional structures in the United States. These models both help to identify recurring patterns of constitutional discourse and underscore the existing order's open texture.

II

Other persons have dealt with a number of the interpretive issues that I confront in this book. For example, Edward S. Corwin, Charles L. Black Jr., and John Hart Ely have examined general problems of constitutional structure.[3] Bruce A. Ackerman, Akhil Reed Amar, and William F. Harris II have examined the people's collective prerogatives and structures of federalism in connection with exploring principles of popular sovereignty and problems of constitutional change.[4]

[3] See, e.g., Charles L. Black Jr., *Decision According to Law* (New York: Norton, 1981), and Black, *Structure and Relationship in Constitutional Law* (Baton Rouge: Louisiana State University Press, 1969); Edward S. Corwin, *The Commerce Power versus States Rights* (Gloucester: Peter Smith, 1962); Corwin, *Constitutional Revolution, Ltd.* (Claremont, Calif.: Claremont Colleges Press, 1941); Corwin, *Liberty Against Government: The Rise, Flowering, and Decline of a Famous Juridical Concept* (Baton Rouge: Louisiana State University Press, 1948); and John Hart Ely, *Democracy and Distrust: A Theory of Judicial Review* (Cambridge: Harvard University Press, 1980). This note and the ones that follow do not, of course, include exhaustive listings of pertinent sources.

[4] See, e.g., Bruce A. Ackerman, "Constitutional Politics/Constitutional Law," 99 Yale L. J. 453 (1989); Ackerman, "The Storrs Lectures: Discovering the Constitution," 93 Yale L. J. 1013 (1984); Ackerman, *We the People: Foundations* (Cambridge: Harvard University Press, 1991); Akhil Reed Amar, "The Bill of Rights as a Constitution," 100 Yale L. J. 1131 (1991); Amar, "The Consent of the Governed: Constitutional Amendment Outside Article

A number of scholars have also sought to locate constitutional adjudication within broader political contexts. For example, Sanford Levinson has examined the multifaceted character of constitutional meaning and authority, along with dimensions of constitutional citizenship and arrangements of interpretive authority.[5] Robert A. Burt, Louis Fisher, and Walter F. Murphy have also emphasized the plural character of constitutional discourse, as have Ackerman, Harris, and others like Frank I. Michelman and Cass R. Sunstein, who have directed attention toward the United States Constitution's "republican" lineage.[6] Robert M. Cover has examined the status of unofficial normative commitments—including popular contributions to making, affirming, and changing the law of the Constitution.[7]

My analysis overlaps these persons' works, but it also departs in significant respects. For example, instead of advancing one dimension of popular sovereignty, I explore intersections among a number of competing facets. Harris emphasizes the people's unitary character; Amar, majoritarianism; Ackerman, electoral representation; Ely, judicial enforcement and individual rights. Each underscores an important component of the constitutional design, but no single perspective fully captures the plural

V," 94 Colum. L. Rev. 457 (1994); Amar, "Of Sovereignty and Federalism," 96 Yale L. J. 1425 (1987); Amar, "Philadelphia Revisited: Amending the Constitution Outside Article V," 55 U. Chi. L. Rev. 1043 (1988); William F. Harris II, *The Interpretable Constitution* (Baltimore: Johns Hopkins University Press, 1993). See also Sanford Levinson, ed., *Responding to Imperfection: The Theory and Practice of Constitutional Amendment* (Princeton: Princeton University Press, 1995). Necessary companions for analyzing the concept of popular sovereignty from historical perspectives include Edmund S. Morgan, *Inventing the People: The Rise of Popular Sovereignty in England and America* (New York: Norton, 1988), and Gordon S. Wood, *The Creation of the American Republic, 1776–1787* (Chapel Hill: University of North Carolina Press, 1969; rpt., New York: Norton, 1972).

[5] See, e.g., Levinson, *Constitutional Faith* (Princeton: Princeton University Press, 1988). For thoughtful analyses of principles of popular sovereignty and the Constitution's place in popular culture, see Michael Kammen, *A Machine That Would Go of Itself: The Constitution in American Culture* (New York: Knopf, 1986), and Kammen, *Sovereignty and Liberty: Constitutional Discourse in American Culture* (Madison: University of Wisconsin Press, 1988).

[6] See, e.g., Robert A. Burt, *The Constitution in Conflict* (Cambridge: Harvard University Press, 1992); Louis Fisher, *Constitutional Dialogues: Interpretation as Political Process* (Princeton: Princeton University Press, 1988); Frank Michelman, "Law's Republic," 97 Yale L. J. 1493 (1988), and Michelman, "The Supreme Court 1985 Term—Foreword: Traces of Self-Government," 100 Harv. L. Rev. 4 (1986); Walter F. Murphy, "Who Shall Interpret? The Quest for the Ultimate Constitutional Interpreter," 48 Rev. Pol. 401 (1986); Cass R. Sunstein, "Beyond the Republican Revival," 97 Yale L. J. 1539 (1988), and Sunstein, *The Partial Constitution* (Cambridge: Harvard University Press, 1993); and the sources cited in n. 4, above.

[7] See, e.g., Robert M. Cover, "The Supreme Court 1982 Term—Foreword: *Nomos* and Narrative," 97 Harv. L. Rev. 4 (1983).

character of "the people" and the constitutional norms they create and sustain.

For similar reasons, I do not confine myself to analyzing interpretive dialogue at the federal level, as emphasized by Burt, Fisher, and Murphy. It is also important to take into account claims of state and individual interpretive autonomy. In this respect, my analysis overlaps Cover's.

Many who have studied constitutional politics broadly have done so to serve relatively narrow ends. Although scholars such as Ackerman, Amar, and Michelman have developed complex interpretive theories, they have repeatedly linked their arguments to claims about how *judges* should decide cases. A recurring premise, in short, has been that constitutional scholars should remain focused on the Constitution's attributes as *judicially enforceable law*.[8]

There are certainly good reasons to be attentive to the Constitution's character as "law" and to issues of judicial review. But the study of constitutional politics may be more encompassing and serve broader ends. As Harris has explained, the Constitution is both more and less than "law" as traditionally conceived. It plays roles in the formation of political identities, antedates formal legal structures, and is not appropriately reducible to specialized or professional understandings.[9] Accordingly, I do not presume that the Constitution is *merely* law or that the law of the Constitution flows entirely from or pertains exclusively to official choices. On the contrary, I seek to account for ways that the people at large may play roles in creating and sustaining constitutional norms—including "legal" norms that do not fit readily within professional narratives.

Taking a broader view of constitutional politics is liberating in several respects. First, there is no need to assume that constitutional meanings are dichotomous. Although judges must decide cases or controversies in favor of one party or another, the Constitution as a whole can accommo-

---

[8] For example, in "Constitutional Politics/Constitutional Law," at 453–61 and 545–47, Ackerman presents analysis leading to conclusions about how *judges* should synthesize the "higher law" made during major constitutional moments. At a strategic moment in "Philadelphia Revisited," at 1046, Amar invites his readers to assume they are judges. In "Traces of Self-Government," at 74, Michelman concludes that active self-governance is impractical "in the national constitutional setting"; he emphasizes instead how "courts, and especially the Supreme Court, seem to take on as one of their ascribed functions the modeling of active self-government that citizens find practically beyond their reach." Even Burt, who repudiates models of judicial interpretive supremacy in *The Constitution in Conflict*, addresses his arguments primarily to judges and judicial scholars. On page 6 of the book, he announces that his goal is to develop "an egalitarian conception of judicial authority." Sunstein's arguments in *The Partial Constitution* are refreshing insofar as he addresses them to legislative and administrative bodies, but I depart significantly from his historical claims and his other efforts to achieve constitutional determinacy.

[9] Harris, *The Interpretable Constitution*, at 9 and 24–26.

date interpretive plurality. Those who study constitutional politics should allow room for its rich texture rather than confine themselves to searching historical sources and other materials for so-called "right answers."

In addition, students of the Constitution should account for its dynamic character. Ackerman is within the mainstream of legal scholarship insofar as he emphasizes the fundamentally preservative role of judicial decision-making. But other actors within the constitutional system are not equally so constrained. Judges have typically been followers, not leaders, of constitutional change; and even when they have led, judges have depended on others to respect or give effect to their decisions.

Incremental changes have been as significant as major transformations. Ackerman is correct that there have been several pivotal epochs in American constitutionalism. But he and others have paid insufficient attention to broader-based, grass-roots components of constitutional transformations. In addition to having intrinsic normative significance, popular political activity has provided foundations for further, larger-scale changes to the Constitution.

To be sure, representative structures and legacies from past decisions impose substantial constraints and narrow the options available to those bound by the United States Constitution. In addition, any particular person's choices are limited by those of contemporaries. But citizens and governmental officials may nevertheless act as authors of the Constitution, even as they are subject to its authority. Constitutional vitality depends on awareness of possibilities, not only acceptance of restraints.

CHAPTER 1

Toward Constitutional Citizenship: Official Pronouncements

> The words "people of the United States" and "citizens" are synonymous terms, and mean the same thing. They both describe the political body who, according to our republican institutions, form the sovereignty, and who hold the power and conduct the Government through their representatives. They are what we familiarly call the "sovereign people," and every citizen is one of this people, and a constituent member of this sovereignty.[1]

IN *Dred Scott v. Sandford*, justices of the United States Supreme Court addressed fundamental questions of American constitutionalism: Who was included among "the people" upon whose authority the U.S. Constitution purported to rest? Who could legitimately claim rights as "citizens"? What, if any, legal obligations did members of the polity have toward those excluded from such membership?

One of the pivotal issues in the case was whether Dred Scott, a black man, had standing to sue as a citizen of Missouri. Scott claimed that John Emerson, his former master, had emancipated him by taking him into a free state and a free territory. He sued John Sanford, a citizen of New York who then claimed to own Scott as his slave. Scott sought jurisdiction based on diversity of state citizenship.[2]

A majority of the justices decided in favor of Sanford.[3] Chief Justice Roger B. Taney wrote the majority opinion, arguing that Scott had no standing to sue in a federal court as a citizen of Missouri. The Chief Justice claimed that a black person (in Taney's words, a "negro") could

---

[1] *Dred Scott v. Sandford*, 60 U.S. (19 How.) 393, 404 (1857).

[2] See generally Don E. Fehrenbacher, *The Dred Scott Case: Its Significance in American Law and Politics* (New York: Oxford University Press, 1987), at 1–7 and chs. 9–11. Because the defendant's name was misspelled in the official Supreme Court report, following convention I use "*Sandford*" in referring to the case but "Sanford" to refer to the individual.

[3] The Court was fractured; the nine justices wrote nine opinions, which span 241 pages in the United States Reports. Justices Wayne, Nelson, Grier, Daniel, Campbell, and Catron concurred; Justices McLean and Curtis dissented. There remains dispute about which of the concurring judges concurred in which parts of Taney's opinion. See Fehrenbacher, *The Dred Scott Case*, ch. 14.

not sue in a federal court even if he were free. Taney argued, moreover, that Scott was not free and could not have been made free by the Missouri Compromise of 1820—a federal law that had prohibited slavery in certain territories. For only the second time, the Supreme Court declared invalid part of an act of Congress.[4]

The case abounds with ironies. The Supreme Court—a *national* institution—committed itself to the cause of slavery, even as members of the majority claimed that prohibiting or allowing slavery was a matter reserved to the states. The judges claimed to be basing their decision on the commands of the Constitution, but personal biases transparently influenced the outcome. Opinions that aspired to settle controversy over slavery through the calmness and deliberation of judicial decision-making instead exacerbated political divisions. Positions that were purportedly grounded in analysis of the Constitution's original meaning did not survive the Civil War or reconstruction amendments. Chief Justice Taney and others relied on the authority of the American people to deny that blacks ever could be "citizens," or members of that people. Justice Curtis in his dissent committed himself to denying the citizenship of Dred Scott and others similarly situated, even as he argued that Scott was a free man.

Taney's and Curtis's opinions are especially instructive because they present opposing conceptions of "the people," or "citizens."[5] Both also relied on formal and participatory conceptions of citizenship that were difficult to reconcile with one another and with political practices at the time. In addition to providing necessary background for analyzing Frederick Douglass's claims of citizenship, these two opinions direct attention toward enduring problems of American constitutionalism.

COMPETING CONCEPTIONS OF CITIZENSHIP

Taney's opinion moves back and forth between two predominant conceptions of citizenship. The decision rests primarily upon a categorical asser-

---

[4] The first time had been *Marbury v. Madison*, 5 U.S. (1 Cranch) 137 (1803). As with the earlier case, the Court's decision in *Dred Scott* had limited immediate effects. John Marshall's interpretation of section 13 of the Judiciary Act of 1789 had been largely constructed, and the Missouri Compromise of 1820 had been expressly repealed by the Kansas-Nebraska Act of 1854.

[5] For present purposes, I follow Taney in not distinguishing "citizens" from "the people." But as explained below, this conflation is problematic in several respects.

In *The Interpretable Constitution* (Baltimore: Johns Hopkins University Press, 1993), at 201–208, William F. Harris II draws a further distinction between the "sovereign people" and the "constitutional people." I do not rely on that distinction here, because Harris would identify as the "constitutional people" those whom Taney described as the "sovereign people." Also, Harris's distinction is problematic insofar as he identifies "sovereignty" as an attribute of the "constitutional people." I shall return to issues raised by these distinctions in subsequent chapters.

tion that blacks were not formally citizens. The Chief Justice assumed that a particular person either was, or was not, a "citizen" with standing to sue in federal courts. Throughout his opinion, however, Taney also relied on a participatory conception of citizenship that competed with his formal analysis of the concept.

He ran these two conceptions together early in his opinion, where he asserted that "[t]he words 'people of the United States' and 'citizens' are synonymous terms, and mean the same thing." Taney argued that "both describe the political body who, according to our republican institutions, form the sovereignty, and who *hold the power* and *conduct the Government* through their representatives." He claimed that every citizen was a member of the "sovereign people" and thus could claim "the rights and privileges which [the Constitution] provides for and secures to citizens of the United States." In this passage, he articulated a distinctive conception of national citizenship and suggested that this status carried with it the right or power to participate in representative processes. He emphasized these points by way of contrast, moreover, by distinguishing "citizens" from constitutional "subject[s]" who "had no rights or privileges but such as those who *hold the power* and the Government might choose to grant them."[6]

The Chief Justice's treatment of federalism complicated his analysis of attributes of national citizenship. He distinguished "the rights of citizenship which a State may confer within its own limits, [from] the rights of citizenship as a member of the Union." He claimed, moreover, that someone could have "all the rights and privileges of a citizen of a State" and still not be "a citizen of the United States." His position was that each state could treat any person as one of its citizens, for purely internal purposes. But a state could not, by itself, make that person "a citizen in the sense in which that word is used in the Constitution of the United States." Only the Constitution itself, or Congress through its power of naturalization, could confer that status.[7]

Taney was concerned not only about standing to sue based on article III. He also focused on the privileges and immunities clause of article IV, section 2: "The citizens of each state shall be entitled to all privileges and immunities of citizens in the several states." He denied that this provision "put it in the power of a single State to make [a member of the negro African race] a citizen of the United States, and endue him with the *full rights of citizenship* in every other State without their consent." Allowing the states to have such a power would, he claimed, "be much more dangerous to the peace and safety of a large portion of the Union, than the few foreigners one of the States might improperly naturalize." He appar-

---

[6] *Dred Scott*, 60 U.S. at 404–405 (emphasis added).
[7] Ibid., at 405.

ently feared that free blacks from one state, if treated as "citizens," might cause agitation within other states seeking to maintain the institution of slavery.[8]

Taney conceived of the "full rights of citizenship" as prerogatives of *state* citizenship that article IV of the United States Constitution extended to all "citizens." If blacks were "citizens" for purposes of article IV, the Chief Justice suggested, these persons would have "all the privileges of a citizen in every other State, and in its own courts."[9] Each state would have to afford to black citizens of other states the same rights that it afforded its own citizens. Taney found that conclusion unacceptable.

He avoided it by denying that the Constitution afforded any rights to black persons. Taney relied heavily on historical sources which, he claimed, compelled a conclusion that blacks had not been among "the people" in whose name the Constitution had been ratified. He also denied that the Declaration of Independence referred to blacks as among "all men" who had been "created equal . . . with certain inalienable rights." The Chief Justice's position was categorical: "[N]either the class of persons who had been imported as slaves, nor their descendants, whether they had become free or not, were [at the time of the Constitution's adoption] acknowledged as a part of the people, nor intended to be included in the general words of that memorable instrument."[10]

He went further and argued that blacks could not, under the existing law of the Constitution, *become* members of that political body. No black, including Dred Scott, could have standing to sue in federal courts as a "citizen." Nor did such persons have any other rights based on the Constitution: blacks "had no rights which the white man was bound to respect."[11]

Taney recognized, however, that formal status and political practices had been (and had remained) disjunctive in several respects. He conceded, for example, that several states had conferred rights of state citizenship, including the franchise, upon free black persons both at the time of the Constitution's ratification and thereafter. These persons had *exercised* "rights of citizenship" not only for a state's internal purposes but

---

[8] See ibid., at 406 (emphasis added) and 417–18.

[9] Ibid., at 406.

[10] See ibid., at 407–23. For critical analysis of Taney's effort to reconstruct "original intentions" on these issues, see Paul Finkelman, "The Constitution and the Intentions of the Framers: The Limits of Historical Analysis," 50 U. Pitt. L. Rev. 349 (1989) at 371–98; Christopher L. Eisgruber, "*Dred* Again: Originalism's Forgotten Past," 10 Constl. Comm. 37 (1993). For background on slavery and the Constitution, see Finkelman, "Slavery and the Constitutional Convention: Making a Covenant with Death," in Richard Beeman, Stephen Botein, and Edward C. Carter, eds., *Beyond Confederation: Origins of the Constitution and American National Identity* (Chapel Hill: University of North Carolina Press, 1987).

[11] *Dred Scott*, 60 U.S. at 407.

also for national purposes such as approving the Constitution, electing members of Congress, and the like. Thus it would appear that these persons satisfied Taney's criteria for membership among "the people," or "citizens": black individuals had *acted* as parts of the "political body" that "form[ed] the sovereignty" and "[held] the power and conduct[ed] the Government through their representatives." Nevertheless, the Chief Justice denied that the Constitution regarded these persons as "citizens" of a state or the United States.

Taney sought to defend this position by distinguishing blacks from other persons who were, in his view, formally citizens (and thus members of "the people") even though they did not hold particular rights. He contradicted his earlier characterization of "citizens," or members of "the people," as those who "hold the power and conduct the government through their representatives": "Undoubtedly, a person may be a citizen, that is, a member of the community who form the sovereignty, although he exercises *no share of the political power,* and is incapacitated from holding particular offices."[12] Taney was referring in this passage to women, minors, and persons who did not satisfy property qualifications to vote or hold particular offices. He assumed these persons were "citizens," or members of "the political family," even if they held "no share of the political power."[13] These examples further highlighted tensions between the Chief Justice's formal and participatory conceptions of citizenship.

Because he contemplated the states' affording different rights to different categories of citizens, Taney's logic did not, as he claimed, commit him to a position that states would have to afford blacks "the full rights of citizenship" if these persons were "citizens" within the meaning of the Constitution. As he interpreted it, article IV would not oblige a state to afford the *same* rights to *all* citizens. This provision would only require the states to afford the same rights to citizens within various *categories,* without regard to their state citizenship.[14]

Taney drove yet another wedge between his formal and participatory conceptions of citizenship by claiming that a person's holding a particular right was not conclusive evidence of that person's citizenship. He pointed out that some states allowed aliens ("foreigners not naturalized") to vote and declared that the status of blacks was analogous in this respect to that of foreigners: "[A] State may give the right [to vote] to free negroes and mulattoes, but that does not make them citizens of the State, and still less

---

[12] Ibid., at 422 (emphasis added).
[13] Ibid.
[14] See ibid., at 406 and 422. As explained below, Justice Curtis in his dissent developed such argument more fully.
[15] Ibid., at 422.

of the United States. And the provision in the Constitution giving privileges and immunities in other States, does not apply to them."[15] Even though he was aware that some noncitizens held and exercised a "share of the political power" denied to many citizens, he did not qualify his claim that holding such power was the principal defining attribute of citizenship. And he continued to overstate the implications of article IV by claiming that it gave all citizens "privileges and immunities in other states." His position was that these rights were primarily a function of state classifications, not federal law.

In an attempt to block another possible avenue of black citizenship, the Chief Justice *distinguished* blacks from unnaturalized foreigners in terms of their eligibility for naturalization. He claimed that the Constitution delegated the power of naturalizing aliens exclusively to Congress.[16] But he asserted that because blacks were not "persons born in a foreign country, under a foreign Government," Congress could not provide for their naturalization. Taney described members of "the African race imported or born in this country" as "one[s]" who "from birth or parentage, by the laws of the country, belong[] to an inferior and subordinate class." Thus he regarded blacks in America, whether free or enslaved, as persons having *no* nationality. Plus he treated such persons as doubly cursed by taking a position that they could never, under the existing Constitution, have any nationality as long as they remained (or were forced to remain) within its jurisdiction.[17]

It is apparent that Taney's primary objectives in *Dred Scott* did not include writing a perfectly consistent or consistently principled opinion. He sought, at every opportunity, to deny rights of citizenship to blacks. He frequently ran together analysis of the status of free blacks and black slaves. He relied on crosscutting distinctions among white males, blacks, women, and resident aliens. He constructed layers of analysis, with re-

[16] Article I, sec. 8, has provided: "The Congress shall have power . . . to establish an uniform rule of naturalization." Taney presumed, however, that a state could regard aliens as citizens "so far as the State alone was concerned" (see ibid., at 405–406). Most of his opinion was concerned primarily with the power to naturalize persons as "citizens" *of the United States*, with the rights afforded to the "citizens" recognized by the *federal* Constitution.

[17] See *Dred Scott*, 60 U.S. at 417 and 420. Among other things, Taney referred to the federal naturalization law of 1790, which confined naturalization to "aliens being free white persons." He claimed this act supported his conclusion that only members of the white race "constituted the sovereignty in the Government" at the time of the Constitution's ratification. But he did not take a position that Congress could only provide for the naturalization of white persons. He conceded that Congress could naturalize Indians, since they were "aliens and foreigners." But he gratuitously characterized Indians as persons in an "untutored and savage state" whom no one at the time of the Constitution's ratification would have considered "capable of enjoying the privileges of an American citizen." See ibid., at 404 and 419–20.

dundancies and fallback positions. Perhaps he thought that the weight of his arguments would add to their force.

Exploring Some Implications of Taney's Reasoning

The example of Frederick Douglass demonstrates how Taney's reasoning would apply outside the context of *Dred Scott*. Douglass was born in 1818 having the status of a slave according to the laws of Maryland. His mother had been a black slave, and his father apparently had been white. In 1838 Douglass escaped from Maryland to Massachusetts and became prominently involved as a fugitive in abolitionist political activity. His publication of an autobiography in 1845 led to concerns that he might be apprehended and returned to Maryland as a slave. For this reason and others, he went to England. While there, a number of individuals purchased Douglass's freedom from his purported Maryland owner. In 1847 the former slave returned to Massachusetts as a free man. Shortly thereafter, he and his family moved to Rochester, New York.[18]

According to Taney's reasoning in *Dred Scott*, Douglass was not and could not become a "citizen," as contemplated by the United States Constitution. For these purposes, it would not matter whether Douglass was formally free or enslaved. His skin color would disqualify him from suing in federal courts, claiming "privileges and immunities" of state citizenship based on article IV, or otherwise claiming "rights" or "powers" as a member of "the people." The reference in the Declaration of Independence to "all men" who were "created equal" did not include Douglass, his black ancestors, or their progeny. Nor were such persons included among "the people" for whom the Constitution had been "ordained and established." Nor could such persons join that people's "posterity." Douglass and other black persons were members of a "subordinate

---

[18] For accounts of Douglass's life see his biography, *Life and Times of Frederick Douglass* (New York: Macmillan, 1962; reprinted from the revised edition of 1892); Philip S. Foner, ed., *The Life and Writings of Frederick Douglass*, vols. 1–4 (New York: International Publishers, 1950–1955); William F. McFeely, *Frederick Douglass* (New York: Norton, 1955). On his political thinking generally, see David W. Blight, *Frederick Douglass' Civil War: Keeping Faith in Jubilee* (Baton Rouge: Louisiana State University Press, 1989); Waldo E. Martin Jr., *The Mind of Frederick Douglass* (Chapel Hill: University of North Carolina Press, 1984). For analysis of his constitutional perspective, see Sanford Levinson, *Constitutional Faith* (Princeton: Princeton University Press, 1988), at 31 and 38 (explains how Douglass exemplified "protestant" approaches to issues of constitutional inclusion and interpretive authority). Many of Douglass's speeches and writings are included in John W. Blassingame, ed., *The Frederick Douglass Papers*, ser. 1, vols. 1–4 (New Haven: Yale University Press, 1979–1991). But because Foner's collection includes selections from a wider range of sources (including the *North Star*), I cite herein to that collection.

and inferior class of beings" who had "no rights that the white man was bound to respect." Douglass was not even a member of a foreign nation and thus could not become naturalized as a citizen of the United States.

When he was held as a slave in Maryland (Taney's home state), Douglass possessed few attributes of citizenship. His owner and others treated him as property and repeatedly placed his life in jeopardy. State officials did not allow him to vote, he could not sue in the state's courts, his liberty was severely restricted, and his right to own property was limited. His role in national politics was minimal—a function largely of his place within a complex matrix of economic and social forces that were heightening tensions over slavery across the political landscape. His predicament was, in short, generally representative of black slaves during the antebellum period.[19]

As a fugitive slave, his formal status remained relatively clear in some respects, but in many ways his situation became convoluted. He defied the coercive powers of several states and of the United States to gain freedom in practice, even if not in law. While in Massachusetts, he was vulnerable to being reclaimed by his owner (or others acting on his owner's behalf) and of being returned to the condition of slavery. The federal Constitution and laws backed Maryland law in this respect. As a slave according to the laws of Maryland, he formally remained a slave throughout the United States. The fugitive slave clause of the federal Constitution forbade other states from "discharg[ing]" him from that condition, and the Fugitive Slave Act of 1793 reinforced that clause by establishing procedures for the rendition of escaped slaves.[20]

Long before his formal emancipation, however, Douglass tasted freedom in Massachusetts and enjoyed prerogatives that persons had denied him in Maryland. He gained personal liberty, earned wages, and acquired property. He became active in abolitionist activities and played an increasingly important role in national political debates. He apparently did not vote during this period in state or national elections and thus did not hold a share of the "political power" that Taney treated (at times) as an incident of citizenship. In addition, he was not in a good position to *demand* privileges or immunities of state citizenship from white citizens or their governmental representatives. Even so, he enjoyed the protective umbrella of the Massachusetts constitution and laws, along with some

[19] See generally James M. McPherson, *Battle Cry of Freedom: The Civil War Era* (New York: Oxford University Press, 1988).

[20] See *Prigg v. Pennsylvania*, 41 U.S. (16 Pet.) 536 (1842). See also Robert M. Cover, *Justice Accused: Antislavery and the Political Process* (New Haven: Yale University Press, 1975).

measure of good will from its people. Taney would deny that these persons had the legal right to treat Douglass as a free person, but in practice many did so anyway.[21]

There was an even wider gulf between Taney's theory of citizenship and political practices involving Douglass after he gained his formal freedom. After moving to New York, he established a newspaper and participated in local, state, and national politics. Among other things, he exercised rights of speech, the press, and religious liberty—rights secured to "the people" by the first amendment to the United States Constitution. After satisfying New York's residency requirement, he also voted in state and national elections.[22]

New York's constitution of 1846 explicitly contemplated that "persons of color" would be among its citizens and its voters. Article II, section 1, of the state charter generally extended the franchise to "male citizen[s] of the age of twenty-one years, who shall have been a citizen for ten days, and an inhabitant of this State one year next preceding any election." The constitutional charter contained additional requirements for "person[s] of color": a requirement of three years' citizenship and ownership of "a freehold estate of the value of two hundred and fifty dollars, over and above all debts and incumbrances charged thereon."[23]

Douglass not only held part of the "political power" of the state for internal purposes but also for purposes of electing national representatives. Along with article I, section 2, of the federal Constitution, the New York constitution made blacks like Douglass members, in practice, of "the people" of the state. The federal Constitution equated "the people of the several states" with "the Electors in each state" who had "the qualifications requisite for electors of the most numerous branch of the state legislature." Douglass satisfied these criteria. He also voted in national presidential elections and participated in electing state legislators who, in turn, selected members of the United States Senate.

Article I, section 2, of the federal Constitution apparently presupposed, as did Taney, that holding the franchise was a defining attribute of "the people." Taney might have attempted to distinguish "the people" (as identified in the preamble and article I) from "citizens" (as identified in

---

[21] See Douglass, *Life and Times*, at 197–258.

[22] See Douglass, "The Suffrage Question," April 25, 1856, and "What Is My Duty as an Anti-Slavery Voter," April 25, 1856, in Foner, ed., *Life and Writings* 2:389–95. See also articles I and II of the New York Constitution of 1821, in Francis N. Thorpe, ed., *The Federal and State Constitutions, Colonial Charters, and Other Organic Laws of the States, Territories, and Colonies Now or Heretofore Forming the United States of America* (Washington, D.C.: GPO, 1909), vol. 5, at 2653–56.

[23] See ibid., at 2656 (article II, sec. 1).

article III).[24] Or he might have argued that a person could be a "citizen" for some purposes (such as article III) but not others (such as article IV).[25] But Taney sought to make no such distinctions. Instead, he insisted that white women who did not vote were both "citizens" and members of "the people," while black men like Douglass fell within neither category— even though they voted and exercised other rights and powers of state and national citizenship.

One of Taney's primary objectives, it appears, was to undercut arguments that he and other federal officials, or state officials from Maryland and other slave states, had a constitutional *obligation* to regard Douglass and persons like him as "citizens." He knew blacks were voting in many of the states, as they had before the Constitution went into effect. Perhaps he could tolerate that practice. And perhaps he could tolerate states' treating free blacks as citizens in other respects. But he would not accept claims that federal or state officials were obliged to treat blacks as citizens with rights based on the United States Constitution.

Taney's position was consistent with Douglass's treatment, pursuant to Maryland law, as a slave prior to his formal emancipation. Article IV and the Fugitive Slave Act reinforced that status. After his formal emancipation, Massachusetts and New York afforded Douglass privileges and immunities of state citizenship, including the right and power to vote. But Taney would not conceive of these prerogatives as "rights" or "powers" within the contemplation of the United States Constitution. His arguments committed him to denying that Douglass had *any* prerogatives that were recognized or protected by the federal Constitution.

Taney thought the Constitution did, however, recognize and secure rights and powers of "the people." He declared in *Dred Scott* that the Missouri Compromise was unconstitutional because it deprived persons of their "property" in slaves without "due process of law," in violation of the fifth amendment to the United States Constitution. Article IV and the fugitive slave law also protected rights of slave ownership. The ninth and

---

[24] See Alexander M. Bickel, "Citizenship in the American Constitution," 15 Ariz. L. Rev. 369 (1973); Herbert J. Storing, "Slavery and the Moral Foundations of the American Republic," in Robert H. Horwitz, ed., *The Moral Foundations of the American Republic*, 2d ed. (Charlottesville: University Press of Virginia, 1979), at 214–33 (distinguishes references to "citizens" and "the people" from that in the Declaration of Independence to "all men" with the rights affirmed therein).

[25] Judge Robert W. Wells apparently relied on such a distinction to decide *Dred Scott v. Sandford* at the trial court level (see Fehrenbacher, *The Dred Scott Case*, at 276–77). According to Fehrenbacher, there is evidence that "free Negroes did sometimes appear as parties in federal suits without being challenged on racial grounds. Indeed, the leading attorney in one such case was Roger B. Taney" (ibid., at 72; citation omitted). Fehrenbacher suggested, moreover, that the idea of blacks' having limited rights of citizenship would have been consistent with other jurisdictional criteria (ibid., at 277).

tenth amendments could support arguments that slave owners held other (unenumerated) rights and powers. Justice John A. Campbell suggested as much in his concurrence.[26]

Ironically, a majority of the Court relied on article III to deny that a lower federal court had jurisdiction to decide the action brought by Dred Scott. In addition, Taney extended Marshall's reasoning in *Marbury* by presuming that article III allowed the Supreme Court to review Congress's interpretation of the scope of its legislative powers. Taney asserted, more specifically, authority to invalidate an act of Congress which had excluded slavery from the territories.[27] Thus he argued that the United States Constitution delegated federal power to *protect* rights of slave ownership but withheld federal power to *interfere* (in at least some ways) with such rights. Two years later, he wrote a complementary opinion for a unanimous Court in *Ableman v. Booth*, upholding the Fugitive Slave Act of 1850.[28]

Taney took corresponding positions on the scope of powers prohibited to the states. In *Dred Scott* he denied that states had authority to naturalize blacks or otherwise to give them the status of United States citizens. In *Ableman* he sought to undercut efforts by state officials to interfere with federal enforcement of the 1850 Act.[29] But he argued that states were not prohibited from treating blacks as slaves or from denying any and all rights to blacks—whether free or enslaved. Even if another state treated a black person as one of its citizens, as New York did Douglass, other states had no obligation to treat him as a "citizen" within the meaning of article IV or other parts of the Constitution.[30]

[26] See *Dred Scott*, 60 U.S. at 511 (Campbell, J., concurring) (The people "demanded an explicit declaration that no more power was to be exercised than they had delegated. And the ninth and tenth amendments to the Constitution were designed to include the reserved rights of the States, and the people, with all the sanctions of that instrument, and to bind the authorities, State and Federal, by the judicial oath it prescribes, to their recognition and observance").

[27] For more thorough analysis of Taney's handling of this issue, see Fehrenbacher, *The Dred Scott Case*, esp. chs. 14 and 16.

[28] 62 U.S. (21 How.) 506 (1859). See also Jenni Parrish, "The *Booth* Cases: Final Step to the Civil War," 29 Willamette L. Rev. 237 (1993); William M. Wiecek, "Slavery and Abolition Before the United States Supreme Court, 1820–1860," 65 J. Am. Hist. 34 (1978).

[29] In this connection, Taney declared that there was a "line of division" between federal and state powers and defended federal judicial powers as necessary to preserve the supremacy of the Constitution and federal laws. With considerable hubris, he suggested that the main alternative to final settlement of "irritating and angry controversies" through "the calmness and deliberation of judicial inquiry" was resolution by "military and physical force." See *Ableman*, 62 U.S. at 516–21.

[30] See Paul Finkelman, *An Imperfect Union: Slavery, Federalism, and Comity* (Chapel Hill: University of North Carolina Press, 1981), for analysis of issues of comity and federalism with reference to *Dred Scott*, *Ableman*, and other cases involving slavery.

The bottom line for Taney was that the Constitution reserved to the states substantial powers regarding the treatment of black persons. At a high level of generality, his position on this issue was largely in accord with actual political practices. Some states treated blacks as citizens and allowed them to exercise a share of the "political power." In other states, blacks were treated as slaves, second-class citizens, or noncitizens.

The life of Frederick Douglass spanned these practices. He lived in a state that used its reserved powers to establish and maintain slavery. He also resided within states that used their reserved powers to oppose slavery. Public officials and citizens of Maryland treated him as property. Before and after his emancipation, he was doubtless subjected to numerous forms of official and unofficial discrimination in Northern states. At the same time, many of the residents and public officials of Massachusetts and New York (along with several other states) treated him as a citizen. In practice, Frederick Douglass held part of the "political power" of more than one state. His actions had national dimensions, even when he was not, according to Chief Justice Taney's opinion, a member of "the people."

STATE CITIZENSHIP, MAYBE

Justice Benjamin R. Curtis countered Taney's position that black persons could not be "citizens" or members of "the people" for purposes of article III and other parts of the United States Constitution. Curtis was a native of Massachusetts, the state where Douglass resided for seven years as a fugitive. One might have expected his dissenting opinion to provide strong support for free blacks claiming equal rights of citizenship.

Those advocating racial equality could endorse much of Curtis's analysis. But a careful reading of his opinion reveals substantial qualifications and concessions. He did not regard all free black men as "citizens." Plus he interpreted the Constitution as consistent with states' denying a wide range of rights to those who were citizens. In short, the dissenting opinion fell far short of the ideals to which Douglass and other abolitionists were committed.

State of Birth and/or Political Participation?

As did Taney, Curtis equivocated between two conceptions of citizenship. The dissenting justice's criteria for formal citizenship were more expansive than the Chief Justice's. But Curtis would accept even greater disparities between formal status and its incidents. He defended a form of citizenship that was, in substance, largely hollow.

Curtis also followed Taney by approaching the issue of standing to sue at a high level of generality. According to the dissenter, the issue was "whether *any* person of African descent, whose ancestors were sold as slaves in the United States, *can be* a citizen of the United States." He argued that "[i]f *any* such person can be a citizen, this plaintiff has the right to the judgment of the court that he is so."[31]

In these passages Curtis relied on rules of pleading. He argued that judges only had authority to address issues raised by the parties in a timely manner. In his view, because "the plea to the jurisdiction in this case shows no facts, except that the plaintiff was of African descent, and his ancestors were sold as slaves, and [because] these facts are not inconsistent with his citizenship of the United States, and his residence in the State of Missouri, the plea [challenging] jurisdiction was bad." He insisted that "the law has been settled, that when the declaration or bill contains the necessary averments of citizenship, this court cannot look at the record, to see whether those averments are true, except so far as they are put into issue by a plea to the jurisdiction." Curtis denied that the justices had authority, based on the pleadings, to reconsider whether or not Dred Scott was a citizen of Missouri.[32]

Curtis's attempt to narrow the scope of judicial inquiry was important, because Scott did not qualify as a citizen of Missouri according to the criteria Curtis announced in *Dred Scott*. Curtis argued that it was "left to each State to determine what free persons, *born within its limits*, shall be citizens of such State, and *thereby* be citizens of the United States."[33] He repeatedly emphasized that "allegiance and citizenship spring from the place of birth."[34] Evidence not considered by the justices indicates that Dred Scott had been born in Virginia, not Missouri.[35] But Scott did not claim to be a citizen of Virginia.

Curtis argued that "[u]nder the Constitution of the United States, each State has retained th[e] power of determining the political status of *its* native-born inhabitants, and no exception thereto can be found in the Constitution."[36] He gave the example of a master who took a slave to a

[31] *Dred Scott*, 60 U.S. at 571 (emphasis added) (Curtis, J., dissenting).

[32] See ibid., at 588–90.

[33] Ibid., at 577 (emphasis on "thereby" in the original; other emphasis added).

[34] Ibid., at 586.

[35] See Fehrenbacher, *The Dred Scott Case*, at 240, 405–408. The location of Scott's birth did not appear in the pleading or the opinions, and none of the judges addressed the issue or considered it necessary to do so.

[36] *Dred Scott*, 60 U.S. at 585–86 (emphasis on "status" removed; emphasis on "its" added).

free state and thereby emancipated him. Curtis claimed that this action would not (and, by definition, could not) make the former slave a native-born citizen of the free state. He explained:

> [W]hatever powers the States may exercise to confer privileges of citizenship on persons not born on their soil, the Constitution of the United States does not recognize such citizens. . . . It does not allow to the States the power to make aliens citizens, or permit one State to take persons born on the soil of another State, and, contrary to the laws and policy of the State where they were born, make them its citizens, and so citizens of the United States.[37]

The residents and public officials of Virginia (or Missouri) certainly would not have approved of another state's making blacks like Dred Scott "citizens" with privileges and immunities and other rights guaranteed by the United States Constitution.

Curtis also denied that Congress had authority to decide what persons born within the several states were "citizens." He interpreted narrowly Congress's power of naturalization as "confined to the removal of the disabilities of foreign birth."[38] On this point, Curtis's analysis overlapped Taney's.

Curtis's main concern, like the Chief Justice's, was not the scope of Congress's powers of naturalization. The dissenter, like Taney, focused on the scope of *state* powers. Curtis argued that the states had greater latitude to decide which persons, born on their soil, were "citizens" as a matter of federal law—not just for the state's internal purposes.

According to Curtis, "Among the powers unquestionably possessed by the several States, was that of determining what persons should and what persons should not be citizens." He claimed that this power embraced "three parts": removing disabilities of alienage; "determining what persons should enjoy the privileges of citizenship, in respect to the internal affairs of the several States"; and determining "[w]hat native-born persons should be citizens of the United States." His position was that "[t]he first named power, that of establishing a uniform rule of naturalization, was granted, and here the grant, according to its terms, stopped." In article I, "a particular part of this entire power [was] separated from the residue," thereby giving rise to "a strong presumption that this is all which is granted, and that the residue is left to the States and to the people." Without expressly citing the tenth amendment, he clearly echoed its terms.[39]

These arguments supported his conclusion that "those persons born

---

[37] Ibid., at 586.
[38] Ibid., at 578. See also ibid., at 577.
[39] The quoted passages are from ibid., at 579.

within the several States, who, by force of their respective Constitutions and laws, are citizens of the State, are thereby citizens of the United States."[40] At least *some* blacks could be "citizens" with standing to sue in federal courts. Blacks born into a free state, if the state treated them as citizens, could even rely on article IV to claim "the privileges and immunities of citizens in the several states."

Not surprisingly, Curtis relied on political practices to support his position. He emphasized that when the Articles of Confederation went into effect, "all free native-born inhabitants" of at least five states "were not only citizens of those States, but such of them as had the other necessary qualifications possessed the franchise of electors, on equal terms with other citizens." He argued that the Constitution of the United States did not deprive such persons or their descendants of citizenship:

> That Constitution was ordained and established by the people of the United States, through the action, in each State, of those persons who were qualified by its laws to act thereon, in behalf of themselves and all other citizens of that State. In some of the States, as we have seen, colored persons were among those qualified by law to act on this subject. These colored persons were not only included in the body of "the people of the United States," by whom the Constitution was ordained and established, but in at least five of the States they had the power to act, and doubtless did act, by their suffrages, upon the question of its adoption. It would be strange, if we were to find in that instrument anything which deprived of their citizenship any part of the people of the United States who were among those by whom it was established.

Curtis, like Taney, equated "citizens" with members of "the people." But the dissenter not only argued that "the elective franchise . . . is one of the chiefest attributes of citizenship under the American Constitutions." He went further and claimed that "the just and constitutional possession of this right is decisive evidence of citizenship."[41]

Curtis did not, however, argue that "enjoyment of the elective franchise [was] *essential* to citizenship." Whereas Taney had suggested that constitutional citizenship carried with it significant rights, in part based on article IV, Curtis denied that this status afforded any particular privileges or immunities. He sought to allay concerns that article IV required a conclusion that "colored persons could vote, and be eligible to not only Federal offices, but offices even in those States whose Constitutions and laws disqualify colored persons from voting or being elected to office." He explained:

[40] Ibid., at 582.
[41] Ibid., at 572–73, 576, and 581.

> The truth is, that citizenship, under the Constitution of the United States, is not dependent on the possession of any particular political or even of all civil rights; and any attempt so to define it must lead to error. To what citizens the elective franchise shall be confided, is a question to be determined by each State, in accordance with its own views of the necessities or expediencies of its condition. What civil rights shall be enjoyed by citizens, and whether all shall enjoy the same, or how they may be gained or lost, are to be determined in the same way.

According to this line of reasoning, article IV was consistent with a state's denying any particular privilege or immunity to certain categories of its citizens and to citizens of other states based on criteria other than "mere citizenship."[42]

Curtis gave several examples. He suggested that a state could, among other things, confine the right of suffrage to white male citizens or could limit the right to hold office or convey property based on age, sex, marital status, or sanity. He suggested, furthermore, that a state could legitimately deny any and all "privileges and immunities" of state citizenship, to natives and nonnatives alike (including "citizens" of another state, for purposes of interpreting article IV), based solely on racial or ethnic criteria. He declared that "[i]t rests with the States themselves so to frame their Constitutions and laws as not to attach a particular privilege or immunity to *mere naked citizenship*."[43]

His position on this issue was doubly in tension with analysis that he had endorsed early in his dissent. Curtis cited with approval an opinion by Judge William Gaston of North Carolina in a state case that had been decided in 1828. According to Gaston, American law did not recognize different classes of free inhabitants:

> Whatever distinctions may have existed in the Roman law between citizens and free inhabitants, they are unknown to our institutions . . . . Slaves manumitted here become freemen—and therefore if born within North Carolina are citizens of North Carolina—and all free persons born within the State are born citizens of the State.[44]

Curtis relied on this passage to rebut Justice Peter V. Daniel's argument, concurring in *Dred Scott*, that free blacks in America had an intermediate status similar to that of Roman subjects who were neither slaves nor Roman citizens. Daniel had denied that all free persons residing in a state were "citizens"; he claimed that this word referred only to those who shared *equally* in political authority, or sovereignty. Gaston, the North

---

[42] See ibid., at 581 (emphasis on "essential" added) and 582–84.
[43] See ibid., at 583–84 (emphasis added).
[44] *State v. Manuel*, 20 N.C. (Dev. & Bat.) 144 (1838), at 151.

Carolina judge, had affirmed these principles of equality in his opinion and had claimed that rights of citizenship, including the franchise, had attached to all free persons within the state "without regard to color." In short, Gaston had denied that the status of free blacks within the state had been any different from that of other citizens.[45]

Curtis's reliance on Gaston's analysis reveals at least two important tensions within Curtis's opinion. First, although he repeatedly emphasized the importance of blacks' holding "the franchise of electors, on equal terms with other citizens,"[46] the dissenting justice backed away from a conclusion that voting was a necessary attribute of citizenship. He suggested that a state could deny the franchise to some of its citizens, based solely on their race. Thus Curtis indicated that a state could legitimately treat "citizens" differently with respect to a right the equal holding of which, in his view, conclusively established citizenship. It is odd that Curtis was so willing to allow a state to deny "citizens" a right that had figured so prominently in his analysis of whether persons were "citizens."

In addition, Curtis's reliance on Gaston's reasoning was problematic in light of the former's conclusion that states had no obligation to regard native-born free inhabitants as "citizens." That was precisely the position Gaston had rejected: the possibility of an intermediate status between slaves and citizens. According to Gaston, all native-born persons within a state were either slaves or citizens; all other persons were aliens until made members of the state. Ironically, Curtis reached a conclusion that overlapped Justice Daniel's in this respect: a state could treat free blacks, born within the state, as noncitizens. Although Curtis, unlike Daniel, regarded some blacks as citizens, both justices would have accepted second-class status for blacks, both in free and slave states. Curtis apparently thought such a conclusion was consistent with affirming the formal "citizenship" of some blacks.

Thus Justice Curtis's criteria for citizenship included significant exceptions and afforded qualified rights. He did not regard citizenship, within a state or the United States, as a birthright. His position in *Dred Scott* was that the Constitution permitted states to maintain slavery and to deny all rights of citizenship to slaves. He did not even take a position that America's fundamental law required slave or nonslave states to treat native-

---

[45] See ibid.; *Dred Scott*, 60 U.S. at 573 (Curtis, J., dissenting) (quoting *State v. Manuel*, 20 N.C. at 152. See also *Dred Scott*, 60 U.S. at 476–82 (Daniel, J., concurring).

[46] See *Dred Scott*, 60 U.S. at 573 (Curtis, J., dissenting) and passim. See also ibid., at 581 (Curtis claimed that "there can be no doubt [the elective franchise] is one of the chiefest attributes of citizenship under the American Constitutions; and the just and constitutional possession of this right is decisive of citizenship"). Taney, in contrast, presumed that a state could allow noncitizens to vote (60 U.S. at 422).

born *free* inhabitants as citizens. He also indicated that if a state did not consider such persons as its citizens, they would not constitute citizens of the United States. According to Curtis, moreover, those designated by a state as its citizens, even if they qualified as such for purposes of the federal Constitution, could nevertheless be denied rights of citizenship by other states through criteria that also applied to state citizens.

More Problems of Theory and Practice

According to Curtis's reasoning, not just the majority opinion, Frederick Douglass was not a "citizen" or a member of "the people" whose rights and powers the Constitution secured. Douglass had not been born in New York, so that state could not make him a "citizen" for purposes of the federal Constitution. The state of his birth, Maryland, did not regard Douglass as one of its "citizens" and almost certainly would not have done so if he had returned there to reside.[47] Federal laws at the time did not provide for the naturalization of black persons; Douglass did not qualify as a "foreign" subject falling within Congress's powers of naturalization; and Curtis denied that Congress had any authority to "declare what free persons, born within the several States, shall be citizens of the United States."

Curtis sought to reduce disparities between political practices and constitutional norms, but he was not completely successful.[48] In order to support his conclusion that blacks had been citizens at the time of the Constitution's ratification, he claimed that "the just and constitutional possession" of the franchise was "decisive evidence of citizenship."[49]

[47] See James M. Wright, *The Free Negro in Maryland, 1634–1860* (New York: Octagon, 1971).

[48] His analysis of the Declaration of Independence was revealing. He explained: "My own opinion is, that a calm comparison of these assertions of universal abstract truths, and of their own individual opinions and acts, would not leave these men under any reproach of inconsistency; that the great truths they asserted on that solemn occasion, they were ready and anxious to make effectual, wherever a necessary regard to the circumstances, which no statesman can disregard without producing more evil than good, would allow" (60 U.S. at 574–75). A similar perspective informed his interpretation of the Constitution. He assumed that political constraints had hindered the full realization, in practice, of aspirations such as those set forth in the constitutional text's preamble and the Declaration of Independence. But he nevertheless invoked those ideals and sought to interpret the Constitution consistently with them, to the extent possible taking into account all the relevant "circumstances." As explained in chapter 2, Frederick Douglass's approach was similar insofar as he treated historical sources as authoritative statements of constitutional aspirations. But Douglass was less willing than Curtis to treat disparities between ideals and aspirations as constitutionally permissible.

[49] Ibid., at 581. See also n. 41, above, and accompanying text.

Douglass held the franchise, as a citizen of New York. Article I, section 2, of the United States Constitution qualified Douglass as a voter in elections to the House of Representatives. That article implied, moreover, that such electors constituted "the People" of New York. It is doubtful Curtis would have taken a position that Douglass's acting as a voter was unjust or unconstitutional, as a matter of state or federal law.

Curtis located primary authority to determine citizenship at the state level. In addition, he relied on the idea of native-born citizenship, but qualified it to allow state discretion. This qualification was apparently a concession to slavery and the practice of Southern states' denying that free blacks were citizens. Treating all native-born subjects as citizens would have squared even less with political practices than did Taney's denial of citizenship to all free blacks.

In light of his dual commitments to state autonomy and the concept of native-born citizenship, two parts of the United States Constitution placed Curtis in an awkward position. One was article I's provisions regarding naturalization of aliens. From the perspective of state citizenship, being born in another state was a disability of alienage. Because he had been born in Maryland, Douglass was an alien in terms of eligibility for New York citizenship. If *Congress* had exclusive powers of naturalization, the Northern *state* could not remove this disability.

If Curtis were only concerned with disabilities of state citizenship, he could have easily gotten around article I. As did Taney, Curtis interpreted that article as contemplating only the naturalization of foreigners. Both presumed that only Congress could remove disabilities of *national* citizenship (for persons born outside the United States). But it still might be possible for states to remove disabilities of *state* citizenship (for those born outside the naturalizing state but within the United States).

The more serious obstacle for Curtis was the privileges and immunities clause of article IV. That clause attached national consequences to findings of state citizenship. Along with other parts of the U.S. Constitution, article IV in effect secured limited rights of national citizenship. Curtis was aware that Southern states would object to a conclusion that the Constitution "permit[ted] one State to take persons born on the soil of another State, and, contrary to the laws and policy of the State where they were born, make them its citizens, and so citizens of the United States."

Thus Curtis retreated to a distinction between national and state citizenship. He sought to accommodate divergent state practices without attaching national implications to all such practices. As a concession to slave states, he adhered to the concept of native-born citizenship. Free states could not make national citizens of persons born in other states. But in his view the Constitution also required a concession from Southern states: native-born citizens of free states, including blacks, were citizens of the United States. In addition, any state could afford privileges and immunities of state citizenship, "in respect of internal affairs," upon natives of other states. Yet these persons would not have rights as "citizens" based on the U.S. Constitution.

Douglass fell into this last category. Curtis presumably would have approved New York's affording Douglass privileges and immunities of state citizenship. But despite the national dimensions of Douglass's exercising those rights and powers, Curtis's reasoning in *Dred Scott* would compel a conclusion that those prerogatives were solely rights of state citizenship. Exercising them did not give rise to national citizenship.

Further Considerations

If Curtis actually considered the predicament of Frederick Douglass (or the fact of Dred Scott's Virginia roots), it is possible the justice would have employed different reasoning. Under other circumstances, he might have attached less importance to a person's state of birth. His reasoning allowed room for flexibility, moreover, in dealing with whether a more expansive conception of national citizenship was actually inconsistent with "the laws and polic[ies]" of particular states where individuals had been born.

A black person like Douglass who sought to claim rights of citizenship would encounter additional obstacles, however, even if he satisfied Curtis's criteria for formal citizenship. Curtis conceived of "citizenship," in the form recognized by article IV, as a hollow shell. Recall his words: "It rests with the States themselves so to frame their Constitutions and laws as not to attach a particular privilege or immunity to *mere naked citizenship*."

Northern and Southern states enacted "black codes." Those in the South were especially harsh. Some prohibited the entry of free blacks, while others required free black immigrants to give proof of their industry and honesty and to post bonds and pay special taxes. Almost all Southern states required free blacks to carry "freedom papers." Many of the codes also required such persons to register themselves and restricted movement. Those who did not comply with these requirements—and even some who did—were vulnerable to imprisonment, harsh punishment, and in many cases enslavement. In addition, Southern states barred blacks from voting, holding office, carrying guns, testifying against whites in court, or distributing "incendiary" publications. Some states denied blacks the right to trial by jury and other rights of due process. Historian Ira Berlin has summarized the plight of free blacks in the South during the antebellum period: "Like slaves, free Negroes were generally without political rights, were unable to move freely, were prohibited from testifying against whites, and were often punished with the lash."[50] Although blacks enjoyed substantially greater freedom in the North, even there free blacks had limited civil and political rights.[51]

Curtis's reasoning in *Dred Scott* was consistent with the enforcement of black codes not only against state residents but also against free blacks who were formally "citizens" of another state. As a matter of political practice, blacks residing in the North certainly knew they were vulnerable to harsh treatment if they entered slave states and sought to claim rights of citizenship.[52] Under the circumstances, it was unlikely that a judicial decision—particularly a dissent—would have had much immediate impact on these conditions.[53] It is remarkable, nevertheless, that Curtis treated racially discriminatory state practices as consistent with article IV's imperatives. Because Curtis did not need to reach this issue, it is significant that he went out of his way to support, rather than undercut, such practices.

His opinion appears to be motivated by a concern to affirm, not simply undercut, claims of state autonomy regarding the treatment of blacks. As much as they were opposed to Southern states' *denying* rights of citizenship to blacks, Curtis and others like him were also committed to upholding the power of free states to *secure* rights of black persons. Taking a weak position on rights of citizenship enabled Curtis to affirm principles

---

[50] Ira Berlin, *Slaves Without Masters: The Free Negro in the Antebellum South* (New York: Pantheon, 1974), at 97. See generally ibid., esp. ch. 3, for a more thorough account of the status of free blacks in the South during this period.

[51] See Paul Finkelman, "Prelude to the Fourteenth Amendment: Black Legal Rights in the Antebellum North," 17 Rutgers L. Rev. 415 (1986), for a review of the legal status of free blacks in the North.

[52] Free blacks from the North presumably had various reasons to enter the South at least temporarily, even if not to reside there permanently. Some individuals would want to visit their relatives, including family members held in bondage. Others might seek to travel through the South. Various jobs would require individuals to leave their home states and to enter the jurisdictions of other states. The plight of black seamen was a particularly thorny issue during the antebellum period. For a review of Southern laws that applied to such persons and controversy surrounding the laws' enforcement, see Paul Finkelman, "States' Rights North and South in Antebellum America," in Kermit Hall and James W. Ely Jr., eds., *An Uncertain Tradition: Constitutionalism and the History of the South* (Athens: University of Georgia Press, 1989), at 130–33 and 151 n. 24 (includes a reference to related literature on the seamen's acts); William W. Freehling, *Prelude to Civil War: The Nullification Controversy in South Carolina, 1816–1836* (New York: Harper and Row, 1966), at 113–15; William M. Wiecek, *The Sources of Antislavery Constitutionalism in America, 1760–1848* (Ithaca, N.Y.: Cornell University Press, 1977), at 132–40.

[53] The sources cited in the previous note explain how persons in the South successfully defied efforts by federal and state officials and other individuals to oppose the black seamen acts and their enforcement. The rights of white persons, along with blacks, were insecure in the South.

of state autonomy that benefited free as well as slave states. Particularly in light of precedents that supported an expanding federal role to *protect* slavery, it was important for free states to defend their power to treat blacks as citizens and to secure their rights even in opposition to opposing claims of federal and slave-state power.[54] Parts of Curtis's opinion are difficult to understand except as dimensions of this sort of defensive posture.

Thus Curtis's opinion in *Dred Scott*, like Taney's, led in many directions. Unlike the Chief Justice, the dissenter argued that at least some black men were among "the people" to whom the constitutional text referred. But his criteria for citizenship were less nationalistic than Taney's: Curtis emphasized state of birth and allowed states to define attributes of citizenship. He took corresponding positions on the scope of federal and state powers and limitations on each.

The bottom line for Curtis, like Taney, was that the states had substantial discretion regarding the treatment of black persons. Both judges thought states had the power to treat free black men as "citizens," at least for domestic purposes. Curtis presumed, moreover, that states could deny this status to some or all blacks. The dissenting justice also presumed that the national Constitution did not prohibit slavery in the United States.

Curtis took opposing positions from Taney's on the scope of federal powers. The Northerner argued that federal courts had jurisdiction to decide some cases in which blacks sued as "citizens" of a state. Having access to federal courts was a substantial right, particularly for those seeking a formal declaration of their freedom. In addition, Curtis argued that the Missouri Compromise of 1820 was a valid federal law. But even as he supported exercises of federal power to limit slavery and to protect rights of free black persons, he sought to guard against possible encroachment by federal officials on free states' exercising their reserved powers to protect rights of their citizens.

LOOKING BACK, LOOKING FORWARD

Section 1 of the fourteenth amendment overturned Taney's position on who constituted (or *would* constitute) "citizens" for purposes of the United States Constitution. The amendment declares: "All persons born or naturalized in the United States and subject to the jurisdiction thereof, are citizens of the United States and of the State wherein they reside." Setting

---

[54] See Parrish, "The *Booth* Cases"; Finkelman, *An Imperfect Union*, chs. 8–10.

aside for now problems associated with the amendment's origins,[55] it formally affirmed the concept of native-born, national citizenship.[56]

The amendment also superseded Curtis's position, as articulated in *Dred Scott*. Native-born citizenship was automatic, not a matter of governmental discretion. In addition, the fourteenth amendment established *national* criteria for citizenship, thereby supplanting Curtis's claim that the Constitution reserved to the states authority to decide which native-born persons constituted "citizens" for purposes of the United States Constitution.

The fourteenth amendment did not, however, make obsolete the concept of formal citizenship.[57] Section 1's criteria for citizenship are more expansive than Taney's and Curtis's, but the more recent standards are still exclusive. Every "person" does not satisfy these criteria. Not even all residents of the United States qualify for the privileges and immunities and other rights and powers of federal and state citizenship that are secured by the Constitution. (The constitutional text does, however, purport to secure some rights to all "persons," regardless of whether they are formally "citizens.")

In addition, not all who have qualified formally as citizens have shared equally in the "political power" to which Taney and Curtis referred. As a result, these judges' references to ideals of active, participatory, representative government continue to offer critical perspectives for evaluating constitutional norms and political practices that the Constitution has justified, reinforced, or tolerated. Taney and Curtis were willing to accept significant disparities between formal criteria and participatory ideals.

[55] See Bruce A. Ackerman, "Discovering the Constitution," 93 Yale L. J. 1013 (1984), at 1063–70, along with the sources cited therein at 1063–64 n. 88. Chapter 3 examines critically Ackerman's position on legitimate means of constitutional change.

[56] It would remain open to debate whether Frederick Douglass and others like him formally became "citizens" when the fourteenth amendment went into effect. In addition to problems of historical pedigree and consistency with antecedent norms, there would be questions about whether the amendment extended citizenship to persons *already born* in the United States. One could reasonably argue (as did Frederick Douglass) that *all* native-born persons were citizens even before the Civil War; or that such persons had become citizens upon the thirteenth amendment's ratification; or that the fourteenth amendment recognized the citizenship of persons that had *already* been born in the United States. But Sanford Levinson has pointed out that the language of the fourteenth amendment does not explicitly address situations like Douglass's. For analysis of similar problems, see Peter H. Schuck and Rogers M. Smith, *Citizenship Without Consent: Illegal Aliens in the American Polity* (New Haven: Yale University Press, 1985).

[57] Nor did it overrule Taney's and Curtis's shared premise of dual citizenship, national and state. The amendment identifies persons as "citizens of the United States *and* of the State wherein they reside." Subsequent chapters return to this issue and explore its significance more fully.

But now as before, disparities among constitutional norms, along with those between such norms and actual practices, represent tensions within the normative landscape.

The fourteenth amendment's expansive criteria for formal citizenship have exacerbated some such tensions even as they have eliminated others. The more inclusive criteria reflect and justify changes in configurations of political power that have become, in certain respects, more in accord with egalitarian ideals of American constitutionalism. *All* persons born or naturalized in the United States and subject to the jurisdiction thereof, not just some categories of such persons, are "citizens." But adding to the constitutional text an expansive conception of formal citizenship has not automatically led to corresponding changes in the holding or exercise of "political power."[58]

Acting through representative institutions and independently of them, those holding coercive power in America have excluded others from sharing effectively in the "political power" that the Constitution has justified and reinforced. Blacks, members of other racial and ethnic groups, women, and others have been denied the right to vote and otherwise to participate in governing themselves through representatives of their choosing. Several amendments have been responsive to these disparities, but gaps between participatory ideals and actual practices have remained. There are also further questions about whether those who *have* had opportunities to participate in representative processes have done so—or have done so consistently with constitutional norms that have governed the exercise by citizens of *their* rights and powers.

The example of Frederick Douglass is instructive. He argued that disparities between authoritative ideals and actual political practices represented failures of law, not its limits. He also exhibited attributes of citizenship in opposition to predominant understandings of the law of the Constitution—including who constituted "citizens." The next chapter examines more closely these contributions.

---

[58] Sec. 2 of the fourteenth amendment (which alters criteria for apportionment) and accompanying changes in practices have been significant in this respect—as have the amendment's equal protection clause and interpretations of it.

CHAPTER 2

Toward Constitutional Citizenship: Unofficial Commitments

> I hold that every American citizen has a right to form an opinion of the constitution, and to propagate that opinion, and to use all honorable means to make his opinion the prevailing one.[1]

IN AN important article on several cultural dimensions of the formation, maintenance, and destruction of legal meanings, Robert M. Cover used the example of radical antislavery constitutionalism during the antebellum period to illustrate a dilemma confronted by those who seek to assert normative visions at odds with official interpretations of law. He explained how that movement, like the later civil rights, women's, and right-to-life movements, "set out to liberate persons and the law and to raise them from a fallen state." He described how the radical antislavery constitutionalists, more specifically, embraced "a vision of an alternative world in which the entire order of American slavery would be without foundation in law." Cover claimed, moreover, that their vision, unlike Garrisonian abolitionism, "require[d] for its fulfillment the participation of the larger community that exercise[d] state power." Because a *popular* movement depended on changes in *official* practices, the radicals risked "the failure of the conversion of vision into reality."[2]

Cover was doubtless correct that one component of radical antislavery constitutionalism was the complete elimination of legal support for slavery. The movement was, in this respect, "utopian." From the perspective of whether its ideals were fully realized in practice, therefore, William Wiecek's appraisal (which Cover supported) was correct: "In the short run, radical constitutionalism was a failure." The movement's "efforts to construe slavery out of the Constitution" did not achieve prominence,

---

[1] Frederick Douglass, "The Meaning of July Fourth for the Negro," speech at Rochester, New York, on July 5, 1852, in Philip S. Foner, ed., *The Life and Writings of Frederick Douglass* (New York: International Publishers, 1950–1955), vol. 2, at 202.

[2] See Robert M. Cover, "Foreword: *Nomos* and Narrative" (hereafter, "*Nomos* and Narrative"), 97 Harv. L. Rev. 4 (1983), at 35 and passim.

either within society at large or by governmental action, at least through the beginning of the Civil War.[3]

Cover had good reasons to distinguish radical antislavery constitutionalism, as a form of "redemptive" legal movement, from "insular" forms of constitutional criticism such as Garrisonian abolitionism. As Cover explained, the latter group interpreted the Constitution as providing legal protection for slavery. On that basis, they "eschewed participation in and renounced obligation to government under such a Constitution." Rather than advocating a "redemptive" vision of the existing Constitution, as did the radicals, the Garrisonians sought "disengagement from participation in the state." Cover characterized their efforts as a form of "nomian insularity" that involved "the pursuit of a pure *nomos* without a polis."[4]

Cover's efforts to distinguish "redemptive" constitutionalism from "insular" forms of normative criticism were helpful in some respects. But his analysis of issues raised by that distinction obscured an important feature of radical antislavery constitutionalism: the importance of its vision of the Constitution as a source of "law" independently of whether that vision achieved prominence within society or became fully realized in practice. In a complex and puzzling paragraph, Cover suggested that whether (or how much) radical antislavery constitutionalism was a "movement of the law" depended on whether (or how much) its vision was converted into practice:

> If law reflects a tension between what is and what might be, law can be maintained only as long as the two are close enough to reveal a line of hu-

---

[3] William M. Wiecek, *The Sources of Antislavery Constitutionalism in America, 1760–1848* (Ithaca, N.Y.: Cornell University Press, 1977), at 274. Cover quoted and endorsed Wiecek's conclusion in "*Nomos* and Narrative," at 38–39 (except that Cover challenged Wiecek's characterization of radical antislavery constitutionalism as a "sectarian" movement). For purposes of this work, it is not necessary to evaluate the longer-term legacy of radical antislavery constitutionalism. It should be sufficient to note that the issue is more complex than considering the movement's success before the Civil War. The movement's aspirations regarding the abolition of legal support for slavery were eventually accomplished, but by the force of arms and formal constitutional amendment, not a reinterpretation of the existing text. But it is not clear how much the radicals' efforts contributed to that cause. Nor is it clear that their interpretive methodology has ever achieved official prominence. But see Wiecek's suggestion, on pp. 274–75 of his book, that the radicals' natural law approach prevailed; and Cover's comment, on p. 36 of his article, that those who claimed that the federal Constitution protected slavery "interpreted and analyzed the Constitution in a manner consistent with the dominant professional methods of their day (*and of our day as well*)."

[4] Cover, "*Nomos* and Narrative," at 35–39. For descriptions of Garrisonian thought, see James B. Stewart, *Holy Warriors* (New York: Hill and Wang, 1976); John L. Thomas, *The Liberator: William Lloyd Garrison* (Boston: Little, Brown, 1963); Wiecek, *Sources of Antislavery Constitutionalism*, ch. 10.

man endeavor that brings them into temporary or partial reconciliation. All utopian or eschatological movements that do not withdraw to insularity risk the failure of the conversion of vision into reality and, thus, the breaking of the tension. At that point, they become movements, but no longer movements of the law.

Complicating this puzzle, Cover suggested that "[w]hile their movement lasted, the radical constitutionalists contributed to an immense growth of law," even though he had just explained how the full realization of their vision depended on changes in political practices that did not occur, at least in the short term. Moreover, he had earlier made clear that he sought to study "the organization of law as meaning," not just "the social organization of law as power." He repeatedly allowed for the possibility of legal meanings in addition to "the official 'law,'" and he criticized others for "confus[ing] the status of interpretation with the status of political domination."[5]

It is important to read these passages in light of Cover's subsequent analysis of how legal meanings are created. He claimed that such meanings depend at least on commitment and objectification. He asserted, moreover, that a community creates law by positing norms external to itself and by making a commitment to obey, and by obeying in practice, its understanding of that law. According to this conception of "law," the radical antislavery constitutionalists were in a very difficult position. Their conception of legal redemption depended on public officials bringing *official* practices into compliance with *the radicals'* vision, not more simply on the radicals bringing *their* practices into line with *their* conception of the law.

Cover claimed, in addition, that individuals and communities could create legal meanings by asserting opposing *interpretations* of law. He used the example of the civil rights sit-in movement from 1961 to 1964 to illustrate how a "community that has created and proposed to live by its own, divergent understanding of the law makes a claim not of justifiable disobedience, but rather of radical reinterpretation." Although members of the civil rights movement conceded that they had a moral obligation to comply with valid laws, they conformed *their* behavior to *their* interpretation of the fourteenth amendment's equal protection clause, not "the official 'law.'" From the "official" perspective, there was civil disobedience; but from the point of view of the civil rights community, there was "obedience to the movement's own interpretation of the Constitution." Cover suggested that it would be inappropriate to privilege official conceptions of law—positions taken by governmental officials—other than

[5] Cover, "*Nomos* and Narrative," at 18, 40–44, and 47.

to recognize "as a sociological datum" that "courts in the United States do wield the heaviest stick and, as a result, are often the voice most carefully attended to." To regard only official interpretations as legal meanings would, according to Cover, "deny to the jurisgenerative community out of which legal meanings arise the integrity of a law of its own."[6]

These considerations underlay his comment that an important challenge to legal theory and practice has been "to maintain a sense of legal meaning despite the destruction of any pretense of superiority of one *nomos* over another." He claimed that "[b]y exercising its superior brute force, however, the agency of state law shuts down the creative hermeneutic of principle that is spread throughout our communities." At the same time, he endorsed official coercion as "necessary for the maintenance of minimum conditions for the creation of legal meaning in autonomous interpretive communities." Thus Cover regarded official power as valuable to maintaining order but as problematic insofar as judges "assert that *this one* [meaning] is law and destroy or try to destroy the rest."[7]

His emphasis on the potentially violent role of legal institutions, particularly on how judges have typically killed rather than created law, informed his analysis of the radical antislavery movement. Insofar as that movement had "redemptive" elements that depended on change in the "official law," judges and other governmental officials had the coercive power to block realization of the redemptive vision. As a result, those seeking to abolish legally sanctioned slavery could not be successful as a "movement of the law," at least at the official level, without changes in governmental officials' practices. The civil rights movement of the 1960s had a similar redemptive vision. But it, unlike the radical antislavery constitutionalists' vision, was largely realized in practice through reinterpretation of the fourteenth amendment *by governmental officials*. In 1964 Congress enacted a Civil Rights Act that invalidated many of the forms of racial discrimination the protesters had opposed as unlawful. That year, for Cover, was a definitive moment for the civil rights movement.[8]

Cover's sensitivity to this difference between radical antislavery constitutionalism and the civil rights movement—whether officials endorsed the respective movements' reinterpretive aspirations—diverted his attention from something common to these two movements: both were

---

[6] Ibid., at 46–47.

[7] See ibid., at 44 and 53. See also ibid., at 53 and 68, on how courts kill legal meanings; and see Robert M. Cover, "The Bonds of Constitutional Interpretation: Of the Word, the Deed, and the Role," 20 Ga. L. Rev. 815 (1986).

[8] See Cover, "*Nomos* and Narrative," at 47.

"movements of the law" independently of positions taken by governmental officials. Cover explained how the civil rights movement created unofficial legal meanings, even before its vision of that law was affirmed by Congress, executive officials, judges, and other governmental actors. His analysis also supports a parallel conclusion with respect to the radical constitutionalists of the antebellum period, a conclusion that Cover did not articulate in his article: interpretations of the Constitution by radical antislavery constitutionalists were "legal interpretations," even when not "official interpretations," insofar as members of that movement ordered *their* (unofficial) conduct by *their* visions of constitutional meanings.

The fact that radical constitutionalists suffered short-term setbacks highlights the importance of Cover's distinction between "the social organization of law as power and the organization of law as meaning."[9] Part of the radicals' vision was transformation of the social organization of power, something accomplished by war and reconstruction and not primarily through changes in practices based on different interpretations of the existing Constitution. But change in the "official law" through radical reinterpretation was not the radicals' only vision. They also sought to conform *their* (unofficial) practices to *their* interpretations of the Constitution. Officials could attempt to suppress these meanings and could otherwise oppose their realization in practice but could only kill them by doing away with the ideas themselves and the forms of popular interpretive autonomy that sustained them. Rather than killing the radical antislavery constitutionalists' normative vision, however, governmental decisions such as *Dred Scott* appear to have provoked and crystallized political opposition, much of which later became channeled through official actions and larger-scale changes in the law of the Constitution.

Unofficial components of the radical antislavery redemptive vision, not just their eventual failures and successes in relation to "official law," deserve fuller consideration. The life of Frederick Douglass, which Cover used to highlight differences between Garrisonian perfectionism and radical constitutionalism, also sheds light on affinities between these two movements. It is not surprising that Douglass's life would bridge these two approaches to abolitionism, since he shifted his affiliation from the former to the latter group. An analysis of several components of that shift suggests important linkages between legal criticism and constitutional affirmation, official and unofficial interpretations, legal continuity and change, constitutional meanings and coercive power, and related problems of constitutional theory and practice that are of central concern to this work.

[9] See ibid., at 18.

CRITICISM AND AFFIRMATION

Although Douglass eventually argued that the United States Constitution was incompatible with legally sanctioned slavery, he had earlier "denounce[d] the Constitution and government of the United States as a most foul and bloody conspiracy."[10] Before he advocated radical reinterpretation, Douglass treated the Constitution as "a compact demanding immediate disannulment, and one which, with our view of its wicked requirements, we can never enter."[11] These earlier views were not surprising, considering his status as a former slave and his identification with blacks still held in bondage. Douglass's reasons for initially opposing the Constitution remained important, moreover, since they informed his later analysis.

Opposition

Douglass repeatedly defied and otherwise opposed "official law," both as interpreted and as enforced. In 1838, at the age of twenty, he evaded the coercive powers of several states and of the United States by escaping from bondage. According to federal and state laws, which persons in official positions interpreted and enforced as valid, Douglass remained a fugitive until 1847 when some of his friends purchased his freedom. Even while formally a fugitive, however, Douglass lived in Massachusetts as if he were a free person. After his formal emancipation from slavery, Douglass continued to defy authoritative legal precedents by claiming to be a citizen of New York and of the United States and by exercising a wide range of rights and powers of state and federal citizenship. He voted in national and state elections, owned property, gave speeches, edited a newspaper, traveled among the states and internationally, gave advice to President Abraham Lincoln, and otherwise expressed commitment to norms of American constitutionalism.[12]

Douglass described in an autobiography how he had initially been a "faithful disciple" of William Lloyd Garrison and had been "fully committed to his doctrine touching the pro-slavery character of the Constitution of the United States, also the non-voting principle of which he was

[10] Douglass, "Comments on Gerrit Smith's Address," from the *North Star*, March 30, 1849, in Foner, ed., *Life and Writings* 1:374–79.

[11] Douglass, "The Constitution and Slavery," from the *North Star*, March 16, 1849, in Foner, ed., *Life and Writings* 1:366.

[12] See ch. 1, n. 18, above, for a reference to biographies of Douglass, along with his autobiography.

the known and distinguished advocate." Opponents of slavery, not just its defenders, interpreted the Constitution as protecting slavery:

> Brought directly, when I escaped from slavery, into contact with abolitionists who regarded the Constitution as a slaveholding instrument, and finding their views supported by the united and entire history of every department of the government, it is not strange that I assumed the Constitution to be just what these friends made it seem to be.[13]

Thus he initially endorsed what William Wiecek has called the "federal consensus," whose correlative central tenets were that the Constitution allowed slavery within the states and precluded the federal government from abolishing slavery.[14]

In speeches, articles, and correspondence, Douglass effectively criticized the Constitution as a pro-slavery compact. He pointed out that the constitutional text, "standing alone, and construed *only* in the light of its letter, without reference to the opinions of the men who framed and adopted it, or to the uniform, universal and undeviating practice of the nation under it, from the time of its adoption until now, is not a pro-slavery instrument." But he claimed that the Constitution, "having a terrestrial, and not a celestial origin," had to be "explained in the light of those maxims and principles which human beings have laid down as guides to the understanding of all written instruments, covenants, contracts and agreements emanating from human beings, and to which human beings are parties both on the first and second part." Interpreted in that light, Douglass argued, the Constitution was "a most cunningly-devised and wicked compact," one "made in view of the existence of slavery, and in a manner well calculated to aid and strengthen that heaven-daring crime." To support that conclusion, he referred to parts of the constitutional text that distorted representation in favor of slave states, gave Congress power to suppress insurrections, precluded Congress from outlawing the slave trade until 1808, provided for the return of "person[s] held to service or labour," and purportedly justified the use of national power to protect slaveholders from domestic violence.[15]

---

[13] See Douglass, *Life and Times* (New York: Macmillan, 1962), at 260–61. See also Douglass, "Comments on Gerrit Smith's Address," in Foner, ed., *Life and Writings* 1:374–79.

[14] See Wiecek, *Sources of Antislavery Constitutionalism*, at 15–19 and passim.

[15] See Douglass, "The Constitution and Slavery," in Foner, ed., *Life and Writings* 1:361–67 (emphasis on "only" in original). See also ibid., at 366 ("The parties that made the Constitution, aimed to cheat and defraud the slave, who was not himself a party to the compact or agreement. It was entered into understandingly on both sides"); Douglass, "American Slavery," speech delivered in New York City on October 22, 1847, in Foner, ed., *Life and Writings* 1:274 ("The Constitution I hold to be radically and essentially slave-holding, in that it gives the physical and numerical power of the nation to keep the slave in

As did other Garrisonians, Douglass at first relied primarily on moral suasion, rather than representative institutions, for legal change. He rejected Gerrit Smith's argument for change through voting and official actions. According to moral perfectionists with whom Douglass associated, those who relied on corrupt governmental structures would become tainted by association, even if these persons' motives were good and their actions helped to bring about good results. Based on a premise that the Constitution was a pro-slavery pact, the Garrisonians also argued that federal officials would be acting illegally if they used their positions to abolish slavery.[16]

Hence their commitment to moral integrity led the Garrisonians to repudiate both popular and governmental efforts to construe the Constitution as pro-slavery. They regarded such efforts as forms of "do[ing] evil that good may come." Invoking perfectionist commitments, Douglass claimed that "a man is lame, impotent, and worse than weak, when he ceases to regard clear convictions of his understanding, to accomplish anything, no matter how desirable that thing may be."[17]

Thus he initially argued against "mending old clothes with new cloth, or putting new wine into old bottles." Instead, he treated the Constitution as a "compact demanding immediate disannulment, and one which, with our view of its wicked requirements, we can never enter." He sought, in short, to expose the Constitution's wickedness to moral condemnation as a way to "hasten the day of deliverance" from the present Union. He pledged that until then, he would not defile himself by engaging in unholy practices: "For my part I had rather that my right hand should wither by my side than cast a single ballot under the Constitution of the United States."[18]

Even as he criticized the Constitution and argued against seeking to

---

his chains by promising that that power shall in any emergency be brought to bear upon the slave, to crush him in obedience"); Douglass, "The Revolution of 1848," speech delivered in Rochester, New York, on August 1, 1848, in Foner, ed., *Life and Writings* 1:328 ("The people of this country are held together by a Constitution. That Constitution contains certain compromises in favor of slavery, and which bind the citizens to uphold slavery"). See generally Paul Finkelman, "Slavery and the Constitutional Convention," in Beeman, Botein, and Carter, eds., *Beyond Confederation* (Chapel Hill: University of North Carolina Press, 1987); William M. Wiecek, *The Guarantee Clause of the U.S. Constitution* (Ithaca, N.Y.: Cornell University Press, 1972).

[16] See the sources cited at n. 4, above. See also nn. 13–14, above, and accompanying text.

[17] Douglass, "Comments on Gerrit Smith's Address," in Foner, ed., *Life and Writings* 1:374–79.

[18] See ibid., at 375, 379; Douglass, "The Constitution and Slavery," in Foner, ed., *Life and Writings* 1:366; Douglass, "American Slavery," in Foner, ed., *Life and Writings* 1:269–70, 275.

eliminate slavery by relying on representative structures, Douglass held out the possibility of radical reinterpretation as a morally commendable rather than corrupt source of popular empowerment. Reflecting his confidence that truth would prevail in an unfettered environment, Douglass wrote in the *North Star* on March 16, 1849, that he was "prepared to hear all sides," including Smith's argument that the Constitution could be used as "a *rightful* instrument against slavery." In his initial response to Smith's arguments, Douglass commended his adversary's moral position but was unpersuaded by his analysis of what the Constitution meant. Almost two years later, he confessed to Smith that he was "sick and tired of arguing on the slaveholders' side of this question." Yet he still could not understand how it was possible to interpret the Constitution, as law, other than as a pro-slavery compact. Douglass questioned whether the antislavery movement could legitimately avail itself of "legal rules which enable us to defeat the wicked intentions of our Constitution makers." Douglass wanted to make *legal* arguments for interpreting the Constitution as an antislavery charter, not only *prudential* arguments. He was especially concerned about whether it was "good morality to take advantage of a legal flaw and put a meaning upon a legal instrument the very opposite of what we have good reason to believe was the intention of the men who framed it."[19]

Thus Douglass considered himself bound by conventions of legal interpretation. He assumed that "law" had positive attributes, making it potentially divergent from norms of morality or principles of justice. In addition, he implicitly denied that it would be permissible for him to claim that the "law" of the Constitution meant whatever he wanted it to mean. He sought to rely on legal meanings that transcended his own will, even as he searched for a conception of such meanings grounded in something other than the will of the Constitution's original makers.[20]

Four months later, Douglass announced a breakthrough in his thinking. He wrote to Smith that he was then "prepared to contend for those rules of interpretation which when applied to the Constitution make its details harmonize with its declared objects in the preamble." The *North Star* also announced Douglass's break from the Garrisonians:

[W]e had arrived at the firm conviction that the Constitution, construed in the light of well established rules of legal interpretation, might be made con-

[19] Douglass, "The Constitution and Slavery," in Foner, ed., *Life and Writings* 1:366 (emphasis on "rightful" added); Douglass, "Comments on Gerrit Smith's Address," in Foner, ed., *Life and Writings* 1:374–79; Douglass, Letter to Gerrit Smith, Esqr., January 21, 1851, in Foner, ed., *Life and Writings* 2:149–50.

[20] See, e.g., Douglass's criticism of "forced and latitudinarian construction[s] of the Constitution," in his "Comments on Gerrit Smith's Address," in Foner, ed., *Life and Writings* 1:378.

sistent in its details with the noble purposes avowed in its preamble; and that hereafter we should insist upon the application of such rules to that instrument, and demand that it be wielded in behalf of emancipation.[21]

Douglass did not deny what he had earlier argued: some "established rules of legal interpretation," including literal reading of particular provisions and/or analysis of framers' intentions, might lead to objectionable results. But he asserted the possibility of a different blend of literalism and purposive analysis: interpreting "the intentions of those who framed the Constitution *in the Constitution itself.*"[22] He also expressed a willingness to rely on the latter approach, at least when its results would promote rather than undercut moral ideals.

As indicated, Douglass used the preamble as the cornerstone for his revised interpretive approach. The purposes set forth in the preamble supplied him with alternatives to framers' intentions as guides for analyzing constitutional purposes. The preamble's writtenness also enabled him to link ideals that he affirmed independently of the Constitution to the positive law of the constitutional text itself. Douglass claimed, moreover, that the Constitution's authority as "supreme law," as a matter of internal coherence, depended on reconciliation among it parts and its self-proclaimed ideals:

> [A] careful consideration of the subject convinced me that . . . the Constitution of the United States not only contains no guarantees in favor of slavery, but, on the contrary, was in its letter and spirit an antislavery instrument, demanding the abolition of slavery as a condition of its own existence as the supreme law of the land. . . .
>
> I was conducted to the conclusion that the Constitution of the United States—inaugurated to "form a more perfect union, establish justice, insure domestic tranquility, provide for the common defense, promote the general welfare, and secure the blessings of liberty"—could not well have been designed at the same time to maintain and perpetuate a system of rapine and murder like slavery, especially as not one word can be found in the Constitution to authorize such a belief. Then, again, if the declared purposes of an instrument are to govern the meaning of all its parts and details, as they clearly should, the Constitution of our country is our warrant for the abolition of slavery in every state of the Union.[23]

---

[21] See Douglass, "Change of Opinion Announced," from the *North Star*, May 23, 1851, in Foner, ed., *Life and Writings* 2:155–56.

[22] See Douglass's Letter to Gerrit Smith, Esqr., May 21, 1851, in Foner, ed., *Life and Writings* 2:157 (emphasis in original).

[23] See Douglass, *Life and Times*, at 260–62.

This interpretive approach—a hybrid of textualism and purposive analysis—enabled Douglass to reconcile his commitments to affirming the rule of law, acting morally, and seeking to abolish slavery.

Radical Reinterpretation

Douglass's change of opinion on how to interpret the Constitution, and hence on what it meant, enabled him to endorse a wider range of political activity. Beginning in 1851, Douglass urged every American "to use his *political* as well as his *moral* power" to overthrow slavery.[24] But rather than advocating dissolution of the Union, he sought its preservation.

Douglass adhered to a Garrisonian premise that the North was responsible for slavery as long as it remained in a Union with slaveholding states. But he repudiated Garrison's argument that dissolving the Union would dissolve that responsibility. Douglass explained: "There now, clearly, is no freedom from responsibility for slavery, but in the Abolition of slavery." He pointed out that "[t]o dissolve the Union would be to withdraw the emancipating power from the field," thereby leaving no remedy for slaves left in bondage within slaveholding states.[25] In Robert Cover's terms, "Douglass' greatest need was for a vision of law that both validated his freedom and integrated norms with a future redemptive possibility for his people."[26]

Douglass recognized a profound truth: the Constitution could accommodate radical change, even without any formal amendment of the constitutional text. Douglass was aware that several parts of the constitutional text had generally been *interpreted* to support slavery. He even conceded that members of the founding generation may have designed such provisions to serve that goal. But he denied that these understandings or objectives were, or had to remain, parts of the law of the Constitution itself.

In a speech on July 5, 1852, shortly after his break with the Garrisonians, Douglass explained how the Constitution could realize a greater potential, as law, if interpreters broke away from conventional understandings of the text. He relied on the Declaration of Independence to highlight gaps between constitutive national ideals and actual political practices: "What, to the American slave, is your 4th of July? I answer; a

[24] See Douglass, "Change of Opinion Announced," in Foner, ed., *Life and Writings* 2:156 (emphasis in original).

[25] Douglass, "The Dred Scott Decision," speech delivered before the American Anti-Slavery Society, New York, on May 11, 1857, in Foner, ed., *Life and Writings* 2:416–17.

[26] Cover, "*Nomos* and Narrative," at 38.

day that reveals to him, more than all other days of the year, the gross injustice and cruelty to which he is the constant victim."[27] He repeatedly distanced himself from "the people" of the United States by referring to "*your* 'sovereign people,'" "*your* nation's history," "the birthday of *your* National Independence, and of *your* political freedom."[28] Not surprisingly, he denied that the "great principles of political freedom and of natural justice, embodied in that Declaration of Independence," had been extended to persons of color. Thus he refused to join in celebrating the nation's independence: "This Fourth of July is *yours*, not *mine*."[29]

Douglass did not, however, consider himself bound by past understandings of what the Constitution meant, including the scope of "the people" for whom it had been ordained and established. He sought to shift the focus of constitutional analysis from studying the past to bringing about a very different future: "My business, if I have any here to-day, is with the present. . . . We have to do with the past only as we can make it useful to the present and to the future."[30] Accordingly, Douglass sought to put the most favorable gloss possible on the constitutional document: a gloss that would bring interpretations of it into line with the ideals set forth in the Declaration of Independence and in the constitutional text's own preamble.

He suggested that persons of color would be able to celebrate the nation's independence and to affirm the Constitution as supreme law only if this sort of change in interpretive practices occurred. Thus his willingness to affirm the Constitution was tentative and forward-looking rather than grounded in maintaining continuity with America's constitutional past. In short, he concentrated not on how the Constitution had *been* interpreted but on how it could "*become* the inheritance of all the inhabitants of this highly favoured country."[31]

Douglass emphasized, moreover, how all the land's inhabitants could regard the United States Constitution as "a glorious liberty document" and "not a sentence or syllable of the Constitution need be altered."[32] He later compared constitutional compromises and original understandings regarding slavery to artifices, or parts of an "unwritten constitution," that could be removed from the main structure: "If in its origin siavery had any

---

[27] Douglass, "July Fourth and the Negro," in Foner, ed., *Life and Writings* 2:192. See also ibid., at 201 ("The existence of slavery in this country brands your republicanism as a sham, your humanity as a base pretense, and your Christianity as a lie").

[28] Ibid., at 182, 183, and 185 (emphasis added).

[29] Ibid., at 188–89 (emphasis in original).

[30] Ibid., at 188.

[31] Ibid., at 202.

[32] Ibid.; Douglass, "Address for the Promotion of Colored Enlistments," delivered at a mass meeting in Philadelphia on July 6, 1863, in Foner, ed., *Life and Writings* 3:365.

relation to the government, it was only as the scaffolding to the magnificent structure, to be removed as soon as the building was complete."[33] In addition, he claimed that if the text were interpreted with reference to the goals set forth in the preamble rather than used to perpetuate historical compromises regarding slavery, "it will be found to contain principles and purposes, entirely hostile to the existence of slavery."[34] Accordingly, he exhorted all Americans to "live up to the Constitution, adopt its principles, imbibe its spirit, and enforce its provisions."[35]

These passages indicate how Douglass linked forms of constitutional criticism and affirmation. He recognized the organizing functions of the Constitution as a symbol of national ideals and as an instrument of collective power.[36] Rather than conceding those functions to his opponents, he sought to enlist them in the cause of radical change: eliminating slavery. As with revolutionaries preceding and following him, including leading members of the founding generation, he presented radical change as more faithful to past traditions and to existing ideals than were the practices of his day. Thus he claimed that affirming his conception of the Constitution, along with corresponding changes in federal and state laws and their enforcement, would be fundamentally preservative. Paradoxically and profoundly, he was advocating fundamental continuity through radical change.[37]

LIMITATIONS OF OFFICIAL LAW

The Supreme Court's decision in *Dred Scott* was, of course, a setback to those who sought to abolish legally sanctioned slavery.[38] Not sur-

[33] Douglass, "The Dred Scott Decision," in Foner, ed., *Life and Writings* 2:419; Douglass, "Address for the Promotion of Colored Enlistments," in Foner, ed., *Life and Writings* 3:365.

[34] Douglass, "July Fourth and the Negro," in Foner, ed., *Life and Writings* 2:202.

[35] Douglass, "The Dred Scott Decision," in Foner, ed., *Life and Writings* 2:424.

[36] See generally Edward S. Corwin, "The Constitution as Instrument and as Symbol," 30 Am. Pol. Sci. Rev. 1071 (1936).

[37] By maintaining that the Constitution can accommodate radical change through reinterpretation, I am not claiming that such change brings about a radically different constitutional order, conceived as a whole. Chapter 3 returns to this issue in the context of exploring distinctions between amending the Constitution and bringing about a fundamentally different regime.

[38] I am not here ignoring (or dismissing) the possibility that *Dred Scott* may have provoked political responses that, along with other developments, ultimately culminated in abolition of slavery. My comment here pertains to the more direct and immediate consequences of the Court's decision. I should note, moreover, that the setback proved to be relatively short-lived. For analysis of the decision's broader political ramifications, see Don E. Fehrenbacher, *The Dred Scott Case* (New York: Oxford University Press, 1987).

prisingly, Douglass criticized the majority decision and similar official pronouncements that upheld slavery.[39] But Douglass and others of like mind were relatively powerless to bring about change in the "official law" regarding slavery under the conditions that prevailed during the antebellum period.

The radicals' failure to transform official law was primarily a function of limitations imposed by representative structures. These structures precluded individuals and groups, acting separately, from preempting a range of authoritative choices that were entrusted by the Constitution and other laws to mechanisms of collective determination. More specifically, the Constitution delegated legislative, executive, and judicial powers to federal officials in ways that precluded or superseded separate claims of official lawmaking and enforcement authority. These governmental powers included official interpretive prerogatives that likewise precluded a range of separate interpretive claims. By definition, those who were not governmental officials could not make legally authoritative *official* decisions, including interpretive decisions on matters of constitutional law.

Political power accompanied delegations of governmental authority, such that force backed official normative claims. In addition to facing opposing claims of lawmaking, law-enforcing, and law-interpreting prerogatives, persons like Douglass confronted institutions of collective power that were operating, in practice, to coerce or enforce compliance with legally authoritative decisions. Douglass did not have the power, by himself or in concert with other radical antislavery constitutionalists, to free all blacks from the practical operations of a legal system that protected slavery. On the contrary, representative structures were used, along with other devices, to maintain institutions of slavery against the will of many persons.

Constitutional structures provided individuals and groups with some means of directly and indirectly affecting official choices. For example, electoral structures enabled members of the people at large, through coordinated voting, to select a range of official representatives. Those who exercised rights of speech, association, assembly, petitioning, and the like also had opportunities to influence governmental choices and thus to affect how representatives, including unelected officials, acted through constitutional structures. Then as now, individuals were able to rely separately and collectively on a variety of political processes as means of reinforcing and/or opposing governmental choices—to promote continuity and/or change in the official law, including the law of the Constitution itself.

Frederick Douglass recognized the potential value of popular political

---

[39] See Douglass, "The Dred Scott Decision," in Foner, ed., *Life and Writings* 2:407–24.

participation as an instrument of legal change. After breaking from the Garrisonians, Douglass urged abolitionists to channel their efforts through representative structures, not just independently of them. He became active in partisan politics, voted, and exercised other rights and powers of political expression by writing, speaking, and using similar means to voice opposition to slavery.[40]

Douglass recognized, however, that the representational structures upon which he relied would not necessarily ensure governmental compliance with constitutional norms. On the contrary, his position was that public officials had acted inconsistently with the constitutional text's self-proclaimed ideals since its ratification. He was aware, moreover, that proponents of change faced substantial political obstacles.

During the antebellum period, political processes were distorted in at least two ways of immediate relevance to controversy over slavery. First, those in power within many of the states excluded blacks (among others) from voting and exercising other rights and powers of political participation. Persons held as slaves were, of course, denied these prerogatives. In addition, free blacks in the North and South were subjected, in varying degrees, to various forms of official and unofficial discrimination that deprived them of opportunities for political expression.[41]

Representative structures did not, moreover, count all persons' votes equally, even among those holding the franchise. Article I enhanced the relative political power of voters in slave states, at the expense of voters in free states, for purposes of apportionment within the House of Representatives. In addition, electoral rules within states further diminished the relative power of voting blacks.[42]

The United States Constitution did not, of course, contemplate simply majoritarian, popular decision-making. Even if members of the House had been chosen through procedures that counted equally the votes of all

[40] See Douglass, "The Suffrage Question," April 25, 1856, and "What Is My Duty as an Anti-Slavery Voter," April 25, 1856, in Foner, ed., *Life and Writings* 2:389–95. See also ch. 1 hereof, nn. 22–23, and accompanying text.

[41] For historical overviews of restrictions on suffrage in the United States, see Kirk H. Porter, *A History of Suffrage in the United States* (New York: Greenwood, 1918); Chilton Williamson, *American Suffrage: From Property to Democracy, 1760–1860* (Princeton: Princeton University Press, 1960). See also James H. Kettner, *The Development of American Citizenship, 1608–1870* (Chapel Hill: University of North Carolina Press, 1978), esp. ch. 10; Finkelman, "Prelude to the Fourteenth Amendment," 17 Rutgers L. Rev. 415 (1986); Judith N. Shklar, *American Citizenship: The Quest for Inclusion* (Cambridge: Harvard University Press, 1991). These sources also identify obstacles confronting members of other racial and ethnic groups (not just blacks), women, and even white men who failed to meet property qualifications.

[42] See generally Charles L. Black Jr., "Representation in Law and Equity," in J. Roland Pennock and John W. Chapman, eds., *Representation* (Nomos X) (New York: Atherton, 1968), at 131–43; Finkelman, "Slavery and the Constitutional Convention."

residents of the United States (including slaves, free blacks, women, and others), and even if a majority of those persons supported federal efforts to abolish slavery,[43] other obstacles to achieving that objective would have remained. The Constitution placed substantive limits on federal powers and established complex structures of popular representation that removed important collective choices from immediate popular control.

The people at large made legally authoritative decisions, but so did state officials, members of the U.S. Congress, presidents, federal judges, and other governmental officials. The Constitution's complex configuration of political power had been designed to enable public officials to act *consistently* with constitutional norms even in the face of widespread popular opposition.[44] But these same structures, along with informal norms such as the functioning of political parties, also made it possible for those holding power to act independently of popular opinion in a manner *inconsistent* with constitutional imperatives. Changing electoral rules would not have eliminated that possibility.

Although Frederick Douglass might have argued that unconstitutional governmental actions were void, he treated them as legally authoritative. As would Abraham Lincoln, Douglass regarded governmental actions as legally preclusive for some purposes even as he argued they went against constitutional ideals. For example, he did not deny that acts of Congress had authority as positive law, even though he criticized some such acts as unconstitutional. Likewise, he accepted *Dred Scott* as final for purposes of resolving the lawsuit, even though he argued that the decision was based on constitutional errors.[45] He did not presume that persons other

[43] The opposite assumption is equally plausible: a majority of Americans (broadly conceived) may have opposed efforts by the federal government to abolish slavery throughout the United States. It is difficult to gauge public sentiment at such a high level of generality on such a complex issue, especially as it might have existed under imagined, counterfactual circumstances.

[44] See, e.g., James Madison's treatment of this issue in the 10th *Federalist*.

[45] See Douglass, "The Dred Scott Decision," in Foner, ed., *Life and Writings* 2:407–24. Compare Abraham Lincoln's speech at Springfield, Illinois, on July 17, 1858 ("[I]n so far as [the Court's decision] decided in favor of Dred Scott's master and against Dred Scott and his family, I do not propose to disturb or resist the decision. . . . [Stephen Douglas] would have the citizen conform his vote to that decision; the member of Congress, his; the President, his use of the veto power. He would make it a rule of political action for the people and all the departments of government. I would not. By resisting it as a political rule, I disturb no right of property, create no disorder, excite no mobs"). The speech is reprinted in Roy P. Basler, ed., *The Collected Works of Abraham Lincoln* (New Brunswick, N.J.: Rutgers University Press, 1953), vol. 2, at 504–20. See also Lincoln's speech at Springfield, Illinois, on June 26, 1857, in Basler, ibid., at 398–410.

Some persons might dismiss as incoherent a position that governmental decisions have been legally authoritative even if they have been inconsistent with the law of the Constitution itself. One could rely, for example, on Chief Justice John Marshall's reasoning in *Marbury v. Madison*, 5 U.S. (1 Cranch) 137 (1803), to argue that governmental actions not in

than governmental officials, whether citizens or not, had authority to exercise governmental powers. Many of his efforts, on the contrary, were directed toward influencing *who* would hold office and how *they* would exercise *their* powers.

Douglass's predicament thus highlights possibilities of constitutional failure, obstacles in the way of correcting official interpretive mistakes, and limitations on popular efforts to bring about legal change. Representative processes gave some persons means of influencing official choices, but these processes excluded many voices from important channels of public discourse. Complex allocations of governing authority gave a variety of officials opportunities to block others' efforts to make or enforce unconstitutional laws, but representative structures did not ensure that all legally authoritative decisions measured up, in practice, to constitutional standards. Those seeking legal reform did not have the prerogative, based only on claims of constitutional error, to substitute their judgments for official decisions.

UNOFFICIAL COMMITMENTS

The fact that public officials continued to interpret the Constitution as consistent with (and supportive of) slavery during the antebellum period does not mean that radical antislavery constitutionalists' efforts to change law failed entirely. Insofar as persons like Douglass called attention to discrepancies between basic legal ideals and actual political practices, the radicals contributed to analyzing problems of constitutional meaning and authority. Some of the tensions between ideals and practices were allevi-

---

accord with the Constitution have been void, and hence not validly enforceable, even if officials have *regarded* them as valid. To be sure, it would be incoherent for the Constitution to sanction its own breach. But neither constitutional logic nor Marshall's reasoning in *Marbury* is inconsistent with the possibility, *in practice*, of legally authoritative but constitutionally erroneous decisions.

Marshall argued in *Marbury* that members of the Supreme Court had authority to decide for themselves whether an act of Congress was valid, at least for purposes of deciding how (or whether) to exercise their judicial powers in a case over which they presumably had some jurisdiction. But the Chief Justice did not suggest that other persons (including other officials) had discretion to disregard the Court's decision, based on their independent interpretations of applicable norms. On the contrary, his implicit premise was that other persons were obliged to accept the Court's decision as final, at least for purposes of resolving the case brought by Marbury to the Supreme Court. Although Marshall's reasoning suggested the possibility of judicial mistakes, as measured with reference to standards of the Constitution itself, he apparently did not think others had authority to disregard *judicial* orders as void. Marshall, like others since him, have presumed that judges have had preeminent interpretive powers in at least some contexts and for at least some purposes, even if not in all contexts and for all purposes.

ated through force, formal amendments, and later interpretive changes. Certainly the radicals were not solely responsible for bringing about the ends they sought, but neither should their contributions be dismissed as insignificant.

The radicals also contributed to transforming law in a more immediate way: by acting consistently with their conceptions of the Constitution. In the process, these individuals expressed commitment to constitutional norms, as they understood them. It makes sense to regard the norms these persons created, through articulation and commitment, as important forms of unofficial law. These norms were, moreover, cornerstones of the Constitution's own authority as "supreme law."

Creating Meanings and Enhancing Authority

There are good reasons to acknowledge the existence of legal norms, including constitutional norms, that go beyond "official law." Governmental decisions have preempted a range of unofficial lawmaking, law-interpreting, and law-enforcing claims, but such decisions have not preempted all important forms of popular constitutional activity. While the Constitution has entrusted certain types of decisions to governmental officials for authoritative determination, it has also reserved a variety of constitutional rights and powers to the people at large for their collective and/or separate exercise. This chapter has already explained how persons could directly and indirectly influence official actions through voting and exercising other rights and powers of speech, the press, petitioning, assembly, and the like. By interpreting and exercising these prerogatives, individuals have also been able to create and reinforce *un*official constitutional norms that have been integral components of the law of the land.

It is important to distinguish individuals' exercising what they claim as *their* rights and powers from their seeking to exercise *other persons'* constitutional prerogatives, including those entrusted by the Constitution to governmental officials. Douglass did not presume that he had authority to adjudicate lawsuits or to act as a legislative or executive official. But he did claim to hold rights, as an individual, that *he* could exercise as *he* chose.

Among other things, Douglass asserted that he could legitimately interpret the Constitution independently of governmental officials, at least for purposes of deciding what his rights were and how to exercise them. In one of his most important speeches, on July 5, 1852, Douglass proclaimed: "I hold that every American citizen has a right to form an opinion of the constitution, and to propagate that opinion, and to use all honorable means to make his opinion the prevailing one."[46] By characterizing his position as a "hold[ing]," Douglass presumed that his opinions had intrinsic normative significance. Thus the form and substance of his comments were complementary: each expressed a conviction that the course of American constitutionalism could be shaped by ordinary persons, not just public officials.

Douglass adhered to this conviction even after the Supreme Court's decision in *Dred Scott*. As would Abraham Lincoln, Douglass denied that the case resolved finally the scope of Congress's power to prohibit slavery. He underscored the tentative and precarious character of official pronouncements by associating the judges' decision with previous and increasingly short-lived efforts to settle controversy over slavery through compromise. He alluded, moreover, to extrajudicial interpretive and enforcement powers by noting that "[t]he Supreme Court of the United States is not the only power in this world."[47]

Douglass's approach to voting epitomized his commitment to individuals' exercising their separately held rights and powers consistently with *their* conceptions of constitutional ideals. Because he depended on formal and informal electoral practices in New York, his ability to vote and express positions on candidates was not entirely independent of others' (including state officials') actions. But within the range of discretion allowed by these practices, Douglass exercised a large measure of political autonomy.

Although he rejected Garrisonian arguments that voting was itself morally impermissible, Douglass remained concerned about moral dimensions of voting. He became associated with the Liberty Party, which was committed to the complete abolition of slavery. But as the Republican Party became stronger, Douglass and other abolitionists were encouraged to join its ranks. Writing in 1856, however, Douglass declined to support Republicans in the upcoming elections and urged fellow members of the Liberty Party to support its candidates even if they were not likely to prevail.[48]

Douglass criticized the Republicans for moving away from commitment to complete abolition of slavery. For this reason, he argued that voting for Republicans would weaken the antislavery movement. He even expressed a willingness to sacrifice an end he sought, saving Kansas from slavery, in order to preserve the antislavery movement's moral integrity. He recognized that supporting members of the Liberty Party rather than

---

[46] Douglass, "July Fourth and the Negro," in Foner, ed., *Life and Writings* 2:202.

[47] Douglass, "The Dred Scott Decision," in Foner, ed., *Life and Writings* 2:410–11. See the passages quoted in n. 45, above, for Lincoln's treatment of these issues.

[48] See Douglass, "What Is My Duty as an Anti-Slavery Voter," in Foner, ed., *Life and Writings* 2:390–95.

Republicans might "give the Government into the hands of the Democratic Party, and thereby establish Slavery in Kansas." But he claimed that "tenfold greater would be the misfortune, should Kansas be saved by means which must certainly demoralize the Anti-Slavery sentiment of the North, and render it weak and inefficient for the greater work of saving the entire country to Liberty." Emphasizing that "our aim is the entire abolition of Slavery," he argued that it was preferable to vote based on principle, even if it led to a short-term loss, rather than to sacrifice integrity by joining a party of compromise: "With Kansas saved, and our Anti-Slavery integrity gone, our cause is ruined."[49]

Being able to convince himself that it was reasonable to interpret the Constitution as consistent with efforts to abolish slavery was only one among numerous hurdles that Douglass confronted in seeking to reconcile his commitment to acting morally with his recognition of the value, in practice, of acting through constitutional structures. Even after he became willing to endorse voting and other forms of constitutionally sanctioned political action, not just moral suasion, he remained unwilling to rely on those forms in ways that he thought would undercut claims of moral integrity. As he had been unwilling to advocate unconstitutional actions by governmental officials based on his earlier position on what the Constitution meant, he treated supporting Republicans as an impermissible means to accomplish a valid end. In both cases, he sought to avoid undercutting moral claims upon which he thought the antislavery cause depended.

Douglass eventually changed his position on whether to support the Republican Party, as he had changed his position on how to interpret the Constitution. Later in 1856 he defended acting within the Republican Party, rather than becoming isolated from it, as most likely to promote the ultimate end of abolishing slavery.[50] It was possible for Douglass to reconcile each approach to principles of morality, though based on different premises regarding matters of instrumental rationality. He also appears to have been more willing to rely on prudential considerations and to accept compromise as appropriate in the political arena.[51]

For present purposes, the fact that Douglass changed his position on how he and others like him should have voted is less important than his position that those seeking to abolish slavery should have voted at all. Rather than repudiating participation in constitutional forms, he affirmed

[49] Ibid.

[50] See Douglass, "Freemont and Dayton," from the *North Star*, August 15, 1856, in Foner, ed., *Life and Writings* 2:396–401; Foner, *Life and Writings* 2:84–85.

[51] Along with the sources cited in the previous note, see Waldo E. Martin Jr., *The Mind of Frederick Douglass* (Chapel Hill: University of North Carolina Press, 1984), at 182–85; David W. Blight, *Frederick Douglass' Civil War* (Baton Rouge: Louisiana State University Press, 1989), at 50–58.

acting in one of the ways contemplated by the Constitution itself as a valid means of seeking change: through representative structures. Douglass affirmed this form of participation, moreover, even when he predicted loss at the polls.[52] Thus he treated voting as valuable independently of its success or failure in electing the candidate of his (or others') choice.

Douglass did not articulate all the ways that he regarded voting as intrinsically significant, but several considerations may have informed his analysis. First, he might have been concerned about how votes could enhance or detract from the authority of particular governmental officials. Political authority is, in some respects, categorical in nature: a specific person either has, or does not have, authority to exercise official powers as a governmental representative based on forms established or sanctioned by the Constitution. But there are also gradations, or degrees, of governing authority. For those whose offices depend on electoral results, political power is a function, at least in part, of the depth and breadth of popular support. As a result, those who voted for a victorious candidate could enhance his authority, while those who voted otherwise would withhold their endorsement. These types of considerations may have informed Douglass's analysis of whether radical abolitionists should have voted for Republican candidates. His comments on the likely success of Republican candidates indicate, however, that his remarks were primarily driven by other concerns.

Douglass's reversal from opposing to supporting voting, as explained above, accompanied his shift from repudiating to endorsing structures of constitutional representation. He recognized that voting not only provided mechanisms through which the people chose governmental officials. It is clear that Douglass also considered voting to be a vehicle for endorsing constitutional norms of popular participation.

In addition, Douglass understood that voting was a means of expressing positions on broader issues of constitutional meaning and authority. He was committed in particular to voting for candidates who both opposed slavery and favored governmental efforts to eliminate it (or, in the case of Republicans, limit its spread). More generally, he suggested that voting and other forms of popular participation enabled individuals and groups to take positions on a variety of issues of constitutional law.[53]

Douglass's example indicates, moreover, that popular endorsement of

---

[52] See the source cited at n. 49, above, and accompanying text.

[53] But see Stanley Kelley Jr., *Interpreting Elections* (Princeton: Princeton University Press, 1983), for analysis of problems associated with efforts to treat election results as evidence of popular support for (or opposition to) particular positions. The book's focus is policy positions, but there are analogous problems associated with efforts to construct popular positions on constitutional issues. Evidentiary problems are distinct, however, from the normative implications of persons' regarding their votes as means of expressing positions on constitutional issues.

constitutional norms could, in practice, be qualified. His willingness to support the Constitution was contingent on his ability to interpret the constitutional text as an antislavery rather than pro-slavery charter. In addition, his conceptions of constitutional meaning and authority were tentative and forward-looking rather than grounded primarily in historical practices. He was likewise willing to affirm some governmental decisions as consistent with constitutional ideals but criticized others.

For these reasons, there is a need to qualify conclusions regarding the failure of radical antislavery constitutionalism. Douglass and others may have failed to bring about a change in the *official* law, but they were effective in changing *unofficial* practices—including, but not limited to, those expressed through voting. It makes sense, moreover, to regard the unofficial norms these persons created as forms of constitutional "law."

The redemptive vision of radical abolitionists did not depend entirely on changes in official practices. Part of the radicals' vision was for abolitionists to conform *their* actions to *their* understandings of the law of the Constitution, even if in opposition to official positions. Ordinary citizens, or aspiring citizens, *could* bring about these changes in unofficial practices: abolitionists could change *their* practices.

Douglass, like constitutional interpreters since before the Constitution's ratification, offered interpretive positions on a variety of issues. Others, during the antebellum period and afterward, would be able to evaluate and affirm or reject these positions based on *their* understandings of historical practices, *their* interpretations of the constitutional text, *their* analysis of other parts of the Constitution, *their* conceptions of rights and powers of the people, *their* grasp of constitutional ideals, and *their* other normative commitments. Thus Douglass and other abolitionists contributed to sustaining, reinforcing, and enhancing the Constitution's meaning and authority during their lives. They also suggested ways that others could later do likewise—whether by affirming the Constitution in its entirety and/or partially, in a tentative and/or unequivocal manner, before and/or after the text's formal amendment to abolish slavery and expand formal citizenship. Before the Civil War, as during earlier and subsequent times, the Constitution's meaning and authority were in part constituted by, not just dependent upon, popular commitments.

It would be a mistake not to treat those commitments as important components of the "law of the land" independently of whether they received official endorsement or became parts of a broader social consensus. Several parts of the constitutional text, along with general principles of American constitutionalism, indicate that the Constitution's meaning and authority have rested at least in part on the people's foundational commitment to constitutional norms. The preamble presumes that constitutional norms have been established by positive acts of the people at large and implies that "the people" have been able in some manner to withdraw support for such norms. Articles V and VII complement the preamble by providing for ratification and amendment of the constitutional text through conventions chosen by the people at large and from among their members. The ninth and tenth amendments further reinforce premises regarding the people's original and continuing political authority. The electoral provisions of articles I and II likewise attach normative significance to the people's continuing to endorse representative structures.

Many persons committed to abolishing slavery during the antebellum period, including radical constitutionalists, were doubtless formally "citizens" and members of "the people" within the embrace of the U.S. Constitution. If anyone could create constitutional norms through unofficial practices, these persons did. They created and supported antislavery norms through voting, signing petitions, writing in the media, giving speeches, participating in public dialogue, and otherwise expressing positions on constitutional issues. In short, some persons were not only formally "citizens"; they made themselves active, participating members of "the people" through their political practices.

The status of Douglass and others who were *not* formally "citizens," according to official pronouncements, was more complex. It is less clear whether he or other black persons could, through their own actions, become "citizens" in the formal and/or participatory sense(s). At issue was not only whether governmental officials were obliged to treat him as a "citizen." The preceding analysis also raises questions about whether he had independent powers of citizenship—including power to create, sustain, or change the law of the Constitution through unofficial practices.[54]

Reconceiving Citizenship

Douglass claimed to be a "citizen" and a member of the American "people" despite the Supreme Court's decision in *Dred Scott* and similar official pronouncements. He conceded that some or all of "the people" who made the Constitution had designed it to secure "the blessings of liberty" to themselves and *their* posterity, not "the colored persons of

---

[54] I am not claiming here that the only way persons may reshape the law of the Constitution is by exercising rights and powers of citizenship as members of the constitutional "people." Others, such as foreigners and resident aliens (who may be constitutional citizens or members of "the people" for some purposes), may play similar roles—including through influencing other persons' commitments. My focus here is on ways that principles of popular sovereignty support attributing normative significance to a range of unofficial practices. Other lines of reasoning may support other types of claims.

African descent."[55] But he claimed that the Constitution itself drew no such distinction:

> "We, the people"—not we, the white people—not we, the citizens, or the legal voters—not we, the privileged class, and excluding all other classes but we, the people; not we, the horses and cattle, but we the people—the men and women, the human inhabitants of the United States, do ordain and establish this Constitution, &c.[56]

In a later speech, he affirmed a corresponding conception of native-born, national citizenship: "There is in the Constitution no East, no West, no North, no South, no black, no white, no slave, no slaveholder, but *all are citizens who are of American birth*."[57]

There are at least three ways to regard these claims. First, one may dismiss them as based on mistaken conceptions of constitutional meaning and authority. Douglass's position became vindicated by the fourteenth amendment, but that amendment arguably changed the law rather than reinforced preexisting norms.[58] Conversely, it is possible to endorse Douglass's interpretive claims as correct and to reject opposing positions as erroneous. Perhaps Douglass was correct on the meaning of the Constitution, even before the fourteenth amendment ratified his position.[59] Or one may explore how Douglass's arguments illuminate dimensions of constitutional citizenship that are graded and continuous rather than dichotomous. According to this perspective, an important question was the *extent* to which Douglass had attributes of "citizenship," or membership

[55] See Douglass, "The Dred Scott Decision," in Foner, ed., *Life and Writings* 2:424. See also nn. 27–29, above, and accompanying text.

[56] Douglass, "The Dred Scott Decision," in Foner, ed., *Life and Writings* 2:419. See also ibid., at 424 ("The Constitution knows all the human inhabitants of this country as 'the people'"); Douglass, "The Constitution and Slavery," in Foner, ed., *Life and Writings* 2:477 ("Its language is 'we the people;' not we the white people, not even we the citizens, not we the privileged class, not we the high, not we the low, but we the people; not we the horses, sheep, and swine, and wheel-barrows, but we the people, we the human inhabitants; and, if Negroes are people, they are included in the benefits for which the Constitution of America was ordained and established").

[57] Douglass, "Address for the Promotion of Colored Enlistments," in Foner, ed., *Life and Writings* 3:365 (emphasis added).

[58] For arguments that blacks were not "citizens" before the fourteenth amendment became part of the Constitution, see, e.g., Edward S. Corwin, "The Dred Scott Decision in the Light of Contemporary Legal Doctrines," 17 Am. Hist. Rev. 52 (1911); Herbert J. Storing, "Slavery and the Moral Foundations of the American Republic," in Robert H. Horwitz, ed., *The Moral Foundations of the American Republic*, 2d ed. (Charlottesville: University Press of Virginia, 1979), at 214–33.

[59] For arguments that free blacks, at least, had been "citizens" from the time of the Constitution's ratification, see, e.g., Fehrenbacher, *The Dred Scott Case*, esp. 64–73, 337–64, 405–408, and 575–76; Finkelman, *An Imperfect Union* (Chapel Hill: University of North Carolina Press, 1981), at 279–80.

among "the people." Among other things, the third approach makes it possible to grasp issues that cut across problems posed by the first two.

According to some conceptions of constitutional meaning and authority, it could not have been true that Douglass both *was* a "citizen" and was *not* a "citizen" as a matter of constitutional law.[60] Likewise, some persons may claim that constitutional logic compels a conclusion that Douglass either *was* a member of "the people" or was *not* a member of "the people." By extension, if interpretive powers depended on an individual's status as a "citizen" or membership among "the people," then perhaps Douglass's authority to interpret the Constitution as a citizen or member of "the people" depended on whether he fell inside or outside these categories.

For some purposes, this type of categorical analysis is appropriate. The Supreme Court has repeatedly had to decide whether or not particular individuals (such as Dred Scott) have had standing to sue in federal courts based on the criteria set forth in article III and applicable statutes. When judges have taken jurisdiction, they have been presented with opposing normative claims—including questions about whether or not governmental officials have acted within delegated authority or violated constitutional rights. The adversarial process complements a judicial system and other governmental practices that have revolved in large measure around dichotomous conceptions of constitutional meaning and authority.

But dichotomies fail to account adequately for diversities of opinion on constitutional issues, particularly among unofficial interpreters. Assuming for now that the existing constitutional order embraces authorship of constitutional norms by "the people" but not others,[61] there remain serious questions about whether all "citizens" are members of "the people."[62] Setting aside that distinction for now, there are further questions about how "the people" may re-authorize existing parts of the Constitution and perhaps change their meanings in the process—whether through interpretive practices or otherwise. Going further yet, what roles may "the people" play in adding text or other objects of interpretation to the Constitution, whether through formal channels or otherwise?

At least when dealing with interpretive practices, there are good rea-

---

[60] But see ch. 1, n. 25 (judges have treated particular persons as "citizens" for some purposes but not others).

[61] But see n. 54, above.

[62] In this connection, consider again Harris's distinction between the "constitutional people" and the "sovereign people" (see William F. Harris II, *The Interpretable Constitution* [Baltimore: Johns Hopkins University Press, 1993], at 201–208). More simply, consider whether it makes sense to conceive of infants as members of "the people" even if they are formally "citizens," if they are not yet capable of the sort of critical reflection that may well be assumed to be a defining attribute of sovereign capacity.

sons to account for diverging positions, not just overlapping ones.[63] From the beginning, the Constitution has been at the center of political controversy, not just a source of integration and unification.[64] Both dimensions have shaped the course of American constitutionalism. Thus it is impossible to account fully for the richness of America's fundamental law without exploring disagreement among interpreters, not just agreement.

It is particularly important to account for disagreement among citizens, or members of "the people," when studying unofficial constitutional norms. There is no need to assume that the most important components of such norms have been dichotomous. On the contrary, it is possible to gain insight into distinctive attributes of American constitutionalism by being attentive to *ranges* or *degrees* of consistency or inconsistency among popular conceptions of constitutional meaning and authority, not just the presence or absence of consistency among such positions.

The American "people," or "citizens" (whether conceived narrowly and/or broadly, organized as members of states and/or a nation), were deeply divided on several basic issues of American constitutionalism during the antebellum period. Disagreement among such persons included, but was not limited to, the status of free blacks. Instead of (or in addition to) searching for a definitive answer to the question of *whether or not* persons like Frederick Douglass were "citizens" or members of "the people" as contemplated by the United States Constitution, much may be gained from paying attention to the problematic status of such persons. Rather than beginning with an assumption that the unofficial law of the Constitution on this issue must have been fully coherent, as a matter of constitutional logic, it is more appropriate to allow for variations or gradations of constitutional meaning and authority.

Following such a line of reasoning, one might conclude that constitutional norms were not perfectly consistent on the status of free blacks such as Douglass. (Nor was the Constitution entirely consistent on many other issues, particularly those involving slavery.) One could argue reasonably that Douglass was neither a "citizen" nor included among "the people" upon whose authority the Constitution rested. One could also argue reasonably that he fell within both categories, or one but not the other. There was solid support for each position in various parts of the constitutional text, general principles and structures of American constitutionalism, a wide range of interpretive precedents, and other relevant sources. The Constitution neither fully supported nor completely under-

[63] My focus in this chapter has been unofficial interpretive practices. The following chapter deals, among other things, with issues involving the founding of constitutional text and the creation of constitutional norms more generally.

[64] See Sanford Levinson, *Constitutional Faith* (Princeton: Princeton University Press, 1988), for an exemplary treatment of both components of American constitutionalism.

cut Douglass's inclusive claims (for himself and other blacks, free and enslaved).[65]

Allowing for degrees or variations of constitutional coherence is also suitable for analyzing problems of political membership because the concepts of membership and participation are themselves variable and not simply dichotomous. Citizenship has not only been present or absent but also is something persons have *become* through their actions. Individuals have not simply acted consistently or inconsistently with norms of constitutional citizenship—they have expressed commitment to the Constitution and abided by its imperatives in varying degrees.[66]

Douglass solidified his claims of citizenship in these terms by exercising rights and powers of citizenship. He owned property, voted, wrote publicly, spoke at political gatherings, petitioned governmental officials, offered and affirmed coherent conceptions of constitutional meaning and authority, criticized official and unofficial actions that he regarded as constitutionally flawed, and otherwise participated actively in political and extrapolitical life at the national and state levels. He supported his claim to be a "citizen" and a member of "the people" by bringing his practices into line with his conceptions of constitutional imperatives. In this connection, he invoked not only his own will but also the preamble's authoritative statement of foundational political ideals and claimed to be acting consistently with them even in opposition to others' assertions of political power. Thus he assumed attributes of citizenship long before public officials endorsed his position through legislation, judicial decisions, constitutional amendments, and other formal governmental and extragovernmental actions.

Douglass, in short, exemplified forms of active self-constitution: becoming a member of the polity through his actions and not just those of other persons. Because of his age, he was obviously not among those who *originally* formed—and were formed by—the Constitution.[67] Because of his race, it was not clear that he was among that people's "posterity." Of

[65] By acknowledging here problems of consistency among constitutional norms, I am not denying that normative coherence is a value for the polity as a whole or that individuals should strive for consistency among their interpretive commitments. On the contrary, I endorse and rely on ideals of normative coherence throughout this book. My point here is that such ideals have not been achieved fully through the *practices* that have constituted norms of American constitutionalism.

[66] See Shklar, *American Citizenship*, at 1–23 and passim, for a complementary treatment of citizenship. Her work identifies four conceptions of citizenship, at least three of which are variable rather than dichotomous: citizenship as standing, active participation, and republican virtue. The problematic status of blacks in the antebellum period indicates that even the idea of citizenship as nationality admits of gradations in meaning.

[67] On the Constitution's mediation of these two functions, see Harris, *The Interpretable Constitution*, at 74, 115 n. 4, and passim.

greater importance to Douglass was gaining membership among "the people" who re-formed—and were re-formed by—the Constitution to sustain its ongoing authority. The Constitution could embrace persons falling within the last category, according to Douglass, even if they were not included within the former two.

Thus Douglass in effect incrementally gained new identities as constitutional author and subject. By claiming membership among "the people," he presumed to be among those able to maintain (re-authorize) constitutional forms to represent the people's collective and separate political identities. He affirmed institutions of national representation while gaining attributes of national citizenship. He likewise endorsed mechanisms of state representation while acting as a citizen of New York. He was a member of religious organizations, antislavery associations, and other groups that also had distinct identities and corresponding constitutional prerogatives. As an individual, he asserted rights of speech, the press, conscience, property ownership, and the like.

A corollary of Douglass's assuming constitutional authorship and endorsing these elements of the constitutional design was deepening his status as constitutional citizen-subject. As Michael Warner has explained, "[T]he people who give law [implicitly] vow that they will take their place as its subjects."[68] In this respect, Douglass is an example of someone who became, in William Harris's terms, "domesticated" in the sense that Douglass redefined his identity as a subject of the existing order rather than remained detached from it.[69] The former Garrisonian moved away from repudiation of the Constitution and toward committing himself to act consistently with its imperatives.

Yet even as he became politically re-formed and assumed the status of a "citizen," Douglass maintained a critical posture toward constitutional norms. As explained above, his endorsement of the Constitution was tentative and qualified. Instead of presuming the validity and continuing viability of constitutional norms, he treated these matters as contingent and open to scrutiny. Unwilling to accept disparities between constitutional

[68] Michael Warner, *The Letters of the Republic: Publication and the Public Sphere in Eighteenth-Century America* (Cambridge: Harvard University Press, 1990), at 110 (also explained that "with the Constitution, consent is to sovereignty as readership is to authorship").

[69] See Harris, *The Interpretable Constitution*, at 202 (distinguished "[t]he Constitutional People who has been domesticated and civilized to the Constitution" and for whom the Constitution "supplies the political categories of their thought" from "the popular sovereign who is a wild and natural people, a potentially new constitution maker outside the bounds of the constitutional order"). William Lloyd Garrison would qualify as someone not "domesticated" in this sense; he repudiated the Constitution and expressly disavowed forms of political participation that he viewed as attributes of membership *within* the existing order.

ideals and political practices, he sought to bring about changes in the practices and thus to reconcile tensions within the constitutional terrain. He looked forward, not only backward, to identify constitutional possibilities.

Persons inhabiting the United States today occupy similar terrain and face similar prospects. Constitutional politics is a function of unofficial along with official choices. There are still wide gaps between constitutional ideals and actual political practices. Membership within the polity continues to offer meaningful possibilities and impose serious constraints. Whether the U.S. Constitution can withstand critical scrutiny remains an open question. Those seeking to become citizens and to make the Constitution worthy of respect have good reasons to offer critical perspectives and commit themselves to change, not only to confine themselves to reinforcing existing norms.

CHAPTER 3

Acting through Government
and Independently

[T]he people have an indubitable, unalienable, and indefeasible right to reform or change their Government,
whenever it be found adverse or inadequate to the purposes of its institution.[1]

IN THE CONTEXT of analyzing Frederick Douglass's claims of constitutional citizenship, I have suggested that the Constitution has had multiple
authors—at least for some purposes. I have not, however, claimed that
individuals acting separately have been the exclusive—or even the
primary—authors of constitutional meaning and authority. My position,
on the contrary, is that "the people" have had multiple identities and have
acted in various capacities to achieve a range of constitutional ends.

For some purposes, the Constitution has depended on coordinated actions by "the people" or those acting on their behalf. For example, article
VII has attributed normative significance to the Constitution's initial ratification by state conventions. The delegates at those conventions arguably represented "the people" of the respective states, each as a whole. One
may also conceive of "the people" as joined into a single political community, "the United States."[2] Articles I and II provide for coordinated actions by "the people" to select representatives; and governmental structures, in turn, require coordinated actions by public officials. Article V

---

[1] From Madison's first proposed amendment to the constitutional text (to precede the
preamble), introduced into the House of Representatives on August 8, 1789, reprinted in
Helen E. Veit, Kenneth R. Bowling, and Charlene Bangs Bickford, eds., *Creating the Bill of
Rights: The Documentary Record from the First Federal Congress* (Baltimore: Johns Hopkins University Press, 1991), at 11–12.

[2] See generally Akhil Reed Amar, "Of Sovereignty and Federalism," 96 Yale L. J. 1425
(1987). Though defending a unitary conception of "the people," Amar has conceded that
the constitutional text can also accommodate plural conceptions of "the people." In this
connection, he has pointed out that the text refers consistently to "the United States" as a
plural noun (see ibid., at 1455 and n. 125). See also William F. Harris II, *The Interpretable
Constitution* (Baltimore: Johns Hopkins University Press, 1993), for an argument that the
logic of American constitutionalism depends on the idea of the Constitution's authorship by
the whole people of the United States, conceived as a single author. Later in this chapter, I
draw upon and evaluate critically Amar's and Harris's arguments.

also establishes mechanisms for amending the constitutional text through coordinated actions, not merely separate decisions.

Yet the Constitution also refers to "rights" and "powers" of "the people." It makes sense to conceive of some such prerogatives as held by "the people" individually and as members of various "private" associations (such as religious organizations). Douglass claimed interpretive powers as an individual, and there are good reasons to conclude that he reshaped constitutional norms by exercising those powers.

It is no simple matter, therefore, analyzing how "the people" have acted or may continue to act—whether to authorize constitutional norms or otherwise. One must confront basic issues of constitutional structure. How do "the people" and their "rights" and "powers" intersect with governmental powers? How may "the people" act through representative structures and independently of them? What constraints do governmental actions place upon "the people" and/or its members?

These basic problems of political theory came to the surface in debates over the Constitution's ratification and initial amending. Those favoring ratification, known as "Federalists," emphasized ways that "the people" could act *through* representative structures. The Constitution would rest upon the foundational political authority of "the people," expressed *through* coordinated action by state ratifying conventions. Following ratification, the people would continue to act *through* representative structures established or endorsed by the Constitution. Thus it would not be necessary, according to the Constitution's proponents, to enumerate rights or powers of the people as *distinct from* those of government.[3]

Those seeking to block ratification, the "Anti-Federalists," objected to the proposed mode of ratification and criticized the structures that would result. The Constitution's opponents emphasized principles of state sovereignty, argued against consolidation of political power, criticized the proposed structures as undemocratic, opposed the scope of delegated powers, and objected to the absence of a bill of rights. In making these arguments, prominent Anti-Federalists repeatedly relied on distinctions between "the people" and "government." Of particular importance, they argued that an enumeration of rights would affirm the right of citizens to

---

[3] See Alexander Hamilton, John Jay, and James Madison, *The Federalist Papers* (New York: New American Library, Mentor Books, 1961). It is important to remember that *The Federalist Papers* were political propaganda. Thomas Jefferson, in a letter to James Madison dated November 18, 1788, observed that the authors of *The Federalist* had not necessarily advocated in the Constitutional Convention of 1787 the constitutional structures that they subsequently defended. The letter is reprinted in Julian P. Boyd, ed., *Papers of Thomas Jefferson* (Princeton: Princeton University Press, 1958), vol. 14, at 187–90. See also Walter F. Murphy, "Constitutional Interpretation: The Art of the Historian, Magician, or Statesman?" 87 Yale L. J. 1752 (1978), at 1765.

act *independently* of government. It would also guard separate preroga-tives: the autonomy of states and individuals.[4]

The Federalists prevailed in securing the Constitution's ratification. But the Anti-Federalists gained concessions from the Federalists—including a commitment to interpret federal powers as intrinsically limited and to sponsor amendments enumerating popular rights in the constitutional text. As a result, the original text and its initial amendments would have mixed lineages. Pivotal parts of the text could accommodate variations of Federalist and Anti-Federalist interpretive frameworks.[5]

Much may be gained, therefore, from studying Federalist and Anti-Federalist positions on problems of constitutional structure. This chapter focuses on competing views of principles of representation and preroga-tives of constitutional change. More specifically, I review arguments from the founding period that "the people" may act *through* representative structures and *independently* of them—including to establish and/or amend the law of the Constitution. Remaining chapters deal with further questions involving relationships among popular rights and governmen-tal powers.

COMMON AND DIVIDED IDENTITIES AND INTERESTS

As Gordon S. Wood has explained, discussions of political power in eighteenth-century America "can only be understood in the context of th[e] ancient notion of the Crown's prerogatives, the bundle of rights and powers adhering in the King's authority to rule, set *against* the rights and liberties of the people, or the ruled, represented in the House of Com-

---

[4] Anti-Federalist sources are collected in Herbert J. Storing, ed., *The Complete Anti-Federalist*, 7 vols. (Chicago: University of Chicago Press, 1981). Debates in state ratifying conventions and related documents are collected in Merrill Jensen, John P. Kaminski et al., eds., *The Documentary History of the Ratification of the Constitution* (Madison: State Historical Society, 1976–86). Bernard Schwartz, ed., *The Bill of Rights: A Documentary History*, 2 vols. (New York: McGraw-Hill, 1971), contains a helpful selection of Federalist and Anti-Federalist commentaries on the Constitution.

[5] Although I refer throughout this work, by convention and for reasons of convenience, to "Federalist" and "Anti-Federalist" positions, it is important to recognize that persons on various sides of debates over ratification were not of identical mind. See Paul Finkelman, "Antifederalists: The Loyal Opposition and the American Constitution," 70 Cornell L. Rev. 182 (1984) (noted the diversity of Anti-Federalist thought and emphasized limits of Stor-ing's collection); Saul Cornell, "Moving Beyond the Canon of Traditional Constitutional History: Anti-Federalists, the Bill of Rights, and the Promise of Post-Modern Historiogra-phy," 12 Law and Hist. Rev. 1 (1994) (emphasized the diversity of Anti-Federalist thought). In addition, some persons (such as Thomas Jefferson) did not identify themselves as "Feder-alist" or "Anti-Federalist," and others (such as James Madison) advocated positions associ-ated with each side. Adding further complication, it is apparent that persons on both sides presented arguments to which they were not personally committed.

mons." According to various formulations of English constitutional the-ory, the people's prerogatives differed from those of their rulers. The people's rights and interests were conceived as being *aligned* with those of their elected representatives and as *opposing* royal, or hereditary, claims of authority.[6]

As had their English counterparts, the American colonists asserted rights and privileges *against* the Crown and claimed they were being de-prived of rights to govern themselves *through* representatives chosen by the people and from among their ranks. For example, the first Continen-tal Congress declared that the people's two greatest rights were "having a share in their own government by representatives chosen of themselves" and the "great right . . . of trial by jury.[7] John Adams had likewise argued that "[t]hese two popular powers," participation through representatives in making and enforcing laws, were "the heart and lungs, the mainspring and the centre wheel," of representative government. He had urged that "[i]n these two powers consist wholly the liberty and security of the people."[8] The American Declaration of Independence also invoked the colonists' rights to legislative representation and trial by jury.[9]

In the 84th *Federalist*, Alexander Hamilton stood some of these argu-ments on their heads to defend the proposed Constitution from criticism owing to its omission of a bill of rights. He claimed that the Constitution already was "itself, in every rational sense, and to every useful purpose, A BILL OF RIGHTS." Because the people would hold all governing power through *their* representatives, a bill of rights in its traditional sense would be inappropriate.

Several considerations converged to support Hamilton's claim that "the people [would] surrender nothing" in the case of the federal Consti-tution. He referred to the preamble and explained that the Constitution would be "founded upon the power of the people and executed by their immediate representatives and servants."[10] According to this line of rea-soning, the people would "ordain and establish" the Constitution to gov-

---

[6] See Wood, *The Creation of the American Republic* (1969; rpt., New York: Norton, 1972), at 19 (emphasis added). See also Edmund S. Morgan, *Inventing the People* (New York: Norton, 1988); Philip Kurland and Ralph Lerner, eds., *The Founders' Constitution*, 5 vols. (New York: University of Chicago Press, 1987), esp. vol. 5, at 388–407.

[7] "Letter to the Inhabitants of the Province of Quebec," drafted by John Dickinson and adopted by the Continental Congress on October 26, 1774, quoted by Clinton Rossiter, *Seedtime of the Republic: The Origin of the American Tradition of Political Liberty* (New York: Harcourt, Brace, 1953), at 398–99.

[8] John Adams, "Letter from the Earl of Clarendon to William Pym," January 27, 1766, quoted by Rossiter, *Seedtime of the Republic*, at 388–89.

[9] Also underlying the Declaration of Independence was another (weaker) conception of representation as flowing from consent. See generally Carl L. Becker, *The Declaration of Independence: A Study in the History of Political Ideas* (New York: Vintage, 1958).

[10] *The Federalist*, no. 84, at 513.

ern themselves, and thus there was no need for them to place constraints on others who might claim authority based on another source.

In addition, Hamilton stressed the fact that all the people's governing representatives would be chosen from among the people themselves. In this connection, he emphasized the importance of the constitutional text's prohibition on titles of nobility. He claimed that this prohibition would preclude the government from ever being "other than that of the people." He was arguing that the new government would be completely "of the people" because ordinary citizens, not kings or members of a nobility, would hold all governmental posts. In this sense, he urged, "the people [would] retain everything."

Pushing this line of reasoning, Hamilton proclaimed that the people "ha[d] no need of particular reservations." He characterized bills of rights, in the form inherited from Great Britain, as "stipulations between kings and their subjects, abridgements of prerogative in favor of privilege, reservations of rights not surrendered to the prince." Hamilton insisted that because the people in America would surrender no powers to a prince, a bill of rights in its "primitive signification" would be superfluous.[11]

Furthermore, Hamilton alluded to a third type of "representation" that governmental structures would provide: the people's right to participate in choosing governmental officials. He called attention to "various prerogatives for the public security" which "declare and specify the political privileges of the citizens in the structure and administration of the government." He was apparently referring to constitutional structures that would provide, among other things, for the people's periodic election of some officials, make other officials more indirectly accountable to the people, and establish complex checks on the operations of each part of the government. He claimed that the constitutional text specified these privileges in "the most ample and precise manner."

Hamilton's comments on this type of representation, popular accountability, were most responsive to the Anti-Federalists' principal criticisms of the proposed Constitution and their main reasons for advocating a bill of rights. Many of these critics objected to the Constitution's "undemocratic" components, particularly its distancing of offices from the people at large. They expressed concern that the national government would grow large, distant, unresponsive to the rights and interests of ordinary persons, and eventually tyrannical. Their first lines of attack thus focused

[11] It is significant that Hamilton, in the 78th and 84th *Federalist*, characterized judges as representatives of the people, even though judges are not elected by the people. He apparently conceived of judges as "representatives" of "the people" in at least two senses: judges derived their governing authority from the Constitution that was "ordained and established" in the people's name, and judges were chosen from among the people at large.

on the size of the government and the scope of delegated powers. But once ratification became likely, Anti-Federalists shifted their efforts to securing an enumeration of rights. Their purported goals included providing security for rights of political minorities and validating some measure of popular participation—for the benefit of majorities as well as minorities.

In the 84th *Federalist*, Hamilton acknowledged arguments that the new government might become remote but dismissed them by claiming that the states would serve as "sentinels" and thereby overcome "the impediments to a prompt communication which distance might create." He assumed, moreover, that those closest to the seat of government would be vigilant in representing all the people:

> It ought also to be remembered that the citizens who inhabit the country at and near the seat of government will, in all questions that affect the general liberty and prosperity, have the same interest with those who are at a distance, and that they will be ready to sound the alarm when necessary, and to point out the actors in any pernicious project. The public papers will be expeditious messengers of intelligence to the most remote inhabitants of the Union.[12]

His assertion that the people would have "the same interest" in this connection was significant.

As with his other arguments against a bill of rights, he relied on the people's common identity. But this time, instead of emphasizing how governmental officials were chosen from among "the people," he acknowledged a dichotomy between "the people" and governmental officials. A variation of that dichotomy had underlain other persons' arguments *for* a bill of rights.

In addition, Hamilton's assertion that the people would have "the same interest" in opposing improper actions by the national government went against many of his and Madison's arguments throughout *The Federalist*. They had argued forcefully in those essays that the Constitution would provide security for rights in America by joining together within an "extended republic" persons having very diverse interests. It is thus appropriate to turn briefly to those arguments for the light they shed on Hamilton's comments in the 84th *Federalist*.

Reconceiving Republicanism

In the 1st *Federalist*, Hamilton set forth one of the objectives of those papers: to discuss "[t]he conformity of the proposed Constitution to the

[12] *The Federalist*, no. 84, at 516.

true principles of republican government." He recognized that not all republics of the past had been "popular governments," but he repeatedly used the republics of Greece and Rome as models. He claimed, moreover, that one of the "great improvements" in "the science of politics" had been the "wholly new discover[y]" of principles that included "the representation of the people in the legislature by deputies of their own election."[13]

Madison likewise assumed that the framers were committed to "preserv[ing] the spirit and the form of popular government" even as they sought to secure the public good and private rights against the dangers of majority factions. But he argued in the 10th *Federalist* that a "pure democracy," direct rule by the people, "can admit of no cure for the mischiefs of faction." On the other hand, he claimed that a "republic," which he defined as "a government in which the scheme of representation takes place," offered the prospect of curing those mischiefs.[14]

He conceded that in a republic, or representative government, the people did not, strictly speaking, govern themselves. But he claimed that this feature made a republic preferable to a "pure democracy." More specifically, Madison argued that representative structures would "refine and enlarge the public views by passing them through the medium of a chosen body of citizens, whose wisdom may best discern the true interest of their country."[15] Here Madison emphasized the common identity of rulers and ruled as "citizens." At the same time, he implicitly presumed that governmental officials and the people at large would have distinct prerogatives.

Later, he again distinguished government by representatives *of* the people from government *by* the people themselves. In the 63rd *Federalist*, Madison remarked that "the true distinction" between ancient republics and American governments was "the total exclusion of the people in their collective capacity, from any share in the latter [governments]." He claimed that this total exclusion of the people at large from government provided "a most advantageous superiority in favor of the United States." Similarly, Hamilton described government in America as "in the hands of *representatives* of the people." He urged that this arrangement was "the essential, and, after all, the only efficacious security for the rights and privileges of the people which is attainable in civil society."[16]

As indicated, both thinkers drew distinctions between "the people"

---

[13] See *The Federalist*, esp. nos. 1, 6, and 9.

[14] *The Federalist*, no. 10, at 78–81.

[15] *The Federalist*, no. 10, at 82.

[16] Madison, *The Federalist*, no. 63, at 387 (emphasis removed); Hamilton, *The Federalist*, no. 28, at 180 (emphasis added). But see Hamilton's earlier claim in the 21st *Federalist*, at 140, that "the whole power of the government *is in the hands of the people*" (emphasis added). The later formulation was more precise, although the earlier one paralleled more closely his arguments in the 84th *Federalist*.

and their "representatives" that called into question Hamilton's emphasis on their common identity in the 84th *Federalist*. In addition, Madison and Hamilton played into Anti-Federalist arguments that national officials would be unaccountable to the people at large. The Constitution's critics were not so much opposed to some form of representation as to the complex structures established by the Constitution.

The Federalists were challenged to rebut arguments that these complex structures were cause for concern. Madison argued just the opposite. The 10th *Federalist* contains his classic argument that a large republic would provide remedies for the problems of "factions" that reputedly plagued popular governments.[17] He elaborated on that argument in the 51st *Federalist*, where he described how an enlarged republic would embrace such a multiplicity of interests that majority coalitions would be unlikely except on principles of justice and the general welfare. He claimed that this diversity of interests in the United States would make the proposed government more trustworthy than smaller state governments. In making these arguments, however, he presented a significantly different conception of "the people" from that expressed by Hamilton in the 84th *Federalist*. Thus Madison's emphasis on diversity within America cast a shadow over Hamilton's claims of common interest.

Yet Madison, like Hamilton, assumed that the American people had a common *identity* despite their divergent *interests*. (Both also assumed that the people had *some* common interests.) In defending the proposed Constitution as "strictly republican" in character, Madison emphasized how "the people" would be united for at least one purpose: to establish the Constitution's authority. He defined a "republic" as "a government which derives *all* its powers directly or indirectly from the great body of the people, and is administered by persons holding their offices during pleasure or for a limited period, or during good behavior."[18] In this passage, he was claiming that the American people, as a whole, could act as a "great body" despite the nation's size and the complexity of its governing institutions.

Madison urged, moreover, that because the proposed Constitution would constitute a "republic," as defined, the new charter would be consistent with "fundamental principles of the Revolution" and "the determination . . . to rest all our political experiments on the capacity of mankind for self-government."[19] Thus Madison and Hamilton each relied on distinctions between the people and their representatives, but each also invoked the rhetoric of "self-government." When defending the Constitu-

---

[17] Chapter 5 examines more thoroughly Madison's arguments in the 10th and 51st *Federalist*.

[18] *The Federalist*, no. 39, at 240 and 241 (emphasis added).

[19] *The Federalist*, no. 39, at 240.

tion's popular character, these two men repeatedly emphasized connections between the people and their representatives.

These arguments addressed some of the Anti-Federalists' criticisms but did not meet their strongest objections. The proposed Constitution's opponents argued that popular checks and democratic participation were essential attributes of republican government. Without such checks, the Constitution's critics warned, rulers would become independent of the people and would abuse their powers. As a result, the people would withdraw their support from the government. That tendency would be exacerbated by an absence of meaningful political involvement of the sort necessary to promote attachment to the *res publica*, or public affairs. According to this line of reasoning, the Constitution would undermine rather than support sentiments of mutual interest and attachment, and the inevitable result would be tyranny by force.

Competing Conceptions of Rights and Powers

Madison, Hamilton, and other Federalists emphasized the importance of representative structures and sought to weaken popular control over government. The constitutional design did not eliminate opportunities for citizens to participate actively in government at the state and local levels. But the original text created few structures through which the people of the United States could act in their combined capacity, as active *national* citizens.

The people as a whole would not even directly choose presidents, and members of the House would be chosen by the people of the respective electoral districts or states. State legislators would select senators. Accordingly, much of the original Constitution would minimize rather than enhance opportunities for active citizenship. An apparent premise was that public support for the new government would not depend on high levels of popular participation, at least at the national level.

One of the proposed constitutional amendments that Madison introduced into the House of Representatives on June 8, 1789, pertained to the size of the House. It was carried forward as the first proposal but was not ratified by three-quarters of the state legislatures.[20] Thus it appears that the Bill of Rights did not fundamentally alter structures or processes of federal representation.[21]

---

[20] See Veit, Bowling, and Bickford, eds., *Creating the Bill of Rights*, at xvi, 3, and 12.

[21] As explained in ch. 4, there were also a number of efforts to add an amendment confining the federal government to expressly enumerated powers. These proposals also failed. They might have affected the scope of delegated powers, not representative structures as such.

Several of the express prohibitions could, however, affect the practical *functioning* of these structures. The first amendment's guarantees pertain most directly to political processes: Congress may not make any law "abridging the freedom of speech, or of the press, or the right of the people peaceably to assemble, and to petition the Government for a redress of grievances." The second amendment guarantees "the right of the people to keep and bear arms." In addition, the amendment affirms militias as "necessary to the security of a free state," thereby validating participation by the people in the use of physical power. Perhaps the amendment also presumes that the people, acting through state militias, may under some circumstances legitimately oppose and check abuses of federal military power.[22] The fifth amendment requires indictment by a grand jury for serious criminal offenses, the sixth (along with article III) secures the right of trial by jury in criminal prosecutions, and the seventh guarantees this right in civil suits. Thus the people would be ensured rights to participate in the administration of justice, along with electing legislative representatives and influencing the choice of executive officials and judges.

These provisions could accommodate Federalist and Anti-Federalist conceptions of popular rights of political participation. Federalists were able to concede that the people could legitimately act in various ways *through* established representative structures. By exercising rights of speech, the press, assembly, and petitioning, the people at large might be able to influence how federal officials exercised their powers. Declaring these rights would not, however, restrict the scope of powers delegated by the Constitution or change their character. To the extent (and in the manner) provided by the original text, the people would govern themselves through complex representative structures.

Anti-Federalists, in contrast, would be able to argue that the Bill of Rights contemplated the people's acting *independently* of government. By exercising retained rights and reserved powers, citizens might be able to oppose improper exercises of national power—including attempts to abridge these popular prerogatives. The Bill of Rights also went beyond the original text by validating a wider range of popular participation than voting for distant representatives. In addition, even if the new provisions did not change governmental structures, they might influence popular

---

[22] See Sanford Levinson, "The Embarrassing Second Amendment," 99 Yale L. J. 637 (1989). See also Amar, "The Bill of Rights as a Constitution," 100 Yale L. J. 1131 (1991) (emphasizes how many of the rights enumerated in the Bill of Rights may be exercised collectively). The April 19, 1995, bombing of the Alfred P. Murrah federal building in Oklahoma City has brought to the fore debates about the constitutional standing of citizen militias. I am not presuming here that all types of militias—or all activities of particular militias—are constitutionally sanctioned.

culture. By enumerating popular rights to participate in making and enforcing laws and in opposing governmental tyranny, the Bill of Rights would remind the people that republican government ultimately depended on active citizenship. Structures of popular participation would supplement and possibly limit exercises of governmental power.

RIGHTS AND POWERS OF CONSTITUTIONAL CHANGE

Even without the Bill of Rights, the constitutional text presupposed that "the people" could take authoritative actions *independently* of governmental structures, not just *through* them. Article V has relied in part on established representative institutions as vehicles for formally amending the constitutional text. But it has also provided for ad hoc conventions as alternative vehicles for proposing and/or ratifying amendments.

As a result, the constitutional text's amending provisions may be understood as providing means through which "the people" may, under some circumstances, participate in formally amending the Constitution. Not all persons would concede that Congress's proposing amendments or calling a national convention have constituted (or would have constituted) an authoritative action of "the people." For similar reasons, it would be reasonable to deny that state legislatures' applying for a convention or ratifying proposed amendments have been (or would be) actions of "the people." But even those who distinguish these governmental actions from those of "the people" could reasonably conceive of conventions as vehicles through which "the people" may formally act. Such a position finds support in the preamble and article VII, along with article V of the original text. It would be reinforced by the ninth and tenth amendments.

Those amendments would, in turn, provide critical perspectives for analyzing rights and powers of constitutional change.[23] The ninth, for example, calls into question arguments that article V's amending provisions contain an exhaustive listing of the people's rights of constitutional change. The tenth likewise challenges interpreters to consider whether the Constitution has reserved powers of constitutional change that have gone beyond those specified in article V. These positions also find support in article VII and the preamble, along with various sources from the founding period.

Article V's amending provisions thus provide several points of departure for analyzing possibilities of constitutional change. The amending

---

[23] I am not denying that there may be good reasons to distinguish "rights" of constitutional change from "powers." Here I am exploring interpretive possibilities. In addition, I am tracking other interpretive precedents that appear to use these terms interchangeably.

provisions offer viable conceptions of "rights" and "powers" of "the people." As a result, article V sheds light on how "the people" may act through governmental institutions and independently of them. In addition, the resulting models provide conceptual frameworks for analyzing rights and powers of constitutional change that go beyond those secured by article V.

Acting through Article V

Madison's first proposed amendment to the constitutional text, as introduced to the House of Representatives on June 8, 1789, would have amended the preamble. The proposal emphasized the people's foundational political authority and corresponding rights and powers of constitutional reform:

> First. That there be prefixed to the constitution a declaration, that all power is originally vested in, and consequently derived from, the people.
>
> That Government is instituted and ought to be exercised for the benefit of the people; which consists in the enjoyment of life and liberty, with the right of acquiring and using property, and generally of pursuing and obtaining happiness and safety.
>
> That the people have an indubitable, unalienable, and indefeasible right to reform or change their Government, whenever it be found adverse or inadequate to the purposes of its institution.[24]

Although the proposal did not survive in its entirety, it informs analysis of problems of constitutional continuity and change.

On first impression, it may appear odd that Madison would propose an amendment that emphasized foundational rights and powers of constitutional reform. In the 49th *Federalist*, he had warned against "frequent appeals" to the people at large. He claimed that such appeals would "disturb[] the public tranquility," "carry an implication of some defect in the government," and "in great measure, deprive the government of that veneration" without which "the wisest and freest governments would not possess the requisite stability."[25] Even after presenting his proposed amendments to the House, he criticized Jefferson's argument that constitutions ought to expire every nineteen years.[26] According to Madison, "a

[24] Veit, Bowling, and Bickford, eds., *Creating the Bill of Rights*, at 11–12.

[25] *The Federalist*, no. 49, at 314–15.

[26] In a letter to James Madison dated September 6, 1789, Jefferson argued that public law should be consistent with the principle that "the earth belongs always to the living generation." The letter is reprinted in Boyd, ed., *Papers of Thomas Jefferson* 15:392–97. See also Jefferson's letter to Madison, January 30, 1787, in ibid., 11:93 ("I hold that a little

Government so often revised [would] become too mutable to retain those prejudices in its favor which antiquity inspires, and which are perhaps a salutary aid to the most rational Government in the most enlightened age."[27]

Yet Federalists and Anti-Federalists alike had emphasized rights and powers of constitutional reform throughout debates over ratification of the federal Constitution. James Wilson, for example, had reportedly argued in the Pennsylvania Convention that "the people may change the constitutions whenever and however they please." He had claimed that "[a]s our constitutions are superior to our legislatures, so the people are superior to our constitutions." Echoing the preamble, he declared that "[t]hose who ordain and establish have the power, if they think proper, to repeal and annul." Although his main concern was to rebut arguments that the proposed Constitution required approval by state legislatures, he also presupposed that the people would continue to exercise their "direct authority" by "amending and improving their own work."[28]

Madison had likewise relied on principles of popular sovereignty when defending the Constitution's method of ratification. In the 40th *Federalist*, he conceded that the Constitutional Convention of 1787 had exceeded its authority in "one particular." "Instead of reporting a plan requiring the confirmation of *all the States*," the delegates "reported a plan which is to be carried into effect by *nine States only*." But he characterized the Convention's powers as "merely advisory and recommendatory." What emerged was "a Constitution which is to be of no more consequence than the paper on which it is written, unless it is stamped with the approbation of those to whom it is addressed." Since the pro-

---

rebellion now and then is a good thing, and as necessary in the political world as storms in the physical"); Jefferson's letter to Samuel Kercheval, July 12, 1816, in Paul L. Ford, ed., *Writings of Thomas Jefferson* (New York: Putnam, 1899), vol. 10, at 37–45 (developed his argument that constitutions ought to provide for revision every nineteen years).

[27] Madison, Letter to Jefferson, February 4, 1790, in *Papers of James Madison* 13:19 (vols. 1–10, Chicago: University of Chicago Press, 1962–77; vols. 11–17, Charlottesville: University Press of Virginia, 1977–92).

[28] James Wilson, Speech at Pennsylvania Ratifying Convention, November 24, 1787, as reported by Thomas Lloyd, in *Documentary History of Ratification* 2:362; ibid., at 383 (November 28, 1787); ibid., at 556 (December 11, 1787). As with the subsequent debates in the First Congress, Lloyd was not the only person to publish accounts of the debates in the Pennsylvania Convention (see "Note on Sources," *Documentary History of Ratification* 2:36–44). The reliability of Lloyd's account of the earlier proceedings has likewise been severely criticized (see James H. Hutson, "The Creation of the Constitution: The Integrity of the Documentary Record," 65 Tex. L. Rev. 1, 20–24 [1986]). Even so, I rely on Lloyd's account, which appears to be the most complete, though without assuming its reliability. The caveats that apply to reliance on the *Annals*, as explained below in n. 43, apply equally to this context.

posal was "to be submitted to the people themselves, the disapprobation of this supreme authority would destroy it forever; its approbation blot out antecedent errors and irregularities."[29]

Madison suggested that "the people" depended upon extralegal/unauthorized actions to bring about "great changes of established governmental forms." He cited the Declaration of Independence for the proposition that the people had a "transcendent and precious right" to "abolish or alter their governments as to them shall seem most likely to effect their safety and happiness." But he presumed that "it is impossible for the people spontaneously and universally to move in concert towards their object." He claimed that "it is therefore essential that such changes be instituted by some *informal and unauthorized propositions*, made by some patriotic and respectable citizen or number of citizens." The people were dependent, in short, on founders who were willing to act outside established forms by proposing a new constitution when existing structures failed.[30]

Madison and other Federalists were hopeful, of course, that the new Constitution would gain the people's acceptance and veneration and thus make fundamental constitutional re-formation unnecessary at least for a while. They were aware, however, that some changes to the Constitution might be necessary to enable it to survive. Thus article V contemplates revision of the constitutional text as an alternative to more fundamental constitutional re-formation.[31]

Members of the founding generation had learned important lessons from problems posed by the Articles of Confederation. That charter had declared the union "perpetual." In addition, article XIII permitted amendments to the articles only upon confirmation "by the legislatures of every state" of alterations "agreed to in a congress of the united states." Article V of the 1787 text, in contrast, requires the approval of proposed amendments only by three-fourths of the states. Plus the option of ratification by state *conventions* has made it unnecessary to gain the approval of state *legislatures*.

Article V's move away from requiring unanimity for approval of proposed amendments parallels more closely article VII's provisions regarding ratification. In the 40th *Federalist*, Madison argued that it would be absurd to allow one state to veto the proposed Constitution. Later, in the 43rd *Federalist*, he elaborated on this issue. He posed the question: "On

---

[29] *The Federalist*, no. 40, at 251–53 (emphasis in original).

[30] Ibid., at 253 (emphasis in original).

[31] See Wood, *Creation of the American Republic*, at 612–14. See also Walter F. Murphy, "*Slaughter-House, Civil Rights*, and Limits on Constitutional Change," 32 Am. J. Juris. 1 (1987), for analysis of distinctions between amending a constitution and more fundamental forms of constitutional re-formation.

what principle the Confederation, which stands in the solemn form of a compact among the States, can be superseded without the unanimous consent of the parties?" He claimed that the question "is answered at once by recurring to the absolute necessity of the case; to the great principle of self-preservation; and to the transcendent law of nature and of nature's God."[32]

Upon the Constitution's ratification, article V would reinforce arguments that constitutional change could be accomplished legitimately without the unanimous consent of all the states or their residents.[33] Article VII, interpreted in conjunction with the preamble, presupposed that ratification by "conventions of nine states" would constitute an authoritative action by or on behalf of "the people of the United States."[34] Article V established corresponding structures for further change in America's fundamental law. Proposed amendments would become part of the Constitution "when ratified by the legislatures of three fourths of the several states, or by conventions in three fourths thereof." It would be possible to view such amendments, like the Constitution's initial ratification, as authoritative actions by or on behalf of "the people of the United States."

Like much of the original text, article V has attributed normative significance to actions by established representative institutions. It has allowed *Congress*, upon the approval of two-thirds of both Houses, to propose amendments. It has also obliged *Congress* to call a convention to propose amendments should *legislatures* of two-thirds of the states petition for such a convention. In addition, *Congress* has had authority to decide on the mode of ratification, and one route has been ratification by *state legislatures*.

Article V has not, however, confined "the people" to acting only through established institutions of federal and state government. The constitutional text has also contemplated more direct actions by "the people"

[32] *The Federalist*, no. 43, at 279. In addition, he suggested that "perhaps" the Articles had been dissolved by repeated infractions of the "compact" which had "no higher validity than a league or treaty" (ibid).

[33] It is noteworthy that article VII provided for the Constitution to go into effect only among the states that ratified it. As explained below, William F. Harris has emphasized this "unanimity principle." In practice, however, the establishment of a new constitution by at least nine states would supersede the Articles of Confederation and affect all the states, including those that might not ratify. Constitutional structures were changed even for states like North Carolina and Rhode Island which did not ratify the Constitution until after it went into effect. These states did eventually ratify the Constitution, making unanimity the historical practice.

[34] The idea of a union of nine states being "more perfect" than the arrangement established by the Articles of Confederation is worth exploring, particularly in relation to arguments that the constitutional text contemplated continuation of the union established by the Articles of Confederation. See generally Kenneth M. Stampp, "The Concept of a Perpetual Union," 65 J. Am. Hist. 5 (1978).

through ad hoc conventions called for proposing and/or ratifying amendments. These two types of conventions would correspond, respectively, to those that proposed and ratified the original Constitution.[35]

As a result, article V has presupposed that "the people" may formally overrule actions by federal or state officials. Against the federal government, the people may act through the amending power of a national convention and ratification by state legislatures or state conventions.[36] Against state governments, the people may act through the amending power of Congress or a national convention and state conventions.[37] In either case, article V has attributed normative significance to actions taken by "the people" (or their immediate representatives) independently of established governmental institutions.[38]

Madison's first proposed amendment would have reaffirmed this principle that "the people" continued to have authority, even after the Constitution's ratification, to bring about fundamental constitutional reform. Federalists were not in a good position to deny this principle, considering their reliance on it to justify the Constitution itself. Even so, it is not surprising that they favored amending the text, if possible, through *established* representative structures. Madison wrote in the 49th *Federalist* that "a constitutional road to the decision of the people ought to be marked out and kept open, for certain great and extraordinary occasions." In context, it appears he was suggesting such a road ought to be kept open *only* for cases of extreme constitutional failure.[39]

It required unusual circumstances, therefore, for Madison to endorse significant changes to the constitutional text. Many of his commitments led him to resist, not favor, amending the text.[40] But he also had several

---

[35] As indicated in the text, however, there were problems of legitimacy, as measured with reference to existing constitutional norms, associated with the Philadelphia Convention of 1787. In addition, the delegates to this convention invoked primarily the authority of the separate states, not that of the people of the combined "United States." Upon its ratification, the federal Constitution would reinforce the authority of national conventions as contemplated by article V, but relationships between delegates to such a convention and the delegates' constituents would remain murky.

[36] Article V provides that Congress *shall* call a convention upon the application of the legislatures of two-thirds of the states, making Congress's involvement in such an event mandatory rather than discretionary.

[37] It is also possible to overrule state actions through Congress's legislative powers and/or federal judicial powers (with judges enforcing federal laws and/or the Constitution itself).

[38] Articles I and II of the original constitutional text also appear to contemplate independent actions by "the people." Article V's amending provisions are located between political activity during times of ordinary politics and during extraordinary constitutional reformation.

[39] See *The Federalist*, no. 49, at 314.

[40] Madison's letter to Richard Peters, dated August 19, 1789, indicates that his support for the proposed amendments remained lukewarm at best. During the House's consideration of his proposals, he referred to the "nauseous project of amendments." He apparently

tactical reasons for advocating the initial amendments. Among other things, they might eliminate the need for an additional "decision of the people."

Madison apparently thought enumerating rights would diffuse opposition to the Constitution and mute calls for more fundamental change. There had been strong pressure in several state conventions, including Virginia's, for conditional ratification or a second national convention. Madison had objected that a second convention would "be fatal"—"the Constitution, and the Union will be both endangered." But he suggested there would be no harm in states proposing amendments for subsequent consideration, as Massachusetts had done. After the Constitution's ratification, Congress, acting in a responsible manner, could propose amendments that were "not objectionable, or unsafe." The additions would quiet, not arouse, public opinion. They would promote, rather than undercut, stability and veneration for the Constitution.[41]

He also had personal reasons for advocating subsequent amendments. After the Constitution's ratification, his political opponents in Virginia blocked his appointment to the Senate. Madison also faced substantial opposition in elections to the House. Patrick Henry, among others, painted Madison as an opponent of popular rights. In response, the latter pledged to work for amendments if elected to the House. He explained to a friend that this strategy might, if done properly, "serve the double purpose of satisfying the minds of well meaning opponents, and of providing additional guards in favour of liberty." Subsequent amendments would be "the safest mode" of changing the Constitution: "Congress, who will be appointed to execute as well as to amend the Government, will probably be careful not to destroy or endanger it." A second convention, in contrast, would "be but too likely to turn every thing into confusion and uncertainty."[42]

Madison faced a reluctant House of Representatives. But he carried

---

felt bound by tacit compacts, compelled by electoral pressures, and motivated more by strategic considerations than personal commitment to enumerating rights. The letter is reprinted in *Papers of James Madison* 12:346–48.

[41] Madison, Letter to George Nichols, April 8, 1788, in *Papers of James Madison* 11:11–14; Madison, Letter to Jefferson, April 22, 1788, in ibid., at 27–29; Madison, Speech at Virginia Ratifying Convention, June 20, 1788, as reported by David Robertson, in ibid., at 177 (also in *Documentary History of Ratification* 10:1504). For criticism of the reliability of Robertson's account, see Hutson, "Creation of the Constitution," at 23–24; *Documentary History of Ratification* 9:901–906. For analysis of Madison's reasons for sponsoring proposed amendments, see Paul Finkelman, "James Madison and the Bill of Rights: A Reluctant Paternity," 1990 Sup. Ct. Rev. 301 (1990). My analysis herein relies heavily on this work.

[42] Madison, Letter to George Eve, January 2, 1789, in *Papers of James Madison* 11:404–405. See also Finkelman, "James Madison and the Bill of Rights," at 334–36.

through on his campaign commitments and sought to undercut opposition to the new Constitution. He repeatedly expressed unwillingness, however, "to see a door opened for a reconsideration of the whole structure of the Constitution—for a reconsideration of the principles and structure of the powers given."[43]

In light of these commitments, his first proposed amendment still appears to be anomalous, even upon closer examination. Although it would not have directly altered the original Constitution's "structure of power," the proposal dealt with fundamental principles that called into question the character of those powers. Articles I through VI reflect a primary commitment to mediating political activity of "the people" through established institutions. The proposed amendment, in contrast, would have underscored the qualified and tentative character of federal power. The proposal would have brought to the fore popular rights and powers of

---

[43] James Madison, Speech to the House of Representatives, June 8, 1789, reprinted in *The Debates and Proceedings in the Congress of the United States* (the *"Annals of Congress,"* or *"Annals"*) (Washington: Gales and Seaton, 1834), vol. 1, at 433. See also ibid., at 738 (August 15, 1789) (Madison reportedly urged colleagues to confine themselves to "an enumeration of simple, acknowledged propositions [whose] ratification will meet with little difficulty"; he argued against "[a]mendments of a doubtful nature [which] will prejudge the whole system").

The *Annals of Congress* for the first session of Congress are based on *The Congressional Register*, published by shorthand writer Thomas Lloyd. This account is incomplete and unreliable, not a verbatim transcript. Newspaper summaries are even more partial. Proceedings in the Senate were closed to the public, and the *Senate Journal* reports only official actions relating to the proposed amendments. The *House Journal* likewise reports official actions but not debates. See generally Laurence F. Schmeckebier and Roy B. Eastin, *Government Publications and Their Use* (Washington: Brookings Institute, 1961), ch. 6; Hutson, "Creation of the Constitution," at 35–38; Veit, Bowling, and Bickford, eds., *Creating the Bill of Rights*, at 55–56. The structure of Madison's speech to the House as reported in the *Annals*, but not more, is corroborated by his notes of the speech, which are reprinted in *Papers of James Madison* 2:193–95.

Because Lloyd's account is more complete and appears to be more reliable than alternative sources on the issues examined herein, I rely primarily on the *Annals*. In several places I also refer to alternative accounts, such as those included in the *Gazette of the United States*. Crucial passages from the *Congressional Register* and the *Gazette* are omitted from *Creating the Bill of Rights*, and thus for accounts of debates I refer directly to the original sources. References herein to the *Annals* are to volume 1 except where otherwise indicated.

This book refers to remarks made by particular persons without repeatedly adding the qualification that in many cases we have access only to unreliable and incomplete *accounts* of such remarks. For example, rather than referring awkwardly to "Madison's speech on June 8, 1798, *as reported by the Annals,*" I review what Madison reportedly said in that speech. I do so for reasons of convenience and clarity but without assuming that the *Annals* report exactly what Madison said. I likewise describe the positions of Madison and other individuals, as reported in particular sources, without repeating my caveat that such individuals might not have been personally committed to the positions they articulated. The available evidence suggests that in many cases individuals were *not* personally committed to the arguments they advanced.

constitutional change which Madison and other Federalists regarded as prerogatives of last resort. Instead of emphasizing the need for governmental stability and constitutional veneration, the proposal articulated critical standards for evaluating governmental performance and advocating change.[44]

Although Madison's amendments would have been integrated into the body of the constitutional text, his first proposal took the form of a preface to the Constitution. At the head of the text, the statement of fundamental principles could have performed exhortatory functions along the lines of those favored by many advocates of a federal bill of rights. The proposal could have served "the kind of standard-setting, maxim-describing, teaching function of bills of rights that the Antifederalists thought so important."[45]

The three paragraphs corresponded closely to the first three paragraphs in Virginia's Declaration of Rights. Madison's draft did not include the state charter's additional declaration that "no free government, or the blessings of liberty, can be preserved to any people but by a firm adherence to justice, moderation, temperance, frugality, and virtue, and by a *frequent recurrence to fundamental principles*."[46] But the draft had a similar thrust.

Edmund Randolph would later characterize Virginia's Declaration of Rights as the "cornerstone" upon which Virginia's constitution of 1776 had been erected. He attributed two purposes to the charter: placing limits on the legislature, and erecting "a perpetual standard . . . around which the people might rally, and by a notorious record be forever admonished to be watchful, firm and virtuous."[47] Randolph and others of like mind made similar arguments for adding a bill of rights to the federal Constitution.[48] Madison's first proposal appears to have been responsive to these demands.

---

[44] For an insightful analysis of the tension, see Sanford Levinson, "'Veneration' and Constitutional Change: James Madison Confronts the Possibility of Constitutional Amendment," 21 Tex. Tech L. Rev. 2443 (1990).

[45] Herbert J. Storing, "The Constitution and the Bill of Rights," in Gary L. McDowell, ed., *Taking the Constitution Seriously* (Dubuque, Iowa: Kendall/Hunt, 1981), at 278.

[46] Virginia Declaration of Rights, 1776, para. 15 (emphasis added), in Schwartz, ed., *Bill of Rights* 1:236.

[47] Randolph, "Essay on the Revolutionary History of Virginia," ca. 1809–1813, in Schwartz, ed., *Bill of Rights* 1:249.

[48] See Randolph, Speech at Virginia Ratifying Convention, June 17, 21, and 24, 1788, as reported by David Robertson, in *Documentary History of Ratification* 10:1347–54, 1450–56, and 1481–88. See also the account of Patrick Henry's Speech at the Convention, June 7, 1788, in ibid., vol. 9, at 1036 ("There are certain maxims by which every wise and enlightened people will regulate their conduct. . . . We have one, Sir, *That all men are by nature free and independent, and have certain inherent rights, of which, when they enter society, they cannot by any compact divest their posterity*") (paraphrasing article 1 of the Virginia Decla-

From Exhortation to Addendum

Herbert Storing has argued that Madison and other Federalists in the First Congress eliminated "all the 'oughts,' all the statements of general principle," from the initial draft that Madison presented to the First Congress. Storing suggested that the Federalists eliminated these statements of principle out of concern that they would "endanger government" and deprive it of "a presumption of legitimacy and permanence." Storing claimed, moreover, that Madison's proposed amendment to the preamble was "dropped altogether."[49]

Storing had good reasons for attributing to members of the First Congress (not just Federalists) an effort to move away from broad statements of constitutional principle. But he ignored roles that the proposal appears to have played in debates over the tenth amendment's precursor. In addition, he overstated the extent to which the eventual Bill of Rights became only "specific protections of traditional civil rights" and not "maxims" that could play roles in fostering active citizenship.

Madison's proposed amendment to the preamble, as quoted above, would have articulated three principles that were arguably implicit in the preamble itself. First, "all power is originally vested in, and consequently derived from, the people." Second, as a result, government "ought to be exercised for the benefit of the people; which consists in the enjoyment of life and liberty, with the right of acquiring and using property, and generally of pursuing and obtaining happiness and safety." Third, "the people have an indubitable, unalienable, and indefeasible right to reform or change their Government, whenever it be found adverse or inadequate to the purposes of its institution."

A more abbreviated proposal emerged from the House select committee, which the House appointed to consider and report on Madison's proposals:

> In the introductory paragraph, before the words "We the people," add "Government being intended for the benefit of the people, and the rightful establishment thereof being derived from their authority alone."[50]

---

ration of Rights); the comments of "A Delegate Who Has Catched a Cold," *Virginia Independent Chronicle*, June 18 and 25, 1788, in ibid., vol. 10, 1640–43 and 1681–84 (also in Storing, ed., *The Complete Anti-Federalist* 5:268–74) (an enumeration of rights, at the "head of the new constitution, can inspire and conserve the affection for the native country"; emphasized the importance of "invigorat[ing] our government" by "renewing and giving it a fresh spring at stated periods"). According to Herbert Storing, "Virtually all the advocates of a bill of rights assumed that it should come at the head of the Constitution" (see Storing, "The Constitution and the Bill of Rights," at 278).

[49] Storing, "The Constitution and the Bill of Rights," at 279.

[50] See Veit, Bowling, and Bickford, eds., *Creating the Bill of Rights*, at 29. According to the *Senate Journal*, at 124, a motion was made in the Senate on Tuesday, September 8, 1789,

Madison was a member of the select committee, along with ten other individuals.[51] Apparently he was not alone in having reasons to favor weakening the draft. It no longer declared that the people had foundational rights and powers of constitutional reform or revolution.

On August 14, the House began considering the revised proposal. The *Annals* report various comments on it by Elbridge Gerry, William Smith, James Madison, Thomas Tucker, Thomas Sumter, John Page, and Roger Sherman. Each reportedly endorsed the general principles underlying it. According to the *Annals*, however, the latter four individuals questioned the appropriateness of amending the preamble. Tucker (an Anti-Federalist) suggested that "if it was necessary to retain the principle, it might come in at some other place." Sumter (another Anti-Federalist) "thought this was not a proper place." Page (a Federalist) "did not doubt the truth of the proposition, . . . but he doubted its necessity in this place." Sherman (another Federalist) urged that it "ought not to come in in this place."[52]

Sherman advocated adding alterations "by way of supplement" instead of integrating them into the original text. He reportedly argued that "[w]e might as well endeavor to mix brass, iron, and clay, as to incorporate such heterogeneous articles; the one contradictory to the other." He characterized the original text as "the act of the people" and suggested that it "ought to remain entire[ly so]." He presumed that the amendments, in contrast, would be "the act of the State Governments." His position, in short, was that using the form of supplemental amendments would preserve the purity of the original Constitution and weaken the force of enumerated rights.[53]

Debate on this issue carried over into a second day. Tucker reportedly suggested on August 15 that the principles articulated in the revised first

---

to add the following amendment: "That Government ought to be instituted for the common benefit, protection, and security of the people; and that the doctrine of non-resistance against arbitrary power and oppression, is absurd, slavish, and destructive of the good and happiness of mankind." The *Senate Journal* reports that the motion "passed in the Negative." Vol. 1 of the *Senate Journal* (for 1789) is reprinted along with vol. 1 of the *House Journal* (for the same period) in Martin P. Claussen, ed., *The Congressional Journals of the United States*, among the *National State Papers of the United States* (Wilmington, Del.: Michael Glazier, 1977).

[51] The other members were Baldwin, Benson, Boudinot, Burke, Clymer, Gale, Gilman, Goodhue, Sherman, and Vining. Most of these men were Federalists.

[52] *Annals*, at 717–19 (August 14, 1789). Except where indicated, I do not distinguish the House's acting as a Committee of the Whole House from its acting more formally. See generally Veit, Bowling, and Bickford, eds., *Creating the Bill of Rights*, at 55–56.

[53] *Annals*, at 707–708 (August 13, 1789). His suggestion was debated by the House but not initially accepted. On August 19, 1789, Sherman renewed his proposal to add the amendments as supplementary articles, and his proposal was then "agreed to" (ibid., at 766).

proposal "may be introduced into a bill of rights." Madison did not directly counter this suggestion, but he claimed that "gentlemen, who admit [the addition] should come in somewhere, will be puzzled to find a better place."[54]

The House proceeded to discuss other proposals and eventually reached the tenth amendment's precursor. Madison had offered the following amendment as one of two clauses in a new article VII: "The powers not delegated by this constitution, nor prohibited by it to the States, are reserved to the States respectively."[55] An identical proposal had emerged from the House select committee.[56]

The *Annals* for August 18 report a motion by Tucker to amend the tenth amendment's precursor. He apparently renewed his suggestion to relocate, in condensed form, the proposed amendment to the preamble:

> Mr. Tucker proposed to amend the [tenth amendment's precursor], by prefixing to it "all powers being derived from the people." He thought this a better place to make this assertion than the introductory clause of the constitution, where a similar sentiment was proposed by the committee. He extended his motion also, to add the word "expressly," so as to read "the powers not expressly delegated by this constitution."[57]

[54] Ibid., at 717–19 (August 14, 1789). Livermore also commented on the proposal, but he expressed doubt as to its likely success within the full House. He reportedly said he "did not care" about the proposal's form.

[55] See ibid., at 435–36 (June 8, 1789). The other clause of Madison's proposed article VII would have concerned the Constitution's separation of powers, but the clause (which became the House's sixteenth proposal) was not approved by the Senate. See ibid., at 760 (August 18, 1789) (debate in the House); ibid., at 767 (August 21, 1789) (House approval); *House Journal*, at 108 (August 21, 1789) (listing of amendments approved by the House); *Senate Journal*, at 106 (August 25, 1789) (listing of amendments approved by the House); ibid., at 122 (September 7, 1789) (Senate disapproval of the sixteenth proposal). These considerations undercut Randy E. Barnett's claim that two concerns "ran together" in Madison's draft of the ninth amendment—a prohibition on unwarranted expansions of federal power and the danger that unenumerated rights would be jeopardized. According to Barnett, these two ideas were "unpacked," with one concern being "handled" by the tenth amendment and the other "addressed" by the ninth. Barnett, "Reconceiving the Ninth Amendment," 74 Cornell L. Rev. 1, 10 (1988). Cf. John Hart Ely, *Democracy and Distrust* (Cambridge: Harvard University Press, 1980), at 36 (Ely explained that Madison, in his draft of the ninth amendment, "wished to forestall *both* the implication of unexpressed powers *and* the disparagement of unenumerated rights" [emphasis in original]; Ely asserted that "just as the Tenth Amendment clearly expresses the former point, the Ninth Amendment clearly expresses the latter"). It is important to note that Madison's original proposals included predecessors to *both* the ninth and tenth amendments. The structure of the latter was preserved, and an additional clause, reserving powers to "the people," was added after the amendment's reference to powers reserved to the states. This proposal and changes to it are examined below and in ch. 4.

[56] See Veit, Bowling, and Bickford, eds., *Creating the Bill of Rights*, at 33.

[57] *Annals*, at 761 (August 18, 1789). The *Gazette* reports the debates as having occurred on *Tuesday*, August *19* and reports the first part of Tucker's proposal. The *Gazette* was

Madison reportedly responded only to the latter part of Tucker's motion, and the House defeated it.[58] The *Annals* indicate, however, that Carroll renewed the first part of the motion by "propos[ing] to add at the end of the proposition, 'or to the people.'" This time, Carroll's motion "was agreed to" by the House, acting as a committee of the whole.[59] Three days later, during the House's formal consideration of the amendments,

> Mr. Sherman moved to alter the last clause, so as to make it read, "the powers not delegated to the United States by the constitution, nor prohibited by it to the States, are reserved to the States, respectively, or to the people."

Although the *Annals* report the adoption of this motion "without debate," neither the *House Journal* nor the *Senate Journal* reflects any change from the select committee's proposal.[60]

---

mistaken on the date, because Tuesday was the *18th*. The error is obvious on the face of the *Gazette*, since it reports *both* Wednesday and Thursday as August 20, 1789. Thereafter, its days and dates accord with the *Annals*. See *Gazette* 1:50, cols. 1 and 2.

In addition, there is an obvious problem with the *Gazette*'s account of the substance of Tucker's proposal, because (according to both accounts) Madison responded to the addition of "expressly," not to the proposal to add an introductory clause. The *Annals* are also apparently correct on the date, since it is internally consistent and accords with the amendments' having been considered sequentially by the House, acting as such, beginning on *Wednesday*, August 19. See *Annals*, at 766 (August 19, 1789).

[58] Madison's response is cited and analyzed in ch. 4.

[59] *Annals*, at 761 (August 18, 1789). According to the *Gazette*, Carrol (spelled with one "l") *opposed Gerry's* proposal to add "*and* people thereof" on the rationale that "it tended to create a distinction between the people and their legislature." "The motion was negatived, and the amendment agreed to." See *Gazette* 1:50, col. 1 (reportedly for August 19, 1789). Peculiarly, *Creating the Bill of Rights* does not reprint either account but does refer to both on p. 33 at n. 34.

[60] See *Annals*, at 768 (August 21, 1789). According to the *House Journal* and *Senate Journal*, the amendment passed by the House on August 21 and 24 was substantially identical to that approved by the select committee: "The powers not delegated by the Constitution, nor prohibited by it to the States, are reserved to the States respectively." See *House Journal*, at 108 (August 21, 1789); *Senate Journal*, at 106 (August 25, 1789).

According to the *Gazette*, Sherman proposed the following amendment to the tenth amendment's precursor on August 21: "after the words, 'prohibited by it to the,' *government of the United*; and after the words, 'reserved to the,' *individuals* should be inserted." According to the *Gazette*, this motion was "acceded to, and the clause was then adopted." See *Gazette* 1:50, col. 3 (August 21, 1789). *Creating the Bill of Rights* also omits this portion of the *Gazette*.

As William W. Crosskey has observed, there is an obvious problem with the *Gazette*'s account. Powers cannot be reserved to "the individuals states respectively." He suggested that Sherman actually proposed the following: "The powers not delegated by this Constitution, nor prohibited by it, to the *government of the United States*, are reserved to the *individuals of the* States respectively" (Crosskey, *Politics and the Constitution in the History of the United States* [Chicago: University of Chicago Press, 1953], vol. 1, at 703–704). For

The available accounts of proceedings in the First Congress are incomplete and unreliable. None of the available sources contains a verbatim transcript. The reporters faced substantial obstacles in practice, and their accounts reflect partisan commitments. There are few records of the Senate's debates in executive session. The House and Senate journals include limited accounts. The possibilities for errors in recording or communicating actions abounded.

None of these limitations detracts, however, from the ability of available sources to identify a range of possible meanings. Sources that are unreliable as evidence of the actual debates may nevertheless provide access to competing conceptions of "the people" and their "rights" and "powers." Many of these positions offer critical perspectives for analyzing basic principles and structures of American constitutionalism.

The tenth amendment would be a fitting place to refer—even if only obliquely—to powers of constitutional reform. The amendment uses the rhetoric of "delegated" powers. Articles I, II, and III of the original text, in contrast, specify powers "granted to" or "vested in" governmental institutions. The language of "delegated" powers connotes a more tentative assignment of authority to these institutions than does the text of 1787. The amendment's implicit premise is that those who have delegated powers, for their benefit, may withdraw such powers—particularly if they do not accomplish the purposes for which they had been delegated. The concept of delegated powers echoes back, therefore, to the preamble and article V, along with articles I, II, and III.

Various drafts of the tenth amendment referred to powers as delegated (or not delegated) "by the Constitution." Accordingly, the drafts consistently reflect a presumption underlying the original text: federal officials would depend for their authority on that of the Constitution itself. This authority would be a function of affirmative delegation, nothing else.

Early drafts referred to powers as reserved "to the states." In this form, the amendment would have reinforced arguments that federal powers derived from delegations of power by the states, acting together through the Constitution. These drafts likewise would have reinforced arguments that the Constitution reserved powers of constitutional change to the states. Such arguments would have complemented articles V and VII. According to article VII, the Constitution had been ratified by "the states." Article V would depend on ratification of proposed amendments by "the states," acting either through their legislatures or ad hoc conventions.

Not all members of the First Congress (or of the founding generation

---

reasons discussed in the text below, such a proposal would have been unlikely. A more likely possibility, though not the most likely, was that Sherman proposed reserving powers to the *individual* states.

more generally) would have conceded, however, that the Constitution depended for its authority primarily or exclusively upon that of "the states." The issue appears to have been complicated then, as it is now, by the equivocal character of references to "the states." As Madison would later explain, individuals could reasonably interpret references to "the states" as denoting territories *and/or* political communities *and/or* the people composing those communities *and/or* governmental institutions for these territories and their residents.[61]

The problematic character of references to "the states" came to the surface in arguments during the founding generation about the location of sovereignty within America. Opponents of the Constitution, as well as those seeking to circumscribe the new government's authority, continued to advocate the idea of state legislative sovereignty. Federalists, in contrast, criticized these arguments and argued that "the people" were sovereign. A number of Federalists were unclear, however, on how "the people" were (or might be) politically configured for various purposes.

James Wilson, for example, argued that the Constitution would flow from the authority of "the states" as well as "the people." In addition, he suggested that "the states" and "the people" would join together and form a national community upon the Constitution's ratification. Even so, he presupposed that "the people" and "the states" would continue to hold distinct prerogatives following ratification. But he was unclear on how he thought "the people" and/or "the states" might legitimately act to repudiate the Constitution itself and perhaps abolish the union.[62]

Wilson's arguments, like many others at the time, raised complex questions about whether "the people of the United States" were (or would be) constituted as members of one political community or only as members of states. Could "the people" act as a national community (or through institutions representing it) and not only through "the states" and their governing institutions? Alternatively or in addition, would the Constitution depend on the people's acting through the states, including in their combined capacity as "United States"? Would different norms apply if "the people" and/or "the states" sought to act independently of constitutional forms rather than consistently with them?

[61] See Madison's "Report on the Virginia Resolutions" (January 7, 1800), in *Papers of James Madison* 17:308–309 (examined in ch. 8 hereof).

[62] Chapter 4 examines Wilson's treatment of relationships among various constitutional prerogatives. For present purposes, the important point is that Wilson assumed that establishing a republican government entailed two theoretically and/or chronologically distinct stages: forming a political society, and delegating governmental powers to representative institutions. In a letter to N. P. Trist, February 15, 1830, Madison likewise distinguished these two stages and claimed they were "blended in the Constitution of the U.S." (see ch. 8, n. 65). Neither Wilson nor Madison explained how "the people" could dissolve a political society once they created one.

The tenth amendment's declaration that powers were reserved to "the people," not *only* "the states," may be understood (among other things) as a means of accommodating Federalist and Anti-Federalist positions on these issues. The addendum would reinforce Federalist arguments that "the people" held sovereign powers within America, including ultimate powers of constitutional change. Some Federalists might concede that "the people" held these powers as members of the states, but the reference to "the people" could also accommodate unitary, nationalistic conceptions of "the people." Meanwhile, Anti-Federalists gained a textual peg upon which to base arguments that the states held residual governing powers. It would be possible to regard these powers, like those delegated to "the United States," as powers of established institutions and/or as powers of sovereignty.

As a result, the addition strengthened bridges between the tenth amendment and article V. The former's reference to powers of "the people" has reinforced arguments that "the people" have continued to hold ultimate powers of constitutional change. According to this line of reasoning, the people have held authority to exercise powers of constitutional change through ad hoc conventions and not just legislatures. The people of the United States could act in their combined capacity through a national convention, and the people of the respective states could act through separate ratifying conventions. Ratification by state conventions, if nine states ratified, would constitute an authoritative action by or on behalf of "the people of the United States" even if ratification by state legislatures would not.

The tenth amendment, along with the preamble and other parts of the Constitution, would be able to accommodate unitary and plural conceptions of "the people." The combined actions of "the people" of the respective states (or their representatives) would also constitute combined actions by or on behalf of "the states." For many purposes, it would not be necessary to resolve whether "the people" referred to a single body or to persons otherwise constituted (i.e., as members of separate states that have together composed the United States).

Acting outside Article V

One may identify at least three conceivable forms of constitutional change in addition to those contemplated by article V. First, interpretive practices may have changed the meanings of provisions whose terms have not changed. Second, "the people" and/or their representatives may have amended the constitutional text, not just reinterpreted its terms, without complying with article V. Third, there may have been fundamental constitutional re-formation, or re-creation, not sanctioned by article V. Efforts to evaluate these forms of change redirect attention to problems associated with analyzing how "the people" have been politically configured and how they have acted or may act.

A number of scholars have stimulated reconsideration of these problems. Bruce Ackerman, for example, has argued that the fourteenth amendment gained legitimacy through procedures that did not comply with the formal requirements of article V.[63] He has likewise argued that, during the 1930s, a judicial precedent—*Lochner v. New York*—was "promoted . . . to the status of a constitutional text . . . with all the potency of a formal amendment under Article V."[64] He claimed that both times, "We the People of the United States expressed its will through a higher lawmaking process that relied primarily upon the structural interaction of Articles I, II and III of the Constitution."[65] In both cases, moreover, the victors "subordinated the states in nationalizing the higher lawmaking system."[66]

Although there are serious problems with his historical claims and his conception of judicial role,[67] Ackerman's arguments are perceptive in several respects. First, he has called attention to possibilities of informal constitutional change.[68] Second, he has been alert to ways that governmental

---

[63] See Ackerman, "Discovering the Constitution," at 1063–69; Ackerman, "Constitutional Politics," at 503–10. In the earlier work, he relied on the idea of extra-legal "conventions." See "Discovering the Constitution," at 1058–63. This suggestion is not developed in the later works, including his book, *We The People: Foundations*.

[64] Ackerman, "Discovering the Constitution," 93 Yale L. J. 1013 (1984), at 1051–57 (the quoted passage is at p. 1056). See also Ackerman, "Constitutional Politics/Constitutional Law," 99 Yale L. J. 453 (1989), at 510–15.

[65] See Ackerman, "Discovering the Constitution," at 1054; ibid., at 1056 ("The democratic struggle over constitutional principle will not end until a series of decisive victories at the polls permits the newly triumphant spokesmen of the People to proclaim their new higher law from *all three* of the branches constituted by the first three Articles") (emphasis in original).

[66] Ackerman, "Constitutional Politics," at 512.

[67] For serious criticism of Ackerman's historical claims, see Suzanna Sherry, "The Ghost of Liberalism Past," 105 Harv. L. Rev. 918 (1992). For criticism of his backward-looking conception of judicial interpretive norms, see Frank Michelman, "Law's Republic," 97 Yale L. J. 1493 (1988), at 1519–24. See also David R. Dow, "The Plain Meaning of Article V," in Sanford Levinson, ed., *Responding to Imperfection* (Princeton: Princeton University Press, 1995), ch. 6 (criticizes Ackerman for paying insufficient attention to deliberative ideals and the importance of states as holders of residual sovereign powers).

[68] But there are serious problems with his collapsing distinctions between constitutional changes that take the form of amendments to the constitutional text and those achieved by reinterpreting its provisions. I set aside these issues for now and deal with them in part by examining instances of the latter in subsequent chapters. I plan to deal more fully in a future work with problems of contemporary ratification as they relate to adding provisions (such as the fourteenth amendment) to the constitutional text.

officials may claim authority to act on behalf of "the people," at least in some contexts and for limited purposes. Third, he has tied constitutional lawmaking to expressions of popular will.[69] Thus he has evaluated the normative significance of actions by "the people" both through representative structures and independently of them.

Akhil Reed Amar has also dealt with these issues. Unlike Ackerman, he has presupposed that "[i]f ordinary branches of government are to amend the Constitution, both state and national levels must be involved." But he has endorsed Ackerman's argument that "the people" may legitimately alter the supreme law without complying with article V and without ratification by state legislatures or state conventions. According to Amar, a majority of "the people" have an unenumerated "right" or "power" to "alter or abolish their government" through a national convention or popular referendum.[70]

He has relied heavily on the ninth and tenth amendments to support his position. According to Amar, both amendments "underscore the revolutionary theory of popular sovereignty." He claimed that "the first, most undeniable, inalienable and important, if unenumerated, right of the People is the right of a majority of voters to amend the Constitution—even in ways not expressly provided for by Article V." In addition, he relied on the tenth amendment to support his claim that sovereignty has resided in "the people" of the whole nation, not "the people" constituted as members of separate states.[71]

[69] But see Stanley Kelley Jr., *Interpreting Elections* (Princeton: Princeton University Press, 1983) (underscores problems associated with relying on popular elections as reliable evidence of the people's considered views); Philip J. Weiser, "Ackerman's Proposal for Popular Constitutional Lawmaking: Can It Realize His Aspirations for Dualist Democracy," 68 NYU L. Rev. 907 (1993) (analyzes corresponding problems posed by popular referenda). Recognizing the interpretive problems and deliberative deficiencies associated with voting and similar forms of popular action does not, however, undercut viewing them as constitutionally authoritative for some purposes.

[70] See Amar, "Philadelphia Revisited," 55 U. Chi. L. Rev. 1043 (1988), at 1056–57 and passim.

[71] See ibid., at 1044, 1056–57, and 1062; Amar, "Of Sovereignty and Federalism," 96 Yale L. J. 1425 (1987), esp. at 1456. See also Amar, "Philadelphia Revisited," at 1057–58 n. 47 ("[I]f there be any 'unenumerated' rights at all—and the Ninth Amendment insists that there must be—the right that legalizes the Constitution itself must surely be one of them"); ibid., at 1062–63 (Amar assumed that this right was held by a majority of the people of the United States and claimed that it was inconsistent with principles of divided sovereignty; he suggested, moreover, that conceiving of sovereignty as divided between the people of the United States and the people of the respective states "was almost always universally recognized as a theoretical impossibility"); "Of Sovereignty and Federalism," at 1448–64 (he argued that "the people" formed a unitary body from founding, but this principle was disputed during the antebellum period; then it was "perfected" through the fourteenth amendment); Amar, "Consent of the Governed," 94 Colum. L. Rev. 457 (1994), passim (reinforced prior arguments as to majoritarian principles). For a complementary treatment

Amar has equivocated on how "the people" may legitimately exercise sovereign powers of constitutional change. His essay, "Philadelphia Revisited: Amending the Constitution Outside Article V," focuses on a hypothetical amendment proposed by a national convention and approved by a national referendum "at which a majority of voters ratify the amendment." In defending such an action, Amar underscored the majoritarian character of ratification by state conventions, as required by article VII. But he has repeatedly run together analysis of approval by a majority of the people at large and approval by a majority of the delegates in conventions.[72]

At one point in his essay, Amar conceded that differences between a direct referendum and a ratifying convention "may be important." But he declared that he would "not explore [the] admitted intricacies here." He suggested that this difference "at most" would suggest the need for a "special national ratifying convention, whose delegates are chosen in a special election." Peculiarly, he announced that his "tentative view"—notwithstanding the essay's contrary thrust—was that "since the amending majority must be deliberative, a convention may well be necessary for both the proposing and ratifying stages."[73]

---

of these issues, see Matthew J. Herrington, "Popular Sovereignty in Pennsylvania, 1776–1791," 67 Temp. L. Rev. 575 (1994).

As explained below, however, it is not clear that the Constitution has rested solely upon majoritarian premises. Nor is it clear that the idea of limited federal sovereignty (and thus a form of divided sovereignty) has ever been theoretically incoherent. Consider Chief Justice John Marshall's claim in *McCulloch v. Maryland*, 17 U.S. (4 Wheat.) 316 (1819), at 410: "In America, the powers of sovereignty are divided between the government of the Union, and those of the states. They are each sovereign, with respect to the objects committed to it, and neither sovereign, with respect to the objects committed to the other." Justice James Iredell likewise declared in *Chisholm v. Georgia*, 2 U.S. (2 Dall.) 419 (1793), at 435: "Every state in the union in every instance where its sovereignty has not been delegated to the United States, I consider to be as completely sovereign, as the United States are in respect to the powers surrendered." Similar examples abound, especially during the Republic's early years and throughout the antebellum period. In addition, the fourteenth amendment (upon which Amar relies heavily) affirmed the idea of *dual* citizenship—an idea that complements principles of limited federal sovereignty, with residual sovereignty reserved to "the states" and "the people." I return to this issue below and in subsequent chapters.

72 See Amar, "Philadelphia Revisited," at 1044–45, 1050–54, and 1058 (claimed that the first amendment "encompasses the *corporate* right of the People to assemble *in convention*, and, by a majority vote, to peaceably exercise their sovereign right to alter or abolish government" (emphasis in original). See also ibid., at 1065 (suggested that "Congress could be constitutionally obliged to convene a proposing convention if a bare majority of Americans so petitioned Congress").

73 Ibid., at 1064–1066 (here he was addressing the question of whether "a petition could demand not a Philadelphia-style proposing convention, but simply a Congressionally called referendum on a proposed amendment text specified in the petition itself"). Later in the article, he considered whether "Congress, by simple majorities in each house (and present-

But in a later article, Amar strengthened claims that "the people" may act directly to amend or replace the Constitution, not only through a convention. He argued that "Congress would be obliged to call a convention to propose revisions if a majority of American voters so petition[ed]; and that an amendment or new Constitution could be lawfully ratified by a simple majority of the American electorate."[74] According to Amar, voting in a national referendum would be a direct expression of the will of "the people." Such an action would, in his view, be lawful even if it supplanted the entire Constitution.

William F. Harris II has explored dimensions of popular sovereignty that call into question some of Ackerman's and Amar's central claims. In his book, *The Interpretable Constitution*, Harris emphasizes distinctions between structures of governmental representation and decisions made through ad hoc conventions. He presumes that "a government (either a legislature or a combination of governmental agents) cannot constitute, since political creatures cannot plausibly define the terms of their creation."[75] Thus he has implicitly repudiated Ackerman's claims that "the people" may legitimately exercise their sovereign constitution-(re)making authority by acting through ordinary structures of governmental representation.[76] In addition, Harris's analysis reinforces materials from the founding period, as summarized above, which do not support Amar's claim that the Constitution may be legitimately amended simply through a majority vote of the people at large.

Relying on article VII, Harris has linked powers of constitutional change to a "unanimity principle."[77] It is significant, in his view, that the

---

ment) [could] propose an amendment to be ratified by a simple majority in a national referendum (or a national convention)." In this context, he suggested that his "tentative inclination" was that it would be permissible for Congress, by two-thirds vote of each house, to "propose amendments for popular ratification" (see ibid., at 1094 n. 102). Here, as elsewhere, his distinction between referenda and conventions appears to have been added by way of afterthought. His analysis of deliberative requirements is contained primarily in a footnote—at 1064–65 n. 79. For further analysis of principles of deliberative democracy, see, e.g., James S. Fishkin, *Democracy and Deliberation: New Directions for Democratic Reform* (New Haven: Yale University Press, 1991).

[74] Amar, "Consent of the Governed," at 459.

[75] Harris, *The Interpretable Constitution*, at 192.

[76] See, e.g., ibid., at 77 ("[T]he term 'popular sovereignty' does not aptly refer to the power of the dominant part of a segmentable voting population to select incumbents to hold office in the institutions of the Constitution. That process is a mere proxy of the sovereign people—an institutionalization itself, *under* the terms of the Constitution. Their sovereign power is the capacity, acting as a whole people seeking a fully collective identity, to speak the Constitution's terms and make its institutions in the first place").

[77] As had Amar, Harris also linked his arguments to the tenth amendment. In his view, "the most obvious power held by the people . . . is the 'original' power to refashion their government, to make new Constitutions, both state and national—to resume constitutive

Constitution would bind only the states that ratified it. In addition, Harris has claimed that the Constitution has constituted a whole people, not just parts. Extending these principles, he has argued that "the people" may only exercise sovereign powers of constitutional change "as a whole people seeking a fully collective identity."[78]

Harris conceded that "[t]he precise historical veracity of [his] story of the whole people as constituting themselves into [a] polity may well be open to qualification." But he argued that "disproof would not invalidate it," because "[t]he purpose for reciting the story is not historical but ritual." The concept of popular sovereignty "is part of a sequence of justification validated because it is used as a principle on which interpretation is grounded."[79]

One of Harris's main objectives has been to develop "a theory of the Constitution's ongoing ratification." He presumed that "the fundamental dynamics of the constitutional enterprise" depend on "the continuing ratification that occurs in the process of mutually adjusting the linguistic and political texts." Among other things, "what goes on in the constitutional order must be kept compatible with the *account* of origins which proposes that the sovereign people as a whole made it." Through a process of "after-the-fact justification," interpretation maintains "the conditions of the Constitution's authority, sustaining (from within) the Constitution's creation of a foundation for itself."[80]

---

speech." Thus the tenth amendment "can be read most plausibly as a textually internal acknowledgement of the putatively external collective sovereignty." The amendment "signifies the people's residual constitution-making power, whether reinforcing the unused popular track of Article V amendment or suggesting a prior and more radical mode of constitutional change" (ibid., at 78).

[78] See ibid., at 73–83. See also ibid., at 190 ("[I]f a supposed sovereign acts partially and whimsically it has not maintained its identity as represented in and what it has made"); ibid., at 116–17 n. 5 ("[E]ven the major part is still partial and not equivalent to the constitutional People"); ibid., at 184–85 n. 15 (refers to but does not endorse Amar's majoritarian conception of how "the people" may act). But as the previous note indicates, Harris has endorsed "the unused popular track of Article V amendment" as an adequate expression of the will of "the people." Article V does not, of course, require unanimity. Instead, its super-majoritarian requirements parallel article VI's premise that the Constitution would go into effect upon its ratification by nine of the thirteen states. Perhaps Harris is presuming that ratification by conventions of three-fourths of the states would be an action of (or on behalf of) "the whole people."

[79] Ibid., at 73. See also ibid., at 111 (suggested that the credo of the whole people as constitutional author may well be historically incomplete).

[80] Ibid., at 115 (emphasis added), 115 n. 4, and 161. See also ibid., at 104–13 (Harris distinguishes the "Constitution" as a written text from the "constitution" as a political order); ibid., at 7–11 (distinguishes "internal" and "external" perspectives, following H. L. A. Hart's *The Concept of Law*). For another sophisticated effort to deal with problems associated with maintaining constitutional authority across time, see Paul W. Kahn, *Legitimacy and History: Self-Government in American Constitutional Theory* (New Haven: Yale University Press, 1992).

According to this line of reasoning, a constitution becomes, through its ongoing interpretation, "a symbolization of the whole people who have no other immanent identity." The text "stands for the presence of the whole." But it is only a *representation* of the sovereign power, which has "retired into the clouds." This perspective informs Harris's analysis of powers delegated to governmental officials, along with those held by "the people" at large.[81] He urges that it would be anomalous to treat majoritarian actions, whether taken through established representative structures or by the people independently of such structures, as exercises of sovereign power.

There are disjunctions, however, between Harris's emphasis on the *myth* of the whole people and the importance he attaches to separate interpretive *practices*. One of his underlying insights is that the Constitution has not merely empowered majorities. Nor has its authority flowed only from those who originally approved the text, either directly or through representatives. Constitutional norms have protected forms of autonomy and depended for their vitality on interpretive practices involving whole communities, not just majorities.[82]

It is common to treat the Constitution as a Federalist creation. The early successes of the constitutional enterprise depended, however, in large measure on support among Anti-Federalists, not just Federalists. In addition, parts of the constitutional design—particularly the Bill of Rights—reflect Anti-Federalist input. Even before ratification, Anti-Federalists shaped interpretive dialogue.

From the beginning, constitutional practices have reflected multiple influences, not only those of a dominant faction or party. At a later time, the example of Frederick Douglass illustrates how out-of-favor positions have played roles in reinforcing and re-creating the supreme law. The states separately, not just collectively or by acting through federal structures, have also contributed to the creation and preservation of constitutional meaning and authority. Much would be missed by failing to be attentive to ways that various persons with competing viewpoints have created, sustained, and remade the law of the Constitution. An awareness of the plural character of American constitutionalism, *in practice*, makes intelligible aspects of the enterprise that are difficult to reconcile with a supposed *myth* of unanimity.

It makes sense, therefore, to invert Harris's claims regarding the imperfect character of political practices as representations of "the people." Constitutional conventions, as with governmental institutions, have only partially represented "the people." Harris was correct that the conven-

---

[81] The quotes are from Harris, *The Interpretable Constitution*, at 193. See also ibid., at 115–21 and 193–208.

[82] See ibid., at 162 and 162 n. 30, on distinctions between "liberal" and "democratic" principles of American constitutionalism.

tions which ratified the Constitution *purported* to represent "the people." It is not clear, however, that these conventions (or their members) separately or collectively purported to represent a unitary, or whole, people. But even if they did (in limited capacities or for some purposes), the delegates did not equally or adequately represent all members of "a political body, one and indivisible, made up of the citizens of the United States, without distinction of age, sex, color, or condition in life."[83] In addition, even if one concedes that the idea of a whole people is a commendable constitutional ideal, it is worth studying and remembering disparities between representational ideals and actual political practices. There is a need for constitutional theory and practice to account for the disparities, not dismiss them as insignificant or gloss over them by emphasizing interpretive "myths."

Relationships between "the people" and governmental officials have been analogous in many respects to those between "the people" and ad hoc conventions. Rich interpretive traditions, along with several parts of the constitutional text, support Ackerman's claim that federal officials have represented "the people of the United States" in their combined capacity. The majoritarian principles that Amar has emphasized have also supported exercises of governmental power. Popular majorities have elected individuals to federal offices, and elected and unelected officials have acted through majoritarian processes. Congress, presidents, and the Supreme Court have all represented "the people" in some capacities, though none has done so fully. Variations of Federalist arguments have remained viable: the people have acted in some capacities *through* institutions created and sustained by the United States Constitution.

Variations of Anti-Federalist arguments have also remained viable. The people have continued to act in some capacities through institutions of *state* government. Distinctions between the representative functions of state conventions and state governmental institutions should not obscure understanding of how both have partially represented "the people."

Even the fourteenth amendment preserves state citizenship and sup-

[83] John Alexander Jameson, *A Treatise on Constitutional Conventions* (New York: Da Capo, 1972) (reprint of 1887 edition), at 54. Harris endorsed this expansive definition of the sovereign people on p. 193 of *The Interpretable Constitution*, adding the caveat that "the people" were "configured into states." In Jameson's words, "sovereignty, so far as relates to its regular exercise, inheres in the people of the United States, *as discriminated into groups by States*" (*Treatise on Constitutional Conventions*, at 61; emphasis in original). It is difficult even for proponents of unitary conceptions of "sovereignty" to deny that its *exercise* has been segmented (not unitary—as it might be if there were a national referendum). Even if state conventions (or members of Congress) have *together* represented a unitary people, it is reasonable to regard them *separately* as representatives of parts of that people (not "one political body"). It is even more obvious that representatives in conventions have never, in practice, represented all citizens without regard to "age, sex, color, or condition of life."

ports arguments that "the people" are constituted in part as members of the respective states. Section 1 identifies persons born or naturalized in the United States as "citizens of the United States *and of the state wherein they reside*" (emphasis added). As a result, it affirms one of the premises underlying Taney's opinion in *Dred Scott* (as well as Curtis's dissent): citizens have dual identities, as members of a nation and as members of states. It supports corresponding conceptions of "the people" and their sovereign powers.

Harris, Ackerman, and Amar have been correct to emphasize that this pivotal amendment reinforces arguments that "the people" have been joined as members of one political community. But the amendment does not compel a conclusion that national authority has occupied the normative field. Federal authority has remained limited by the manner of its delegation, and the Constitution has continued to reserve powers to the respective states. The people are constituted as members of the states and may act through institutions of state government, not just as national citizens and through institutions of national representation.

It is equally important to account for how "the people" have been configured as members of other communities and as individuals. Federalist arguments about the diversity of interests within an extended republic underscore this need. No representative institution or set of institutions, including ad hoc conventions, has ever fully represented all dimensions of "the people."[84] Yet members of the people, separately as well as collectively, have had parts in making and remaking the law of the Constitution. It makes good sense to conceive of these activities, like more formal determinations, as exercises of power by "the people."

It would be wrong to settle on any type of political activity as adequate to account for how "the people" have exercised constitutional power. The people have exercised governing prerogatives through conventions and a variety of federal and state institutions. But the people have also exercised constitutional rights and powers independently of representative structures. There are many members, yet one body. But the people have acted—and may continue to act—not *only* as members of that body.

PROBLEMS OF INTERNAL COHERENCE

There remain serious questions about whether it is coherent to interpret the ninth amendment and/or the tenth as affirming a right and/or power of "the people" (or their representatives) to bring about changes that may

[84] See Pauline Marie Rosenau, *Post-Modernism and the Social Sciences* (Princeton: Princeton University Press, 1992), ch. 6 (reviews postmodern criticism of the concept of representation).

be inconsistent with antecedent constitutional norms. Abraham Lincoln posed the issue in stark form in his First Inaugural Address: "Perpetuity is implied, if not expressed, in the fundamental law of all national governments. It is safe to assert that no government proper, ever had a provision in its organic law for its own termination."[85]

One might also question whether it would be coherent for a constitution to contemplate more modest constitutional changes. For example, may the states, acting through the means contemplated by article V, withdraw powers from federal officials? May federal and/or state officials, acting through article V and/or independently of it, nullify enumerations of rights? Would it be permissible to amend the Constitution to withdraw powers of constitutional change from the people? Have "the people" and/or their representatives legitimately amended the Constitution in ways that have directly or indirectly narrowed the range of other rights "retained by the people"?

There are several ways to approach these issues. First, one may criticize Lincoln's remarks as based on a flawed premise that the Constitution was a creation of "the government," not "the people" or "the states." Perhaps the federal "government," understood as a set of governmental institutions, may not terminate itself. But it does not follow that the creators of that government may not legitimately abolish it—or the Constitution itself.

Lincoln's reference to "its organic law" was ambiguous. He may have been referring to the organic law that created "the government," not vice versa. According to this reading, Lincoln was assuming that no organic law creating a national government had a provision for the termination of the organic law itself. Though strained, this reading complements other parts of Lincoln's speech in which he emphasized the perpetuity of "the *Union* of these States."[86]

In addition, Lincoln commented explicitly on prerogatives of constitutional change. He distinguished "revolutionary" from "constitutional" rights: "Whenever [the people] shall grow weary of the existing government, they can exercise their *constitutional* right of amending it, or their

---

[85] Lincoln, "First Inaugural," in Roy P. Basler, ed., *Collected Works of Abraham Lincoln* (New Brunswick, N.J.: Rutgers University Press, 1953), vol. 4, at 264. Lincoln asserted in like vein that it was "impossible" to destroy "our national Constitution . . . except by some action not provided for in the instrument itself" (ibid., at 265).

[86] Ibid., at 264. See Stampp, "The Concept of a Perpetual Union," for criticism of Lincoln's argument that the union was perpetual—especially his reliance on the preamble to argue that the idea of a "more perfect Union" implied continuation of the union established by the Articles of Confederation. According to Stampp, the Constitution re-formed a Union, rather than continued the old one. See also Mark E. Brandon, "No Exit? Secession and Constitutional Order," Paper delivered at the 1992 Annual Meeting of the American Political Science Association, Chicago, Ill., September 3–6, 1992; Cass R. Sunstein, "Constitutionalism and Secession," 58 U. Chi. L. Rev. 633 (1991).

revolutionary right to dismember, or overthrow it."[87] He had suggested that if the Union were merely a contract (not a "government proper"), it could not "be peaceably unmade, by less than all the parties who made it." But he rejected contractual analogies in favor of an analogy to marital unions. He also referred to majoritarian principles, though it is not clear whether he endorsed them as controlling secession or other forms of constitutional change.[88]

Despite Lincoln's suggestions to the contrary, the idea of a *constitutional* right of revolution has not been logically inconsistent with principles of American constitutionalism. An analogy to powers of governmental institutions *does* suggest obstacles to claiming that a constitution may *create* a right of revolution. There would be problems of internal coherence if a constitution sought to *authorize* its own repudiation. But such problems have not been present if the Constitution has merely *acknowledged* norms having independent authority.[89]

The distinction is not trivial. It pertains to the identity and character of "the people"—particularly whether they have had *constitutional* authority to act independently of a Constitution that they have created and whose authority they continue to sustain. In this connection, the ninth amendment's reference to rights as "retained" is significant. The amendment presupposes that "rights" of "the people"—some of which are enumerated in the constitutional text and others of which are not—have not depended for their authority on the Constitution itself. It would be anomalous to deny that these rights have been "constitutional" rights. The text has acknowledged, affirmed, and been instrumental in providing security for them. But it has not purported to *create* these prerogatives.

The concept of "reserved" powers has been more equivocal. One may reasonably take a position that some such powers have depended for their authority on the Constitution itself.[90] But there are also good reasons for conceiving of some reserved powers as having independent authority. The

[87] Lincoln, "First Inaugural," in Basler, ed., *Works of Abraham Lincoln* 4:269 (emphasis in original). The quoted passage immediately follows a sentence in which Lincoln remarked: "This country, with its institutions, belongs to the people who inhabit it."

[88] See ibid., at 265 and 267–69.

[89] For an insightful analysis of problems of internal coherence associated with various forms of constitutional change, see Peter Suber, *The Paradox of Self-Amendment: A Study of Logic, Law, Omnipotence, and Change* (New York: Peter Lang, 1990).

[90] See, e.g., T. E. Tomlins, *The Law-Dictionary: Explaining the Rise, Progress, and Present State of the English Law, in Theory and Practice* (London: Andrew Strahan, 1797), vol. 2, under "Reservation" ("[A] Reservation is of a thing not in being, but is newly created out of the lands or tenements demised; though Exception and Reservation have been used promiscuously"); Henry Campbell Black, *Black's Law Dictionary*, 4th ed. (St. Paul: West Publishing, 1951), at 1472 (a "reservation" is a "clause in a deed or other instrument of conveyance by which the grantor creates, or reserves to himself, some right, interest, or profit in the estate granted, which had no previous existence as such, but is first called into being by the instrument reserving it; such as rent, or an easement").

powers of constitutional change examined in this chapter provide examples of each position. One may likewise conceive of other prerogatives of "the people" and "the states" as depending on the Constitution and/or as having independent authority.

For example, state governmental powers antedated the federal Constitution. These powers have also been conceptually prior to federal governmental powers, since the latter have presupposed the former but not vice versa. Even so, as explained more thoroughly in subsequent chapters, federal structures have provided security for state institutions. In addition, state powers have been subject to preemption by the federal Constitution and limitations imposed by it.

There is no need to rule out the possibility of the people's holding constitutional "powers," not just "rights," whose authority has not depended on the Constitution itself. Perhaps the Constitution has recognized and sought to reinforce the exercise of those powers, even if it has not purported to create them. In addition to reinforcing fundamental powers of constitutional change, the tenth amendment may acknowledge the authority of "the people" to exercise and provide security for enumerated and unenumerated rights, for example. Separately and collectively, the people have exercised much political "power" independently of government, not just through representative structures. Popular political activity has supported the Constitution, not only brought about fundamental change. Thus there have been good reasons for the constitutional text to acknowledge these prerogatives.

But these types of relationships have been precarious. Since the Constitution has acknowledged the concept of popular sovereignty, it has conceded the possibility of its own repudiation. Since the constitutional text has affirmed norms having independent authority, it has invited critical scrutiny with reference to those norms. The successes of American constitutionalism have depended on conjunctions among actions and ideals. But the Constitution has also underscored possibilities of constitutional failure. In practice, members of "the people" may have repudiated rather than endorsed the norms created or affirmed by the Constitution that has purported to represent them.

It is helpful to distinguish various levels of consistency or inconsistency among norms. Amendments that have purported to clarify rather than alter the law of the Constitution have posed relatively few threats to antecedent norms. For example, the first amendment may be understood as having reinforced rather than altered limits on delegated powers. The concept of "amending" the Constitution has also been able to accommodate incremental changes in the fundamental law. The fourth, fifth, and sixth amendments may have altered constitutional norms without fundamentally changing the character or scope of federal executive and judicial powers. These types of incremental changes have not been especially difficult to reconcile with antecedent conceptions of "the people" or the norms that have configured their political affairs.[91]

More significant changes in governmental structures may have also promoted rather than undercut congruity among constitutional norms. In this connection, authoritative articulations of ends have provided criteria for adjusting means to accomplish them. Antecedent norms—such as those articulated in the preamble and enumerations of rights—have supported expanding federal powers, withdrawing powers from the states acting separately, and reinforcing limits on state governmental powers. Although these changes may have entailed reconfiguration of "the people" and repudiation of antecedent constitutional norms, the result has arguably been greater coherence in the law of the Constitution.[92] It also appears that similar changes have been achieved less formally through reinterpretation of existing parts of the Constitution.[93]

Attempts to reconcile conflicting articulations of constitutional ends have been more difficult to justify with reference to antecedent norms. The constitutional text has affirmed a commitment to "Union" and "Justice," but these ideals have not always been understood as complementary in practice.[94] Commitments to state autonomy and individual rights have sometimes conflicted. Governmental efforts to secure "liberty" and "equality" have converged in some respects but diverged in others. The Constitution itself has not necessarily provided criteria for mediating these controversies, or the means have been inadequate.

Efforts to resolve these types of problems have bordered on reformation of the Constitution, not just amending it. The people or their representatives have apparently imported into the Constitution "external" criteria in order to bring about changes that have been difficult to justify with reference to norms "internal" to the Constitution itself. The preamble and the ninth and tenth amendments, along with other open-ended parts of the Constitution, have blurred "internal" and "external" perspectives; but they have not made such distinctions inapplicable.[95]

---

[91] There *have* been problems, though, reconceiving these limits as they have applied to the states since the fourteenth amendment's ratification. For a thoughtful treatment of this issue, see Akhil Reed Amar, "The Bill of Rights and the Fourteenth Amendment," 101 Yale L. J. 1193 (1992).

[92] See Murphy, "*Slaughter-House, Civil Rights*, and Limits on Constitutional Change," for an argument that the fourteenth amendment promoted greater congruity among constitutional norms.

[93] See generally Sanford Levinson, "How Many Times Has the United States Constitution Been Amended? (A) < 26; (B) 26; (C) 27; (D) > 27: Accounting for Constitutional Change," in Levinson, ed., *Responding to Imperfection*, ch. 2.

[94] The Garrisonians, for example, argued that commitment to justice required abolishing the Union. See ch. 2 and sources cited therein.

[95] See, e.g., H. L. A. Hart, *The Concept of Law* (Oxford: Oxford University Press, 1961), and Harris, *The Interpretable Constitution*, for thoughtful treatments of this distinction.

For these amendments to be (or remain) coherent as parts of the Constitution, it appears necessary for their conceptions of "the people" and their "rights" and "powers" to be harmonious with one another and the remainder of the Constitution. It would be anomalous, at best, for these amendments to presuppose different conceptions of "the people" from those necessary to sustain the constitutional enterprise itself. The amendments may be able to *reflect* re-formation of "the people." But it would be problematic to interpret them as *justifying* such a change.[96]

One may question whether repudiation of a particular constitution and the structures created by it would necessarily entail dissolution (and perhaps re-formation) of "the people" themselves. The preamble to the United States Constitution has presupposed that "the people" could "ordain and establish" the supreme law. To what extent might "the people" maintain the same identity (or identities) even when abolishing the Constitution and creating a new one? The answer seems to hinge on the extent to which norms in the new constitution would be consistent with those being supplanted.[97]

These considerations lead back to questions about the identity of "the people" and how their "rights" and "powers" have related to those of federal and state governmental officials. The character and magnitude of particular changes to the fundamental law have depended in part on the extent to which they have been consistent with antecedent norms, along with those that have survived.

It is appropriate, therefore, to consult sources that shed further light on how the people have created, sustained, and changed American constitutionalism by acting through government and independently. Constitutional norms have been deeply embedded in practices, some of which have left lasting legacies. Among the more important legacies are bridges to constitutional change, not just continuity.

---

[96] From points of view *outside* the Constitution, by contrast, alternative conceptions of "the people" may be possible—though perhaps difficult to reconcile with norms affirmed from *within* the constitutional enterprise. In addition, ends such as those set forth in the preamble might support reconfiguration or reconstitution of "the people." Both types of norms might be capable of providing justification for constitutional changes *post hoc*, even if not *ex ante*.

For a complementary treatment of issues of normative consistency, see Mark E. Brandon, "The 'Original' Thirteenth Amendment and the Limits to Formal Constitutional Change," in Levinson, ed., *Responding to Imperfection*, ch. 10.

[97] In order to deal with similar issues, William Harris has distinguished "the Constitutional People" from "the sovereign constitution-making people" (see ch. 2, n. 69).

CHAPTER 4

Enumerations and Implications

[B]ills of rights, in the sense and to the extent in which they are contended for, are not only unnecessary in the proposed Constitution but would even be dangerous.[1]

ANTI-FEDERALIST criticisms of the Constitution converged on a central issue: power. Critics of the proposed scheme argued repeatedly that the new government would hold too much concentrated, coercive power. The people at large would not be able to control those who purported to represent them, either through public opinion or political participation. The central government would neither respect rights of individuals nor the autonomy of the respective states. Rights and powers of constitutional change, like other principles of republicanism, would be hollow shells. In practice, the Constitution's ratification would set in motion a course of events that ordinary persons would not be able to resist or turn back.

There were good reasons for concern. Federalists argued that the Articles of Confederation did not provide for sufficient centralized power. In addition, there is evidence that many of the Constitution's proponents favored even greater concentrations of governmental power than authorized by the constitutional text of 1787. Changes following ratification might weaken rather than reinforce popular checks. Gaps between the people and government might become greater, not narrower.

Men like Alexander Hamilton aspired to create a commercial empire. He claimed that power was necessary to secure rights, but he apparently had in mind a different set of rights from those emphasized by his political opponents. He celebrated rather than apologized for expectations that complex representative structures would enable federal officials to resist popular movements. The people at large might interfere, after all, with governmental policies designed to achieve military and commercial greatness.

Even so, in debates over ratification the Federalists committed themselves to a position that the Constitution would delegate *limited* powers. That premise supported their main arguments against enumerating rights. In addition to claiming that a bill of rights was unnecessary, Ham-

---

[1] Alexander Hamilton, *The Federalist*, no. 84, at 513.

ilton and others argued that doing so would be harmful. Some persons might construe a bill of rights as an exhaustive listing of popular prerogatives. Such reasoning might support *broader* exercises of power than would be permitted by the Constitution's affirmative delegations.

Federalist and Anti-Federalist positions were ironic. Those arguing *against* enumerating rights expressed commitment to interpreting federal powers as limited. Those arguing *for* amendments argued that the Constitution in its original form would delegate vast powers. After ratification, the sides would switch positions. Federalists would defend expansive interpretations of national authority. Their critics would rely on rights and the idea of residual powers to support inferences of narrower (not broader) conceptions of delegated power.[2]

After more than two centuries, variations of Federalist and Anti-Federalist arguments have remained viable. An assumption underlying much constitutional rhetoric is that federal powers are intrinsically limited by the manner of their delegation. Even so, federal officials exercise vast powers and defend them as consistent with the constitutional design. It is still possible to conceive of some rights as beyond the reach of federal governmental authority, and one may extend this model to analyze limits on state powers. Federalists were correct that enumerations of rights could support inferences of expanded governmental power: notwithstanding the ninth amendment, judges and others have treated express prohibitions as an exhaustive set of limits on governmental authority. Anti-Federalists were also correct that such prohibitions could provide security for rights, conceived as crosscutting limits on governmental powers. The character and identity of unenumerated rights, including their relationships to federal and state governmental powers, have remained controversial.

There have been analogous problems analyzing relationships among federal and state governmental powers. Models of "dual federalism" flourished during the antebellum period and into the twentieth century. It is still possible to conceive of some state powers as residuals, defined negatively in relation to national powers. One may also conceive of state powers as crosscutting limitations capable of precluding otherwise legitimate exercises of federal power. Conversely, it is common to treat federal powers as capable of preempting otherwise legitimate exercises of state power. Competing theoretical paradigms have sometimes overlapped but have also diverged in their practical implications.

---

[2] See Kenneth R. Bowling, *Politics in the First Congress, 1789–1791* (New York: Garland, 1990), for an examination of the historical origins of the Federalist and Republican parties, including their relationships to divisions between the Federalists and Anti-Federalists of the 1780s.

One may consult sources from the founding period for the insights they offer into these problems of theory and practice without assuming that relationships among constitutional prerogatives have remained constant or that early interpretive positions are privileged. Some of the positions taken during formative stages provide vantage points for analyzing current interpretive options. From the beginning, the constitutional text has been able to accommodate competing conceptions of relationships among constitutional rights and powers. Understanding the text's ability to do so is essential to grasping the open-ended character of constitutional norms.

RIGHTS AND POWERS AS RESIDUALS

During debates over ratification in Pennsylvania, James Wilson defended the constitutional text's omission of a separate bill of rights. As would Hamilton, he argued that such an enumeration was unnecessary and might be harmful. Wilson's arguments are particularly instructive because Madison claimed that the ninth amendment's precursor was responsive to them. Wilson's analysis is also valuable because he offered a distinctive framework for analyzing relationships among various categories of constitutional rights and powers. He presumed, in short, that powers of the United States government, powers reserved to the respective states, and some of the people's rights and powers were mutually exclusive normative categories.

Whereas Hamilton's arguments from principles of republican government would apply by analogy to state constitutions, Wilson distinguished the character of the United States Constitution from that of state constitutions. In addition, whereas Hamilton would emphasize connections among the American people and their governments, Wilson presupposed that the people at large and governmental officials had distinct prerogatives. Wilson actually relied on distinctions and concerns underlying arguments *for* enumerating rights to argue *against* such an enumeration.

Wilson argued that the proposed Constitution's delegations would differ in manner and scope from those in state constitutions. Although he presumed that in both instances governmental powers had to flow from the people themselves and could be recalled by them at will, he argued that different ways of delegating powers led to different results. He urged that with state constitutions, "everything which is not reserved, is given." In contrast, he claimed that with the United States Constitution, "the reverse of the proposition holds, and every thing which is not given, is reserved." Although he assumed that the people of the respective states had delegated to state governments implied along with express powers, he asserted that the United States Constitution would delegate *only* the powers "expressed in the instrument of union."[3]

He elaborated on this argument in the Pennsylvania Ratifying Convention. He presumed that "in all societies, there are many powers and rights which cannot be particularly enumerated." Furthermore, he assumed that a specific prerogative was *either* delegated/granted to government *or* retained/reserved by the people. Thus he claimed that the people could either delegate all governmental powers subject to express reservations or delegate only express powers and retain the residual. His position was that the people had delegated powers to state governments using the former method but would use the latter method if they approved the proposed federal Constitution.[4]

Wilson described the proposed Constitution as establishing a "federal republic," or "confederate republic," rather than "one government, in which the separate existence of the states shall be entirely absorbed." The federal republic would be "composed" not only of individuals but also of states, conceived as political communities: "When a confederate republic is instituted, the communities of which it is composed surrender to it a part of their political independence, which they before enjoyed as states." He reasoned that "[s]ince *states*, as well as *citizens*, are represented in the Constitution before us, and form the objects on which that Constitution is proposed to operate, it was necessary to notice and define *federal* as well as *civil* liberty."[5]

He defined "civil liberty" as "natural liberty itself, divested of only that part which, placed in the government, produces more good and happiness to the community than if it had remained in the individual." He argued that analogous principles applied to the formation of confederate republics: "The states should resign to the national government that part, and

---

[3] Wilson, Speech in the State House Yard, Philadelphia, October 6, 1787, in *Documentary History of Ratification* 2:167–68 (Wilson's "State House Speech"). The available account of this speech is from the *Pennsylvania Herald*, which was edited by Alexander Dallas. For criticism of the reliability of this account, see ibid., at 38–40.

[4] See ibid.; Wilson, Speech at Pennsylvania Ratifying Convention, November 28, 1787, as reported by Thomas Lloyd, in *Documentary History of Ratification* 2:388 (the "Pennsylvania Convention," cited herein by date and page number in this source). See ch. 3, n. 28, on matters of selection and reliability.

[5] Ibid., at 357, 359 (November 24, 1787) (emphasis in original). Wilson's comments on how "the people" could act in a single government also applied by analogy to his model of a compound republic. He presumed that "[i]n forming [a single] government, and carrying it into execution, it is *essential* that the *interest* and *authority* of the whole community should be binding in every part of it" (ibid., at 356–57; emphasis in original). Thus he implied that in the case of the federal republic, the Constitution would depend on the authority of "the whole community"—i.e., the people of the United States in their combined capacity.

that part only, of their political liberty, which, placed in that government, will produce more good to the whole than if it had remained in the several states."[6]

According to this scheme, the states (including the individuals of which they were composed) would join together in limited capacities to form a national community. This national community would form a "government," but it would not entirely eliminate the separate communities constituting the states. The states would, therefore, continue to hold residual governing powers. Individuals would, in turn, hold residual "civil liberty."

This theoretical framework would nicely parallel the structure of the tenth amendment. One could conceive of powers "delegated to the United States" as governmental powers entrusted by the people of the United States to the representative institutions created by the Constitution. Residual governing powers would be held by "the states," each of which had established representative institutions to act on behalf of the people of that state. Yet other powers—those not delegated by "the people" to institutions of federal *or* state government—would be held separately by "the people" as individuals.[7]

Wilson denied, however, that "the people" could delegate sovereign powers. He claimed that a distinguishing feature of "a republic or democracy" was that "the people at large *retain* the supreme power, and act either collectively or by representation." The people did not "part with" their "sovereignty"; hence "the supreme, absolute, and uncontrollable power *remains* in the people." They "only dispensed with such portions of their *power* as were necessary for the public welfare."[8]

---

[6] Ibid., at 359.

[7] Thomas Paine presented similar arguments to distinguish rights retained by individuals from those over which power should be delegated to government. In *Rights of Man* (1791; Penguin ed. 1984), at 68–69, he explained: "[I]t will be easy to distinguish between that class of natural rights which man retains after entering into society, and those which he throws into the common stock as a member of society. The natural rights which he retains, are all those in which the *power* to execute is as perfect in the individual as the right itself. Among this class . . . are all the intellectual rights, or rights of the mind: consequently, religion is one of those rights. The natural rights which are not retained, are all those in which, though the right is perfect in the individual, the power to execute them is defective. . . . [T]he power produced from the aggregate of natural rights, imperfect in power in the individual, cannot be applied to invade the natural rights which are retained in the individual, and in which the power to execute is as perfect as the right itself" (emphasis in original). Wilson relied on similar premises, both to analyze rights retained by individuals and federal liberties retained by states.

[8] Wilson, Pennsylvania Convention, in *Documentary History of Ratification* 2:361, 362 (November 24, 1787) (emphasis in original); ibid., at 448 (December 1, 1787) (emphasis on "power" added). See also ibid., at 383 (November 28, 1787) ("the fee simple remains in the people at large, and, by this Constitution, they do not part with it").

These passages indicate that Wilson distinguished "governmental" powers from "sovereign" powers. In addition, he treated the former as analogous to powers of attorney or powers of trust, not irrevocable transfers or contractual commitments. According to this scheme, "the people" of the states and of the United States collectively held sovereign powers even as they delegated to governmental institutions power to act on their behalf.[9]

As a result, there were several layers to Wilson's analysis of the people's retained rights and reserved powers. Separately, "the people" held power to exercise individual rights. Collectively, "the people" had authority to exercise sovereign powers of constitutional change. While constitutions remained in effect, "the people" did not have authority, separately or collectively, to exercise ordinary governmental powers. Through ratification of the national and state constitutions, the people of the United States and of the respective states would entrust (or had entrusted) these powers to governmental representatives.

Wilson took corresponding positions on protections for rights. A bill of rights was not necessary because the people could recall governmental powers at will: "Those who ordain and establish have the power, if they think proper, to repeal and annul. A proper attention to this principle may, perhaps, give ease to the minds of some who have heard so much concerning the necessity of a bill of rights." He suggested that "[e]ven in a single government, if the powers of the people rest on the same establishment as is expressed in this Constitution, a bill of rights is by no means necessary." He referred in this connection to several state constitutions

---

[9] See ibid., at 554–56 (December 11, 1787) (rejected contractual analogies, claiming that the Constitution neither formed a compact among the states nor one between the people and government). (But see ch. 8, under "Limited, Delegated Powers.") Thomas Paine likewise characterized governmental powers in America as held in trust rather than resulting from contract. In *Rights of Man*, at 68, he explained: "Man did not enter into society to become *worse* than he was before, nor to have fewer rights than he had before, but to have those rights better secured" (emphasis in original). Paine claimed that the people entrusted to government a power over some of their rights but not others, in each case retaining the underlying rights. In his view, governmental officials became responsible, as trustees, for securing the rights over which the people had delegated powers: "Government . . . is altogether a trust, in right of those by whom that trust is delegated and by whom it is always resumable. It has of itself no rights; they are altogether duties" (ibid., at 189). He urged, moreover, that governmental officials were the people's agents when acting pursuant to this trust, but claimed such officials lack delegated authority when acting otherwise: "All delegated power is trust, and all assumed power is usurpation" (ibid., at 185). Jefferson made a similar claim: "Our legislators are not sufficiently apprised of the rightful limits of their power; that their true office is to declare and enforce only our natural rights and duties, and to take none of them from us. . . . [T]he idea is quite unfounded that on entering society we give up any natural right" (Thomas Jefferson, Letter to Francis W. Gilmer, June 7, 1816, in Paul L. Ford, ed., *Writings of Thomas Jefferson* 10:32).

that lacked bills of rights and questioned: "Whence comes this notion, that in the United States there is no security without a bill of rights?"[10]

On the surface, these arguments resembled Hamilton's analysis in the 84th *Federalist*, as reviewed in chapter 3. But beneath the surface, their arguments differed significantly. Instead of defending the adequacy of constitutional structures, Wilson referred to the people's remedies if the government *did not* represent the people. Rather than concentrating on how the people would act *through* their government, he concentrated on the people's ability to act *independently* of government.[11]

Wilson also argued, as would Hamilton, that the Constitution protected rights as residuals. The Pennsylvanian urged that it would have been "superfluous and absurd" to have enumerated rights over which the Constitution delegated no coercive power. In his view, "the proposed system possesses no influence whatever over the press." As a result, "it would have been merely nugatory to have introduced a formal declaration upon the subject."[12]

Wilson went further and suggested that enumerating rights would be harmful. He warned that adding a bill of rights to the new instrument would transform its character by giving rise to interpretive assumptions similar to those governing interpretation of state constitutions. Omitted prerogatives would be conveyed by implication to the national government: "If we attempt an enumeration, every thing that is not enumerated is presumed to be given. The consequence is, that an imperfect enumeration would throw all implied power into the scale of the government, and the rights of the people would be rendered incomplete."[13] Enumerating rights might imply that the people had fewer, not more, residual prerogatives.[14]

[10] Wilson, Pennsylvania Convention, in *Documentary History of Ratification* 2:383, 388 (November 28, 1787).

[11] Wilson outlined means available for correcting errors: "If the error be in the legislature, it may be corrected by the constitution; if in the constitution, it may be corrected by the people. There is a remedy, therefore, for every distemper in government, if the people are not wanting to themselves; if they are wanting to themselves, there is no remedy. From their power, as we have seen, there is no appeal; of their error there is no superior principle of correction" (ibid., at 362; November 24, 1787). Of course, Wilson's arguments on the absence of a need to enumerate rights also converged with Hamilton's in some respects. For example, both emphasized that governmental authority flowed from the people's original authority.

[12] Wilson, State House Speech, in ibid., at 162. Compare Hamilton's arguments in the 84th *Federalist* (examined in ch. 3 and below).

[13] Wilson, Pennsylvania Convention, in *Documentary History of Ratification* 2:388 (November 28, 1787).

[14] In the 84th *Federalist*, Hamilton made a subtly different argument about possibly harmful implications that might arise from enumerating rights: "Why, for instance, should it be said that liberty of the press shall not be restrained, when no power is given by which

Confronting Interpretive Dangers

Wilson's arguments identify serious risks associated with enumerating rights. Those who favored adding an enumeration of rights to the constitutional text had to confront the possibility that such an enumeration might support even more expansive interpretations of the federal government's powers than would the text alone or a similar charter. Such persons could continue to favor an enumeration of some individual rights and state powers at the risk of being confronted by arguments that the new government would have power over all other prerogatives unless and until the American people, acting collectively, amended the Constitution or established a new one. These arguments would have heightened concerns over governmental tyranny.

But approving the unamended Constitution posed similar dangers. According to Thomas Jefferson, for example, Wilson's position was "gratis dictum, opposed by strong inferences from the body of the instrument." The Constitution authorized implied powers, not just express ones. As a result, the constitutional design posed threats to individual rights and state prerogatives of the sort that Wilson claimed would be exacerbated by enumerating rights. Jefferson's remark seemed wise: "Half a loaf is better than no bread. If we cannot secure all our rights, let us secure what we can."[15]

Wilson's arguments, however, cut at least two ways; for they also placed rhetorical constraints upon those who defended the Constitution. He committed himself, and those who endorsed his arguments committed themselves, to the idea that the Constitution would limit powers by the manner of their delegation. More generally, the Federalists committed

---

restrictions might be imposed? I will not contend that such a provision would confer regulating power; but it is evident that it would furnish, to men disposed to usurp, a plausible pretense for claiming that power. They might urge with a semblance of reason that the Constitution ought not to be charged with the absurdity of providing against the abuse of an authority which was not given, and that the provision against restraining the liberty of the press afforded a clear implication that a power to prescribe proper regulations concerning it was intended to be vested in the national government."

Whereas Wilson had expressed concern that a bill of rights might give rise to an assumption that the government had power over rights *omitted* from an enumeration, Hamilton suggested that a bill of rights could support an inference of power over rights *included* in the enumeration. Contrasting Wilson's emphasis on how rights protected normative spheres over which the government had *no* power, Hamilton invoked the concept of rights as limitations on powers that *had* been delegated. He suggested, in sum, that enumerating the liberty of press might imply authority to restrict the press except to the extent specifically prohibited.

[15] Thomas Jefferson, Letters to James Madison, December 20, 1787, and March 15, 1789, in Julian P. Boyd, ed., *Papers of Thomas Jefferson* 12:440, and ibid., vol. 14, at 660.

themselves to interpreting the Constitution consistently with two complementary presumptions: one *against* delegated powers and another *in favor of* the people's rights. Whether and how these presumptions could, should, or would survive an enumeration of rights were questions of central concern to those who supported as well as those who opposed the Constitution's ratification and its initial amending.

Madison later addressed these issues in June 1789, when commenting to the House on his proposed amendments to the constitutional text. He acknowledged concerns that adding a bill of rights might have the unintended effect of supporting broader (not narrower) conceptions of national authority:

> It has been objected also against a bill of rights, that, by enumerating particular exceptions to the grant of power, it would disparage those rights which were not placed in that enumeration; and it might follow by implication, that those rights which were not singled out, were intended to be assigned into the hands of the General Government, and were consequently insecure.

According to the *Annals*, Madison remarked: "This is among the most plausible arguments I have ever heard urged against the admission of a bill of rights into [the constitutional] system."[16]

But he claimed the ninth amendment's precursor "guarded against" such an implication. His proposal read:

> The exceptions here or elsewhere in the constitution, made in favor of particular rights, shall not be so construed as to diminish the just importance of other rights retained by the people, or as to enlarge the powers delegated by the constitution; but either as actual limitations of such powers, or as inserted merely for greater caution.[17]

The draft appears to be responsive, at least in part, to Wilson's argument that enumerating rights would be dangerous because it might imply delegation of power to restrict the exercise of rights not so enumerated.

Significantly, the ninth amendment's precursor dealt with relationships between *enumerated* rights and governmental powers, along with the status of "other rights retained by the people." Madison's analysis of the status of unenumerated rights, like Wilson's, flowed from broader prem-

[16] *Annals*, at 439 (June 8, 1789).

[17] Ibid., at 435. Madison proposed inserting this amendment into article I, sec. 9. The first nine clauses of the fourth proposal were precursors to parts of the first, second, third, fourth, fifth, sixth, and eighth amendments. All of these amendments were to be inserted between the third and fourth clauses of sec. 9. Madison also proposed amending eight other parts of the Constitution. One was incorporated into the fifth, sixth, and seventh amendments; part of another was a precursor to the tenth amendment; and the four remaining resolutions covered other matters. See ibid., at 434–35.

ises about relationships among constitutional norms. At issue were fundamental problems of constitutional structure. Competing positions had profound and sweeping normative and practical implications.

Madison's more general comments on the proposed amendments help to place his analysis of the ninth amendment's precursor into perspective. Before commenting on particular amendments, he had set forth a framework for analyzing them. Among other things, he identified several types of relationships among popular rights and governmental powers.

Of particular relevance for present purposes, Madison claimed that some of the amendments "specif[ied] those rights which are retained when particular powers are given up to be exercised by the Legislature." Plus he suggested that "the great object in view" was "to limit and qualify the powers of Government, by excepting out of the grant of power those cases in which the Government ought not to act, or to act only in a particular mode." Both passages are consistent with a premise that the people *either* retained a particular right *or* delegated power to exercise it.[18]

Madison again relied on a dichotomous conception of retained rights and reserved powers to defend the eventual ninth amendment, not just its precursor. In debates over ratification of the proposed amendments in the Virginia legislature, Edmund Randolph had criticized the phrasing of the eventual ninth and tenth amendments. According to Hardin Burnley, Randolph objected that the proposals did not include a sufficient list of enumerated rights, and "there was no criterion by which it could be determined whether any other particular right was retained or not." Randolph suggested that the ninth amendment's "reservation against constructive power, should operate rather as a provision against extending the powers of Congress by their own authority, than as a protection to rights reducable to no definitive certainty."[19] Madison communicated this objection to President George Washington and characterized Ran-

---

[18] See ibid., at 437.

[19] Hardin Burnley, Letter to James Madison, November 28, 1789, in *Papers of James Madison* 17:455–57. According to Burnley, Randolph would have preferred the form of the first and seventeenth amendments to the body of the Constitution that had been proposed by the Virginia Ratifying Convention. The first (a precursor of the eventual tenth amendment) provided: "That each State in the Union shall respectively retain every power, jurisdiction and right not by this Constitution delegated to the Congress of the United States or to the departments of the Foederal Government." The seventeenth (a precursor of Madison's draft of the ninth amendment) provided: "That those clauses which declare that Congress shall not exercise certain powers be not interpreted in any manner whatsoever to extend the powers of Congress. But that they may be construed either as making exceptions to the specified powers where this shall be the case, or otherwise as inserted merely for greater caution." The proposals are reprinted in Helen E. Veit, Kenneth R. Bowling, and Charlene Bangs Bickford, eds., *Creating the Bill of Rights* (Baltimore: Johns Hopkins University Press, 1991), at 17 and 19.

dolph's distinction as "altogether fanciful." In this context, he invoked the metaphor of a "line" between delegated powers and retained rights: "If a line can be drawn between the powers granted and the rights retained, it would seem to be the same thing, whether the latter be secured by declaring that they shall not be abridged, or that the former shall not be extended." But Madison hedged his analysis by using a conditional sentence structure, which he mirrored in suggesting that "[i]f no line can be drawn, a declaration in either form would amount to nothing."[20]

As explained below, Madison had good reasons to be skeptical about the theoretical assumptions underlying his defense of the ninth amendment and its precursor. But before considering problems with a mutually exclusive conception of retained rights and delegated powers, it is worth exploring some of its possibilities.

Presupposing that rights corresponded to absences of delegated authority would yield distinctive conceptions of enumerated and unenumerated rights and their relationships to delegated powers. Madison's draft of the ninth amendment provided that express prohibitions were "actual limitations of [delegated] powers" or "inserted merely for greater caution." It would be possible to conceive of the prohibitions as complementing perfectly the original Constitution's delegations of limited powers. Supplementing the original text with an enumeration of rights would have provided "greater caution" for interpreting the scope of those powers. The prohibitions would make explicit "actual limitations" that were arguably implicit in the original delegation.

These premises would be tenable even after the First Congress removed from the ninth amendment's precursor its explicit reference to relationships between enumerated rights and delegated powers. If the people *either* retained a particular right *or* delegated to government power over its exercise, it would be logically impossible for both to be true. Finding delegated power would preclude finding a conflicting retained right, and vice versa.

Enumerating particular rights would make this equation more capable in practice of cutting in both directions than would a general but less specific prohibition against denying or disparaging retained rights.[21] Express prohibitions would provide more determinate standards for oppos-

---

[20] See James Madison, Letter to George Washington, December 5, 1789, in *Papers of James Madison* 12:458–59.

[21] A general prohibition against denying, disparaging, or abridging retained but unenumerated rights would, by itself, embrace more specific prohibitions against abridging named rights. Furthermore, interpreters would not have any constitutional warrant to breach either prohibition, nor would they have any warrant to interpret incorrectly the scope of delegated powers even absent any such prohibition. At issue are the specificity of the constitutional text's enumeration of norms and corresponding implications for constitutional practices.

ing improper interpretations of delegated powers. More specifically, if delegated powers and retained rights were mutually exclusive and if the constitutional text declared that the people had a particular right, that declaration (correctly interpreted) would preclude finding that the government had a conflicting power. Conflicting interpretations of delegated powers and retained rights, therefore, would necessarily be based on some type of mistake.[22] That mistake might be owing to an overly expansive conception of delegated powers, retained rights, or both. By enumerating powers *and* rights, the constitutional text would provide additional criteria for identifying and correcting any such mistakes.

For example, the eventual first amendment takes the form of a categorical prohibition. According to its terms, the amendment identifies normative spheres over which Congress has no power. The amendment appears to be an example of what Madison described as a declaration of "cases in which the Government ought not to act." Assuming that delegated powers and retained rights have been perfectly complementary and mutually limiting norms, and assuming that the first amendment has protected some such retained rights, interpreters would be committed to concluding that Congress has not had any power to act in the ways expressly prohibited by the amendment. According to this view, the amendment has reinforced the Constitution's delegation of intrinsically limited authority by identifying some such normative boundaries.

The ninth amendment's precursor would have served a more general function. Rather than identifying particular normative spheres over which Congress had no power, it would have prohibited construing "exceptions . . . in favor of particular rights . . . as to diminish the just importance of other rights retained by the people, or as to enlarge the powers delegated by the constitution." Assuming again a dichotomous conception of delegated powers and retained rights, the proposal would have referred to gaps in delegated authority in addition to those identified by enumerated rights and would have precluded interpreting federal powers as capable of operating within those gaps.

The ninth amendment, as approved, could serve a similar function. It has commanded interpreters not to "deny or disparage" unenumerated rights. One way to violate this prohibition would be through overly expansive interpretations of delegated powers. It would be wrong to claim that the Constitution delegated to the federal government authority to exercise a right retained by the people.

According to these premises, therefore, the ninth amendment (either in the form proposed by Madison or the final version) and express prohibi-

---

[22] Consistent interpretations, on the other hand, would not necessarily be correct. Interpretations of powers and rights might both be mistaken, but consistently so.

tions would have perfectly complemented the Constitution's original delegations. Federal powers would have been on one side of a normative boundary; the people's enumerated and unenumerated rights would have been on the other side. The federal government would have had *no* authority to interfere with the exercise of *any* of the people's retained rights.

Arrangements of Power

In anticipation of the Constitution's initial amending, more states proposed variations of the tenth amendment's precursor than endorsed antecedents to any other amendment.[23] The proposals echoed article II of the Articles of Confederation, which had provided: "Each state retains its sovereignty, freedom, and independence, and every Power, Jurisdiction and right, which is not by this confederation expressly delegated to the United States, in Congress assembled." Following these models, Madison's draft of the tenth amendment reflects a dichotomous view of federal and state governmental authority: "The powers not delegated by this constitution, nor prohibited by it to the States, are reserved to the States respectively."

Unlike several state proposals, Madison's draft did not imply that the Constitution delegated only "express" powers.[24] But like the state pro-

---

[23] Six of the seven states that proposed constitutional amendments, plus the Pennsylvania minority, included one that derived from article II of the Articles of Confederation. By comparison, one state (New Hampshire), along with the Pennsylvania and Maryland minorities, proposed an amendment to enumerate the right of religious liberty. The proposals from the Virginia, Massachusetts, South Carolina, New Hampshire, and New York conventions are reprinted in Veit, Bowling, and Bickford, eds., *Creating the Bill of Rights*, at 14–28. Those from the Pennsylvania minority are reprinted in ibid., vol. 2, at 623–25; and those from the North Carolina Convention (along with the others) are included in the appendix to Edward Dumbauld, *The Constitution and What It Means Today* (Norman: University of Oklahoma Press, 1957). A majority of the Maryland Convention Committee approved a proposal that addressed more directly the scope of federal powers (see n. 24, below). In addition to submitting a proposal along the lines of the eventual tenth amendment, the New York Convention proposed: "[T]hose clauses in the said Constitution, which declare, that Congress shall not have or exercise certain Powers not given by the said Constitution, do not imply that Congress is entitled to any Powers not given by the said Constitution; but such Clauses are to be construed either as exceptions to certain specified Powers, or as inserted merely for greater Caution." The thrust of this proposal, like Virginia's seventeenth (quoted in n. 19, above), was similar to that of Madison's draft of the *ninth* amendment.

[24] Proposals from three of the states (Massachusetts, New Hampshire, and South Carolina) and from the Pennsylvania minority referred to federal powers as "expressly" delegated, a fifth (New York) used the adverb "clearly," and the Maryland Convention Committee's proposal declared more directly that "Congress shall exercise no power but what is *expressly* delegated by this Constitution." Only two states, one of which was Madison's

posals, Madison's version contained no reference to powers reserved to "the people." The draft appears to have presumed that the relevant powers were *either* delegated by the Constitution *or* reserved to the states.

The structure of the amendment is peculiar, especially taking into account the main concerns of those who advocated similar provisions. The amendment is an obtuse way of declaring that the national government could legitimately exercise only the powers delegated to it by the United States Constitution. It is also odd that the amendment identifies the states' reserved powers indirectly as residuals. It provides no affirmative criteria for identifying reserved powers and contains no provision comparable to the ninth's prohibiting the denial or disparagement of reserved powers.

Proponents of the tenth amendment's precursor, those seeking to limit national power and reinforce state prerogatives, evidently thought the formula of reserving all powers not expressly delegated had worked quite well in the Articles of Confederation and would work well enough in the case of the new Constitution. It made sense for critics of centralized power to favor the basic structure of a formula that had proven effective in prior practice. But Anti-Federalist hopes were Federalist concerns. Those who favored a stronger central government were concerned that the Articles had been *too* effective in limiting the confederate congress's powers. Madison's removal of the term "expressly," along with opposition in the First Congress to reinserting that term, reflect those concerns.[25]

The tried formula might have continued to work, even with a more general reference to powers not "delegated" by the Constitution, if interpreters had accepted relatively straightforward assumptions concerning arrangements of governmental authority. If interpreted consistently with an underlying assumption that a particular power could not have been *both* delegated to the national government *and* reserved to the states, the amendment as drafted by Madison would have referred to *all* national and state governmental powers. In addition to protecting *all* of the states' reserved powers, the amendment would have indirectly rebutted findings of undelegated federal power. An explicit declaration that the United States government could only exercise delegated powers would have been unnecessary, because the government logically could not have had any authority over powers reserved to the states. Likewise, the states

---

home state of Virginia—the other was North Carolina—had submitted proposals that referred, without such a qualification, to the federal government's "delegated" powers (see nn. 19 and 23, above).

[25] Accounts of efforts in the First Congress to reinsert "expressly" into the tenth amendment's predecessor, along with responses by Madison and others to such efforts, are cited and reviewed at nn. 27 and 45–47, below, and in the accompanying text.

could not have reserved a power that had been delegated to the central government.

The addition to Madison's proposal of a final phrase, "or to the people," would not have required abandoning these assumptions. Those adhering to a mutually exclusive conception of governmental powers could expand that paradigm to embrace powers of the people themselves within a trichotomous normative framework. Such a framework could have drawn support, moreover, from variations of natural rights theory that were prevalent at the time.

For example, one could reasonably argue that the people could not have reserved power over a particular right, or reserved any other power, if they had "granted" or "delegated" that power to the United States government. Conversely, one could plausibly assume that the people only "retained" the rights and "reserved" the powers they had not "assigned," even if only tentatively, to institutions of national and state government. Those who accepted such premises might have interpreted the revised amendment consistently with such premises: a particular power was *either* delegated to the United States government *or* reserved to the states *or* reserved to the people.[26]

For those who interpreted the tenth amendment consistently with such assumptions, its final phrase would have made the amendment logically complete. It would have referred to three mutually exclusive sets of powers: those delegated to the United States, those reserved to the states, and those reserved to the people as such. The amendment would have made clear that powers prohibited to the states could not have been re-

---

[26] Madison's defense of the ninth amendment using the metaphor of a "line" between retained rights and delegated powers, as quoted in the text accompanying n. 20, above, reflected a similar premise that constitutional prerogatives were mutually exclusive. See also James Wilson's description of relationships between federal and state powers: "[T]here is another subject to which this Constitution deserves approbation. I mean the accuracy with which the *line is drawn* between the powers of the *general government* and those of the *particular state governments*. . . . [I]t is not pretended that the line is drawn with mathematical precision; the inaccuracy of language must, to a certain degree, prevent the accomplishment of such a desire." Pennsylvania Convention, in *Documentary History of Ratification* 2:496 (December 4) (emphasis in original).

Wilson claimed that even if there was "some difficulty in ascertaining where the true line lies," there was no need for "despair," because the two governments, each in the service of the people, would not be "enemies of each other, or resemble comets in conflicting orbits, mutually operating destruction." On the contrary, he gave assurances that "their motions will be better represented by that of the planetary system, where each part moves harmoniously within its proper sphere, and no injury arises by interference or opposition" (ibid). Wilson's image was of distinct bodies, moving in separate orbits, rather than joined bodies or ones moving in overlapping orbits. See also ibid, at 449 (December 1, 1787) (the people can "distribute one portion of power to the more contracted circle, called state governments; they can also furnish another portion to the government of the United States").

served to them or to the people. In addition, its reference to powers of the people would have complemented enumerated rights (i.e., rights over which the people continued to hold power) and the ninth amendment's command not to deny or disparage other rights retained by the people (i.e., other rights beyond the legitimate reach of governmental power).

The preceding formulas would have been even more suitable if the tenth amendment or some other provision declared or implied clearly that the United States government only had authority to exercise the powers "expressly delegated" to it by the Constitution. Then it would have been easier to identify the scope of the central government's powers by applying assumptions similar to those appropriate for interpreting the Articles of Confederation. If the tenth amendment took that form, it would have been reasonable to assume its reference to "expressly delegated" powers would have been coextensive with the powers explicitly enumerated in the constitutional text. It would have been relatively straightforward to assume, moreover, that the states and the people held all other constitutionally authoritative powers.

Other parts of the constitutional text also could have accommodated such assumptions. If the tenth amendment indicated that the United States government only had authority to exercise the powers "expressly delegated" to it, the Constitution's prohibitions on the states could have been viewed as redundant safeguards that partially paralleled express delegations. The prohibitions would have thereby provided additional criteria for interpreting federal powers, along with enumerations of the people's rights.

Members of the First Congress repeatedly sought to add "expressly" to drafts of the tenth amendment. But these efforts failed in both the House and Senate, each of which was predominantly Federalist.[27] In order to evaluate more fully the issues at stake, it is helpful to locate these efforts in the context of analyses by Madison and others of the scope of the Constitution's original delegations. Positions taken on this issue inform analysis of relationships between the people's rights and federal powers, along with relationships between delegated and reserved powers.

COMPLICATIONS

Madison's remarks to the House contain mixed signals. Although his comments on the ninth amendment's precursor reflect dichotomous con-

---

[27] See *Annals*, at 761 (August 18, 1789) (Tucker's proposal and responses to it; the proposal was "negatived"); ibid., at 767 (August 21, 1789) (a similar proposal by Gerry was also negatived); *House Journal*, at 108 (August 21, 1789) (reported the same vote); *Senate Journal*, at 122 (September 7, 1789) (a similar resolution, not attributed to any particular person, "passed in the negative").

ceptual premises, his analysis of other constitutional provisions called such premises into question. Of particular relevance, he underscored problems associated with identifying the scope of delegated powers.

According to the *Annals of Congress*, Madison dealt separately with the two main prongs of Wilsonian arguments against enumerating rights. Before reaching the problem of possibly harmful implications, he considered the need for express prohibitions. In this context, though, he cast a cloud over his subsequent endorsement of premises that rights and powers were mutually exclusive, with the former protected by the manner of delegating the latter. He reportedly explained:

> It has been said, that in the Federal Government they are unnecessary, because the powers are enumerated, and it follows, that all that are not granted by the constitution are retained; that the constitution is a bill of powers, the great residuum being the rights of the people; and, therefore, a bill of rights cannot be so necessary as if the residuum was thrown into the hands of the Government.

Madison countered that "these arguments are not entirely without foundation; but they are not conclusive to the extent which has been supposed."[28]

He presumed that this objection to enumerating rights was based on the fact that "the powers of the General Government are circumscribed, they are directed to particular objects." But he said that "even if the Government keeps within those limits, it has certain discretionary powers with respect to the means, which may admit of abuse to a certain extent." In this connection, he referred to the necessary and proper clause and indicated that it enabled the federal government "to fulfil every purpose for which [it] was established." To prevent an abuse of these "discretionary powers with respect to means," he suggested, it was desirable to "restrain[] the Federal Government" in the exercise of its powers. Furthermore, he compared powers of the national government to those of state

[28] *Annals*, at 438 (June 8, 1789). In his comments to the House, Madison also addressed a second branch of arguments that a bill of rights was unnecessary in a "republican" government: "It has been said, by way of objection to a bill of rights, by many respectable gentlemen out of doors, and I find opposition on the same principles likely to be made by gentlemen on this floor, that they are unnecessary articles of a Republican Government, upon the presumption that the people have those rights in their own hands, and that is a proper place for them to rest." He reportedly dismissed this objection in a cursory manner by claiming that it "lies against such provisions under the State Government, as well as under the General Government." He suggested that "few gentlemen would push *their* theory so far as to say that a declaration of rights in those cases is either ineffectual or improper" (ibid., at 438; emphasis added). Chapter 3 deals with issues raised by this objection and Madison's response to it. As indicated there, Madison was dealing with an argument that he and Federalist colleagues had made during debates over ratification.

governments, and he urged that similar types of restraints were appropriate in both cases.[29]

He equivocated, however, on whether he conceived of governmental powers as defined only according to objects or also according to the proper means of their exercise. On a parallel issue, he was unclear on whether he was contemplating "abuse" within or beyond the limits of delegated authority. His treatment of these issues was complicated by his mixing *what* the Constitution meant with *who* would interpret it.

Madison's analysis in the 44th *Federalist* of the necessary and proper clause enables a richer understanding of his positions on these issues—or at least the positions he articulated in both places.[30] In that paper, he asserted that "no axiom is more clearly established in law, or in reason, than that wherever the end is required, the means are authorized." In explaining the application of this axiom to the Constitution, he identified two categories of governmental powers: "general" and "particular." He described the former as powers enumerated in the constitutional text, and he defined the latter both as the "means of executing the general powers" and as "the means of attaining the *object[s]* of the general power[s]." If the constitutional text were silent on the means of exercising general powers, Madison claimed, "there can be no doubt that all the particular powers requisite as means of executing the general powers would have resulted to the Government by unavoidable implication."[31]

Madison implicitly denied in the 44th *Federalist*, however, that the "doctrine of construction or implication," as made explicit by the necessary and proper clause, authorized *all* means of attaining the objects of general powers. He assumed that this clause authorized only "necessary and proper" means. He conceded that Congress might "misconstrue this part of the Constitution and exercise powers not warranted by its true meaning." But he characterized such an occurrence as "usurpation."[32]

It is apparent that Madison, in his remarks to the House on enumerating rights, relied implicitly on a similar dichotomy between general and particular powers. Consider again his explanation of federal powers in his remarks to the House: "It is true, the powers of the General Government

[29] *Annals*, at 438 (June 8, 1789).

[30] There are special perils associated with analyzing Madison's arguments in the First Congress with reference to the positions he took in *The Federalist Papers*. In the one context, he was proposing amendments; in the other, he was advocating ratification of the original Constitution. His arguments were not perfectly consistent. Even so, as explained in ch. 3, Madison claimed in the First Congress that he was unwilling to open the door for reconsidering "the principles and structure of the powers given." Not surprisingly, many of his positions are consistent; and his fuller development of arguments in one context sheds light on more cursory analyses in the other.

[31] *The Federalist*, no. 44, at 285 (emphasis in original).

[32] Ibid., at 285–86.

are circumscribed, they are directed to particular objects." Here, he was describing the government's "general" powers.

But he implied that notwithstanding the limited character of such (general) powers, the constitutional text did not clearly specify the legitimate means of executing them: "[E]ven if Government keeps within those [circumscribed] limits, it has certain discretionary powers with respect to the means, which may admit of abuse to a certain extent." Here, he was explaining that the Constitution's delegation of "particular" powers was imprecise. He claimed that this imprecision, which the necessary and proper clause made explicit, was required to enable the government "to fulfill every purpose for which [it] was established."[33] These comments echoed his analysis in the 44th *Federalist* of relationships between "particular" powers and the "objects" of "general" powers.

We may now return to Madison's comments to the House on relationships between rights and certain types of powers. As indicated, he drew connections between who would interpret and what would be interpreted. He claimed that "it is for [Congress] to judge of the necessity and propriety to accomplish those special purposes which they may have in contemplation." Thus the potential for abuse to which he was alluding was the possibility that "laws [may] be *considered* necessary and proper by Congress . . . which laws *in themselves* are neither necessary nor proper." He explained that the Legislature might, for example, consider general warrants as necessary for the purpose of collecting revenues. He claimed it was necessary to "restrain" the national government, like the states, from exercising powers this way. The fourth amendment would specify requirements for obtaining evidence through detailed search warrants supported by probable cause.[34] More generally, amending the constitutional text to enumerate rights would "restrain" officials of the national government from interpreting their general powers or the necessary and proper clause as authorizing the use of prohibited means to achieve the purposes of such delegated powers.[35]

---

[33] See *Annals*, at 438 (June 8, 1789).

[34] See ibid. For convenience of reference, I am now ignoring differences between the fourth amendment's precursor and the eventual fourth amendment. The precursor provided: "The rights of the people to be secure in their persons; their houses, their papers, and their other property, from all unreasonable searches and seizures, shall not be violated by warrants issued without probable cause, supported by oath or affirmation, or not particularly describing the places to be searched, or the persons or things to be seized."

[35] Randy A. Barnett has relied on this passage to argue that Madison viewed rights and powers as overlapping (not mutually exclusive) normative categories (Barnett, "Reconceiving the Ninth Amendment," 74 Cornell L. Rev. 1 [1988], at 10 and 13–14). But a careful reading of Madison's remarks indicates that he did not treat "necessary and proper" laws as capable of legitimately "infringing" the people's rights. Instead, he presumed that laws abridging such rights were *not* necessary and proper and thus were *invalid*. (The idea of

In sum, there were two levels to Madison's response to the objection to enumerating rights based on the lack of necessity in a government of enumerated powers. At one level, he acknowledged that "the powers of the General Government are circumscribed, they are directed to particular objects." He was alluding to the fact that the government had only the "general" powers enumerated in the constitutional text. He claimed that the government had no authority to pursue "objects" or "ends" other than those specified by the Constitution's delegation of "general" powers. Moreover, his analysis of the necessary and proper clause *assumed* satisfaction of this threshold criterion for constitutional legitimacy. He explained that "even if Government keeps within *those limits*," it must comply with a different sort of limitation: the complementary "restraints" of the necessary and proper clause and enumerated rights. He indicated that the government was confined to acting in pursuance of delegated ends *and* to using limited means to accomplish those ends.

What Kind(s) of Limits?

Madison's comments on relationships between "general" and "particular" powers, along with his distinction between "express" powers and the "means" of their execution, suggest a need to explore alternative conceptions of relationships between retained rights and delegated powers. The ninth amendment's precursor is instructive: it would have *required* interpreters to construe the "exceptions . . . in favor of particular rights . . . *either* as actual limitations of [delegated] powers, *or* as inserted merely for greater caution." It also would have *prohibited* construing the exceptions "as to diminish the just importance of other rights retained by the people, or as to enlarge the powers delegated by the constitution."[36]

The draft invited parallel interpretations of its negative and affirmative imperatives. The prohibition on construing the exceptions "as to enlarge the powers delegated" paralleled the command to interpret enumerated rights as "inserted merely for greater caution." Some exceptions would specify "cases in which the Government ought not to act." There was no express power. In some contexts, prohibitions would mirror the Constitution's enumeration of "principal" powers.

"usurpation" implies *ultra vires* actions, or actions unauthorized by the Constitution.) Barnett also cites a judicial precedent, *Lamont v. Postmaster General*, 381 U.S. 301 (1965), for the proposition that "Legislative acts that fall within an enumerated power *can* violate an enumerated right" (ibid., at 7; emphasis in original). But in *Lamont*, the Court *invalidated* an exercise of power on the rationale that it was *not* permissible to abridge an enumerated right.)

36 The draft is cited in full in the main text at n. 17, above.

The proposal's reference to "other rights retained by the people" paralleled "actual limitations of [delegated] powers." Rights might, in some contexts, limit officials to acting "only in a particular mode." The prohibitions would reinforce limits on "means" available when executing "general" powers.

Interpreting the draft along these lines, "actual limitations" would mirror exercises of power authorized by the necessary and proper clause. These limitations would make explicit that some means of exercising delegated powers were not "necessary and proper." The draft's initial prohibition would have precluded viewing the listing of some such limitations as exhaustive; it would have protected "other rights retained by the people" that had "just importance" as constraints on the exercise of delegated powers. As Madison explained in the 44th *Federalist*, enumerating all the permissible or impermissible means of exercising delegated powers would not have been possible.

But the draft would not have required treating all enumerated rights as "actual limitations" of this sort. It was consistent with a finding that other amendments specified rights over which the Constitution had delegated no power. As with "actual limitations," all such spheres of "no power" could not have been enumerated. Thus the draft might reasonably have assumed that some of the latter rights provided "greater caution" in two complementary ways: by making explicit that the people had retained these rights and by reinforcing arguments that the central government had no power to restrict their exercise.[37]

The ninth amendment carries forward only one of the two prohibitions

[37] Madison's distinction between "natural" and "positive" rights merits consideration along with the distinctions discussed in the text. He said that some of his proposals "specif[ied] those rights which are retained when particular powers are given up to be exercised by the Legislature." He said others "result[ed] from the nature of the compact." To explain this distinction, he gave the following example: "Trial by jury cannot be considered as a natural right, but a right resulting from a social compact which regulates the action of the community, but is as essential to secure the liberty of the people as any one of the pre-existing rights of nature" (*Annals*, at 437 [June 8, 1789]). These remarks invite conceiving of "natural" rights as limitations on ends and "positive" rights as limitations on means.

Various implications would flow from these premises, especially when combined with a complementary interpretation of the ninth amendment's precursor. For example, Madison's proposal would imply that the federal government had no power to act in pursuance of some purposes that corresponded to rights retained by the people. Furthermore, "positive" rights in addition to those enumerated in the constitutional text would constitute "actual limitations" on the national government's powers. Both views would link the Constitution to traditions of unwritten fundamental law.

Distinctions between "positive" and "natural" rights are of less importance for present purposes than conceptions of relationships between written and unwritten norms, however conceived. What is most important is that Madison presupposed there were limitations on constitutional ends and means in addition to those specified in the constitutional text.

in Madison's draft and neither of its affirmative clauses. The amendment does not stipulate how to interpret enumerated rights. It only prohibits interpreters from construing them so as to "deny or disparage" other rights "retained by the people."

But it would still be possible to interpret retained rights as capable of serving both purposes identified by the draft. The first amendment could be conceived as "inserted merely for greater caution" to reinforce limits not only on "general" powers but also on the "means" of their execution. Not all enumerated rights, however, would necessarily correspond to limitations on "general" powers. The third, fifth, sixth, and seventh amendments, along with the fourth, might only articulate "actual limitations" on the "means" of exercising the principal delegations.

Following the structure just outlined, one might conceive of other rights "retained by the people" as "actual limitations" only on "means." Without the ninth amendment, someone might argue that the constitutional text implied criminal defendants were entitled *only* to the express guarantees set forth in the text (such as the fifth and sixth amendments). The ninth amendment would rebut such a presumption. The express guarantees would not preclude arguments that principles of equal protection have imposed additional constraints and that defendants have had other rights in criminal trials—such as a presumption of innocence.[38] More generally, the ninth amendment would rebut arguments that the constitutional text contained a complete listing of prohibited or required means of executing delegated powers.

Madison relied on the ninth amendment as capable of serving such a function even before the amendment went into effect. In 1791 he argued at length against the validity of a bill to establish a national bank. He pointed out that the constitutional text did not give Congress express authority to create a bank, and he denied that forming one was necessary to exercise any express power. Madison reportedly referred to "the explanatory amendments" which had been "proposed by Congress" and "ratified by nearly three-fourths of the States." According to the *Annals*, he described the amendments as setting forth "a rule of construction, excluding the latitude" claimed by defenders of the bank bill: "He read several of the articles proposed, remarking particularly on the 11th and 12th; the former, as guarding against a latitude of interpretation; the latter, as excluding every source of power not within the Constitution it-

---

[38] The Supreme Court has made such arguments, without relying explicitly on the ninth amendment. In *Bolling v. Sharpe*, 347 U.S. 497 (1954), the majority held that the fifth amendment's due process clause had an equal protection component); *In re Winship*, 397 U.S. 358 (1970), required a presumption of innocence and proof of guilt beyond a reasonable doubt for criminal proceedings involving juveniles.

self."[39] The eleventh proposal would soon become the ninth amendment; and the twelfth proposal would become the tenth amendment.

Madison invoked these amendments' terms to reinforce arguments that incorporating a national bank did not fall within Congress's delegated authority. The tenth indicated that the federal government was (or would be) confined to the "source[s] of power" enumerated in the text. The ninth would "guard[] against a latitude of interpretation" based on the necessary and proper clause. The bank was not "necessary" but was at most a "convenient" means of exercising a number of express powers.[40]

The account of Madison's references to the terms of the ninth and tenth amendments, if read out of context, suggests he conceived of them as performing different functions. The tenth would deal with express powers, the ninth with the means of their exercise. This dichotomy complemented the structure of his draft of the ninth amendment.

He did not, however, use the idea of reserved powers only to rebut claims of a general "power not within the Constitution itself." He noted that "it is allowed on all hands, a concurrent right to lay and collect taxes." In this context, Madison echoed the structure of the tenth amendment: "This power is secured to [the states], not by its being expressly reserved, but by its not being ceded by the Constitution." He was not denying that Congress had the express power to tax. On the contrary, he invoked what he presumed was a reserved power to oppose claims that Congress's creating a bank was "necessary and proper" as a means of borrowing money. Thus he relied on the concept of reserved powers to reinforce limits both on "general" powers and the "means" of their exercise. He argued that the "essential characteristic of the Government, as composed of limited and enumerated powers, would be destroyed" if his opponents' arguments prevailed.[41]

This example demonstrates how the ninth and tenth amendments could serve complementary but distinct functions. Madison did not specify the retained rights involved; he presumably had in mind rights of eco-

---

[39] *Annals* 2:1901 (February 2, 1791). An identical account is included in *Papers of James Madison* 13:372–81, taken from the *Gazette of the United States*. It is apparent that the *Annals* for this day are taken from the *Gazette*, though other sources were available. See ibid., at 381n. My research repeatedly underscores problems of reliability associated with the *Gazette*. See, e.g., nn. 57, 59, and 60 of ch. 3.

[40] See *Annals* 2:1900–1901. It is noteworthy that Madison assumed that the Constitution placed upon him the responsibility, as a member of Congress, to respect the limits on Congress's authority. As explained in the text, he had presumed when commenting on his proposed amendments that it would be for Congress to decide on whether a law was "necessary and proper" as a means of exercising an enumerated power. Chief Justice John Marshall would take a similar position in *McCulloch v. Maryland* (examined in ch. 6).

[41] *Annals* 2:1898–99.

nomic autonomy that would be affected by the establishment of a national bank. He did identify powers of the states that would be affected. Identifying retained or reserved prerogatives would strengthen his analysis, but he treated the ninth and tenth amendments as complementary parts of a "rule of construction" that did not depend on identifying residuals.

The *Annals* do not report Madison as having gone full circle by relying on the ninth amendment or the idea of retained rights to support his claim that the Constitution excluded "every source of power not within the Constitution itself" (not just to guard against "latitude" interpreting the means of exercising such powers). Even so, the text of the ninth amendment—like the tenth—could rebut presumptions of "general" powers.

Such a function would assume even greater importance following ratification of the other proposed amendments. Although the first amendment's primary thrust is to deny congressional power (thereby guarding the specified popular rights), it appears to presume that the Constitution has delegated *some* legislative power to Congress. Several amendments arguably presume to limit executive and judicial powers. There are good reasons to interpret the ninth amendment as rebutting findings of delegated power based only on these presumptions. In each case, governmental power would depend for its legitimacy on positive delegation rather than negative implication. The Constitution presumably had delegated some powers whose manner of exercise would be limited by some enumerated rights, but it would not be proper to identify the powers by referring to the amendments.[42]

In addition, unenumerated rights might correspond to the limits of express powers, not just the means of their exercise. It would be wrong to

---

[42] One of the provisions dropped from Madison's proposals may further illustrate how individuals might presume powers based on the negative implications of rights. His draft of the second amendment's precursor included an additional clause: "no person religiously scrupulous of bearing arms shall be compelled to render military service in person." This prohibition might reasonably have been interpreted as making two presuppositions: (a) the Constitution gave governmental officials authority to compel military service in person by those who were *not* "religiously scrupulous of bearing arms"; and (b) the Constitution gave governmental officials authority to compel military service *other than in person* by those who *were* "religiously scrupulous of bearing arms." Thomas B. McAffee has argued that the ninth amendment was originally designed *only* to serve this type of function: to deny implied power based on the enumeration of rights (but not place limits on delegated powers). See Thomas B. McAffee, "The Original Meaning of the Ninth Amendment," 90 Colum. L. Rev. 1215 (1990), at 1300 n. 325 ("The ninth amendment reads entirely as a 'hold harmless' provision: It thus says nothing about how to construe the powers of Congress or how broadly to read the doctrine of implied powers; it indicates only that no inference about those powers should be drawn from the mere fact that rights are enumerated in the Bill of Rights"). It is not clear, however, that Madison (or others) expected the amendment to serve *only* this function.

assume that express prohibitions such as the first amendment have contained an exhaustive listing of prerogatives completely outside the reach of federal regulatory authority. On the contrary, constitutional structures have supported the opposite presumption.

It would be coherent to argue, for example, that Congress originally had no authority to regulate sexual or reproductive choices. One might likewise argue that the people have retained rights to make decisions pertaining to employment and education. A large measure of personal autonomy appears to have been outside the reach of delegated authority (though the government might legitimately be able to exercise powers in ways that might *influence* the people's reproductive choices—for example, through taxing and spending policies). It would make more sense to characterize these realms of individual choice as residual prerogatives, not just limits on federal officials' choice of means to exercise the powers expressly delegated to them.[43]

These considerations lead back to questions about the scope of powers reserved to *the states*. Presumably institutions of state government have had authority to restrict the exercise of some rights in ways that federal officials have not. In addition, state constitutions and laws have provided security for rights not enumerated in the federal Constitution.

Madison's distinction between "general" and "particular" powers offers insights into problems associated with analyzing relationships among federal and state powers, including their respective relationships to rights and powers of "the people." Debates over the tenth amendment suggest a need to consider the possibility of conflicting prerogatives, not just dichotomies. As explained below, the idea of "trumps" offers alternative perspectives for analyzing relationships between constitutional rights and powers, along with relationships among powers.

Overlapping Powers?

When Madison introduced his proposals to the House in June, he summarized his draft of the tenth amendment and claimed it "may be consid-

---

[43] Randy Barnett has relied on a similar distinction between "means-constraints" and "ends-constraints." In his view, rights create a rebuttable presumption of constitutional invalidity but are not capable of defeating "a genuinely necessary and proper exercise" of federal power or a "necessary" exercise of a state's "police power." He argues that such a presumption should arise every time a governmental action "infringes upon the rightful liberties of the people." But he has not articulated adequate criteria for deciding what liberties are "rightful" (and which are not) or what exercises of power are "genuinely" necessary (or "necessary and proper" in the case of federal actions). See Barnett, "Reconceiving the Ninth Amendment," at 7, 11–16, 34–42; Barnett, "Introduction: Implementing the Ninth Amendment," in Barnett, ed., *The Rights Retained by the People*, 2 vols. (Fairfax, Va.: George Mason University Press, 1989 and 1993), vol. 2, at 10–19, esp. at 17.

ered as superfluous" or "may be deemed unnecessary." He referred to the amendments proposed by state conventions and noted that "several are particularly anxious that it should be declared in the constitution, that the powers not therein delegated should be reserved to the several States." He reportedly remarked that there would be "no harm in making such a declaration" as long as it did no more than make explicit a principle that he claimed was already implicit in "the whole of the instrument." In other words, he took a position that the tenth amendment, as he proposed it, was acceptable precisely *because* it would not withdraw any powers originally delegated to the federal government.[44]

In contrast, he warned that limiting the federal government to "express" powers would threaten the ability of "the system . . . to retain its present form." The *Annals* report a motion by Thomas Tucker to insert the word "expressly" into the initial clause of Madison's draft.[45] Madison reportedly voiced concern that the insertion would confine the federal government to "expressly delegated" powers and gave that reason for opposing the motion:

> Mr. Madison objected to this amendment, because it was impossible to confine a Government to the exercise of express powers; there must necessarily be admitted powers by implication, unless the constitution descended to recount every minutia. He remembered that the word "expressly" had been moved in the convention of Virginia, by the opponents of ratification, and, after full and fair discussion, was given up by them, and the system allowed to retain its present form.[46]

[44] Madison's remarks on his draft of the tenth amendment, as reported in the *Annals*, were as follows: "I find, from looking into the amendments proposed by the State conventions, that several are particularly anxious that it should be declared in the constitution, that the powers not therein delegated should be reserved to the several States. Perhaps words which may define this more precisely than the whole of the instrument now does, may be considered as superfluous. I admit that they may be deemed unnecessary; but there can be no harm in making such a declaration, if gentlemen will allow that the fact is as stated. I am sure I understand it so, and do therefore propose it. " *Annals*, at 441 (June 8, 1789).

[45] See *Annals*, at 761 (August 18, 1789) (a House select committee had reported a proposal identical to Madison's). According to the *Annals*, Tucker's proposal to add "expressly" to the tenth amendment's precursor was the second part of a two-pronged motion, the first part of which would have prefixed the amendment with the clause: "all powers being derived from the people." Chapter 3 quotes that motion in the text accompanying n. 57.

[46] Ibid. Compare the *Gazette*'s account of Tucker's proposal and Madison's response: "Mr. Tucker proposed an introductory clause to this amendment, *viz. all power being derived from the people.* Mr. Madison objected to this, as confining the government within such limits as to admit of no implied powers, and I believe, said he, that no government ever existed which was not necessarily obliged to exercise powers by implication. This question was agitated in the Convention of Virginia; it was brought forward by those who were opposed to the Constitution, and was finally given up by them" (*Gazette* 1:50 [reportedly

He presumed that limiting the federal government to "express" powers would preclude *any* exercise of implied power.[47]

As Madison characterized it, Tucker's proposal would have effectively repealed the necessary and proper clause. The amendment would no longer be "superfluous." Instead, it would require "a reconsideration of the whole structure of the Government," including "the principles and the substance of the powers given." Madison was reportedly unwilling to "see a door opened" for such fundamental changes.[48]

His response to Tucker's proposal indicates that Madison was unwilling to follow entirely the supposed paradigm of the Articles of Confederation: delegated and reserved "particular" powers. He adhered to the position he had articulated in the 44th *Federalist*. In that context, he had also argued that the Constitution would not confine the central government to *expressly* delegated powers. The Constitution would delegate "more extensive" powers and "real authority" to carry out the "objects" for which the government was formed.[49] This more open-ended conception of the central government's authority, however, posed problems for interpreting relationships between delegated and reserved powers.

Assuming that his conceptions of delegated and reserved powers were symmetrical, he was committed to interpreting the tenth amendment's residuals, like "delegated" powers, as general *and* particular powers. It is not clear, however, that the national government's choice of "particular" means to exercise "general" powers could never, as a matter of constitutional logic, conflict with the states' choice of "particular" means of exercising *their* "general" powers. Likewise, it is not clear that particular exercises of national power could never interfere with the people's exercise of *their* reserved powers or retained rights.

Furthermore, Madison's approach would have made it difficult to iden-

---

for August 19, 1789] [emphasis in original]). The *Annals* contain a more accurate account than the *Gazette* of Tucker's proposal, because Madison was clearly responding to a motion to add "expressly" to the proposal. At least on this issue, the *Gazette*'s account was deficient. See also ch. 3, n. 57, for criticism of the *Gazette*'s dating.

[47] The available sources indicate that Roger Sherman also objected to Tucker's proposal. According to the *Annals*, at 761 (August 18, 1789), Sherman argued that "corporate bodies are supposed to possess all powers incident to a corporate capacity, without being absolutely expressed." According to the *Gazette*, at 50, he argued that "all corporations are supposed to possess all the powers incident to their corporate capacity."

[48] See ch. 3, n. 43, and accompanying text.

[49] Madison, *The Federalist*, no. 44, at 284–85. Madison had argued here that limiting Congress to "expressly delegated" powers would have exposed legislators under the proposed Constitution, "as their predecessors ha[d] been, to the alternative of construing the term '*expressly*' with so much rigor as to disarm the government of all real authority, or with so much latitude as to destroy altogether the force of the restriction." Ibid., at 284 (emphasis in original).

tify the scope of reserved "particular" powers. Did the Constitution re-serve to the states and the people "particular" powers that were incapable of interfering with *possible* exercises of federal powers (means that *might have been* "necessary and proper"), or did it reserve means other than those *actually* chosen by Congress? Under each scenario, the states and the people might have been deprived of "particular" means that would be "necessary and proper" to exercising their reserved "general" powers.

In addition, under the latter scenario, the scope of residual powers ap-parently could have varied, depending on Congress's choice of means. If Congress used a wide range of means to exercise its "general" powers, the residual would diminish; if Congress used a more limited range of means, reserved powers would correspondingly expand. Such a conception of "reserved" powers, however, would have been at odds with the idea of powers reserved to the states and the people *by the Constitution*, not Congress. Congress could effectively "prohibit" the exercise of powers by the states, or withdraw previously "reserved" powers.[50]

One way of avoiding these conceptual puzzles would be to assume that "powers not delegated to the United States" referred only to absences of "enumerated" powers, or "principal" powers, even if such powers carried with them "particular" means of their execution. That approach would complement interpreting the Constitution's "reservations" as "principal" powers other than those delegated to the United States government. Such a conception of "delegated" and "reserved" powers underlay, for ex-ample, Marshall's arguments in *McCulloch v. Maryland* that the people had committed different "objects" to the national and state govern-ments.[51] Similarly, it would be reasonable to view the people's reserved powers as "objects" over which the people had not delegated governmen-tal power.

Interpreting the tenth amendment at this level of generality, unlike a more inclusive conception of delegated and reserved powers, would treat the amendment as conceptually complete in a different way from that just discussed. The amendment could be interpreted as referring to all general rather than particular powers. According to this reading, its references to "delegated" and "reserved" powers would not address conflicting exer-cises of "particular" powers, but the amendment would rebut claims of undelegated "general" powers. The necessary and proper clause, prohibi-tions on the exercise of federal and state powers, enumerated and un-enumerated rights, the supremacy clause, and other parts of the Constitu-tion might have addressed conflicting exercises of "particular" powers

---

50 Marshall effectively took this position in *McCulloch* (discussed in ch. 6).
51 See *McCulloch v. Maryland*, 17 U.S. (4 Wheat.) 316, 410 (1819).

without detracting from the logical coherence of the Constitution's principal delegations and reservations.[52]

Madison implicitly rejected such an approach. In the 44th *Federalist*, he had assumed that limiting the central government to "express" powers would preclude it from exercising any implied powers. Constitutional delegations would be conceived as enumerations of "particular" powers, not "general" authorizations. Madison was unwilling to endorse such a scheme, either in *The Federalist* or in his remarks to the House.

Instead, he conceived of the tenth amendment's precursor as mirroring *all* powers delegated by the Constitution, implied as well as express. According to this alternative paradigm, the tenth amendment (like its precursor) referred only to the general and particular powers *not* delegated to the United States. Assuming the necessary and proper clause authorized a finite range of particular powers, all other particular powers would presumably be reserved as residuals to the states and the people.

It would be possible to interpret the tenth amendment along these lines and still to regard it as a complete reference to reserved powers. The Constitution would reserve to the states and the people *only* residuals, defined negatively with reference to delegated powers. But such an approach would have defeated rather than promoted the goals that many sought to achieve by favoring addition to the constitutional text of a provision like the tenth amendment. The amendment would have preserved conceptual neatness by committing interpreters to a narrow conception of reserved powers, thereby upsetting prevalent assumptions concerning the scope of state powers, means of exercising them, and limitations on their exercise.

Constitutional structures as a whole were more congruent with assuming, notwithstanding the tenth amendment, that exercises of delegated and reserved powers might conflict.[53] Conceding that possibility, however, would logically entail abandoning an assumption that the tenth amendment referred to all delegated and reserved powers. Abandoning that assumption, in turn, would partially undercut the amendment's logical and practical ability to serve as a critical standard for interpreting the scope of delegated powers.

[52] The amendment's reference to powers "prohibited" to the states might have operated at this same (general) level, but also might have operated at the level of "particular" powers. As suggested in the text, there are good reasons for interpreting "prohibitions" as restrictions on "particular" exercises of "general" powers, whether or not they have restricted the "objects" reserved to the states.

[53] Chapter 6 focuses on this issue, particularly as it relates to powers of taxation (which Hamilton characterized as "concurrent" in *The Federalist*, nos. 32–34). Note that Madison also characterized such powers as "concurrent" in his analysis of the validity of the national bank bill. (See the text accompanying n. 41, above.)

The language of the tenth amendment has been consistent with arguing that the states and the people have had "reserved" powers in addition to residuals, even if it has not referred to those powers. But the idea of overlapping delegated and reserved powers would not have been attractive to the Constitution's critics. One of the primary objectives of that amendment's sponsors (or sponsors of more restrictive drafts) was to gain a textual peg for rebutting overly broad interpretations of national authority. Those favoring such a provision would have realized, however, that the idea of overlapping delegated and reserved powers would not have the same critical bite as the idea of mutually exclusive powers.

Finding that a state was exercising a reserved power would not, by itself, entail a conclusion that conflicting exercises of national power were impermissible. Only finding that a power was reserved *exclusively* to the states or the people would compel such a conclusion. But once critics of national power conceded the possibility of overlapping means, they would have more difficulty arguing that a given power was exclusively reserved. The necessary and proper clause and the idea of potentially conflicting powers would be consistent with simultaneously broad interpretations of national and state powers. It would not be difficult to support a claim of reserved power, but it would be difficult to prevail in arguing that a power was reserved *exclusively*. The latter determination, not simply the former, would be necessary to rebut claims of central authority.

Furthermore, the idea of potentially conflicting delegated and reserved powers would raise questions about which powers would have priority in cases of conflict: those of the United States government, the states, or the people? More specifically, would the central government's "particular" powers have priority over conflicting claims of reserved power by the states or the people? What would be the constitutional status of the Constitution's "reservations" of "general" and/or "particular" powers, and how would such powers relate to the Constitution's principal delegations and its authorization of implied powers? There would be analogous questions involving claims of enumerated or unenumerated rights.

The available records indicate that Madison did not confront these problems in his remarks to the House. Nevertheless, the accounts frame the issues, offer several theoretical paradigms, and suggest a need for further consideration.

Potentially Crosscutting Rights and Powers?

John Hart Ely has argued that Madison's remarks on the ninth amendment's precursor reflect "confusion" flowing from a "category mistake." Instead of "separating the question of unenumerated powers from the question of unenumerated rights," Madison ran together analysis of these issues. As Ely explained, "the possibility that unenumerated rights will be disparaged is seemingly made to do service as an intermediate premise in an argument that unenumerated powers will be implied (though at the very end of the first sentence it seems to flip again and the possibility that unenumerated powers will be inferred now seems threatening because of what that would mean to unenumerated rights)." Ely claimed that "[t]he confusion is understandable in context," because "a great deal of the debate over a bill of rights was marked by what we would today regard as a category mistake." The "mistake" made by members of the founding generation was "a failure to recognize that rights and powers are not simply the absence of one another but that rights can cut across or 'trump' powers."[54]

The concept of rights as "trumps" has become familiar. It proceeds from an assumption that rights may preclude *otherwise valid* exercises of governmental power. Unlike dichotomous conceptions of constitutional norms, it can accommodate simultaneously expansive interpretations of competing prerogatives.[55]

Ely gave a puzzling example of an enumerated right "trumping" an exercise of governmental power: "A law prohibiting the interstate shipment of books *may* be a regulation of commerce, but it violates the First Amendment and thus must fall."[56] According to dichotomous conceptions of rights and powers which Ely rejected, it would be wrong to entertain arguments that the Constitution *both* delegated power to regulate the shipment of books *and* prohibited such regulations. The Constitution *either* delegated the power *or* prohibited it, not both. If the law violated an enumerated right, therefore, it could not—as a matter of constitutional logic—fall within Congress's delegated authority. Ely suggested such a possibility by equivocating on whether the hypothetical law would constitute a regulation of commerce.

But in order for his example to demonstrate "trumping," Ely had to *presume* that the law would fall within Congress's delegated powers *and* would violate an enumerated right. According to this reading, delegated powers and retained rights are crosscutting prerogatives. In addition, Ely assumed that rights prevail in cases of conflict. The first amendment prohibits *otherwise legitimate* exercises of power (as delegated to Congress by article I of the Constitution).

[54] John Hart Ely, *Democracy and Distrust* (Cambridge: Harvard University Press, 1980), at 36.

[55] See generally Ronald Dworkin, *Taking Rights Seriously* (Cambridge: Harvard University Press, 1978), esp. at xi–xiii and chs. 6 and 7. See also "Symposium: Individual Rights and the Powers of Government," 37 Ga. L. Rev. 343–501 (1993).

[56] Ely, *Democracy and Distrust*, at 36 (emphasis added).

Other examples further illustrate the competing theoretical paradigms. As explained above, it is possible to conceive of prohibitions throughout the Bill of Rights as conceptually redundant (but nevertheless politically significant) articulations of norms. The textual additions arguably did not withdraw powers that had been previously delegated. Instead, the amendments made explicit various limitations that arguably had been implicit. According to this scheme, specific prohibitions have been capable of reinforcing arguments that the Constitution never delegated power to act in the prohibited ways.

Another possibility is that some or all of these amendments established potentially crosscutting norms capable of precluding *otherwise valid* exercises of governmental power. Before the third amendment's ratification, it was arguably permissible for the United States government to quarter soldiers in homes in times of peace without an owner's consent or in times of war without legislative authorization. Upon the Constitution's ratification, Congress may have had authority to issue general warrants to collect taxes or to enforce criminal laws. The limitations set forth in the fifth, sixth, seventh, and eighth amendments conceivably did not apply to the conduct of trials authorized by article III until these amendments went into effect. The first and second amendments may likewise establish crosscutting norms. According to this scheme, the amendments placed new limits on delegated powers and did not merely reinforce the Constitution's original delegations.

This alternative perspective suggests a different reading of Madison's draft of the ninth amendment and his comments on the proposed amendments. The draft provided that some rights would specify "actual limitations" of delegated powers. In his remarks to the House, he reportedly declared that some rights would "limit and qualify the powers of Government, by *excepting* out of the grant of power those cases in which the Government ought not to act, or to act only in a particular mode."[57] It would be possible to conceive of "exceptions" as potentially crosscutting limitations, not articulations of perfectly complementary norms.[58]

Ely argued that despite Madison's "confusion," he "understood what he had written." According to Ely, Madison made *two separate* points:

[57] *Annals*, at 437 (June 8, 1789). This comment is also consistent with the alternative view that limitations on means complemented perfectly the original delegation. Note that Madison also referred to "cases in which the government ought not to act" as "exceptions," although he apparently did not think the government originally had power over all retained rights.

[58] Randy Barnett has argued that rights are "exceptions" of this sort—limitations on means—but not "trumps" (i.e., limits capable of preempting exercises of delegated power). See Barnett, "Reconceiving the Ninth Amendment," at 7–16 and 32–42; Barnett, "Implementing the Ninth Amendment," in Barnett, ed., *Rights Retained by the People* 2:2–6, 10–19, and 22–46.

that "he wished to forestall the implication of unexpressed powers *and* the disparagement of unenumerated rights." Although Madison "linked [these points] in a way that seems unnatural today," the language of the *tenth* amendment "clearly expresses the former point, [and] the Ninth Amendment clearly expresses the latter." Ely referred to Hamilton's analysis in the 84th *Federalist*, moreover, to support an inference that "the possibility of a governmental act's being supported by one of the enumerated powers and at the same time violating one of the enumerated rights is one our forbears were *capable* of contemplating." But in the example Ely cited, Hamilton *denied* there would be such a conflict.[59]

Ely did not rest his analysis exclusively on evidence of the framers' expectations. He emphasized that members of Congress and state legislatures approved the *language* of the amendments. In his view, the language of the *tenth* amendment "completely fulfills" the function historically attributed to the ninth:

> Th[e tenth] amendment . . . says—in language as clearly to the point as the language of the Ninth Amendment is not—that the addition of the Bill of Rights is not to be taken to have changed the fact that powers not delegated are not delegated. It does seem that a similar thought was part of what animated the Ninth Amendment, but if that were *all* that amendment had been calculated to say, it would have been redundant.[60]

In sum, he advocated *separating* analysis of constitutional rights and powers. The tenth amendment would rebut impermissibly broad conceptions of delegated authority, and the ninth would protect unenumerated rights (along with enumerated rights) as potentially crosscutting norms ("trumps").

Although it is not clear that Madison and other Federalists endorsed the idea of rights as crosscutting norms, variations of such a perspective were certainly viable during the founding period. Common preoccupation with Madison's role and the Constitution's Federalist lineage has diverted attention from analysis of *Anti-Federalist* thought. It was the Anti-Federalists, after all, who expressed concern over the breadth of constitutional delegations. The Constitution's critics, not its defenders, argued that original structures would provide insufficient security for rights. Those pressing for an enumeration of rights, not just those opposing such an enumeration, had good reasons to advocate conceiving of rights as trumps.

For example, in his "Objections to the Constitution," George Mason

---

[59] See Ely, *Democracy and Distrust*, at 36 and 202 n. 86 (emphasis on "capable" added); Hamilton, *The Federalist*, no. 84, at 514–15n.

[60] Ely, *Democracy and Distrust*, at 34–35 (emphasis in original).

argued that under the "general clause at the end of enumerated powers, Congress may grant monopolies in trade and commerce, constitute new crimes, inflict unusual and severe punishments, and extend their power as far as they shall think proper." He noted that there was "no declaration of any kind for preserving the liberty of the press, the trial by jury in civil cases, nor against the danger of standing armies in time of peace."[61] It is clear that he conceived of enumerated rights as crosscutting norms.

"Brutus" observed that "[t]he powers, rights and authority, granted to the general government by this Constitution, are as complete, with respect to every object to which they extend, as that of any State government—it reaches to every thing which concerns human happiness—life, liberty, and property are under its control." As a result, there was the same need to restrain its exercise "within proper limits." He identified a number of rights that would not (in his view) be secure under the Constitution, many of which found their way into the eventual Bill of Rights.[62]

He countered arguments that there was no need to enumerate "these exceptions" because "every thing which is not given is reserved." He conceded that the Constitution did not "grant . . . in express terms" the power to abridge rights he had identified. But he claimed that such power was "implied in the general powers granted." He concluded: "With equal truth it may be said, that all the powers which the bills of rights guard against the abuse of, are contained in the general ones granted by this Constitution."[63]

"The Federal Farmer" also referred to arguments that rights would be secure as residuals. He noted that "it is mere matter of opinion" whether the people reserved powers not delegated or assigned those not expressly reserved. He was unwilling to rely on a premise that the Constitution would secure rights based on the former implication, since "men usually take either side of the argument, as will best answer their purposes." Particularly since "men who govern will, in doubtful cases, construe laws and constitutions most favourably for increasing their own powers," it was prudent to "fix limits to their legislators and rulers, which will soon be plainly seen by those who are governed, as well as by those who govern."[64]

---

[61] Mason, "Objections to the Constitution of Government formed by the Convention" (1787), in Herbert J. Storing, ed., *The Complete Anti-Federalist* (Chicago: University of Chicago Press, 1981), vol. 2, at 13.

[62] "Essays of Brutus" (perhaps Robert Yates), no. II, November 1, 1787, in ibid., vol. 2, at 374–77.

[63] Ibid., at 374 and 376.

[64] Richard Henry Lee, "Letters from the Federal Farmer," nos. II and IV, October 9 and 12, 1787, in ibid., vol. 2, at 231–32 and 247–48.

Examples like these abound. Anti-Federalists repeatedly emphasized the breadth of delegated powers. They expressed concern that popular rights would not be secure under the Constitution, particularly if not enumerated in the constitutional text. Such an enumeration would potentially limit the United States government's powers several ways. Specific prohibitions would guard against the tendency of rulers to interpret open-ended delegations of authority expansively. More importantly, an express declaration of rights would establish potentially crosscutting limitations. Those in power would be more likely to comply with the limits. But if such persons did not comply with the prohibitions, they would reinforce potentially crosscutting exercises of political power by the people at large. The enumerations would not only amend the law formally; they would also change equations of governing power.[65]

Anti-Federalists would, therefore, endorse Ely's argument that rights should be understood as potentially crosscutting norms. But they would not accept his claim that a general declaration like the tenth amendment would "completely fulfill" the function of limiting the central government to exercising delegated powers. Nor would the Constitution's critics endorse Ely's recommendation to *separate* analysis of constitutional "rights" and "powers." Enumerating rights and reinforcing the idea of unenumerated rights might affect *what* powers governmental officials would exercise and *how* they would do so.

Anti-Federalists were not only concerned about formal limits. They were also attentive to roles that the text might play in shaping political discourse. They presumed that the rhetoric of rights would constrain practices that otherwise might find support from the rhetoric of powers.

INTERPRETIVE OPTIONS

Precedents from the founding period are not perfectly consistent. During debates over the Constitution's ratification and initial amending, individuals advocated competing conceptions of constitutional structures. There is no need to assume artificially that there has only been one "correct" way to interpret the Constitution, with all others being "mistaken." On the contrary, one may learn much about the open-ended character of constitutional norms by being attentive to ways they have emerged from conflict. Equally important, the Constitution has remained able to accommodate a large measure of interpretive plurality.

[65] See, e.g., Hugh Henry Brackenridge, "Cursory Remarks" (1788); and Robert Yates, "Letters of Sydney" (1788), in Bernard Schwartz, ed., *The Bill of Rights* (New York: McGraw-Hill, 1971), vol. 1, at 521–26.

During the founding generation, many persons had good reasons to advocate conceiving of enumerated and unenumerated rights, like reserved powers, as residuals beyond the reach of delegated authority. But many persons also reasonably conceived of delegated and reserved powers, along with retained rights, as overlapping and potentially conflicting norms. Various combinations and permutations of these positions intersected to create a richly textured interpretive fabric, one that would continue to be woven through subsequent practices containing similar threads.

Some of the principal interpretive frameworks are set forth schematically in figures 1 through 4. The figures approach issues of constitutional design—relationships among basic categories of constitutional discourse—at high levels of generality which correspond to competing strategies that historical sources offer as models. The figures progress in complexity, with even the simpler schemes portraying major features of the constitutional terrain.

A caveat is in order. Two dimensions are not adequate to fully represent any particular conception of the constitutional design, much less intersections among them. Overlapping and concentric circles, arrows, solid and dashed lines, crosscutting axes, and other devices suggest multiple dimensions and various forms of intersection; but the figures still demand imaginative thinking, and each figure supports alternative conceptualizations. The constitutional text does likewise, as it aspires to represent in writing a political order whose contested terrain is composed of features occupying numerous dimensions.

Schemes A and B of *figure 1* represent arguments that the Constitution has delegated intrinsically limited powers. In each case, the spheres designated "F" portray the main delegations as set forth primarily in articles I, II, and III of the constitutional text. In addition, both versions of figure 1 show an area of implied powers arguably surrounding the principal delegations but nevertheless falling within the reach of delegated authority. As explained more fully in chapter 6, however, one may reasonably take a position that the Constitution has not authorized implied powers (whether based on the necessary and proper clause or otherwise) beyond the principal delegations. Even Alexander Hamilton—one of the Constitution's leading proponents—suggested that implied powers were *embraced within* the principal delegations. This issue would come to a head in the context of controversy over Congress's power to establish a national bank, and there would be analogous questions involving judicial powers. (Judicial review, for example, may be conceived as falling within "the judicial power" delegated by article III or as an additional power implied by the principal delegation.) Accordingly, version A of figure 1 includes a tentative reference to implied powers and uses dashed lines to mark some

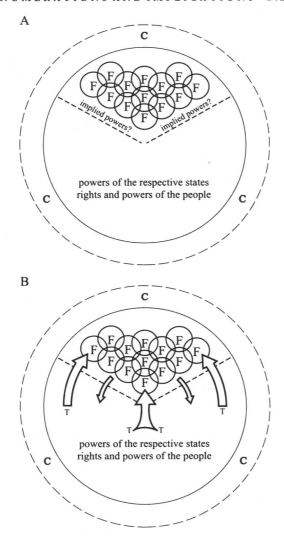

Key:

F = enumerated federal powers

C = rights and powers of constitutional change

T = actions of the people and the states (collectively)
     through federal structures

Fig. 1. Schemes of Delegated Power

of the bounds of constitutional delegations. Version B has corresponding features, except that the explicit reference to implied powers has been removed to eliminate clutter.

Both versions of figure 1 show federal powers as occupying only a portion of the normative terrain. In each case, the constitutional order is portrayed as embracing, in addition, powers reserved to the respective states and rights and powers of the people at large. Following the structure of the tenth amendment, these reserved powers and retained rights are grouped together.

Each scheme also includes rights and powers of constitutional change. As explained above, the Constitution presupposes that its norms may be amended through extraordinary procedures involving established governmental institutions such as Congress and state legislatures. But the constitutional text also sanctions formal change through processes involving actions by ad hoc conventions, and possibilities of more fundamental reformation may be conceived as located outside the bounds of the existing order. Accordingly, figures 1A and 1B place rights and powers of constitutional change at the margins of the primary schemes of governmental powers and residual prerogatives, where they both adjoin established mechanisms of government and extend beyond them. The concentric arrangement has the added benefit, moreover, of conveying the collective and separate components of rights and powers of constitutional change, since they adjoin the full range of delegated and reserved/retained prerogatives.

Despite their common features and superficial resemblances, figures 1A and 1B depict significantly different conceptions of relationships among the rights and powers involved. According to scheme A, constitutional delegations and reservations have been mutually exclusive and reciprocally limiting, composing a zero-sum universe. This scheme mirrors, for example, James Wilson's characterization of relationships between constitutional delegations and residuals.

Alexander Hamilton, however, offered a radically different conception of relationships among these norms. He joined Thomas Paine and Thomas Jefferson in arguing that some rights and powers were coextensive and overlapping. These men argued, more specifically, that the people would continue to hold all rights even after the Constitution's ratification.[66] Following similar reasoning, it has been possible to conceive of the states as continuing to hold even the powers delegated to the federal government, since the Constitution has enabled the states (collectively, along

---

[66] See n. 9 of this chapter for references to Paine's and Jefferson's arguments, along with chapter 3 for analysis of Hamilton's.

with the people) to act *through* federal structures.[67] Thus it has been reasonable to conceive of popular rights (and, according to some schemes, state powers) as coextensive with powers delegated to national institutions. In sum, delegating federal powers has not necessarily implied surrendering or narrowing retained rights or reserved powers. Figure 1B uses arrows pointing toward and through the area of federal powers to portray this alternative conceptualization in which federal structures are viewed as vehicles *through which* the states and the people may act in their combined capacities.

The smaller arrows pointing in the opposite direction—proceeding *from* federal powers—depict a complementary type of normative overlap. Madison, Hamilton, and other prominent Federalists repeatedly argued that the people's retained rights and reserved powers, along with the states' reserved powers, would gain security from exercises of federal power. Thus federal power may be conceived as undergirding or reinforcing realms of autonomous choice. This scheme is consistent with conceiving of retained rights and reserved powers as residuals, but with the added feature that they are viewed as depending in some respects on complementary assertions of centralized power. For example, as explained more fully in chapter 7, it appears that Congress and other federal institutions (including federal courts) have reinforced the states' commercial powers and secured personal rights of economic autonomy. Federal judges exercising judicial review have likewise secured popular rights and reserved powers. Most exercises of national power may be conceived as serving this type of function in some manner since governmental actions reinforce some claims precisely *because* they preempt others.[68]

Figure 2 goes beyond figure 1 by portraying not only limits implied by the original Constitution but also those contained in the Bill of Rights. As with figures 1A and 1B, prerogatives of constitutional change surround the primary scheme of governmental powers and residual prerogatives. But figure 2 also reflects changes imported into that scheme by the initial textual amendments.

This figure depicts several of the functions that prohibitions in the Bill of Rights, like those in the original text, have been capable of serving. Some have negated federal power, for the benefit of the states and/or the people at large. These limits may be conceived as reinforcing intrinsically limited delegations of power and/or as potentially crosscutting norms. A

---

[67] For a more recent argument along these lines, see Herbert Wechsler, "The Political Safeguards of Federalism: The Role of the States in the Composition and Selection of the National Government," 54 Colum. L. Rev. 543 (1954).

[68] Offering further support for such a position, the Declaration of Independence presupposes that government is instituted to *secure* rights.

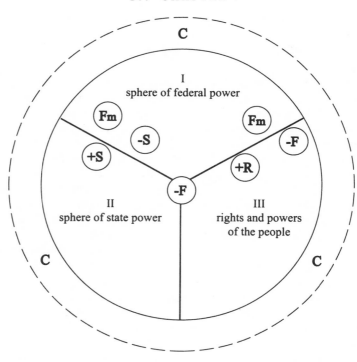

Key:
-F = absence of federal power
-S = absence of separate state power
Fm = limit on federal means
+S = enumerated state power
+R = enumerated rights of the people
C   = rights and powers of constitutional change

Possible areas of overlap:
II and III (collectively) through I
III (collectively) through II
II and/or III dependent on I
III dependent on II

Fig. 2. Accounting for Normative Boundaries

number of provisions have guaranteed rights more affirmatively by speci-
fying legitimate means of exercising powers. These rights may likewise be
conceived as mirroring the original delegations and/or as new restrictions. The location of various provisions on this scheme hinges on their
characterization according to these types of criteria.

Figure 2 also has the added feature of calling attention to possible distinctions among prerogatives of the states and those of the people as such (although it continues to group together the people's reserved powers and retained rights). In addition, its portrayal of federal powers, state powers, and the people's rights and powers within a single sphere with lines of division between them helps to account for the rhetoric of "lines of division" or "boundaries" between rights and powers or between powers. The figure leaves open whether these sets of norms are arrayed coordinately ("horizontally") or hierarchically ("vertically"). I return to this issue below.

The figure suggests a need to examine whether prohibitions on the federal government have also applied to the states, acting separately. At least during the Republic's early years, it was common to presume that the Bill of Rights did not apply to the states.[69] But one could also plausibly argue that the Constitution's internal logic was inconsistent from the beginning with states' abridging the rights protected by those guarantees.[70] In any event, the fourteenth amendment and other developments have made it necessary to reconsider these issues.

Yet trichotomous conceptions of relationships among constitutional norms have survived that amendment's addition to the constitutional text. As explained in chapter 7, judges in the early twentieth century treated federal and state commercial powers and the people's economic liberties as mutually exclusive and reciprocally limiting spheres of choice. Current claims of sexual and reproductive autonomy reflect similar premises, and the Court has expressed renewed willingness to enforce limitations on federal powers.[71]

There is not a separate figure modifying figure 2 to portray representative structures as vehicles through which constituents may act. But the notations at the base of the figure deal with this issue, suggesting variations of the main scheme portrayed by this figure. The notations also refer to the idea that governmental powers may provide security for separately held rights and powers. Thus figure 2 can bear alternative conceptualizations, with the respective versions paralleling the models of constitutional structures designated as A and B of figure 1.

[69] The leading judicial precedent on this issue was, of course, John Marshall's opinion in *Barron v. Baltimore*, 32 U.S. (7 Pet.) 243 (1833). But see Marshall's opinion in *Fletcher v. Peck*, 10 U.S. (6 Cranch) 87 (1810) (quoted in n. 64 of ch. 6).

[70] See, e.g., Sotirios A. Barber, *On What the Constitution Means* (Baltimore: Johns Hopkins University Press, 1984), at 154–59. Several prominent members of the reconstruction Congress who backed the fourteenth amendment presented similar views. See generally Michael Kent Curtis, *No State Shall Abridge: The Fourteenth Amendment and the Bill of Rights* (Durham: Duke University Press, 1986).

[71] See ch. 7, including n. 40 and accompanying text.

In confronting issues of normative overlap, the trichotomous framework of figure 2 makes further refinements possible. The idea of three distinct sets of prerogatives reinforces the need to distinguish ways that the states and the people at large may act differently through federal structures. For example, the people at large may act through national elections; state legislatures could originally choose senators and can still petition for a constitutional convention to propose amendments. Chapter 8 deals with these issues in the context of examining arrangements of constitutional interpretive authority.

Figure 2 also suggests a need to distinguish ways that national representational structures may, conversely, provide different forms of security for various categories of retained or reserved prerogatives. Chapter 7 explores, among other things, how national regulations of the economy have reinforced individual rights and state governmental powers in distinct ways.

Distinguishing prerogatives of the states from those of the people also makes transparent other relationships involving these categories of norms. As suggested by the notations accompanying figure 2, the people may act in distinct ways through institutions of state government. These structures, in turn, go beyond federal structures in securing a range of popular rights. Figure 2 complements arguments that federal and state powers have, for example, reinforced different popular rights.

Figure 3 portrays an additional type of overlap among constitutional rights and powers. The figure may be understood as representing original structures or those brought about by subsequent changes. The three main categories of prerogatives—powers delegated to the federal government, powers reserved to respective states, and rights and powers of the people at large—are each shown to be expansive. According to this scheme, the Constitution has embraced a wider range of overlapping normative claims than the schemes represented by figures 1 and 2 would allow. Rights and powers of change are again portrayed as located at the margins of the constitutional order. This figure, like the others, can also accommodate arguments that representational structures offer vehicles through which constituents may act—including to provide security for separately held rights and powers.[72] Rights and powers of constitutional

---

[72] According to this alternative conceptualization of figure 3, normative overlapping extends beyond that portrayed by the areas within which the three primary spheres intersect with one another. As with figures 1 and 2, rights and powers of the people (including prerogatives of constitutional change) may be conceived as occupying the entire normative field and thus as overlapping (and gaining security from) state and federal powers. State powers may likewise be viewed as underlying (and gaining security from) federal powers—and thus as occupying at least the two spheres designated "federal powers" and "state powers."

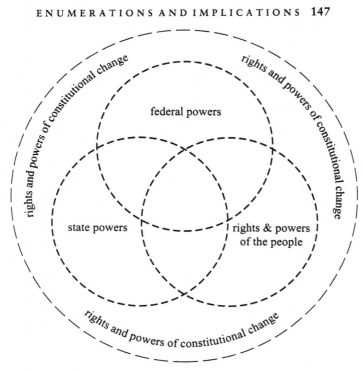

Fig. 3. Accounting for Normative Overlap

change may likewise be conceived as distinct from the other categories of norms and/or as overlapping them.

Allowing for the possibility of greater overlap among various categories of constitutional norms leads to further questions. For example, are the overlapping norms complementary or potentially conflicting? If conflicting, do some have priority over others? Or does the Constitution allow for conflict without assigning priority?

Figure 4 provides an additional framework for examining these matters. Among other things, the figure joins several issues raised by the other three figures. The two main axes form four primary quadrants, with normative overlap, boundaries, priority, and its absence at the respective poles. The figure enables both the mapping of particular interpretive commitments and the conceptualization of intersections among competing contributions to constitutional discourse and other features of the constitutional terrain.

The respective quadrants depict recurring conceptions of relationships among particular norms or categories of norms. *Quadrant I* represents arguments that various rights and powers have been arrayed across

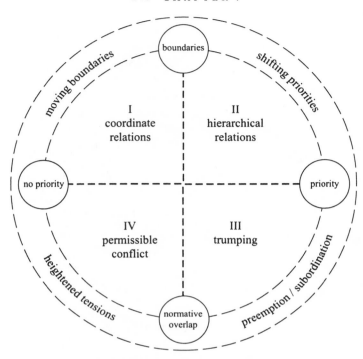

Fig. 4. Competing Conceptions of Constitutional Structures

boundaries but not hierarchically configured. Precedents involving claims of "dual federalism" reflect variations of these relational premises.[73] One may conceive of federal and state powers as equal in authority and thus "horizontally" arranged insofar as all such powers have purportedly flowed from delegations by "the people."

Quadrant I would not, however, embrace all positions flowing from a premise of mutually limiting constitutional norms. If those norms are conceived as hierarchically rather than coordinately arranged, *quadrant II* would more accurately represent their intersection. Taney's arguments in *Ableman v. Booth* regarding the supremacy of federal over state judicial powers reflect such a position. Although he described such powers as separated by a "line of division," he repeatedly characterized federal courts as higher in authority than state courts.[74]

Quadrant III portrays relationships of preemption and subordination.

---

[73] Along with Taney's opinion in *Dred Scott*, see, e.g., his opinion in *License Cases*, 45 U.S. (5 How.) 504 (1847). See also *Hammer v. Dagenhart*, 247 U.S. 251 (1918) (examined in ch. 7).

[74] See *Ableman v. Booth*, 62 U.S. (21 How.) 506 (1859).

This quadrant represents, for example, Ely's arguments that rights may "trump" governmental powers. Trumping is a means of resolving conflicts among assertions of overlapping prerogatives.[75]

Yet one may view various categories of constitutional norms as overlapping without presuming that the Constitution has provided criteria to resolve all conflicts between such norms through preemption and subordination. Instead, one may regard at least some such conflicts as legitimate. For example, it is reasonable to conclude that the Constitution has sanctioned conflicting exercises of congressional and presidential lawmaking powers. The Constitution has arguably reinforced rather than undercut the exercise of rights by individuals like Douglass even when they have opposed legitimate exercises of governmental power. Presidents and members of Congress repeatedly acted inconsistently with judicial precedents during the 1930s. Chapter 8 examines examples of states asserting interpretive autonomy. These types of conflicts would be candidates for inclusion within *quadrant IV* of figure 4.

The figure enables mapping a single interpreter's conception of constitutional structures even if that conception embraces a range of relational premises. For example, a single interpreter may reasonably conceive of relationships between federal legislative and executive powers as coordinately arranged (thus falling within quadrant I) while presuming that individual rights may trump federal legislative powers (as portrayed by quadrant III). An interpreter may likewise conceive of a single norm as intersecting differently with various other norms. Thus one may reasonably conceive of rights of political expression as beyond the legitimate reach of Congress's legislative powers (quadrant I or II), as capable of restraining the means of exercising state legislative powers (quadrant III), and as overlapping assertions of federal judicial powers (quadrant III or IV).

Figure 4 can also account for intersections among interpretive commitments. One may use the figure to juxtapose various positions at any one time and to compare configurations of positions across time. A range of Federalist and Anti-Federalist arguments, for example, may be located within the four quadrants (and perhaps outside them in some instances). The figure as a whole facilitates analyzing intersections among such arguments and directs attention to ways they combined to form the rich texture of American constitutionalism during the founding period.

Equally important, one may use figure 4 to explore relationships among founding expectations, a range of subsequent interpretive com-

---

[75] See Walter F. Murphy, "An Ordering of Constitutional Values," 53 So. Cal. L. Rev. 703 (1980), for an argument that the constitutional system revolves around a ranking of fundamental values.

mitments, changes to the Constitution through formal amendments and otherwise, and the respective relational premises underlying these features of the constitutional terrain (or developments affecting them). The figure can serve this function because it does not presume a static model of constitutional structures or interpretive paradigms. Nor does it assume that any particular structures or paradigms have changed. On the contrary, it can account for dimensions of normative continuity and change. If one or more persons reaffirmed prior conceptions of constitutional norms and relationships among them, these positions could be shown as overlapping on figure 4. But the figure can also be used to plot changing norms and conceptions of them. The areas surrounding the four main quadrants direct attention to these possibilities.

Several problems arise once one allows for possibilities of normative change. Some types of change, for example, may be conceived as taking place within a stable relational framework. In other words, there may be movement within the respective quadrants. Alternatively or in addition, it is possible to conceive of change as involving movement between quadrants.

In order to regard change as occurring within a particular relational paradigm, it is necessary to overcome obstacles associated with adhering to that paradigm. If constitutional change has occurred within quadrant I or II, for example, changes among constitutional norms must not have upset the guiding premise of normative boundaries. Thus if some norms have expanded, as a matter of constitutional logic others must have contracted. Conversely, if some prerogatives have diminished in reach, adjoining ones must have enlarged. Maintaining interpretive commitments within these quadrants depends on a premise, in short, that changes in the scope of constitutional rights and powers have been offsetting.

The main candidates for expansion and/or contraction are federal powers, powers reserved to the states, powers reserved to the people, and rights of the people. (Interpretive prerogatives, along with rights and powers of constitutional change, may be conceived as within these categories.) As various federal powers have been extended, for example, a number of reserved powers and/or rights of the people may have become narrower in scope. Conversely, if one takes a position that some of the people's retained rights and reserved powers have expanded, one may treat intersecting federal and/or state powers as having become more restricted in scope. One may imagine countless possible permutations and combinations of changes involving particular norms within these categories.

An assumption of mutual exclusivity does not, however, apply in the bottom two quadrants (III and IV). Those quadrants can accommodate a position that various categories of norms (or particular norms within these categories) have simultaneously expanded their reach. Simultaneous contractions are also plausible. Thus changes since the Constitution went into effect may have enlarged the scope of federal powers, state powers, and popular rights and powers. At the same time, prerogatives within each category may have become narrower or lapsed.

This scenario calls attention to possibilities of greater overlapping of constitutional rights and powers across time (movement at the macro level from figure 2 to figure 3). As indicated above, such overlapping does not necessarily entail greater conflict. But if one concludes that greater conflict has taken place, it is necessary to confront further questions about whether the Constitution has supplied criteria to resolve these conflicts or been silent on the matter. Quadrants III and IV of figure 4, along with the surrounding zones of constitutional change, may help to place issues like these in perspective.

In addition, figure 4 allows for movement among the quadrants, not only within them. For example, one may conclude that rights and powers which were previously arrayed across normative boundaries (within quadrant I or II) now intersect (within quadrant III or IV). As explained in chapter 7, such a perspective helps to account for reconceptualization of relationships among federal and state commercial powers and individual rights of economic autonomy.

Much of the constructive work of this sort remains to be done. There is a need for further analysis of intersections among parts of the Constitution, interpretive commitments relating to them, and underlying relational premises—including but not limited to variations of those summarized above. This process will be hindered, not furthered, by artificial or overly narrow assumptions about the character or reach of constitutional politics—including assumptions of legal determinacy or normative coherence.

CHAPTER 5

Problems of Practical Politics

Wherever there is an interest and power to do wrong,
wrong will generally be done, and not less readily by a
powerful & interested party than by a powerful and
interested prince."[1]

IT SHOULD BE CLEAR that members of the founding generation were not
only concerned with issues of formal theory. During debates over the
Constitution's ratification and initial amending, there were intense debates about the likely effects, *in practice*, of actions being taken. A constitutional text might attempt to delineate who *should* hold political power
and how they *ought* to exercise it. But the Constitution's proponents and
opponents were concerned about more: Who *would* hold political power
and how *would* they exercise it? How might a constitutional text, in addition to articulating norms, affect the practical workings of politics?

Federalists and Anti-Federalists shared an assumption that political
practices should be consistent with constitutional norms. But they disagreed profoundly about what norms and practices to establish, affirm, or
weaken. Federalists emphasized ways that complex representative structures, not "verbal and nominal distinctions," would provide security for
popular rights and powers. Anti-Federalists, in contrast, emphasized
ways that a bill of rights could instill republican virtue and foster popular
participation. Both perspectives contribute to analyzing central norms
and practices of American constitutionalism.

INTERNAL AND EXTERNAL CHECKS

James Madison's remarks to the House of Representatives on June 8,
1789, were informed by a healthy dose of realism. After examining
whether an enumeration of rights was necessary and proper in the case of
the United States Constitution, he questioned whether the proposed
amendments would affect practices: "It has been said, that it is unnecessary to load the constitution with [a bill of rights], because it was not

[1] James Madison, Letter to Thomas Jefferson, October 17, 1788, in *Papers of James
Madison* 11:298.

found effectual in the constitution of the particular States."[2] Madison was quite familiar with this objection, because he and other Federalists had repeatedly warned that express prohibitions alone would not provide effective security for personal rights.

Madison's subsequent efforts to defend his proposals reflect his continuing sensitivity to the practical limits of parchment barriers. At the same time, he reversed a number of positions that he had previously articulated by arguing that a bill of rights would provide security for rights. In order to understand the issues at stake, it is necessary to locate his remarks within the context of broader debates over problems of constitutional design.

Interest, Faction, and Will

During debates over ratification, Madison exchanged correspondence with Thomas Jefferson, his friend and mentor. The latter was in France serving as foreign minister, as he had been during the Constitutional Convention. In a letter dated December 20, 1787, Jefferson expressed concern about the absence of a bill of rights in the proposed Constitution.[3] Madison responded to those concerns in a letter to Jefferson dated October 17, 1788.[4]

Madison claimed that he had "always been in favor of a bill of rights; provided it be so framed as not to imply powers not meant to be included in the enumeration." But he also denied that the omission of such an enumeration was "a material defect." He indicated that he was not anxious to amend the text to add a bill of rights "for any other reason than that it is anxiously desired by others."

Madison gave several reasons for his ambivalence. In addition to being concerned about the possibly harmful implications of adding an enumeration of rights, he claimed that "experience proves the inefficacy of a bill of rights on those occasions when its controul is most needed." He referred to "repeated violations" of "parchment barriers" in Virginia and

---

[2] *Annals*, at 439 (June 8, 1789). If the account of Madison's remarks is correct, his reference to "this provision," for which I have substituted "a bill of rights," was awkward. Although the quoted passage appears immediately after his discussion of the ninth amendment's precursor, he was not referring only to that proposal as inefficacious. Within context, it is evident that Madison was referring to his entire fourth resolution, which he considered a type of bill of rights. His notes for the speech to the House, in *Papers of James Madison* 12:193–95, support my reading. See also Madison's characterization of his first proposed resolution as "relat[ing] to what may be called a bill of rights" (*Annals*, at 436).

[3] The letter is reprinted in Julian P. Boyd, ed., *Papers of Thomas Jefferson* 12:438–42.

[4] The letter is reprinted in *Papers of James Madison* 11:295–300.

by "overbearing majorities in every State." His prognosis was bleak: "In Virginia I have seen the bill of rights violated in every instance where it has been opposed to a popular current."

Madison compared the efficacy of bills of rights in two types of regimes—republics and monarchies. He assumed that "in a monarchy the latent force of the nation is superior to that of the Sovereign"; he presumed, in contrast, that "in a popular Government, the political and physical power may be considered as vested in the same hands, that is in a majority of the people." He suggested that because of this difference, a bill of rights would make more of a difference in a monarchy than in a republic. If a monarch opposed the people, Madison explained, "a solemn charter of popular rights must have great effect, as a standard for trying the validity of public acts, and as a signal for rousing & uniting the superior force of the community." But in republics, he suggested, there would be no other "force within the community" to check "the tyrannical will of the Sovereign."

Accordingly, Madison claimed that the greatest threat to private rights in republics was from majority factions' acting *through* government rather than from government's acting *against* the people:

> Where the real power in a Government lies, there is the danger of oppression. In our Governments the real power lies in the majority of the Community, and the invasion of private rights is chiefly to be apprehended, not from acts of Government contrary to the sense of its constituents, but from acts in which the Government is the mere instrument of the major number of the Constituents.

He presumed that a bill of rights, to be effective in a republic, would have to limit the people themselves (the opposite of its function in a monarchy, where it would strengthen the people). On this score, however, Madison was skeptical: "Wherever there is an interest and power to do wrong, wrong will generally be done, and not less readily by a powerful & interested party than by a powerful and interested prince."[5]

Madison argued that private rights would nevertheless be more secure in a republic than in a monarchy because of "the less degree of probability that interest may prompt more abuses of power in the former than in the latter." He explained the underlying premises of this argument more fully in the 51st *Federalist*. There he argued that a hereditary or appointed monarchy, although it established a will independent of society capable of limiting majorities, provided "but a precarious security" for

---

[5] See also Madison's skeptical remarks on the efficacy of "parchment barriers" in the 48th *Federalist*, at 308–13. In the 78th *Federalist*, as explained below in the text, Alexander Hamilton expressed a similar view.

rights of minorities and even posed threats to rights of majorities. But Madison suggested that an extended republic such as the United States offered a partial solution: "[A]mong the great variety of interests, parties, and sects which it embraces, a coalition of a majority of the whole society could seldom take place on any other principles than those of justice and the general good."

In the 10th *Federalist*, Madison had argued that an extended republic was also superior to a "pure democracy" or a small republic in protecting rights of minorities. In each case, he suggested, the causes of faction could not be removed except by destroying liberty, and he assumed that such a cure would be worse than the effects of factions. In limiting those effects, moreover, he argued that a large republic would offer two main advantages over other forms of popular government: elected representatives, like a monarch, would be partially insulated from factions among the people; and it would be more difficult for majority factions to form or act in a larger republic than in smaller states. Anticipating his arguments in the 51st *Federalist*, he claimed that with "a greater variety of parties and interests," it would be less likely that "a majority of the whole will have a common motive to invade the rights of other citizens; or if such a motive exists, it will be more difficult for all who feel it to discover their own strength and to act in unison with each other." Thus Madison celebrated diversity among the people and obstacles to communication within a larger polity.[6]

Madison equivocated, however, on whether he expected representatives within the new government to serve primarily the interests of their respective constituents or whether constitutional structures would depend on governmental officials' seeking collective goals even when in opposition to the local interests or expressed views of the public at large. Much of his analysis suggests a skeptical view of human nature and a complementary emphasis on the need for complex structures that would pit interests against each other and enable factional impulses to cancel one another out. For example, he claimed that the Constitution was built on a "policy of supplying, by opposite and rival interests, the defect of better motives." Such passages indicate that Madison was assuming or hoping that national interests (the "permanent and aggregate interests of the community") would emerge from competition and compromise among representatives, each of whom would seek to promote the interests of his (and later her) district.[7]

---

[6] In addition to Madison's analysis in the 10th *Federalist*, see his earlier treatment of these issues in his "Vices of the Political System of the United States" (April 1787), in *Papers of James Madison* 9:345–58.

[7] The quote is from the 51st *Federalist*, at 322. The 10th *Federalist* contains overlapping arguments.

Other passages, however, suggest a faith in the ability of representatives to rise above the partisan, or local, concerns of their constituents. In places, Madison expressed hope that governmental officials would be willing and able to secure the public welfare even in opposition to constituents' wishes, based on the officials' superior "wisdom," "patriotism," and "love of justice"—in short, their virtue. Thus Madison may have been assuming that the people's representatives would have more in common with each other, including more virtue, than with the people at large. But even if his arguments in *The Federalist* rested on such assumptions, he apparently was unwilling to place full trust in the virtue of such officials or their constituents (upon whose trust the officials depended), at least absent structures that would mediate the virtue and filter out other impulses.[8]

Public Opinion and Popular Representation

Madison's defense of larger republics countered arguments by Anti-Federalists that rights were more secure under state governments than they would be under the federal Constitution. Several critics of the proposed scheme disputed Madison's claim that the purpose of constitutional government was to control only the effects and not the causes of faction. According to Melancton Smith, for example, "Government operates upon the spirit of the people, as well as the spirit of the people acts upon it." He suggested that a constitution was not only a frame of government but was also a charter for teaching principles of citizenship. Similarly, "A [Maryland] Farmer" proposed the establishment of local "seminaries of useful learning" that would instruct citizens in "the principles of free government," strengthen the people's attachment to government, and promote their willingness to sacrifice individual interests for collective welfare. Along the same lines, many believed religious conviction was a necessary foundation for public morality and favored mild religious establishments within the states.[9]

Anti-Federalists repeatedly argued that civic education and republican virtue were only possible within small, homogeneous societies. Thus the Constitution's opponents warned that the diversity extolled by Madison

---

[8] The quotes are from the 10th *Federalist*, at 82.

[9] See Melancton Smith, Speech Delivered in the Course of Debate by the Convention of the State of New York on the Adoption of the Federal Constitution, June 21, 1788, in Herbert J. Storing, ed., *The Complete Anti-Federalist* (Chicago: University of Chicago Press, 1981), vol. 6, at 160–61; "Essays by a [Maryland] Farmer" (probably John Francis Mercer), no. V, March 28, 1788, in ibid., vol. 5, at 50. See also Storing, ed., *Complete Anti-Federalist* 1:22–23; and the works included in Josephine F. Pacheco, ed., *To Secure the Blessings of Liberty: Rights in American History* (Fairfax, Va.: George Mason University Press, 1993).

would undermine one of the basic preconditions for republican government. "Brutus" cautioned: "In a republic, the manners, sentiments, and interests of the people should be similar. If this be not the case, there will be a constant clashing of opinions." Whereas Madison argued that diversity within the United States would limit the effects of factions, Brutus claimed that a legislature representing states and people with diverse climates, laws, customs, and wealth "would be composed of such heterogeneous and discordant principles, as would constantly be contending with each other." More specifically, he and other Anti-Federalists expressed concern that there was so much religious diversity within the United States that religion could not provide a common foundation for the kinds of public morality necessary for republican government.[10]

According to these thinkers, two related advantages of small republics were the people's attachment to their representatives and the latter's responsiveness to the former. Richard Henry Lee wrote that within each state, "opinion founded on the knowledge of those who govern, procures obedience without force." But he claimed that in "so widely extended a country" as the entire United States, the people could not remain attached by proximity to their rulers and "force [would] become[] necessary to secure the purposes of civil government." Brutus agreed that in a large republic such as the United States, the people "will have no confidence in their legislature, suspect them of ambitious views, be jealous of every measure they adopt, and will not support the laws they pass." He and his colleagues claimed that these tendencies would be exacerbated by the federal Constitution's insulation of representatives from popular control and by its requiring only shallow participation in government by the people at large.[11]

Leading Anti-Federalists offered these types of arguments, along with others, to support their position that the states should remain the primary political units within America. It is apparent that vocal critics of the Constitution initially advocated preserving the fabric established by the Articles of Confederation, article II of which declared that each state "retain[ed] its sovereignty, freedom, and independence." Yet many of these persons conceded eventually that existing forms were inadequate to secure the likely advantages of united states. In any event, ratification

[10] See "Essays of Brutus," no. I, October 18, 1787, in Storing, ed., *Complete Anti-Federalist* 2:369–90. See also Richard Henry Lee, "Letters from the Federal Farmer," no. II, October 9, 1787, in ibid., vol. 2, at 231–32, for an argument that an inability to agree on a bill of rights would be an argument against forming one society. See generally *Complete Anti-Federalist* 1:22–23.

[11] See Richard Henry Lee, Letter to Samuel Adams, April 28, 1788, in *Documentary History of Ratification* 2:765–66; "Essays of Brutus," no. I, October 18, 1787, in Storing, ed., *Complete Anti-Federalist* 2:371. See also Lee, "Letters from the Federal Farmer," nos. III and VII, October 10 and December 31, 1787, in ibid., vol. 2, at 234–35 and 264–65. See generally *Complete Anti-Federalist*, vol. 1, chs. 1, 3, 6, and 7.

became likely. But Anti-Federalists remained opposed to what they perceived as the consolidating tendencies of the proposed Constitution: the possibility of a complete national government in place of state governments or capable of overrunning them. As a compromise position, efforts shifted to protecting state powers, reinforcing limits on the central government's authority, and ameliorating the alleged dangers of a national government within the areas of its authority.[12]

A number of the Anti-Federalists' objections to the Constitution's omission of a bill of rights and their later calls for amendments flowed from these "republican" concerns. On the surface, their arguments predominantly emphasized the need to limit the national government's powers. Richard Henry Lee, for example, warned that "men who govern, will in doubtful cases, construe laws and constitutions most favourably for increasing their own powers." In light of this natural tendency for governmental powers to expand, he advised, "all wise and prudent people, in forming constitutions, have drawn the line, and carefully described the powers parted with and the powers reserved." He declared that a bill of rights would "fix limits" that would be "plainly seen by those who are governed, as well as by those who govern." He claimed the rulers would know these limits could not be "passed unperceived by [the people], and without giving a general alarm." Hugh Henry Brackenridge likewise advised declaring "what powers are not given" rather than relying solely on the Constitution's enumeration of powers given, while other proponents of a bill of rights emphasized how the people could appeal to it "for the vindication of their wrongs in courts of justice."[13]

Anti-Federalists also pointed out that bills of rights could protect majorities as well as minorities. "Agrippa" (probably James Winthrop) explained that a declaration of rights "serves to secure the minority against the usurpation and tyranny of the majority." He cautioned that "unbridled passions produce the same effect, whether in a king, nobility, or a mob." But Agrippa also alluded to the possibility that a bill of rights

---

[12] See generally *Complete Anti-Federalist*, vol. 1, chs. 3, 4, and 5.

[13] See Lee, "Letters from the Federal Farmer," nos. II and IV, October 9 and 12, 1787, in ibid., vol. 2, at 231–32 and 248; Brackenridge, "Cursory Remarks" (1788), in Bernard Schwartz, ed., *The Bill of Rights* (New York: McGraw-Hill, 1971), vol. 1, at 522 (like Wilson, Brackenridge emphasized the imprecise nature both of delegations and reservations. He drew a useful analogy: "What is the nature of a bill of rights? 'It is a schedule or inventory of those powers which Congress do not possess.' But if it is clearly ascertained what powers they have, what need of a catalogue of those powers they have not? Ah! there is the mistake. A minister preaching, undertook, first, to show what was in his text; second, what was not in it. When it is specified what powers are given, why not also what powers are not given? A bill of rights is wanting, and all those things which are usually secured under it"); "The Address and Reasons of Dissent of the Minority of the Convention of Pennsylvania to Their Constituents," December 18, 1787, in Storing, ed., *Complete Anti-Federalist* 3:162.

might protect the people as a whole from tyranny by an aristocratic elite. He warned that "as a just government protects all alike, it is necessary that the sober and industrious part of the community should be defended from the rapacity and violence of the vicious and idle." As indicated, a recurring criticism of the Constitution was that it would enable a governing elite to promote their interests at the expense of the general welfare within broader communities. Many Anti-Federalists expressed such concerns as reasons for favoring a formal declaration of limitations on governmental authority.[14]

But not all the Constitution's critics conceived of bills of rights only as limitations on government. According to Brutus, such a document should also include a clear statement of the principles "upon which the social compact is founded." Similarly, Agrippa argued that a bill of rights "ought to set forth the purposes for which the compact is made." Herbert J. Storing has explained that bills of rights at the time typically served as preambles, "often of an exhortatory kind," that could serve to promote republican virtue among citizens as well as provide standards for evaluating governmental actions. In addition to enumerating limitations on governmental powers, bills of rights contained authoritative statements of the purposes of government, including the rights to be secured by it.[15]

Richard Henry Lee explained one of the reasons for affirming first principles in governing charters:

> We do not by declarations change the nature of things, or create new truths, but we give existence, or at least establish in the minds of the people truths and principles which they might never otherwise have thought of, or soon forgot. If a nation means its system, religious or political, shall have duration, it ought to recognize the leading principles of them in the front page of every family book.

Thus it was possible to regard bills of rights as important instruments of public education. According to one Anti-Federalist, these charters provided "the first lesson of the young citizens."[16]

In sum, critics of the Constitution indicated that a bill of rights could serve at least two salutary purposes. First, it would provide authoritative

---

[14] See "Letters of Agrippa" (accredited to James Winthrop), no. XVI, February 5, 1788, in *Complete Anti-Federalist* 4:111. See also George Mason, "Objections to the Constitution of Government formed by the Convention" (1787), in ibid., vol. 2, at 11–13. See generally *Complete Anti-Federalist* 1, ch. 6.

[15] See "Essays of Brutus," no. II, November 1, 1787, in *Complete Anti-Federalist* 2:372; "Letters of Agrippa," no. XVI, February 5, 1788, in ibid., vol. 4, at 111; ibid., vol. 1, at 70. State constitutions and bills of rights are reprinted in Schwartz, ed., *Bill of Rights* 1:231– 379.

[16] Lee, "Letters from the Federal Farmer," no. XVI, January 20, 1788, in Storing, ed., *Complete Anti-Federalist* 2:324; Letter from "A Delegate Who Has Catched a Cold," June 25, 1788, in ibid., vol. 5, at 273.

standards for scrutinizing and, if necessary, checking exercises of governmental power. The government's compliance with these limitations would make it more worthy of the people's obedience and respect. Second, the formal declaration would serve as a charter proclaiming fundamental principles of republican government. Hence it would help to foster republican virtue among the citizenry. In both ways, a bill of rights could promote republican sentiment, or attachment to government.

Attachment to Good Government

In the 84th *Federalist*, Alexander Hamilton responded directly to criticism of the proposed Constitution owing to the absence of a bill of rights. His position was similar to that articulated by Madison in his letter to Jefferson. Hamilton repeated arguments that security for rights would depend primarily on governmental structures rather than "verbal and nominal distinctions" or "volumes of aphorisms."

The Federalists lost this argument. The constitutional text now has a bill of rights. The express prohibitions are "parchment guarantees." Even so, those of Federalist persuasion could continue to argue that the effectiveness of these guarantees would depend on the proper functioning of governmental structures. Those of Anti-Federalist persuasion, in contrast, could emphasize the importance of the affirmative limitations.

Federalist and Anti-Federalist arguments converged, however, in attaching importance to public opinion. Echoing Anti-Federalists' arguments about the importance of governmental dependence upon the people, but doing so from a distinctively Federalist perspective, Hamilton argued in the 84th *Federalist* that security for rights "must altogether depend on public opinion, and on the general spirit of the people and of the government." He claimed, moreover, that such public opinion "must be the only solid basis of all our rights." He was building on Madison's arguments earlier in *The Federalist* that the national government would be "substantially dependent upon the great body of the citizens of the United States." Those arguments overlapped positions taken by proponents of state power.[17]

Yet there were subtle differences between Federalist and Anti-Federalist

[17] See Hamilton, *The Federalist*, no. 84, at 514–15; Madison, *The Federalist*, nos. 46 and 51. Federalists endorsed Anti-Federalist arguments that public opinion would provide necessary foundations for constitutional government. Disagreements between the Constitution's proponents and opponents were more subtle: whether pubic opinion would support an extended republic, which pubic sentiments were required, how the necessary public virtues could be fostered, and through what institutions public opinion could constrain exercises of governmental power.

positions on the importance of public opinion. Madison, in claiming that the national government would be "dependen[t] on the people," was referring in part to electoral constraints. In the 51st *Federalist*, he emphasized the fact that appointments to each department would be channeled independently as a way of guaranteeing that no department would be dependent on any other. Earlier, he had similarly argued that "republican liberty" depended not only on all power's being derived from the people but also on keeping those entrusted with power "in dependence on the people by a short duration of their appointments."[18]

Madison had referred, however, to another form of governmental "dependence" on the people: its dependence on "public opinion," or "prejudices of the community." In the context of arguing against periodic or frequent constitutional referenda, he claimed that such referenda would "carry an implication of some defect in the government." They would "disturb[] the public tranquility" and deprive the government of "that veneration which time bestows on everything, and without which perhaps the wisest and freest governments would not possess the requisite stability." Thus he suggested that a "constitutional road to the decision of the people" should be reserved only for "certain great and extraordinary occasions."[19]

Furthermore, he argued that in many cases the people at large would not effectively check constitutional abuse by governmental officials. He claimed that the legislative branch in a representative government was more likely than the other branches to exceed delegated powers by "everywhere extending the sphere of its activity and drawing all power into its impetuous vortex." He explained that state constitutions had relied on "parchment barriers" to oppose "the encroaching spirit of power," but he indicated that experience had proved the inefficacy of those provisions. He suggested that one reason enumerated rights had been ineffective in the face of unconstitutional actions was that legislative powers were "more extensive, and less susceptible of precise limits." Thus he claimed that a legislature could "mask, under complicated and indirect measures,

---

[18] See *The Federalist*, no. 51, at 321–22; *The Federalist*, no. 37, at 227. In the latter passage, Madison treated the government's "energy and stability" as considerations that *opposed* republican liberty. He explained: "Stability, *on the contrary*, requires that the hands in which power is lodged should continue for a length of time the same." His later argument that energy and stability in government were necessary for good government and that good government would protect the people's rights suggest that he did not follow his earlier treatment of relationships among liberty, energy, and stability.

[19] See *The Federalist*, no. 49, at 314–15. Among other things, Madison commented on Thomas Jefferson's proposal that Virginia's constitution provide for periodic appeals to the people to settle constitutional controversies within the state. See also Madison's discussion in the 50th *Federalist* of the Pennsylvania constitution's establishment of a Council of Censors to check constitutional abuse by legislative and executive officials.

the encroachments it makes on the co-ordinate departments." In addition, he suggested that the legislative department would have an advantage over the others in conventions of the people, both in "pleading their cause most successfully with the people" and in "constitut[ing] themselves as judges." Finally, he warned that the people's deliberations would be swayed by preexisting party factions rather than the "true merits of the question." His conclusion on this issue epitomized his skepticism about the general populace's trustworthiness as constitutional arbiters: "The *passions*, therefore, not the *reason*, of the public would sit in judgment."[20]

Madison argued, moreover, that neither "demarcations on parchment" nor direct appeals to the people would provide "a sufficient guard against those [legislative] encroachments which [might] lead to a tyrannical concentration of all the powers of government in the same hands." In the absence of "external" controls, he urged, the only way for "maintaining in practice the necessary partition of power as laid down in the Constitution" was "by so contriving the interior structure of the government as that its several constituent parts may, by their mutual relations, be the means of keeping each other in their proper places." As a result, the "constant aim" was to "divide and arrange the several offices in such a manner that each may be a check on the other."[21]

Madison relied on this principle to defend proposed constitutional structures. Dividing Congress into two branches would weaken the legislative department. On the other hand, giving the president a qualified veto over legislation would "fortify" the executive. He also emphasized "internal" checks when summarizing what he conceived to be the central paradox of constitutional government: "[Y]ou must first enable the government to control the governed; and in the next place oblige it to control itself."[22]

Madison pointed out, however, that the Constitution did not rely *solely* on "internal" checks. He emphasized that with the "compound" division of political authority in America, state *governments* would check the federal *government*, and vice versa. He explained that under the Constitution, "the power surrendered by the people [would be] first divided be-

---

[20] *The Federalist*, no. 49, at 308–10 and 316–17. Cf. *The Federalist*, no. 45, at 291, on how legislators were expected to influence the people. See also *The Federalist*, no. 50, for Madison's assumption that the people would typically act in accord with their passions rather than their reason.

[21] *The Federalist*, nos. 48 and 51, at 313 and 320–22.

[22] *The Federalist*, no. 51, at 322–23. Cf. Madison's comments in the 44th *Federalist*, at 286, on checks against efforts by Congress to exceed the authority delegated by the necessary and proper clause: "In the first instance, the success of the usurpation will depend on the executive and judiciary departments." See also Hamilton's similar arguments in the 33rd *Federalist*, at 203.

tween two distinct governments, and then the portion allotted to each
[would be] subdivided among separate departments." Thus he claimed
that federal structures would provide "a double security" for the people's
rights: "The different governments will control each other, at the same
time that each will be controlled by itself."[23]

Madison and Hamilton assumed that abuses of power by the central
government would abridge prerogatives reserved to state governments
and/or their citizens. These thinkers also relied on the fact that "[p]ower
[is] almost always the rival of power." Accordingly, they claimed that if
the central government exceeded constitutional limits, state legislatures
would be "ever ready to mark the innovation."[24]

Furthermore, Madison and Hamilton argued that state governments
would "have the advantage" in conflicts with the United States government. In this context, Madison again emphasized constitutional structures by relying on the fact that the states would be "constituent and
essential parts of the federal government; whilst the latter is nowise essential to the operation or organization of the former." Hamilton likewise
relied on the closer proximity between the people and state legislatures in
arguing that the latter would "possess[] all the organs of civil power and
the confidence of the people" and could "adopt a regular plan of opposition, in which they can combine all the resources of the community."
Madison explained, more specifically, that state legislatures could oppose
federal representatives directly by replacing senators and/or indirectly by
influencing elections to the House and the Presidency.[25]

The thrust of these arguments was that the states, like "auxiliary pre-

[23] See The Federalist, no. 51, at 323.

[24] See Hamilton, The Federalist, no. 28, at 181; Madison, The Federalist, no. 44, at 286.
See also Hamilton's claim in the 26th Federalist, at 172 (he suggested that state legislatures
"will always be not only vigilant but suspicious and jealous guardians of the rights of the
citizens against encroachments from the federal government . . . and will be ready enough,
if anything improper appears, to sound the alarm to the people, and not only to be the
VOICE, but, if necessary, the ARM of their discontent"); Hamilton's argument in the 28th
Federalist, at 181 (he presumed that "the general government will at all times stand ready to
check the usurpations of the state governments, and these will have the same disposition
towards the general government"); and his argument in the 60th Federalist, at 367 (attempts by the federal government to exclude states from representation "could never be
made without causing an immediate revolt of the great body of the people, headed and
directed by the State governments").

[25] See Madison, The Federalist, no. 45, at 290–91; Hamilton, The Federalist, no. 28, at
181. See also Hamilton, ibid., no. 32, at 197 (he claimed that contests between the federal
and state governments "will be most apt to end to the disadvantage of the Union"); Madison, ibid., no. 46, at 294–96 (he assumed likewise that "the first and most natural attachment of the people will be to the governments of their respective States"). Madison similarly
claimed in the 44th Federalist, at 286, that if the federal government misconstrued its
powers, state legislatures would "sound the alarm to the people, and exert their local influence in effecting a change of the federal representatives."

cautions" within the federal government, would further obviate the need for the people at large to participate directly in overseeing or checking government. According to Hamilton, state legislatures would have "better means of information" than the people at large. Thus he assumed that the former could "readily communicate with each other in the different States, and unite their common forces." As had Madison, Hamilton suggested that the states would serve as intermediaries between the people and the central government in a manner that would keep the former from becoming distant, unresponsive, or unaccountable.[26]

Although Federalists did not deny the people's ultimate authority to act independently of government, they endorsed components of the constitutional design that would channel political participation by the people through established institutions. Madison applauded the ability of state legislatures to "exert their local influence in effecting a change of federal representatives." Hamilton claimed that the people would "hold the scales" in controversies between the two governments, but he contemplated actions by the people predominantly *through* established *governmental* institutions. He explained: "If [the people's] rights are invaded by either [government], they can make use of the other as the instrument of redress." Hamilton assumed that extreme abuses of power by the federal government might lead to "an immediate revolt by the great body of the people," but he also assumed such a revolt would be "headed and directed by the State governments."[27]

As these passages indicate, Madison and Hamilton relied on the ability of state governments to serve important constitutional functions by mediating the people's sentiments in ways that would complement the Constitution's primary structures for insulating federal representatives from factions among the people. Both individuals suggested that popular sentiments should be channeled, if possible, through established institutions even when "auxiliary precautions" within the federal government failed to check abuses of power. In those cases, state governments would

[26] See Hamilton, *The Federalist*, no. 28, at 181. See also Hamilton's argument in the 84th *Federalist*, at 516, where he claimed that impediments to prompt communication among the people would be "overbalanced by the effects of the vigilance of the State governments." He continued: "The executive and legislative bodies of each State will be so many sentinels over the persons employed in every department of the national administration."

[27] Madison, *The Federalist*, no. 44, at 286 (he also claimed that the success of a usurpation of power by Congress would ultimately depend on "the people, who can, by the election of more faithful representatives, annul the acts of the usurpers"); Hamilton, *The Federalist*, nos. 28, 31, and 60, at 181, 197, and 367. In the 60th *Federalist*, at 367, Hamilton gave an example of when the people might revolt against the federal government: if it attempted "to promote the election of some favorite class of men in exclusion of others by confining the places of election to particular districts and rendering it impractical to the citizens at large to partake in the choice."

provide an additional type of "auxiliary precaution" capable of further mediating political activity by the people themselves.

Madison and Hamilton hoped, however, that the people's most important sentiments, their attachment to the national government itself, would not be mediated through institutions of state government. They expected the people to decide for themselves that the national government's actions warranted their approval and acquiescence. Madison suggested, for example, that the people might give greater allegiance to the national government than to the states, despite all the advantages in the states' favor, based on "such manifest and irresistible proofs of a better administration as will overcome all their antecedent propensities." He claimed, moreover, that "the people ought not surely to be precluded from giving most of their confidence where they may discover it to be most due."[28]

These arguments summed up the Federalists' response to Anti-Federalist criticisms of the extended republic and their arguments for reserving the most important powers to the smaller, more homogeneous states. According to leading Federalists, the kind of republican sentiment, or public opinion, that mattered most was attachment to good government. The Constitution's proponents thus offered to measure its success by whether federal structures instilled that type of attachment even without close proximity between rulers and ruled and without high levels of direct participation by the people in government.

FUNDAMENTAL MAXIMS OF FREE GOVERNMENT

Madison eventually defended adding a bill of rights to the United States Constitution. He never backed away from his premise that governmental structures rather than "parchment barriers" or "verbal and nominal distinctions" would provide the most important foundations for the people's attachment to government. But he added important glosses to those arguments.

Even before submitting proposed amendments to Congress, Madison implicitly qualified his arguments in *The Federalist* that it was possible to control the effects but not the causes of faction. After explaining the reasons for his ambivalence about enumerating rights in his 1788 letter to Jefferson, Madison identified two possible advantages of such a listing. In

---

[28] *The Federalist*, no. 46, at 295. See also Hamilton's comment in the 32nd *Federalist*, at 197, that all conjectures regarding the balance of power between the federal and state governments are "extremely vague and fallible." He suggested that everything must be left to "the firmness and prudence of the people" in maintaining a "constitutional equilibrium between the general and State governments." Here again he emphasized political practices rather than parchment limitations.

this context, he endorsed Anti-Federalist arguments that enumerated rights could serve educative functions:

> 1. The political truths declared in that solemn manner acquire by degrees the character of fundamental maxims of free Government, and as they become incorporated with the national sentiment, counteract the impulses of interest and passion.

In addition, he partially retreated from his earlier arguments that "parchment barriers" were inefficacious in controlling the effects of faction:

> 2. Altho. it be generally true as stated that the danger of oppression lies in the interested majorities of the people rather than in usurped acts of the Government, yet there may be occasions on which the evil may spring from the latter source; and on such [occasions], a bill of rights will be a good ground for an appeal to the sense of the community.

Both arguments linked enumerated rights to public opinion and governmental structures.[29]

His argument, in brief, was that a bill of rights might directly shape public opinion by fostering a "national sentiment" protective of rights. The "fundamental maxims of free Government" would oppose "impulses of interest and faction" that might otherwise lead a majority of the community to invade private rights by acting *through* government. Instilling a "national sentiment" protective of rights would complement the Constitution's other means of diffusing factional tendencies. As with many of the checks described in *The Federalist*, the desired result would be to preclude actions other than those in accord with rights of citizens and "the permanent and aggregate interests of the community."[30]

The check provided by "public sentiment" would be distinctive in an important respect. As explained above, Madison argued in the 10th *Federalist* that the causes of faction could not be controlled. His underlying assumptions were that (1) the people's impulses followed their interests and passions, and (2) their actions followed a coincidence of impulse and opportunity. He therefore assumed that the people would act based on majority interests or passions unless the majority, "by their number and local situation, [were] unable to concert and carry into effect schemes of

---

[29] *Papers of James Madison* 11:298–99. It is particularly dangerous to assume that Madison merely presented his own views in this letter. In this context, as with his remarks to the House, his arguments on the possible advantages of enumerating rights were apparently influenced by other thinkers (such as Jefferson) and by the views of his constituents (including those in Virginia who had demanded constitutional amendments).

[30] In the 10th *Federalist*, at 78, Madison defined "factions" as "a number of citizens, whether amounting to a majority or minority of the whole, who are united *and actuated* by some common impulse of passion, or of interest, adverse to the rights of other citizens, or to the permanent and aggregate interests of the community" (emphasis added).

oppression." Thus he sought to preclude (1) a coincidence of interests or passions among a majority of citizens except on principles of justice and the common good or (2) action in accordance with any majority impulses of interest or passion except as provided.[31]

He implicitly qualified these assumptions by suggesting that a national bill of rights could "counteract the impulses of interest and faction." He thereby assumed that a majority of the people might *not* act based on a coincidence of interest or passion and opportunity. He was unclear on whether he was assuming that (1) the people's impulses would not follow their interests and passions and/or (2) their actions would not follow their impulses. Anti-Federalist positions and variations of Federalist positions were consistent with both of these possibilities and with a third: (3) a bill of rights might shape perceptions of interest and/or formation of passions. In any of these ways, a bill of rights might constrain the formation and operation of "factions," as Madison defined them.

His reference to a second benefit of enumerating rights was silent on a different issue: who would "appeal to the sense of the community" if the government "usurped" power contrary to that sense? Madison's remarks to the House were more explicit on this issue. In those remarks, he identified two ways that a bill of rights might have a "salutary effect against the abuse of power." First, he claimed that "independent tribunals of justice [would] consider themselves in a peculiar manner the guardians of those rights; they [would] be an impenetrable bulwark against every assumption of power in the legislative or executive." In this passage, he anticipated judicial enforcement of enumerated rights. Second, he suggested that "State Legislatures [would] jealously and closely watch the operations of th[e Federal] Government, and be able to resist with more effect every assumption of power, than any other Government on earth can do." Thus he speculated that a bill of rights would reinforce the states' ability to act as "sure guardians of the people's liberty."[32]

Reinforcing Judicial Fortitude

In the 78th *Federalist*, Hamilton had claimed that federal judges would have an unconditional obligation to enforce the Constitution, even

---

[31] See *The Federalist*, no. 10, at 78–81, esp. at 81 ("If the impulse and the opportunity be sufficient to coincide, we well know that neither moral nor religious motives can be relied on as an adequate control"). See also Madison, Letter to Jefferson, October 17, 1788 (quoted above in the text accompanying n. 5).

[32] *Annals*, at 439 (June 8, 1789). On March 15, 1789, Jefferson had written Madison: "In the arguments in favor of a declaration of rights, you omit one which has great weight with me, the legal check which it puts into the hands of the judiciary." The letter is in Boyd, ed., *Papers of Thomas Jefferson* 14:659.

against the people themselves and their elected representatives. He presumed that the people would have a right "to alter or abolish the established Constitution whenever they [found] it inconsistent with their happiness." But he argued that the supreme law would be binding upon the people "collectively, as well as individually," until they had "by some solemn and authoritative act, annulled or changed the established forms." Moreover, he emphasized that the people's elected representatives would also be bound by the Constitution unless and until it was formally amended. His position, in brief, was that governmental officials would not be justified in violating the fundamental law "whenever a momentary inclination happen[ed] to lay hold of a majority of their constituents."[33]

Hamilton acknowledged, however, that in practice governmental officials occasionally might not comply with constitutional limitations even though the officials had an obligation to do so and even taking into account the many "internal" checks set up by the Constitution. As a result, he recognized that judges might be called on to check abuses of power by the legislative and executive branches. He suggested that judges would be positioned to "guard the Constitution and the rights of individuals" even without a formal declaration of rights.[34]

[33] See Hamilton, *The Federalist*, no. 78, at 469–70. See also ibid., at 470 (according to Hamilton, "no presumption, or even knowledge of the [people's] sentiments, can warrant their representatives in a departure from [the Constitution] prior to such an act [of amendment]"). Hamilton's arguments on the obligations of governmental officials to comply with the Constitution notwithstanding contrary popular sentiments complemented arguments for insulating governmental officials from the people. His common theme was that government would mitigate factional tendencies of popular government. (Note in this connection that article VI of the Constitution requires the President to take an oath to "preserve, protect and defend the Constitution of the United States.") Madison took a similar position in the First Congress in the context of debates over whether to enumerate a right of the people to instruct their representatives. According to the *Annals*, at 733–47 (August 15, 1789), he observed that "the inhabitants of any district" do not "speak the voice of the people; so far from it, their ideas may contradict the sense of the whole people." He indicated that "the people [could] change the constitution if they please[d]." But he claimed that "while the constitution exists, they must conform themselves to its dictates." His position, in other words, was that part of "the people" could not legitimately "contravene an act established by the whole people." He concluded, therefore, that it was "not true" that "the people have a right to instruct their representatives in such a sense as that the delegates are obliged to conform to those instructions."

[34] *The Federalist*, no. 78. In the 33rd *Federalist*, at 203, Hamilton conceded that the central government might "overpass the just bounds of its authority." Madison likewise acknowledged in the 44th *Federalist*, at 285, that Congress might "misconstrue" its powers. He noted that "the success of the usurpation will depend [in the first instance] on the executive and judiciary departments, which are to expound and give effect to the legislative acts; and in the last resort a remedy must be obtained by the people, who can, by the election of more faithful representatives, annul the acts of the usurpers" (ibid., at 286).

In this context, Hamilton defended the permanent tenure of federal judges and presented classic arguments for judicial review. He suggested that the judiciary's ability to serve as "bulwarks of a limited Constitution" would depend on the judges being "independent" from the other branches and from factional sentiments among the people at large. Emphasizing again how the Constitution—even in its original form—would provide security for popular rights, he declared that "nothing [would] contribute so much as [permanent tenure] to that independent spirit in the judges which must be essential to the faithful performance of so arduous a duty."[35]

Hamilton conceded, however, that judges might still shirk their constitutional responsibilities under some circumstances. He remarked that "it would require an uncommon portion of fortitude in the judges to do their duty as faithful guardians of the Constitution, where legislative invasions of it had been instigated by the major voice of the community." In brief, he recognized that judges would be no match for legislative power backed by predominant popular sentiment.[36]

These comments on the limits, in practice, of judicial power complemented Hamilton's claim that the judiciary would be "the least dangerous to the political rights of the Constitution." He pointed out that judges had "neither FORCE nor WILL but merely judgment." Judges could not even carry out their own decisions, since the judiciary "must ultimately depend upon the aid of the executive even for the efficacy of its judgments." On this issue, Hamilton was largely in agreement with the skeptical Madison: "Wherever there is an interest and power to do wrong, wrong will generally be done."[37]

Madison recognized, however, that a bill of rights would change this equation. As explained above, he suggested that such a declaration would fortify judges by providing formal status to "fundamental maxims of free Government." The constitutional text would purportedly be evidence of the people's *considered* judgments. Declaring rights "in that solemn manner" would make it explicit, as part of America's "supreme law," that legislative and executive officials were obliged to follow principles of republican government rather than momentary inclinations.

Madison assumed in his remarks to the House that judges would "consider themselves in a peculiar manner the guardians of those rights." Notwithstanding his earlier skepticism regarding the political efficacy of enumerated rights, he claimed that judges would be "naturally led to resist every encroachment upon rights expressly stipulated for in the constitu-

---

[35] *The Federalist*, no. 78, at 465–72.
[36] Ibid., at 470.
[37] Ibid., at 465; Madison, Letter to Jefferson, October 17, 1788, in *Papers of James Madison* 11:298.

tion by the declaration of rights." Judges could base their decisions on explicit prohibitions, not only on unwritten principles of fundamental law and the negative implications of constitutional delegations.[38]

Points of Departure

The sources examined above offer several overlapping points of departure for analyzing constitutional developments since the founding period. First, one may evaluate the design and functioning of legislative and executive structures. Second, one may question whether federal judges have, in practice, acted as "impenetrable bulwarks" against violations of constitutional norms. Third, one may examine the political consequences of the constitutional text's inclusion of express prohibitions such as those contained in the Bill of Rights. Fourth, one may study the roles state officials have played in constitutional controversies—including their ability to act on behalf of "the people" in opposing allegedly impermissible exercises of national power. Fifth, one may address questions about how public opinion has fit within equations of governing power.

Each set of issues has many components. For example, Madison argued that representative structures would promote "the permanent and aggregate interests of the community" while providing security for "rights" of individuals. Accordingly, his arguments provide tentative criteria for evaluating the practical functioning of governmental structures. What "rights," "interests," and other ends have governmental officials actually advanced? How might governmental structures be redesigned to achieve these ends more effectively? Are representing diverse interests, seeking the collective welfare, and protecting individual autonomy consistent with one another and with principles of popular sovereignty? What other objectives should government pursue? These remain open questions.

There are further problems involving the evaluation of judicial opinions and the actual effects of express prohibitions such as those contained in the Bill of Rights. In his remarks to the House, Madison presupposed that judges would rely on *express* prohibitions. According to the *Annals*, he did not in that context call attention to the possibility of federal judges' relying on the ninth amendment or the idea of *unenumerated* rights. Nor did he comment on whether judges would rely on the tenth amendment and principles of federalism. These issues would be important, as would

---

[38] See *Annals*, at 439 (June 8, 1789). See also Jefferson's letter to Madison, quoted in n. 32, above; and Wayne D. Moore, "Written and Unwritten Constitutional Law in the Founding Period: The Early New Jersey Cases," 7 Constl. Comm. 341 (1990) (examines relationships among written and unwritten norms, public opinion, judicial powers, and actions by legislative and executive officials).

questions about whether (and how) the Bill of Rights and other parts of the constitutional text would affect decisions by federal and state legislative and executive officials. State officials, for example, have repeatedly relied on the tenth amendment and guarantees of rights to oppose assertions of national power. Problems of federalism and subsequent developments (such as the reconstruction amendments) would further complicate these matters.

There are also numerous vantage points for studying the relevance of public opinion within the constitutional scheme. One may question, for example, whether judges have acted independently of public opinion, as Hamilton predicted. Federalist and Anti-Federalist arguments also suggest a need to consider, conversely, how constitutional provisions and governmental choices have affected popular culture. To what extent, for example, have presidential addresses and decisions by federal courts shaped citizens' conceptions of constitutional ideals? How have popular attitudes and actions influenced, in turn, decisions by legislative and executive officials? To what extent has the rhetoric of constitutional "rights" been prominent within popular culture, and how has it intersected with the rhetoric of "power"?

Individuals have used various techniques to study these types of issues. Modern technology has supported a proliferation of public opinion polls, including surveys to examine relationships between public attitudes and official actions. Individuals have also studied records of governmental deliberations, including judicial opinions, for general patterns of constitutional decision-making. Research tools have enabled analysts to evaluate the impact of judicial opinions and other governmental actions.

Instead of seeking, presenting, or defending general findings of this sort, my analysis in this book draws primarily on case studies and uses them to support more qualified conclusions. I study actual precedents that exemplify distinctive components of constitutional politics. But I generally hold open whether these precedents are representative of predominant practices.

Taney's and Curtis's analyses of constitutional issues in *Dred Scott*, for example, were prominent parts of antebellum political practices. In addition, these two judges' arguments offer models of judicial reasoning and provide access to distinctive conceptions of federal and state powers relating to slavery. Frederick Douglass exemplified forms of popular interpretive criticism. He also offered alternatives to Taney's and Curtis's conceptions of constitutional imperatives. Positions taken by Federalists and Anti-Federalists during debates over the Constitution's ratification and initial amending contribute to analyzing constitutional structures. More importantly, Federalist and Anti-Federalist perspectives also provide frameworks for identifying and evaluating current interpretive options.

The insights offered by these sources are significant independently of whether they were in accord with surrounding practices.

Remaining chapters examine additional precedents that shed further light on the problems of constitutional theory and practice at issue. In addition to studying cases in which judges have sought to enforce constitutional limits, I explore ways that legislative and executive officials have promoted collective ends and reinforced or limited popular choices. I also study efforts by state officials and other persons to protect separately held prerogatives.

The precedents examined below, like those already considered, exemplify diverse attributes of American constitutionalism. The people have, in practice, acted through representative structures and independently of them. Exercises of governmental power have both reinforced and constrained individual choices. Constitutional meaning and authority have continued to rest on complex configurations of political power. Founding aspirations have been realized in some respects, frustrated in others.

CHAPTER 6

Reconceiving Supreme Powers

[T]he government of the Union, though limited in its
powers, is supreme within its sphere of action.[1]

ONE OF THE Republic's first great controversies after the Constitution
went into effect concerned the United States government's establishment
and operation of a national bank. The controversy made it necessary to
confront fundamental questions about the character and scope of federal
and state governmental powers and their respective relationships to rights
and powers of the people at large. Precedents were set by each branch of
the federal government and at the state and local levels.

In 1791 Alexander Hamilton, as Secretary of the Treasury, introduced a
bill to establish a first Bank of the United States. As he conceived it, the
bank would serve as the federal government's principal depository and
fiscal agent, functions that Hamilton considered essential to developing a
vigorous national economy.[2] The Constitutional Convention had considered proposals to include in the constitutional text an express delegation
of power to grant charters of incorporation. But the proposals had
failed.[3]

There were serious questions about the constitutional validity of Ham-

---

[1] *McCulloch v. Maryland*, 17 U.S. (4 Wheat.) 316 (1819), at 405.

[2] Alexander Hamilton's "Report on a National Bank," December 14, 1790, is reprinted
in Harold C. Syrett, ed., *The Papers of Alexander Hamilton* (New York: Columbia University Press, 1963), vol. 7, at 305–42. For an account of House debates over the bank bill, see
Annals 2:1892–1960 (February 1–6, 1791). As explained in ch. 4, n. 39, the *Annals* for this
period were apparently based on the *Gazette of the United States*.

[3] See Max Farrand, ed., *The Records of the Federal Convention of 1787* (New Haven:
Yale University Press, 1966), vol. 2, at 325, 615–16, for an account of proceedings in the
Constitutional Convention of 1787 on this issue. For background on the bank controversy,
see generally M. St. Clair Clarke and D. A. Hall, eds., *Legislative and Documentary History
of the Bank of the United States: Including the Original Bank of North America* (Washington, D.C.: Gales and Seaton, 1832); Paul Finkelman, "The Constitution and the Intentions
of the Framers," 50 U. Pitt. L. Rev. 349 (1989), at 358–71; Gerald Gunther, ed., *John
Marshall's Defense of McCulloch v. Maryland* (Stanford, Calif.: Stanford University Press,
1960), at 1–21; Bray Hammond, *Banks and Politics in America from the Revolution to the
Civil War* (Princeton: Princeton University Press, 1957); John C. Miller, *The Federalist Era*
(New York: Harper and Row, 1960), ch. 4; Charles Warren, *The Supreme Court in United
States History* (Boston: Little, Brown, 1926), vol. 1, at 499–540.

ilton's bill. James Madison, in a speech to the House of Representatives, argued that Congress had neither express nor implied power to create a national bank.[4] Congress nevertheless approved the bill, and it was presented to President George Washington for his signature. The president requested opinions on the bank's validity from Attorney General Edmund Randolph and Secretary of State Thomas Jefferson. Both advocated a veto.[5] Washington submitted their arguments to Hamilton for rebuttal, and he defended the bill as within Congress's implied powers.[6] Despite continuing doubts about the bank's validity, Washington followed Hamilton's advice and signed the bill into law.[7]

During Madison's tenure as president, the political tides shifted dramatically. In 1811, during Madison's first term, the bank's charter expired. Congress initially declined to recharter the bank, then in 1814 passed a bill which Madison vetoed in January 1815.[8] In his veto message, Madison waived constitutional objections and focused on issues of public policy.[9] But he changed course at the policy level by declaring eleven months later in his annual message that "the probable operation of a national bank will merit consideration."[10] The Republican Congress approved a new bill to reestablish a national bank. This time, Madison signed the bill into law.[11]

The bank established branches that began to attract business away from competing state institutions. In response, Maryland enacted a law

---

[4] See *Annals* 2:1894–1902 (February 2, 1791); ibid., at 1956–60 (February 8, 1791). The speech is also reprinted in *Papers of James Madison* 13:372–81.

[5] Randolph's and Jefferson's opinions, dated February 12 and 15, 1791, respectively, are reprinted in Clarke and Hall, eds., *Legislative and Documentary History of the Bank*, at 86–94. Jefferson's opinion is also reprinted in Merrill D. Peterson, ed., *The Portable Thomas Jefferson* (New York: Viking, 1975), at 261–67.

[6] Hamilton's opinion, dated February 23, 1791, is reprinted in Clarke and Hall, eds., *Legislative and Documentary History of the Bank*, at 95–112; and in Syrett, ed., *Papers of Alexander Hamilton* 8:97–134.

[7] President Washington had requested Madison to draft a veto message, which is reprinted in *Papers of James Madison* 13:395.

[8] See Clarke and Hall, eds., *Legislative and Documentary History of the Bank*, chs. 3 and 4.

[9] President Madison's veto message, dated January 30, 1815, is reprinted in ibid., at 594–95.

[10] Madison's Annual Message, December 5, 1815, is reprinted in ibid., at 609.

[11] See ibid., at 713. Madison defended his signing the second bank bill in a letter to Mr. Ingersoll, June 25, 1831, which is reprinted in *Letters and Other Writings of James Madison* (Philadelphia: Lippincott, 1865), vol. 4, at 183–87. The letter echoed Marshall's opinion in *McCulloch* by emphasizing the importance of precedents as settling constitutional meanings. See also his comments in the 37th *Federalist*, at 229 (the meanings of obscure constitutional provisions would be "liquidated and ascertained by a series of particular discussions and adjudications").

that heavily taxed all banks doing business in the state that were not incorporated there. James McCulloch refused to pay the tax. After Maryland obtained a judgment against him, he appealed it to the United States Supreme Court.

In *McCulloch v. Maryland*,[12] the justices confronted two main questions. First, did Congress have authority to establish the bank? If so, could Maryland legitimately tax its operations?

Under the circumstances, it is not surprising that the justices upheld Congress's authority and invalidated the Maryland tax. But the reasoning that Chief Justice John Marshall used to defend these conclusions was remarkable. Instead of deciding the case on narrow grounds, the Chief Justice set broad precedents and announced general interpretive principles that would apply in a wide range of contexts.

The decision provoked substantial opposition. Judge Spencer Roane of Virginia, writing under the pen name "Hampden," argued that the Court had attempted to amend the Constitution by construction, in effect giving "a *general* letter of attorney to future legislators of the union." But Hampden denied that the judges had "power to adjudicate away the *reserved* rights of a sovereign member of the confederacy, and vest them in the government." Insofar as it purported to do so, it was "entirely extra-judicial, and without authority."[13]

Constitutional scholars have suggested that *McCulloch* had the effect that Hampden and his Republican allies feared. Endorsing James Boyd White's characterization, Sanford Levinson has used the case as his leading example of an "amendment" to the Constitution brought about by judicial decision-making.[14] He assumed the case was so "familiar" that it was unnecessary to "rehearse" its significance. According to Levinson,

---

[12] 17 U.S. (4 Wheat.) 316 (1819).

[13] Spencer Roane, "Hampden," Essay No. 1, published in the *Richmond Enquirer* (June 11, 1819), in Gunther, ed., *John Marshall's Defense of McCulloch*, at 111 (emphasis in original). In his introduction, Gunther includes background information on Hampden's four essays (published in the *Richmond Enquirer* between June 11 and 22, 1819), along with similar information on essays written by "Amphictyon" (probably Judge William Brockenbrough of Virginia) and published in the *Enquirer* between March 30 and April 2, 1819.

[14] See Levinson, "How Many Times Has the United States Constitution Been Amended?" in Levinson, ed., *Responding to Imperfection* (Princeton: Princeton University Press, 1995), at 21–26; Levinson, "Accounting for Constitutional Change (Or, How Many Times Has the United States Constitution Been Amended? (A) < 26; (B) 26; (C) > 26; (D) All of the Above)," 8 Constl. Comm. 409 (1991), at 418–21. In both versions of this essay, Levinson endorses James Boyd White's suggestion—in *When Words Lose Their Meaning* (Chicago: University of Chicago Press, 1984), at 263—that *McCulloch* was an "amendment" of the Constitution.

the Court's precedent "functional[ly] eliminat[ed] the tenth amendment and the necessary and proper clause as meaningful limits on the federal government."[15]

For reasons given below, I am not convinced the decision had such significance. The tenth amendment and the necessary and proper clause have continued to serve important functions in subsequent constitutional controversies. Even so, Marshall's opinion has undeniably left lasting legacies. Grasping their significance requires rethinking and not merely rehearsing much of what may be partially obscured by its familiarity.

INTERPRETING DELEGATED POWERS

Marshall began his opinion with two peculiar presumptions. First, he asserted that "the conflicting powers of the government of the Union and of its members, as marked in [the U.S.] constitution, are to be discussed." In addition, he assumed that the duty of deciding the controversy devolved on the Supreme Court "alone." He warned that the alternative was continued "hostility," perhaps even "hostility of a still more serious nature."

His reference to "conflicting powers" was ambiguous. There was obviously a conflict in practice between the national bank's functioning and Maryland's tax. But it would have been odd to assume that all competing political practices were constitutionally impermissible. Even assertions of judicial review entail such a conflict.[16]

The Chief Justice suggested that the case involved conflicting norms, not just conflicting practices. But it would have been circular to *assume*, at the outset of his opinion, that the national bank's functioning fell within delegated authority. Marshall devoted a substantial portion of his opinion to addressing precisely this issue.

One might treat Marshall's assertion as anticipating rather than presuming the positions he thereafter defended. But the second part of his opinion led to a conclusion that Maryland's tax on the national bank did *not* fall within the state's reserved powers. He eventually argued, in short, that there was *not* a conflict between federal and state authority. In the end, he concluded that there was delegated authority but not an opposing reservation.

---

[15] See Levinson, "Accounting for Constitutional Change," at 418. Levinson deleted this passage from his revised version of the essay included in *Responding to Imperfection*, though it is not clear whether he did so for stylistic or substantive reasons (or otherwise).

[16] Article I appears to contemplate conflict at least in the exercise of legislative and executive lawmaking powers. Conflicts between judicial (common law) and legislative (statutory) lawmaking also appear to be consistent with constitutional structures.

It appears that Marshall was laying a foundation to rebut arguments that Congress did not have authority to establish a bank because the Constitution reserved that power to the states. The Chief Justice did not confront that issue head on. But his invocation of the rhetoric of "conflicting powers" signaled his unwillingness to use the concept of reserved powers to rebut expansive interpretations of federal authority. His presumption set the tone, even though he subsequently denied there were conflicting prerogatives in *McCulloch*.

His claim of judicial interpretive authority was also anomalous. McCulloch had argued that because of prior practices, the validity of the national bank "was not now to be considered an open question." Marshall gave credence to that argument: "The principle now contested was introduced at a very early period of our history, has been recognized by many successive legislatures, and has been acted upon by the judicial department, in cases of peculiar delicacy, as a law of undoubted obligation." He explained that consistent practices would not preclude the justices from resisting "a bold and daring usurpation, . . . after an acquiescence still longer and more complete than this." But he characterized the issues in *McCulloch* as "doubtful"; he claimed that "the great principles of liberty [were] not concerned"; and he indicated that judicial invalidation was inappropriate because the controversy only involved "the respective powers of those who are equally the representatives of the people." Under these circumstances, he suggested that the constitutional issue, "if not put at rest by the practice of the government, ought to receive a considerable impression from that practice" and "ought not to be lightly disregarded."

In effect, Marshall endorsed ordinary representative processes as adequate for mediating constitutional conflicts in cases not involving "the great principles of liberty." He noted that the national bank's validity had been contested in "the fair and open field of debate, and afterwards in the executive cabinet." In a similar vein, he claimed later in the opinion that the only "security against the abuse" of the federal taxing power resided in "the structure of the government itself." The people "give to their government a right of taxing themselves and their property, . . . resting confidently on the interest of the legislator, and on the influence of the constituent over their representative, to guard them against its abuse." He suggested that similar principles applied to the federal government's exercise of its other powers and made duly enacted federal laws equally binding on the states, the people thereof, and their respective governments.[17]

---

[17] See *McCulloch*, 17 U.S. at 401–402 and 428. On the weight of constitutional precedents, including those created through "political" practices, Marshall concluded: "It would require no ordinary share of intrepidity, to assert that a measure adopted under these circumstances, was a bold and plain usurpation, to which the constitution gave no countenance" (ibid., at 402). On representative structures, he suggested that because "the legisla-

Marshall assumed that a necessary corollary of the Constitution's establishment as "supreme law" was that the Constitution itself and duly enacted laws bound state governments along with the people, separately as well as collectively. He explained:

> [T]he government of the Union, though limited in its powers, is supreme within its sphere of action. This would seem to result, necessarily from its nature. It is the government of all; its powers are delegated by all; it represents all, and acts for all. . . . The nation, on those subjects on which it can act, must necessarily bind its component parts.[18]

Maryland's counsel had not disputed these basic propositions. But they had argued that establishing the national bank did not fall within delegated authority; and they had claimed that state governments could, in any event, legitimately tax the bank's operations.[19]

Spheres Generally

Maryland's counsel had relied on a conception of relationships between federal and state governmental powers that Marshall acknowledged in his

---

ture acts upon its constituents," constitutional structures are usually "a sufficient security" (ibid., at 428). See also Marshall's position on "political" questions in *Marbury v. Madison*, 5 U.S. (1 Cranch) 137 (1803). In addition, as explained below, Marshall deferred to Congress on one of the pivotal issues in the case: the necessity of the bank as a means of executing express powers.

[18] *McCulloch*, 17 U.S. at 405. Alexander Hamilton presented a similar view of constitutional structures in the 33rd *Federalist*, commenting on the supremacy clause: "A LAW, by the very meaning of the term, includes supremacy. It is a rule which those to whom it is prescribed are bound to observe. This results from every political association. If individuals enter into a state of society, the laws of that society must be the supreme regulator of their conduct. If a number of political societies enter into a larger political society, the laws which the latter may enact, pursuant to the powers intrusted to it by its constitution, must necessarily be supreme over those societies and the individuals of whom they are composed" (*The Federalist*, no. 33, at 204). See also Madison, *The Federalist*, no. 44, at 287.

Marshall dismissed an argument that different principles applied to state governments because they had "sovereign powers." He emphasized that the Constitution had been "submitted to the *people*," from whom it "derive[d] its whole authority." He conceded that "[t]he assent of the states, in their sovereign capacity, [was] implied, in calling a convention, and thus submitting that instrument to the people." He also denied that the people's having acted "in their *states*" made their approval "measures of the state *governments*" (*McCulloch*, 17 U.S. at 403–404) (emphasis on "the people" in original; emphasis on "states" and "governments" added). According to Marshall, the American people, of necessity, had acted "in their states" rather than as "one common mass." Here, of course, he was referring to the "states" as political societies.

[19] See *McCulloch*, 17 U.S. at 330–52 and 362–77 (summary of Maryland counsel's arguments).

opinion. As the passage just quoted indicates, the Chief Justice conceded that the federal government had authority to act within a limited normative "sphere." He also presumed that state governments had authority to act within other spheres. He explained: "In America, powers of sovereignty are divided between the government of the Union, and those of the states. They are each sovereign, with respect to the objects committed to it, and neither sovereign, with respect to the objects committed to the other."[20] This passage evokes images of normative boundaries between powers held by the respective governments.

In a later decision, *Gibbons v. Ogden*, Marshall explained in greater detail his underlying assumptions:

> The genius and character of the whole government seems to be, that its action is to be applied to all the external concerns of the nation, and to those internal concerns which affect the states generally; but not to those which are completely within a particular state, which do not affect other states, and with which it is not necessary to interfere, for the purpose of executing some of the general powers of the government.[21]

Parts of *McCulloch* reflect similar interpretive aspirations. The Chief Justice claimed that measuring the states' reserved powers "by the extent of the sovereignty which the people in a single state possess" would make it possible to interpret federal and state authority as perfectly consistent:

> We have a principle which is safe for the states, and safe for the Union. We are relieved, as we ought to be, from clashing sovereignty; from interfering powers; from a repugnancy between a right in one government to pull down, what there is an acknowledged right in the other to build up.[22]

He assumed, in short, that the two levels of governments had authority to operate within separate normative spheres.

He suggested that these two spheres encompassed the federal government's delegated powers, at one level, and the states' reserved powers, at another. Furthermore, he endorsed the principle, supposedly "acknowledged by all," that the federal government was "one of enumerated powers." Thus he declared that the government "can exercise only the

---

[20] Ibid., at 410 (Marshall, C.J.).

[21] *Gibbons v. Ogden*, 22 U.S. (9 Wheat.) 1 (1824), at 195. Marshall described broadly the scope of the states' reserved powers: "that immense mass of legislation, which embraces everything within the territory of a state, not surrendered to the general government; all which can be most advantageously exercised by the states themselves. Inspection laws, quarantine laws, health laws of every description, as well as laws for regulating the internal commerce of a state, and those which respect turnpikes, ferries, &c., are component parts of this mass" (ibid., at 203).

[22] *McCulloch*, 17 U.S. at 430 (Marshall, C.J.). As explained below, Marshall used a similar approach to interpret the scope of *federal* powers.

powers granted to it," and he asserted that "the whole residuum of power" was reserved to the states.[23] On these issues, his arguments converged at a high level of generality with those of Maryland's counsel.

Marshall's interpretive assumptions were, however, significantly different from those of the attorneys. Among other things, Marshall drew a subtle but important distinction between the federal government's "enumerated" powers and those "delegated" or "granted" to it. He acknowledged that the power to establish a national bank was not among the federal government's "enumerated powers," but he argued that the bank was within the government's "delegated" authority. Thus he conceded that the government was "one of enumerated powers," but he did *not* concede it was one of *only* enumerated powers. He based this distinction on the tenth amendment, "general reasoning," and the original text's necessary and proper clause.[24]

The Chief Justice recognized that his interpretive approach would have been difficult to defend if proposals to conform the tenth amendment to a comparable provision in the Articles of Confederation had succeeded. He explained:

> Among the enumerated powers, we do not find that of establishing a bank or creating a corporation. But there is no phrase in the instrument which, like the articles of confederation, excludes incidental or implied powers; and which requires that everything granted shall be expressly and minutely described. Even the 10th amendment, which was framed for the purpose of quieting excessive jealousies which had been excited, omits the word "expressly," and declares only, that the powers "not delegated to the United States, nor prohibited to the states, are reserved to the states or to the people;" thus leaving the question, whether the particular power which may become the subject of contest, has been delegated to the one government, or prohibited to the other, to depend on a fair construction of the whole instrument.[25]

This passage is important. It relies on distinctions among enumerated, express, or general powers; and incidental, implied, or particular powers. Marshall later overlaid these distinctions with a dichotomy between governmental "ends" and "means" in a manner that set a precedent for a subtle shift in the terms of discourse. Furthermore, by assuming that a

---

[23] Ibid., at 405 and 410. Note, however, that the tenth amendment also refers to powers reserved "to the people." Marshall was most concerned in *McCulloch* with divisions of governmental power and assumed the people had committed the powers at issue to one government or the other.

[24] See ibid., at 405–406 and 411–12.

[25] Ibid., at 406.

power was *either* delegated to the federal government *or* prohibited to the states, he invoked a variation of prevalent conceptual premises even as he laid foundations for undercutting them. He assumed that federal and state powers were distinct, but he interpreted the federal government's implied powers as capable of displacing state powers. He likewise stood the tenth amendment on its head and skirted its main stumbling blocks. Rather than using the idea of reserved powers to rebut an interpretation of federal authority, he argued that exercises of federal power could displace exercises of state power.

The overall structure of his argument was as follows: Instead of using the tenth amendment to reinforce limits on federal authority, he relied on that amendment to rebut arguments that the federal government was confined to exercising *expressly* delegated powers. He also stood the tenth amendment on its head by assuming that some powers that *had* been delegated to the federal government *were* prohibited to the states and thus were *not* reserved to them. In short, rather than affirming the importance of powers that *were* reserved to the states and were *not* delegated to the federal government, he argued that particular powers *were* delegated to that government and were *not* reserved to the states. The structure of the tenth amendment, in contrast, assumes that some powers *not* delegated to the federal government were *not* prohibited to the states and *were* reserved to them. The amendment is silent on whether powers that *were* delegated to the former government were *also* reserved to the latter.

Beyond Spheres

Maryland's counsel (following the lead of Madison, Jefferson, and Randolph, among others) argued that the necessary and proper clause authorized a limited range of implied powers. Their position was that the necessary and proper clause did not authorize *all* means of exercising the express powers or accomplishing their objects—only those necessary and proper. Maryland's counsel urged the justices to scrutinize and uphold as *constitutional* limits the dual requirements of necessity and propriety.

The Chief Justice rejected restrictive interpretations of the necessary and proper clause. He argued that interpreting the clause narrowly would restrict Congress's powers and "abridge, and almost annihilate, this useful and necessary right of the legislature to select its means." He claimed that because the Constitution was "intended to endure for ages to come," its provisions must have been designed "to be adapted to the various *crises* of human affairs." He asserted that the national legislature had to have "the capacity to avail itself of experience, to exercise its reason, and to accommodate its legislation to circumstances" in ways that would not have been possible if it were confined to using means that were "indispensably necessary."[26]

He described the national bank as "necessary" in the broader sense of being "a convenient, a useful, and essential instrument in the prosecution of [Congress's] fiscal operations." In this connection, he compared the bank to other permissible exercises of federal power and claimed that "the right to carry the mail, and to punish those who rob it, is not indispensably necessary to the establishment of a post-office and post-road. This right is indeed essential to the beneficial exercise of the power, but not indispensably necessary to its existence."[27] His use of this example is particularly instructive, because he elaborated on it in subsequent essays.

In response to criticism of *McCulloch*, the Chief Justice used the pen names "A Friend of the Union" and "A Friend of the Constitution" to defend the Court's opinion through a series of essays published in the *Philadelphia Union* and the *Alexandria Gazette*.[28] In the latter essays he emphasized distinctions between "incidental" powers and "means" of exercising expressly delegated powers. Marshall described "[t]he law designating post offices and post roads, with all the provisions relating to that subject," as "means" chosen by Congress to execute the enumerated power. In contrast, he claimed that "the right to punish those who rob the mail is an incidental power, and the question whether it is fairly deducible from the grant is open for argument." In addition, he argued that "a mode of executing that which was granted" is not "an 'additional' or 'incidental' power" but rather "part of the original grant."[29]

The Chief Justice also relied on these categories to distinguish the Constitution's delegations from those made by the Articles of Confederation. He presupposed that the national Congress but not the confederate congress had authority to exercise "incidental" or "implied" powers: "Under the confederation, congress possessed no implied powers, and was therefore unable to punish those who robbed the mail, but was capable of regulating the post office. These regulations were means, not incidents."[30]

---

[26] Ibid., at 412–19 (emphasis in original).

[27] Ibid., at 417 and 422.

[28] The essays signed "A Friend of the Union" were published between April 24 and 28, 1819, in the *Philadelphia Union*, in response to attacks on *McCulloch* by "Amphictyon." The essays signed "A Friend of the Constitution" were published June 20 to July 15, 1819, in the *Alexandria Gazette*, this time in response to further attacks from "Hampden." See n. 13, above, and Gunther's introduction to *Marshall's Defense of McCulloch*.

[29] Marshall, "A Friend of the Constitution," in Gunther, ed., *Marshall's Defense of McCulloch*, at 162–63 and 172.

[30] Ibid., at 172.

Not even Alexander Hamilton had argued that the necessary and proper clause expanded federal powers beyond what the principal delegations (properly understood) would authorize.[31]

In *McCulloch* Marshall blurred distinctions between "means" and "incidental" powers by grouping together "the right to carry the mail, and [the right] to punish those who rob it." He argued that both "rights" were "essential to the beneficial exercise of the [enumerated] power, but not indispensably necessary to its existence."[32] He brushed over the fact that according to his criteria, the example of "carrying the mail along the post-road, from one post office to another," illustrated means of exercising an express power; while his claim that the government had "the right to punish those who steal letters from the post-office, or rob the mail," was an argument for "incidental" power.

This distinction was important to Marshall, because he took a position that the requirements of necessity and propriety applied only to the government's exercise of "incidental" powers, not to its choice of "means" when exercising expressly delegated powers. In his defense of *McCulloch*, he argued that "a rule applicable to powers, which may, strictly speaking, be denominated *incidental*, is not equally applicable to all the *means* of executing enumerated powers."[33] He later adhered to this distinction in *Gibbons v. Ogden*, where he asserted that Congress was not limited to using "necessary and proper" means to exercise its expressly delegated powers.[34] He proclaimed that each "express" power "vested in congress, [was] complete in itself, [could] be exercised to its utmost extent, and acknowledge[d] no limitations, other than are prescribed in the constitution."[35]

In sum, he urged that the necessary and proper clause authorized the federal government to exercise implied powers *in addition*, or "incidental," to those included within the principal delegations.[36] Furthermore,

---

[31] See Hamilton's arguments in the 33rd *Federalist* and in his opinion on the validity of the bill to establish a national bank (cited at n. 6, above).

[32] See *McCulloch*, 17 U.S. at 417.

[33] Marshall, "A Friend of the Constitution," in Gunther, ed., *Marshall's Defense of McCulloch*, at 171 (emphasis added).

[34] See *Gibbons*, 22 U.S. at 187.

[35] Ibid., at 196. As had Madison and Hamilton in *The Federalist*, Marshall relied on governmental structures rather than parchment barriers: "The wisdom and the discretion of congress, their identity with the people, and the influence which their constituents possess at elections, are, in this, as in many other instances, as that, for example, of declaring war, the sole restraints on which they have relied, to secure them from its abuse." See also Marshall, "A Friend of the Constitution," in Gunther, ed., *Marshall's Defense of McCulloch*, at 171.

[36] To support his position that the necessary and proper clause expanded federal powers and did not restrict the government's choice of means, he pointed out in *McCulloch*: "1st.

he claimed that the Constitution authorized the government to use *any* means (except those expressly prohibited) to execute expressly delegated powers and to use *additional* means to the extent "necessary and proper" to ensure the "beneficial exercise" of the principal powers. Thus his conception of "delegated" powers encompassed two unspecified forms of power: means included within express powers and other powers instrumentally related to accomplishing the specified ends. Portions of *McCulloch* supported a finding of each type of unenumerated power.[37]

Early in the opinion, he argued that even without the necessary and proper clause, the national government would have had "the general right, which might otherwise be implied, of selecting means for executing the enumerated powers." Furthermore, he suggested that the necessary and proper clause, if it served no other purpose, at least did not "impair the right of the legislature to exercise its best judgment in the selection of measures to carry into execution the constitutional powers of the government."

His reformulation of the scope of federal powers likewise emphasized the government's prerogative to choose appropriate "means":

> We admit, as all must admit, that the powers of the government are limited, and that its limits are not to be transcended. But we think the sound construction of the constitution must allow to the national legislature that discretion, with respect to the means by which the powers it confers are to be

---

The clause is placed among the powers of congress, not among the limitations on those powers. 2d. Its terms purport to enlarge, not to diminish the powers vested in the government. It purports to be an additional power, not a restriction on those already granted" (17 U.S. at 419–20).

[37] Marshall was able to gloss over his distinction between means and incidental powers by mixing the question of *what* the Constitution required with his comments on *who* had constitutional authority to interpret constitutional boundaries. He claimed that if the bank was "an appropriate measure, . . . the de[g]ree of its necessity . . . is to be discussed in another place." For judges "to inquire into the de[g]ree of necessity," he asserted, "would be to pass the line which circumscribes the judicial department, and to tread on legislative ground" (*McCulloch*, 17 U.S. at 422–23). This passage indicates that he was treating Congress's establishment of the national bank as an exercise of "incidental" power. Furthermore, other portions of the decision address the issue of "necessity," even though Marshall apparently did not treat a finding of necessity as essential to the *Court's* decision. If Marshall were assuming that establishing the national bank had been a means of exercising an express power, he would not have regarded the requirements of necessity and propriety as applicable either to Congress's deliberations or to the Court's determination of constitutionality. Not everyone would have accepted such a position, however, and thus it would have been prudent to deal with the issues of necessity and propriety in any event.

Madison had likewise presumed that "it is for [Congress] to judge of the necessity *and* propriety" of means chosen to exercise its powers (*Annals*, at 438 [June 8, 1789]). As explained in ch. 5, Madison claimed these limits applied to Congress, even if judges could not (or would not) enforce them.

carried into execution, which will enable that body to perform the high duties assigned to it, in the manner most beneficial to the people. Let the end be legitimate, let it be within the scope of the constitution, and all means which are appropriate, which are plainly adapted to that end, which are not prohibited, but consist with the letter and spirit of the constitution, are constitutional.[38]

On the surface, it appears that Marshall was merely claiming that the national government had authority to use appropriate means when exercising its delegated powers. According to one reading of this passage, his reference to "ends" denoted exercising express powers. Interpreted along these lines, the claim was relatively modest: if the government's "end" was to exercise an enumerated power, appropriate "means" of exercising that power (i.e., means not prohibited) were constitutional.

But the passage contained mixed signals, especially because it followed a sentence in which Marshall suggested that the necessary and proper clause authorized Congress to exercise "incidental" powers.[39] He suggested with characteristic understatement that a "sufficient reason" for the necessary and proper clause was "to remove all doubts respecting the right [of Congress] to legislate on that vast mass of *incidental* powers which must be involved in the constitution, if that instrument be not a splendid bauble." Until that point in his opinion, he had claimed only that the necessary and proper clause authorized the government to choose appropriate *means* for exercising its powers.[40]

These considerations suggest an alternative reading of his reformulation of the scope of delegated powers. He suggested that if the government's "end" was to accomplish a legitimate "object" or "purpose," all means that were "necessary and proper" to accomplishing that object were constitutional unless they were prohibited. The government would not be limited to exercising implied powers *included within* express delegations. The necessary and proper clause would also sanction the exercise of additional ("incidental") powers.[41]

---

[38] *McCulloch*, 17 U.S. at 421.

[39] See ibid., at 412–21.

[40] See ibid., at 417 and 420–21.

[41] It is noteworthy that Marshall did not include a requirement of necessity in his formula. There are at least three good ways to account for that omission. First, he may have thought testing whether means were "plainly adapted" would be an adequate proxy for the constitutional standard. Second, he may have conceived of his formula as a guide for judicial review, the standards for which were not coextensive with constitutional limitations. Third, in light of his position that the requirement of necessity did not apply to the government's choice of means to exercise express powers, he might have wanted the formula to be broad enough to encompass that type of implied power without burdening it with the more restrictive standard of "necessity."

According to this scheme, the scope of "incidental" powers would depend, among other things, on the character and scope of constitutional "ends." On this score as well, Marshall articulated an expansive conception of federal authority. He described the government's "vast" powers as embracing "[t]he sword and the purse, all the external relations, and no inconsiderable portion of the industry of the nation." He claimed that "the happiness and prosperity of the nation" would "so vitally depend" on the "due execution" of these powers. Furthermore, he urged that the Constitution marked only the "great outlines" and "important objects" from which "minor ingredients" could be deduced.[42]

Although it would be a mistake to think Marshall sought to circumvent the principle of enumerated powers, he certainly opposed applying that principle in a manner that would preclude the government from securing the advantages of union.[43] He was less committed than Madison to a distinction between "a power necessary and proper for the Government or Union, and a power necessary and proper for executing the enumerated powers."[44] Marshall later explained in *Gibbons* that if the general government did not exercise power over matters of common interest, those common interests would not be secured:

> The grant does not convey power which might be beneficial to the grantor, if retained by himself, or which can inure solely to the benefit of the grantee; but is an investment of power for the general advantage, in the hands of agents selected for that purpose; which power can never be exercised by the people themselves, but must be placed in the hands of agents, or lie dormant.[45]

Rather than allowing federal powers to "lie dormant," he trusted federal structures to ensure their beneficial execution.

FEDERAL PREEMPTION

He trusted those structures even when exercises of federal power conflicted with exercises of state power. The second branch of *McCulloch*

---

[42] *McCulloch*, 17 U.S. at 407–408.

[43] Marshall presumed that the necessary and proper clause did not authorize Congress to circumvent its authority to act only in pursuance of "objects . . . intrusted to the government." He warned that "should congress, under the pretext of executing its powers, pass laws for the accomplishment of objects not intrusted to the government; it would become the painful duty of this tribunal, should a case requiring such a decision come before it, to say, that such an act was not the law of the land" (ibid., at 422). See also Marshall, "A Friend of the Constitution," in Gunther, ed., *Marshall's Defense of McCulloch*, at 173.

[44] See Madison's arguments against the first bank bill, as reported in the *Annals* 2:1900–1901 (February 2, 1791).

[45] *Gibbons*, 22 U.S. at 188–89.

dealt with this conceptually distinct issue. As Maryland's counsel had argued, a finding of delegated authority did not logically entail a conclusion that conflicting exercises of state power were constitutionally impermissible.

Several of Alexander Hamilton's arguments in *The Federalist* supported the state's position on this issue. For example, he had presumed in the 32nd *Federalist* that the states would retain "an independent and uncontrollable authority" to impose taxes on "all articles other than imports and exports." He also proclaimed that "an attempt on the part of the national government to abridge [the states] in the exercise of [that power] would be a violent assumption of power, unwarranted by any article or clause of [the] Constitution." Furthermore, he assumed that taxation powers, except as expressly provided, would be "manifestly a *concurrent and coequal authority* in the United States and in the States." He declared that "this *concurrent jurisdiction* in the articles of taxation was the only admissible substitute for an entire subordination, in respect to this branch of power, of the State authority to that of the Union."[46]

Hamilton had distinguished "concurrent" powers from those delegated "exclusively" to the federal government. He described three forms of "exclusive" delegations to the federal government:

> where the Constitution in express terms granted an exclusive authority to the Union; where it granted in one instance an authority to the Union, and in another prohibited the States from exercising the like authority; and where it granted an authority to the Union to which a similar authority in the States would be absolutely and totally *contradictory* and *repugnant*.

According to Hamilton, "the State governments would clearly retain all the rights of sovereignty which they before had, and which were not, by [the Constitution's adoption], *exclusively* delegated to the United States." He recognized, furthermore, that there might be conflicts in practice between the federal government and the states in the exercise of their respective taxation powers, but he suggested that these "occasional inter-

---

[46] *The Federalist*, no. 32, at 198–99 and 205 (emphasis on "concurrent and coequal authority" added; emphasis on "concurrent jurisdiction" in original). See also ibid., at 205, where Hamilton argued that a federal law "for abrogating or preventing the collection of a tax laid by the authority of a State (unless upon imports and imports) would not be the supreme law of the land, but a usurpation of power not granted by the Constitution." See also Hamilton's argument in the 36th *Federalist*, at 221, that conflicts in practice would not necessarily represent clashes of authority, or repugnancy in "a legal sense." In the 32nd *Federalist*, at 205, he characterized such conflicts as "mutual inconvenience." But compare his comment that a federal law "for the use of the United States would be supreme in its nature and could not legally be opposed or controlled" (ibid.). Compare also the argument of Maryland's counsel that federal and state revenue powers would be "*co-equal*" except as to duties on imports and tonnage. See *McCulloch*, 17 U.S. 343–45 (emphasis in original).

ferences . . . would not imply any direct contradiction or repugnancy in point of constitutional authority."[47]

Relying on these arguments, Maryland's counsel had argued that "the right to incorporate a bank may exist, and be exercised consistently with the right of the state, to tax the property of such bank within its territory . . . although some inconvenience or diminution of advantage may be the consequence." The attorney had claimed that a "direct and necessary consequence" of Hamilton's position was that "whatever jurisdiction the federal government may exercise in this respect, over a bank created by a state, any state may exercise over a bank created by the United States."[48]

The Chief Justice disagreed. Although he characterized federal and state powers of taxation as "concurrent," he did not regard them as equal in authority. He argued that the state's powers of taxation were subordinate not only to the United States Constitution but also to exercises by the "supreme government" of its delegated powers. He conceded that "no express provision" governed resolution of the case, but he claimed to base his opinion on "a principle which so entirely pervades the constitution, is so intermixed with the materials which compose it, so interwoven with its web, so blended with its texture, as to be incapable of being separated from it, without rending it into shreds."[49]

Consistently with his opening premise that the case involved "conflicting powers" of the two governments, Marshall described the case as presenting opposing claims of "supremacy." He argued that Maryland's tax was not only repugnant in practice but also in authority to the federal government's power to establish a bank. Where a repugnancy exists between a power to create and a power to destroy, he asserted, "that authority which is supreme must control, and not yield to that over which it is

[47] *The Federalist*, no. 32, at 198 (emphasis in original). See also *The Federalist*, no. 36, at 221, where Hamilton had argued: "As to the interference of the revenue laws of the Union and of its members, we have already seen that there can be no clashing or repugnancy of authority. The laws cannot, therefore, in a legal sense, interfere with each other; and it is far from impossible to avoid an interference even in the policy of their different systems. . . . As neither can *control* the other, each will have an obvious and sensible interest in this reciprocal forbearance."

[48] *McCulloch*, 17 U.S. at 338 and 351. It is worth noting that the supremacy clause can accommodate arguments that state as well as federal laws are part of the "supreme law of the land" to the extent they are not contradictory.

[49] *McCulloch*, 17 U.S. at 426 (Marshall, C.J.). As Charles L. Black Jr. has characterized *McCulloch*, it is a paradigmatic example of "structural" interpretation. According to Black, in *Structure and Relationship in Constitutional Law* (Baton Rouge: Louisiana State University Press, 1969), at 15, "Marshall's reasoning . . . has to do in great part with what he conceives to be the warranted relational proprieties between the national government and the government of the states, with the structural corollaries of national supremacy—and, at one point, of the mode of formation of the Union."

supreme." He presumed that "the very essence of supremacy [is] to remove all obstacles to its action within its own sphere, and so to modify every power vested in subordinate governments, as to exempt its own operations from their own influence." He claimed that any other conclusion would have rendered the supremacy clause an "empty and unmeaning declamation."[50] In sum, his position was that collective prerogatives superseded opposing separate prerogatives.

He treated that principle as a necessary corollary of constitutional structures. The states were represented in the federal legislature, but not vice versa. As a result, principles of representation provided the states with a type of security that Congress did not have, aside from the supremacy of its laws:

> [W]hen a state taxes the operations of the government of the United States, it acts upon institutions created, not by their own constituents, but by people over whom they claim no control. It acts upon the measures of a government created by others as well as themselves, for the benefit of others in common with themselves. The difference is that which always exists, and must always exist, between the actions of the whole on a part, and the actions of a part on the whole.

He concluded that the state had "no power, by taxation or otherwise, to retard, impede, burden, or in any manner control, the operations of the constitutional laws enacted by congress to carry into execution the powers vested in the general government."[51]

As these passages indicate, Marshall treated the Constitution's express prohibitions on the states as an incomplete listing of powers prohibited to them. Relying on the supremacy clause, he argued that not only the Constitution, but also laws made in pursuance of it, were "supreme" over state constitutions and laws. In his view, the same "paramount character" that restrained the states from taxing imports and exports "would seem to restrain, as it certainly may restrain, a state from such other exercise of this power, as is in its nature incompatible with, and repugnant to, the constitutional laws of the Union."[52] Consistent with these arguments, he misquoted the tenth amendment, claiming that it "declares only, that the powers 'not delegated to the United States, nor prohibited to the states, are reserved to the states or to the people.'"[53] His omissions of "by the

---

[50] See *McCulloch*, 17 U.S. at 403, 426–27, and 433. Marshall argued that "the constitution and the laws made in pursuance thereof are supreme; that they control the constitution and laws of the respective states, and cannot be controlled by them."

[51] See ibid., at 428 and 435–36.

[52] Ibid., at 425.

[53] Ibid., at 406.

Constitution" and "by it" were significant; they allowed him to equivocate on the source of prohibitions and hence on the scope of reserved powers.[54]

The amendment's negative implication is that only the Constitution itself could "prohibit" powers in the sense of withdrawing them from "reserved" status. Nevertheless, Marshall suggested that federal laws could create additional "prohibitions." Much of the opinion treats acts of Congress and judicial decisions as capable of preempting *otherwise legitimate* exercises of state power.

But he equivocated on this issue by suggesting at the end of his opinion that the decision did not deprive the state of any power held by it before the Constitution went into effect. He characterized the state's attempt to tax the bank as a "usurpation of a power which the people of a single state cannot give"—a right that "never existed." Thus he suggested that because the state had no such "original right," the state could not claim the power as a residual prerogative.[55]

The assumption with which he began his opinion, that federal and state powers could conflict, was in tension with his premise that the people had entrusted different "objects" to the federal and state governments. He claimed that the Court's decision was faithful to a principle that made it unnecessary to choose among conflicting normative claims:

> We have a principle which leaves the power of taxing the people and property of a state unimpaired; which leaves to a state the command of all its resources, and which places beyond its reach, all those powers which are conferred by the people of the United States on the government of the Union, and all those means which are given for the purpose of carrying those powers into execution.[56]

According to this line of reasoning, the case did not present normative conflict. In Marshall's terms, the state had "no power" to tax the bank. On one side, there was power; on the other, its absence. Maryland's *claim* of power was fallacious: the state sought to "usurp" a power it did not have.

---

[54] Marshall repeated this ambiguity in stating that the amendment "le[ft] the question, whether the particular power which may become the subject of contest, has been delegated to the one government, or prohibited to the other, to depend on a fair construction of the whole instrument" (ibid). The Chief Justice omitted powers reserved to the states from his formula for interpreting "the whole instrument," and he did not track the tenth amendment's presumption in favor of powers being reserved. Contrast his careful analysis of the tenth amendment's omission of the term "expressly," as discussed above in the text.

[55] See *McCulloch*, 17 U.S. at 429–30. But see ch. 3, n. 90.

[56] Ibid., at 430. See also the passages quoted at nn. 20–23, above.

Marshall was presumably aware that his broad conception of delegated authority would make it impossible to adhere in all contexts to such a conception of constitutional structures. It would be difficult to conceive of all federal and state powers, along with the respective means of their exercise, as arrayed across normative boundaries. In some cases, even if not in *McCulloch*, these prerogatives would overlap. There would be conflicts between *otherwise legitimate* exercises of governmental power.

Marshall announced that he would support federal and not state powers in such a case. More specifically, he claimed that federal structures gave priority to actions by the states and the people as a whole, acting through representative structures. These actions could defeat separate prerogatives.

The rhetoric of "withdrawal" bridged both branches of Marshall's reasoning. He presumed that the federal Constitution and laws could "withdraw" powers from the states.[57] Such "withdrawal" could be conceived as displacement, creating the absence of power where it previously existed. According to this conceptualization, there might be impermissible conflicts in practice but not legitimately conflicting norms.

It would also be reasonable to conceive of federal powers as capable of "withdrawing" from the states means of exercising powers that the Constitution continued to reserve to them. According to twentieth-century rhetoric, the Constitution and laws were capable of "trumping" otherwise legitimate exercises of state power. The idea of "trumping" would be well suited to deal with "conflicting powers." With characteristic foresight, Marshall was establishing normative frameworks to deal with future controversies, not just the one at hand.

UNRESOLVED TENSIONS

Marshall referred obliquely to "prohibitions" on the exercise of federal powers. He also alluded to "the great principles of liberty." He apparently had in mind primarily rights of individuals, including those set forth in the Bill of Rights. In addition, article I, section 9, contains a number of prohibitions for the benefit of the respective states.

Marshall referred to "prohibitions" and "principles of liberty" in two

---

[57] See ibid., at 425. As would Marshall, McCulloch's counsel argued that the bank withdrew no powers from the states. But the attorney argued that even if it did, this would not be a reason for objecting to the validity of the bank (see ibid., at 396–97). See also Madison's argument in the 45th *Federalist*, at 288–89, that the Constitution's withdrawing powers from the states was not a valid objection if such powers were needed to accomplish national ends.

contexts. First, he excluded prohibited means from permissible exercises of national power in his reformulation of the scope of constitutional delegations. In that context, the main issue was the scope of "means" authorized by the necessary and proper clause. He implied that the Constitution would restrain Congress from choosing prohibited means, even if its "object" were legitimate. He also suggested that judges would not be willing to presume constitutional validity in cases involving "the great principles of liberty."

The Chief Justice did not examine closely relationships between federal powers and constitutional prohibitions in *McCulloch*, because he claimed there was no applicable prohibition. As a result, he did not present analysis of relationships between prohibitions for the benefit of the states, the tenth amendment's reference to residual powers of the states and the people, express enumerations of rights, and the ninth amendment's more general prohibition on denying or disparaging unenumerated rights.

The opinion nevertheless implicated the full range of such relationships. His position on the "objects" entrusted by the Constitution to the federal government had implications for conceiving of the scope of residual "objects" reserved to the states and the people. His broad conception of delegated powers increased the likelihood of normative conflict involving rights and powers of the people, not just powers of the states. In addition, his position that federal powers would preempt conflicting exercises of state powers provided a model for analyzing relationships between federal powers and prerogatives of the people at large.

He emphasized the importance of federal powers. Marshall claimed that "the happiness and prosperity of the nation"—its "welfare"— depended on the "due execution" of delegated powers. He presumed that the powers entrusted to the government would "lie dormant" if not exercised by it.[58]

It would have been anomalous for Marshall to treat rights or powers of the people at large, any more than powers of the states, as capable of preempting the federal government's ability to achieve the "great objects" committed to its care. He did not conceive of these prerogatives as zero-sum. Exercises of governmental power would necessarily restrict the exercise of some rights, but the result would be a collective good that individuals could not separately achieve. To allow individual rights to prevail in every case would undercut the very purposes of Union.

Yet he presumed that the Constitution imposed *some* restrictions on federal powers in addition to those implicit in its delegation of limited "objects." His analysis of relationships between federal and state powers

[58] See the passages quoted at nn. 42–45, above.

offers by analogy at least two ways to conceive of relationships among the powers and prohibitions. As federal powers could "trump" state powers, perhaps prohibitions would be capable of "trumping" federal powers. According to this scheme, the hierarchy of constitutional norms, in order of decreasing priority, would be: constitutional prohibitions, delegations of federal authority, and reservations of power to the states (and perhaps the people). Alternatively, he might conceive of the prohibitions as corresponding to absences of federal authority. In that case, as a matter of constitutional logic, there could be no normative conflict. Interpreters would be "relieved, as we ought to be," from "clashing sovereignty"— from "a repugnancy between a right in one . . . to pull down, what there is an acknowledged right in another to build up."[59]

Marshall would be willing to conceive of prohibitions as capable of "trumping" some means of exercising federal powers but not the powers themselves. He apparently thought Congress would have adequate means of securing the "objects" entrusted to it without using prohibited means. In addition, he would presumably attempt to interpret the prohibitions consistently with the delegations. In practice, however, his expansive conception of delegated authority would make it difficult to avoid treating the opposing prerogatives as potentially conflicting.

Marshall and his colleagues left it to others to work out these problems of constitutional theory and practice outside the context of constitutional adjudication. Although he had asserted the power of judicial review in *Marbury v. Madison*, the Supreme Court (but not the Marshall Court) would not exercise that power again to invalidate an act of Congress until 1857 in the case of *Dred Scott v. Sandford*. In that case, as explained in chapter 1, Chief Justice Taney relied on the idea of rights as secured by the fifth amendment to reinforce arguments that the Missouri Compromise of 1820 was invalid. Justice Campbell, concurring, invoked the ninth and tenth amendments to rebut claims of federal power.[60]

The Marshall Court set important precedents involving restrictions on the states. *Cohens v. Virginia*[61] and *Martin v. Hunter's Lessee*[62] rank among the important early cases dealing with conflicting claims of federal and state interpretive authority. The judges also invalidated exercises of state power as inconsistent with federal authority or constitutional prohibitions.[63] In *Fletcher v. Peck*, Marshall suggested that prohibitions on the

---

[59] *McCulloch*, 17 U.S. at 430.

[60] See ch. 1, n. 26.

[61] 19 U.S. (6 Wheat.) 264 (1821).

[62] 14 U.S. (1 Wheat.) 304 (1816).

[63] See, e.g., *Dartmouth College v. Woodward*, 17 U.S. (4 Wheat.) 517 (1819); *Gibbons v. Ogden* (1824); *Brown v. Maryland*, 25 U.S. (12 Wheat.) 419 (1827).

states included more than express guarantees.[64] Then in *Barron v. Baltimore*,[65] he argued that the judges had no authority to enforce the express prohibitions in the Bill of Rights as limits on the states. Much of these decisions would be overshadowed by the Civil War, reconstruction amendments, and other constitutional changes.[66]

In the meantime, Marshall's successor inverted the structural premises underlying *McCulloch*. Chief Justice Taney accepted his predecessor's premise that the Constitution entrusted different "objects" to the federal and state governments. But Taney expressed greater willingness than Marshall to protect state powers from national preemption. Taney's commitment to "dual federalism" culminated in *Dred Scott*, where he argued that Congress had no authority to interfere with rights of slave ownership as defined and secured primarily by state laws.[67]

During his later years, Marshall was aware that there was a wide gap between his interpretive commitments and actual political practices. He expressed concern that the states were too autonomous and the national government too weak to achieve the great ends for which the Constitution had been created. He died pessimistic about the future prospects of the Union.[68]

McCulloch did not even settle controversy over the validity of the national bank. In 1832 Andrew Jackson vetoed a bill to extend the bank's charter. Notwithstanding the Supreme Court's decision, the president argued that the charter was unconstitutional.[69] The man who would soon succeed Marshall as Chief Justice carried out Jackson's order to remove from the bank all funds owned by the United States.

There would be further twists. Among the greatest ironies would be

---

[64] 10 U.S. (6 Cranch) 87 (1810), at 139 ("the state of Georgia was restrained, either by general principles, which are common to our free institutions, or by the particular provisions of the constitution of the United States, from passing a law whereby the estate of the plaintiff in the premises so purchased could be constitutionally and legally impaired and rendered null and void").

[65] 32 U.S. (7 Pet.) 243 (1833).

[66] Much would also remain viable. For example, much constitutional theory still proceeds from an assumption that the Bill of Rights does not apply *directly* to the states. Questions about whether states are confined only by *express* prohibitions have also remained problematic.

[67] See generally Edward S. Corwin, *Liberty Against Government* (Baton Rouge: Louisiana State University Press, 1948); Don E. Fehrenbacher, *The Dred Scott Case* (New York: Oxford University Press, 1987).

[68] See Albert J. Beveridge, *The Life of John Marshall* (New York: Houghton Mifflin, 1919), vol. 4, ch. 10; William W. Crosskey, "Mr. Chief Justice Marshall," in Allison Dunham and Philip B. Kurland, eds., *Mr. Justice* (Chicago: University of Chicago Press, 1956), at 17–46.

[69] See ch. 8, n. 58 and accompanying text, for references to Jackson's veto of the Bank Bill and other assertions of interpretive autonomy in defiance of judicial precedents.

ratification during the twentieth century of Marshall's expansive conception of federal authority. Then, even more than during the nineteenth century, predominant political practices would largely accord with ideals he had expressed.

The subsequent viability of Marshall's interpretive commitments serves as a reminder of possibilities that may attach to out-of-favor positions. An awareness of such possibilities may inform analysis of the constitutional issues in remaining chapters, as well as help to keep in perspective the contributions of this chapter and preceding ones.

CHAPTER 7

Exercising Powers and Securing Rights

We deal with a right of privacy older than the Bill of Rights.[1]

FAR FROM settling the fundamental problems of constitutional design raised in previous chapters, the fourteenth amendment has been at the center of continuing debate. Many of its provisions, like those in the original Constitution and its initial amendments, are radically open-ended. Even after two centuries of practice, the constitutional text can accommodate substantial change through reinterpretation of its imperatives. American constitutionalism still rests on broad-based, multifaceted political activity—not simply judicial decision-making. Interpretive dialogue has continued to have forward-looking along with preservative dimensions.

Precedents involving claims of economic, sexual, and reproductive autonomy underscore these organic components of American constitutionalism. These precedents offer distinctive conceptions of "the people" and their "rights" and "powers." There have been recurring questions about how federal and state officials may act on behalf of "the people." Claims that citizens may act *through* government have been pitted against claims that individuals and groups may act *independently*. Arguments that legislative and executive officials may promote collective interests and secure individual rights have opposed arguments that judges may enforce private rights as limits on legislative and executive powers. Federal and state governmental powers have been conceived as mutually exclusive and reciprocally limiting in some contexts; as overlapping and complementary in others.

The first half of this chapter focuses on cases involving competing claims of economic rights and powers. The second half examines cases involving claims of sexual and reproductive autonomy. Although I cover familiar territory, I point out features of the constitutional design that are commonly overlooked. In addition, my focus again moves beyond judicial opinions toward broader commitments and activities of American constitutionalism.

---

[1] *Griswold v. Connecticut*, 381 U.S. 479 (1965), at 486.

ECONOMIC RIGHTS AND POWERS

Few of the Supreme Court's precedents are more notorious than *Lochner v. New York*.[2] It was at the center of controversy during the New Deal about whether judges may invalidate efforts by federal and state officials to regulate the economy. With its famous "switch in time," the Court in 1937 repudiated *Lochner* and similar efforts to guard economic laissez-faire.[3] Since then, there has been widespread agreement that judges may not invalidate governmental actions merely because they restrict economic liberties.

But it has not been easy to account for these developments. The lessons are not readily apparent. On first impression, it may appear that changes in the course of judicial precedents during the New Deal signaled that economic liberties had lost "constitutional" status. But the Constitution could also accommodate a different perspective: rights of economic autonomy arguably *gained* security even as judges ceased enforcing them as beyond the reach of governmental restriction.

It is instructive to link *Lochner* to cases involving principles of federalism. Being attentive to central components of the constitutional background may enhance understanding of comparable features in the foreground.

Enforcing Normative Boundaries

In *Lochner*, a majority of the Court invalidated a New York statute that prohibited employing bakers for more than sixty hours in any one week. Justice Rufus W. Peckham wrote the majority opinion. He argued that the statute unreasonably interfered with the employer's and employee's contractual liberties. The decision thereby promoted principles of economic laissez-faire that were popular at the time within the American bench and bar.[4]

Justice Peckham characterized the basic issue in *Lochner* as whether the New York law was "within the police power of the State." In order to

---

[2] 198 U.S. 45 (1905).

[3] The commonly understood turning point was *West Coast Hotel v. Parrish*, 300 U.S. 379 (1937). But as indicated below, the turnaround in judicial precedents was more gradual than sudden.

[4] See Edward S. Corwin, *Liberty Against Government* (Baton Rouge: Louisiana State University Press, 1948), ch. 4. Corwin explained that *Lochner* typified a judicial approach to economic regulation that was prevalent but not consistently followed for the next few decades. See generally Laurence H. Tribe, *American Constitutional Law*, 2d ed. (Mineola, N.Y.: Foundation Press, 1988), at 567 and n. 2.

qualify as such, he argued, the law had to have a legitimate "end" and had to be a reasonable "means" to that end:

> The mere assertion that the subject relates though but in a remote degree to the public health does not necessarily render the enactment valid. The act must have a more direct relation, as a means to an end, and the end itself must be appropriate and legitimate, before an act can be held valid which interferes with the general right of an individual to be free in his person and in his power to contract in relation to his own labor.[5]

Referring to the New York law and echoing the necessary and proper clause, he argued that there was "no reasonable foundation for holding this to be *necessary* or *appropriate* as a health law to safeguard the public health or the health of the individuals who are following the trade of a baker." Furthermore, echoing analyses of federal powers in terms of their "ends," he asserted that "the real object and purpose were simply to regulate the hours of labor between the master and his employés (all men being *sui juris*), in a private business, not dangerous in any degree to morals or in any real and substantial degree, to the health of the employés." Finally, echoing decisions that had invalidated exercises of federal powers on the basis that they were *ultra vires* and invaded prerogatives reserved exclusively to the states or retained by the people, he concluded that "the limit of the police power has been reached and passed."[6]

As these passages indicate, Peckham presumed there was a boundary between "public" and "private" prerogatives. He interpreted the fourteenth amendment's general reference to "liberty" as embracing a right to contract over terms of employment. In his view, state officials had no authority to interfere with the people's exercise of that right, at least without a good reason for doing so. On the other hand, he presumed that federal judges had authority to secure economic liberties by exercising their power of judicial review. The alternative, according to Peckham, would be that "the Fourteenth Amendment would have no efficacy and the legislatures of the States would have unbounded power."[7]

The significance of *Lochner* and similar precedents involving *state*

---

[5] *Lochner*, 198 U.S. at 56–58. He described the states' police powers broadly, as follows: "There are . . . certain powers, existing in the sovereignty of each State in the Union, somewhat vaguely termed police powers, the exact description and limitation of which have not been attempted by the courts. Those powers, broadly stated and without, at present, any attempt at a more specific limitation, relate to the safety, health, morals and general welfare of the public" (ibid., at 53).

[6] Ibid., at 58 and 64 (emphasis on "necessary" and "proper" added).

[7] Ibid., at 56. See Cass R. Sunstein, "Lochner's Legacy," 87 Colum. L. Rev. 873 (1987), for analysis of how economic laissez-faire depended on judicial power, not a complete absence of governmental involvement.

powers was magnified by parallel decisions involving *federal* powers. During the late nineteenth and early twentieth centuries, the Supreme Court also invalidated federal laws that regulated terms of employment. Depending on the context, the justices relied on the due process clause of the fifth amendment and/or the tenth amendment. They treated these provisions as complementing one another, the Constitution's delegation of intrinsically limited federal powers, and the limitations of the fourteenth amendment.[8]

In *Hammer v. Dagenhart*, for example, the Supreme Court invalidated a federal law that restricted transportation in "interstate commerce" of goods manufactured in a factory that employed children under specified ages or contrary to various limitations on hours. The defendants argued that the act exceeded Congress's authority to regulate commerce, contravened the tenth amendment, and conflicted with the fifth amendment's due process clause. The justices declared the law invalid on the first two grounds.

Justice William R. Day, writing for the majority, argued that "[t]he act in its effect does not regulate transportation among the States, but aims to standardize the ages at which children may be employed in mining and manufacturing within the States." Furthermore, he asserted that "the production of articles, intended for interstate commerce, [was] a matter of local regulation." He emphasized that the federal government was "one of enumerated powers" and claimed that "[t]he grant of authority over a purely federal matter was not intended to destroy the local power always existing and carefully reserved to the States in the Tenth Amendment." Joining this assumption of mutually exclusive and reciprocally limiting powers to his characterization of the act, his reasoning was straightforward:

> The grant to Congress over the subject of interstate commerce was to enable it to regulate such commerce, and not to give it authority to control the States in their exercise of the police power over local trade and manufacture. . . . The power of the States to regulate their purely internal affairs by such laws as may seem wise to the local authority is inherent and has never been surrendered to the general government. . . . Thus the act in a twofold sense is repugnant to the Constitution. It not only transcends the authority delegated to Congress over commerce but also exerts a power as to a purely local matter to which the federal authority does not extend.[9]

---

[8] See generally Corwin, *The Commerce Power versus States Rights* (Gloucester: Peter Smith, 1962); Corwin, *Constitutional Revolution* (Claremont, Calif.: Claremont Colleges Press, 1941); and Edward S. Corwin, "Introduction to the 1953 Edition," *The Constitution of the United States* (Washington, D.C.: GPO, 1987), at xi–xxvi.

[9] *Hammer v. Dagenhart*, 247 U.S. 251 (1918), at 271–76. See also ibid., at 275, where Justice Day paraphrased the tenth amendment incorrectly by claiming that the Constitution

Day's assumption that federal and state legislative powers were mutually exclusive and reciprocally limiting had solid historical antecedents.[10]

But because the law at issue in *Hammer* concerned employment of children, the justices were able to avoid dealing explicitly with an issue that made the decision distinctive. Justice Day could justify invalidating the federal law by pointing to state laws that regulated employment of children and other labor conditions where there were special considerations of capacity, safety, health, and public welfare. The justices had held that the states' police powers extended to regulating such conditions, notwithstanding the due process clause of the fourteenth amendment.[11] But *Hammer* established a precedent that also applied to restrictions on terms or conditions of employment when no such special circumstances existed.

Distinctions between "interstate" and "intrastate" matters were equally capable of supporting a denial of federal authority to restrict terms or conditions of employment in cases involving ordinary industries that employed healthy, competent, adult workers. In *Lochner*, however, the Court had held that the states did *not* have authority to regulate such general terms of employment. Thus the precedents set by *Lochner* and *Hammer* converged to protect what judges treated as a void in legislative authority. If they adhered to the principles underlying these precedents, the justices were committed to holding that *neither* the federal government *nor* the states had authority to regulate ordinary terms and conditions of employment.

In effect, therefore, these two decisions treated setting general terms of employment as reserved to the people themselves. The justices' approach to economic regulations thus neatly paralleled the tenth amendment's tripartite structure. Based on an assumption that Congress had authority to regulate interstate but not intrastate commerce, the Court held in *Hammer* that the federal government had no authority to regulate manufacturing, a form of intrastate commerce reserved to the states by the tenth amendment. But in *Lochner*, the Court had also held that the states' authority to regulate such manufacturing was limited by the due process

---

reserved to the states and the people "powers not *expressly* delegated to the National Government" (emphasis added). As explained in ch. 5, Madison and his colleagues in the First Congress had refused to accept proposals to revise drafts of the tenth amendment's precursor so that it would include "expressly." Day's misquoting the amendment reveals his assumption of mutually exclusive and reciprocally limiting state and federal powers.

[10] See, e.g., Chief Justice Taney's opinion in *License Cases*, 46 U.S. (5 How.) 504 (1847). See generally Corwin's "Introduction to the 1953 Edition," and Edward S. Corwin, "The Passing of Dual Federalism," 36 Va. L. Rev. 1 (1950).

[11] See, e.g., *Holden v. Hardy*, 169 U.S. 366 (1898) (upheld limits on hours worked in underground mines and smelters); *Muller v. Oregon*, 208 U.S. 412 (1908) (upheld limits on hours worked by women in laundries).

clause of the fourteenth amendment. According to that precedent and complementary decisions, the states could not interfere with contractual liberties unless there were special considerations of health or capacity or in cases involving industries "affected with a public interest."[12]

These lines of reasoning, along with an assumption that most businesses fell outside these exceptions, supported a conclusion that state legislatures had no authority to govern most terms of employment. Moreover, it was reasonable to infer that if the Constitution had not delegated the relevant power to the federal government or reserved such a power to the states, the Constitution must have reserved the power to the people themselves. Various threads of judicial doctrine thus came together to protect a realm of personal economic autonomy: "private" employer-employee relations that judges held were beyond the legitimate reach of governmental regulation.[13]

Transitions

The Court's decision in *Ashwander v. Tennessee Valley Authority*[14] was a bridge between declining and emerging theoretical paradigms. In 1936 the judges upheld the national government's construction and operation of the Wilson Dam, despite arguments that the government exceeded its delegated authority and encroached on the states' reserved powers and the people's retained rights. Much of Chief Justice Charles Evans Hughes's opinion treats these prerogatives as mutually exclusive and reciprocally limiting. But he also anticipated a significantly different framework for analyzing constitutional structures.[15]

For the first time in a majority opinion, Hughes referred explicitly to

[12] See *Munn v. Illinois*, 94 U.S. (4 Otto) 113 (1877) (upheld limits on grain elevator rates). See also the cases cited in the previous note.

[13] Edward S. Corwin observed that precedents concerning the due process clauses of the fifth and fourteenth amendments, along with the justices' approach to issues of federalism, created a void in legislative power. See, e.g., Corwin, *Constitutional Revolution*, at 99 ("a realm of no-power"); Corwin, "The Passing of Dual Federalism," at 22 ("a realm of no-power, 'a twilight zone', 'a no-man's land' in which corporate enterprise was free to roam largely unchecked"). See also Paul W. Kahn, *Legitimacy and History* (New Haven: Yale University Press, 1992), ch. 4, for a complementary treatment of the *Lochner* Court's reliance on categorical analysis (Kahn explains how the Court relied heavily on categories supplied by the common law).

[14] 297 U.S. 288 (1936).

[15] Thus the "constitutional revolution" was well under way, even before the landmark decision in *West Coast*. Argument for *Ashwander* took place in the October term of 1935; and the Court announced its decision in February 1936—well before the elections of 1936 that Bruce A. Ackerman claims were pivotal. (See Ackerman, "Discovering the Constitution," 93 Yale L. J. 1013 (1984), at 1054–56.)

the ninth amendment.[16] His references to that amendment, along with the tenth, are revealing. He suggested that the people's retained rights and the states' reserved powers may have diminished as federal powers expanded. But his opinion contains mixed messages.

The stockholders of a corporation argued that the Tennessee Valley Authority, a federal agency, had no authority to sell electricity generated at the Wilson Dam. According to the stockholders, the national government had invaded "the field of action reserved to the States and the people under the guise of exercising substantive federal powers." More specifically, the TVA was "engaging in business" through "manufacturing" or "production" of electric energy.[17]

Hughes rejected these arguments, along with claims that Congress had no authority to authorize the dam's construction. He emphasized that article IV, section 3 of the Constitution "expressly granted to the Congress" power to dispose of property legally acquired by it. Based on this finding, he dismissed the ninth and tenth amendments as inapplicable:

> To the extent that the power of disposition is thus expressly conferred, it is manifest that the Tenth Amendment is not applicable. And the Ninth Amendment (which petitioners also invoke) in insuring the maintenance of the rights retained by the people does not withdraw the rights which are expressly granted to the Federal Government.

As indicated, he presupposed that the ninth and tenth amendments each referred to residual prerogatives beyond intrinsic limitations of delegated powers. He claimed that the constitutional text settled the issue of power and precluded finding that retained rights or reserved powers had been abridged.

Hughes's opinion points out that the concept of reciprocally limiting constitutional prerogatives may cut several ways, not just *against* the federal government. In *Lochner*, Peckham relied on a finding of retained rights to rebut a claim of state power. In *Hammer*, Day relied on a finding of state power to rebut a claim of national power. Justices in other cases used findings of retained rights to rebut claims of national power.[18] Hughes reasoned in the opposite direction by using a finding of federal power to rebut claims of retained rights and reserved powers.

---

[16] The first reference in any opinion for the Court was Justice Campbell's concurrence in *Dred Scott*, as cited in ch. 1, n. 26. It is possible, of course, that judges have consulted and/or relied on the ninth amendment in other cases but not referred to it in their opinions.

[17] See *Ashwander*, 297 U.S. at 295 and 302 (argument for petitioners).

[18] The most notorious precedent in this respect is *Dred Scott v. Sandford* (relying on the fifth amendment's due process clause). See also *Adair v. United States*, 208 U.S. 161 (1900) (also relying on the fifth amendment's due process clause). For a more recent case, see, e.g., *New York Times v. United States*, 403 U.S. 713 (1971) (relying on the first amendment).

A later case, *United Public Workers v. Mitchell*,[19] demonstrates how such an approach could be used to defend narrow conceptions of enumerated as well as unenumerated rights and powers. The issue in that case was the validity of the Hatch Act. It forbade officers and employees of the executive branch of the federal government from taking "any active part in political management or in political campaigns." Justice Stanley F. Reed, writing for a majority of the Court, upheld the Act.

He presumed that "political rights reserved to the people by the Ninth and Tenth Amendments are involved." He conceded that the Act interfered with "what otherwise would be the freedom of the civil servant under the First, Ninth and Tenth Amendments." In addition, there was an "impairment" of "the guarantee of freedom" secured by the fifth amendment's due process clause. But Reed denied that these rights were "absolutes" and argued that the government could restrict their exercise to satisfy "the elemental need for order." In this context, he treated delegated powers as preemptive:

> The powers granted by the Constitution to the Federal Government are subtracted from the totality of sovereignty originally in the states and the people. Therefore, when objection is made that the exercise of a federal power infringes upon rights reserved by the Ninth and Tenth Amendments, the inquiry must be directed toward the granted power under which the action of the Union was taken. If granted power is found, necessarily the objection of invasion of those rights, reserved by the Ninth and Tenth Amendments, must fail.[20]

Using similar reasoning, Reed argued that the government could legitimately restrict the exercise of rights protected by the first and fifth amendments.

After a majority of the justices repudiated *Lochner* and *Hammer*, it would be possible to conceive of economic liberties as "subtracted" from retained rights. Likewise, one might conceive of authority to regulate manufacturing as taken from the states and surrendered to the national government. Such positions would flow from assumptions that constitutional prerogatives were zero-sum. *Either* the people retained a particular right *or* they surrendered to government the authority to restrict its exercise. Rights falling within the latter category were *either* surrendered to the states *or* delegated to the national government.

While parts of Hughes's opinion in *Ashwander* support such an account, others lead in different directions. After concluding that the government was acting within its delegated powers, the Chief Justice contin-

---

[19] *United Public Workers v. Mitchell*, 330 U.S. 75 (1947).
[20] Ibid., at 94–96.

ued to examine the "method" or "means" chosen by the TVA to dispose of electric energy. He explained:

> That method must, of course, be an appropriate means of disposition according to the nature of the property, it must be one adopted in the public interest as distinguished from private or personal ends, and we may assume that it must be consistent with the foundation [*sic*] principles of our dual system of government and must not be contrived to govern the concerns reserved to the States.

Similarly, he indicated that there would have been a "constitutional question" if the dam's operations had invaded "rights reserved to the State or to the people." He denied, however, that the government was "using the water power at the Wilson Dam to establish any industry or business."[21]

A finding of delegated power was not, according to Hughes, conclusive of constitutional validity. He also indicated that the Constitution precluded the federal government from exercising its principal powers in ways that encroached on "concerns reserved to the states" or "rights reserved to the states or the people." He apparently thought these limitations did not "withdraw" express powers from the federal government but could confine the government's choice of "means" in exercising them.

The structure of Hughes's opinion paralleled Madison's approach to analyzing the validity of the first bank bill. First, Hughes assumed that some retained rights and reserved powers corresponded to inherent limitations on the scope of delegated powers. He also treated retained rights and reserved powers as limitations on the "means" chosen by the national government to exercise its delegated powers.

In dealing with the latter issue, Hughes suggested that limits on means and delegations of power were crosscutting norms. Such a perspective would not necessarily entail a conclusion that retained rights and reserved powers had diminished (or would diminish) as federal powers had expanded (or would expand). Judges and others could coherently affirm simultaneously broad conceptions of overlapping prerogatives.

The Chief Justice did not fully develop this perspective in *Ashwander*. It is helpful to turn to other precedents for fuller elaboration of the idea of overlapping norms. Subsequent decisions upholding other components of the New Deal are instructive in this respect. They challenge common preoccupation with the Constitution's *judicial* interpretation and enforcement. These sources also underscore elements of constitutional continuity that survived radical change. The people arguably *gained* security for

---

[21] I am less concerned here with the actual character of the government's operations than with Hughes's characterization of them. Of most relevance here, he maintained that the dam had valid purposes and served legitimate governmental functions but did not invade state prerogatives or constitute "private enterprise."

economic liberties even as judges retreated from enforcing some such rights as spheres beyond the reach of governmental regulation.

Judicial Retreat

West Coast Hotel v. Parrish[22] upheld a law that set minimum wages and maximum hours for women in the state of Washington. One year earlier, the Court had invalidated a similar New York law on the rationale that it violated contractual liberties.[23] But in *Parrish*, Justice Owen J. Roberts made his famous "switch in time that saved nine." In response to enormous pressure from Congress, the president, state officials, and the people at large, the justices retreated from enforcing economic laissez-faire and began to consistently affirm the validity of New Deal legislation.[24] In an opinion written by Chief Justice Hughes (also the author of *Ashwander*), the Court upheld Washington's law.

The Chief Justice presumed that the due process clause of the fourteenth amendment did not guarantee "absolute and uncontrollable" freedom. He emphasized that liberty existed in the context of "a social organization which requires the protection of law against the evils which menace the health, safety, morals and welfare of the people." His test was not new: "Liberty under the Constitution is thus necessarily subject to the restraints of due process, and regulation which is reasonable in relation to its subject and is adopted in the interests of the community is due process."[25] But this time, the Court upheld the legislation.

Among other things, Hughes reviewed the importance of the state's purported interests and the reasonableness of the state's choice of means to accomplish those interests. More importantly, he indicated that the Constitution entrusted regulation of the economy to legislative rather than judicial oversight. He took a position that judges should *assume* ordinary economic regulation was constitutional unless it was clearly "arbitrary or capricious."[26]

As Corwin explained, the justices shifted away from emphasizing "constitutional liberties" as absences of regulatory authority and affirmed in-

---

[22] 300 U.S. 379 (1937).

[23] See *Morehead v. New York*, 298 U.S. 587 (1936).

[24] See generally Corwin, *Constitutional Revolution*; C. Herman Pritchett, *The Roosevelt Court: A Study in Judicial Politics and Values, 1937–1947* (New York: Macmillan, 1948).

[25] *Parrish*, 300 U.S. at 391. Chief Justice Hughes endorsed a decision in 1911 that had held: "There is no absolute freedom to do as one wills or to contract as one chooses. . . . Liberty implies the absence of arbitrary restraint, not immunity from reasonable regulations and prohibitions imposed in the interests of the community." Ibid., at 392, quoting *Chicago, Burlington and Quincy R. Co. v. McGuire*, 219 U.S. 549 (1911), at 565.

[26] See *Parrish*, 300 U.S. at 391–99.

stead the legislature's prerogative to secure "civil liberties" through active intervention in the economy: "Thus 'liberty' is recognized as something that may be infringed by other forces as well as by government; indeed, something that may require *the positive intervention of government against these other forces.*"[27] Although he claimed that this recognition was "unique" and marked "a development of profound significance," the judges actually returned to variations of earlier conceptions of the scope of the states' reserved powers.[28]

Parrish raised more questions than it resolved. As he had in *Ashwander*, Hughes equivocated on the constitutional status of economic liberties. Parts of his opinion imply a narrower conception of retained rights. Other parts presuppose that government may restrict the exercise of constitutionally protected liberties. He was likewise unclear on whether the justices were endorsing a broader range of governmental purposes and/or clearing the way for states to use means that had been disallowed in prior cases. His deferential posture made it unnecessary to deal thoroughly with these issues in *Parrish*. But they would assume greater importance in other contexts involving analogous claims of governmental power and opposing claims of popular rights.

Of more immediate relevance were problems of federalism. It was not readily apparent whether a commitment to uphold *state* legislation entailed affirming the validity of similar *national* legislation. Predominant models of dual federalism led in the opposite direction. If the states *did* have authority to regulate employment conditions, perhaps the national government did not. Judges might adhere to *Hammer* and guard the states' regulatory powers from national preemption.

The judges were, of course, under tremendous pressure to uphold na-

---

[27] *Constitutional Revolution*, at 67 (emphasis in original). See also ibid., at 79: "[T]he term liberty in the [due process] clause includes 'fundamental rights,' like that of labor to organize and bargain collectively, which can often be more effectively asserted by means of legislation than by judicial review. The clause is, therefore, broad enough to lend positive constitutional sanction to projects of social reform—it is not solely a constitutional barrier." Corwin was not clear what sort of constitutional status he thought these "fundamental rights" had, although it is doubtful he thought they were judicially enforceable as "constitutional law." He did not explain who might "assert" rights by means of legislation, nor did he explain how any such person might make such an "assertion."

[28] The quotes are from Corwin, *Constitutional Revolution*, at 67. Curiously, Corwin observed in another context that the justices "return[ed]" during the constitutional revolution of 1937 to "the constitutional proposition enunciated in *Munn v. Illinois*; namely, 'that courts do not substitute their social and economic beliefs for the judgment of legislative bodies.'" See "Introduction to the 1953 Edition," at xxv, quoting *NLRB v. Jones and Laughlin Steel Corp.*, 301 U.S. 1, 33–34 (1937). By repudiating *Lochner*, the judges in effect returned to the majority's position in *Slaughter-House Cases*, 83 U.S. (16 Wall.) 36 (1873) (held that the fourteenth amendment did not transfer ordinary police powers from the states to the federal government; rejected claims based on the fourteenth amendment's privileges or immunities, due process, and equal protection clauses).

tional along with state commercial regulations. But it was not clear how their doing so would implicate federal structures. Would affirming assertions of national authority entail accepting a narrower conception of reserved powers? Or would it be necessary to reconceive relationships among federal and state commercial powers?

These problems had profound normative and practical implications. What institutions, at the federal and state levels, would assert authority to act on behalf of "the people"? Would constitutional structures continue to provide security for private rights and/or state autonomy? Would assertions of federal and state governmental power diminish the people's retained and reserved prerogatives or give them added security?

Overlapping Rights and Powers

The justices confronted some of these issues in *United States v. Darby Lumber Co.*[29] The case involved a federal law governing terms and conditions of employment. The Court explicitly overturned *Hammer* and announced a revised approach to problems of federalism. The decision also echoed and reinforced *Parrish*'s treatment of relationships between governmental powers and rights of the people at large.

The Fair Labor Standards Act of 1938 (FLSA) set minimum wages and maximum hours for employees engaged in the production of goods for interstate commerce. The law also prohibited the shipment in interstate commerce of any goods produced in violation of those restrictions on wages and hours. A manufacturer of lumber challenged the act as only nominally a regulation of "interstate" commerce and claimed that the law's real motive or purpose was to regulate wages and hours of persons engaged in manufacturing, a form of "intrastate" commerce. Chief Justice Harlan Fiske Stone, writing for the majority in *Darby*, rejected that argument and upheld the federal law.

The case framed even more clearly than *Parrish* issues of constitutional change and relationships between judicial and legislative authority. Stone adhered to distinctions between "interstate" and "intrastate" commerce that had developed from Chief Justice John Marshall's dichotomy between federal and state commercial powers. Both distinctions had become anachronistic, however, because of changes in the character of the U.S. economy. But instead of relying on the text's delegation to Congress of authority to regulate "commerce among the states," Stone effectively revitalized that delegation by relying on Marshall's distinction between expressly delegated and implied powers.[30]

[29] 312 U.S. 100 (1941).
[30] See Marshall's opinions in *McCulloch v. Maryland* (1819) and *Gibbons v. Ogden* (1824)—including the passages quoted in ch. 6 hereof.

In addition, Stone reaffirmed Marshall's position that judges had little authority to review the legitimacy of Congress's choice of means in exercising delegated powers. Stone analyzed separately the FLSA's two principal components: its restrictions on transportation and its regulation of wages and hours. He argued that although "manufacture is not of itself interstate commerce, the shipment of manufactured goods interstate is such commerce and the prohibition of such shipment by Congress is indubitably a regulation of the commerce."[31] Citing *Gibbons v. Ogden*, he argued that "[t]he power of Congress over interstate commerce 'is complete in itself, may be exercised to its utmost extent, and acknowledges no limitations other than are prescribed in the Constitution.' "[32] He declared that "[t]he motive and purpose of a regulation of interstate commerce are matters for the legislative judgment upon the exercise of which the Constitution places no restriction and over which the courts are given no control."[33] Stone's position, in sum, was that the justices were confined to deciding whether Congress was exercising a legitimate power. Accordingly, they had no authority to substitute their "conception of public policy" for Congress's.

In a curious statement, Stone asserted: "The power of Congress over interstate commerce is not confined to the regulation of commerce among the states."[34] In this passage, he awkwardly endorsed Marshall's position that Congress may exercise powers in addition to "regulating commerce among the states" as means of regulating that commerce. In other words, he reaffirmed the concept of incidental powers. He relied on that concept to uphold the FLSA's regulation of wages and hours.

Stone claimed that Congress's power over interstate commerce "extends to those activities intrastate which so affect interstate commerce or the exercise of the power of Congress over it as to make regulation of them appropriate means to the attainment of a legitimate end, the exercise of the granted power of Congress to regulate interstate commerce." He treated the FLSA's restrictions on wages and hours of employment as legitimate "means" of regulating interstate commerce through "the suppression of the production of the condemned goods for interstate commerce." He concluded that these means were "so related to [interstate] commerce and so affect[ed] it as to be within the reach of the commerce power." He argued, in sum, that Congress could regulate intrastate commerce as a means of regulating interstate commerce.[35]

---

[31] *Darby*, 312 U.S. at 113.

[32] Ibid., at 114, quoting *Gibbons*, 22 U.S. at 196.

[33] *Darby*, 312 U.S. at 115.

[34] Ibid., at 118.

[35] Ibid., at 118 and 123. See also ibid., at 119 (Stone indicated that Congress's authority to regulate intrastate commerce as such a means depended on that commerce's having "a substantial effect on interstate commerce").

But Stone was unwilling (or unable, given the Court's makeup) to declare unequivocally that the production of goods for interstate commerce was part of that commerce—or, with more fidelity to the constitutional text, of "commerce among the states." He explained that the FLSA was part of a "comprehensive legislative scheme," and he described some of the ways manufacturing and transportation were integrally related:

> [T]he evils aimed at by the Act are the spread of substandard labor conditions through the use of the facilities of interstate commerce for competition by the goods so produced with those produced under the prescribed or better labor conditions; and the consequent dislocation of the commerce itself caused by the impairment or destruction of local businesses by competition made effective through interstate commerce. The Act is thus directed at the suppression of a method or kind of competition *in interstate commerce* which it has in effect condemned as "unfair."[36]

One might have expected him to declare that the production of goods with substandard labor conditions was a central component of competition in interstate commerce (or "commerce among the states") rather than a prior activity made effective through such commerce. The decision reached a similar result but based on different theoretical premises and with correspondingly different normative and practical implications.

Stone's approach may be attributed to several factors. The decision paralleled the terms of the FLSA, which relied on the concept of "interstate" commerce that judges had articulated in prior decisions. Counsel's arguments had likewise followed judicial precedents by distinguishing "manufacturing" or "production" from "commerce," and there were linguistic obstacles to characterizing manufacturing and production as forms of "commerce." In addition, numerous judicial precedents had held that manufacturing and production were matters of local concern reserved to the states rather than forms of activity falling within the federal government's regulatory authority. Several members of the Court might have been unwilling to overturn these precedents.

Adhering to these distinctions, however, committed the justices to reconsidering relationships between federal and state powers. In this connection, Stone's analysis of the tenth amendment was highly ironic. He implied that the amendment was insignificant by claiming that it "states but a truism that all is retained which has not been surrendered."[37] But as explained above, that truism was capable of cutting several ways. Not only does the amendment declare that powers not delegated are reserved; it also indicates that the states hold some reserved powers that were not delegated to the United States; and it says that the people hold yet other

---

[36] Ibid., at 109 and 122 (emphasis added).
[37] Ibid., at 124.

powers delegated to neither government. Especially because Stone endorsed a broad conception of the states' reserved powers, his reference to the tenth amendment's origins was capable of supporting arguments *against* exercises of federal power.

Stone's analysis of the amendment's purposes was likewise peculiar. He claimed there was "nothing in the history of [the amendment's] adoption to suggest that . . . its purpose was other than to allay fears that the new national government might seek to exercise powers not granted, and that the states might not be able to exercise fully their reserved powers." Those were precisely the arguments against the FLSA's validity: it was not within Congress's delegated powers and interfered with the states' reserved powers. Stone dismissed such arguments by declaring that "[f]rom the beginning and for many years the amendment has been construed as not depriving the national government of authority to resort to all means for the exercise of a granted power which are appropriate and plainly adapted to the permitted end."[38] But this line of reasoning left the opinion vulnerable to arguments that the FLSA's regulation of wages and hours was an inappropriate means of exercising Congress's power over commerce and was a pretextual exercise of power. Such a criticism would not have been pertinent if producing and manufacturing goods for interstate commerce were held to be *part of* that commerce. According to this alternative line of reasoning, Congress would have been exercising one of its powers rather than one reserved to the states.

These different forms of argument could have significantly different practical implications. Among other things, Stone's approach preserved a greater role for judges in reviewing the validity of federal legislation that purportedly interfered with powers reserved to the states or to the people. Thirty-five years later, in *National League of Cities v. Usery*,[39] a majority of the justices accepted this implicit invitation by invalidating an amendment to the FLSA on the grounds that it interfered with state prerogatives. If the judges had been committed to finding that Congress was exercising a delegated power, the decision in *Usery* would have been more difficult to defend. There are good reasons for concluding that principles of national supremacy have afforded more favorable status to enumerated powers than to additional powers purportedly authorized by the necessary and proper clause.[40]

---

[38] Ibid.

[39] 426 U.S. 833 (1976).

[40] Compare Stone's concurring opinion in *New York v. United States*, 326 U.S. 572 (1946), with Justice William Joseph Brennan's dissent in *National League of Cities v. Usery*, 426 U.S. at 856–80. In addition, for criticism of the majority decision in *Usery*, see, e.g., Sotirios A. Barber, "National League of Cities v. Usery: New Meaning for the Tenth Amendment," 1976 Sup. Ct. Rev. 161 (1976); Jeff Powell, "The Compleat Jeffersonian: Justice

Stone's position on the scope of federal and state powers did, however, commit him to abandoning a premise of mutually exclusive governmental powers. Accordingly, he treated delegated and reserved powers as substantially overlapping. Although his position on this issue superficially resembled Marshall's, these two jurists' approaches again diverged in important respects.

Stone assumed greater harmony among federal and state powers than had Marshall. As explained above, the justices had held in *Parrish* that the states held authority to regulate wages and hours of employment. Nothing in *Darby* detracted from that holding. Stone wrote both opinions, and he assumed that the states could continue to exercise reserved powers *consistently* with federal laws. The emerging paradigm, as Corwin described it, was one of "cooperative" rather than "competitive" federalism.[41]

The New Deal apparently depended on cooperation among institutions of federal and state government. Particular states could not have enforced limitations on wages and hours without being at a competitive disadvantage. A uniform policy at the national level was therefore a reasonable means of implementing policies that were sought at different levels of government. The mechanisms of federal representation enabled a majority of the states to work *through* the central government, presumably with a large measure of popular support, in overcoming potential problems of free ridership that might have been associated with a more disjointed regulatory scheme. In a very real sense, the states depended on the federal government to *secure* conditions in which they could effectively exercise their reserved powers.

The New Deal likewise presumed that the central government's superior powers were necessary to secure *the people's* economic rights and powers. A similar principle had underlain *Parrish*, but at the state level. The federal government would *secure* economic liberties by regulating markets and attempting to remedy imbalances of power and opportunity. Through legislation, Congress and state legislatures could pursue objec-

---

Rehnquist and Federalism," 91 Yale L. J. 1317 (1982). For arguments supporting *Usery*, see, e.g., A. E. Dick Howard, "*Garcia* and the Values of Federalism: On the Need for a Recurrence to Fundamental Principles," 19 Ga. L. Rev. 789 (1985); Robert F. Nagel, "Federalism as a Fundamental Value: National League of Cities in Perspective," 1981 Sup. Ct. Rev. 81 (1981). A majority of the justices repudiated *Usery* in *Garcia v. San Antonio Metropolitan Transit*, 469 U.S. 528 (1985). In contrast, Justice Sandra Day O'Connor relied more recently on dual federalist premises to strike down a federal law in *New York v. United States*, 505 U.S. 144 (1992). See also *United States v. Lopez*, 115 S. Ct. 1624 (1995) (held that Congress had exceeded its delegated authority by enacting a law prohibiting possession of firearms within designated school zones).

[41] See Corwin, *Constitutional Revolution*, at 96–102; Corwin, "The Passing of Dual Federalism," at 19 and passim; Corwin, "Introduction to the 1953 Edition," at xiii–xvii.

tives that courts were ill-equipped to promote through more disjointed judicial decision-making. Even as they preempted some persons' separate choices, federal and state laws empowered other persons whose rights had been hollow shells under a regime of judicially supervised markets.

Under these circumstances, therefore, the judges treated separate economic prerogatives as subordinate to exercises of collective power. The people would continue to make economic choices, but within the confines of restraints set primarily by legislatures rather than courts. The role of judges would shift from making economic policy to enforcing legislative choices. State governments would act as intermediaries between the people and the federal government, both in representing their interests and in enforcing national policies.

Securing Constitutional Rights

It is not necessary to conclude that rights and powers of economic autonomy lost constitutional status as federal judges withdrew from enforcing them as limits on legislative and executive authority. On the contrary, it would be reasonable to conclude that legislative and executive officials provided security for *constitutional* prerogatives (characterized as "liberties," "privileges," or "immunities") in ways that the judges alone could not: by making and enforcing laws of general applicability. Judges in effect conceded, moreover, that legislatures had *authority*, based on *the Constitution*, that the judges lacked.[42]

As a result, it became more tenable to conclude that some forms of constitutional power and authority became aligned with each other and with many of the people's economic rights. As judges withdrew from enforcing some of the people's rights as immune from governmental regulation and from enforcing some of the states' reserved powers as absences of federal power, there were fewer obstacles to conceiving of these norms as complementary rather than mutually opposing. Judges backed federal and state legislative and executive officials by treating economic powers at both levels of government as complementary with one another and with the people's rights and powers.

There was no need to assume, moreover, that Congress and the presi-

---

[42] Significantly, Justice Samuel F. Miller assumed in *Slaughter-House Cases* (1873) that Congress and state legislatures would define and secure privileges and immunities of citizenship, with judges playing a subordinate role. One may adhere to his premises regarding legislative enforcement authority but (unlike him) view federal and state powers as overlapping. In this connection, section 5 of the fourteenth amendment is significant because it delegates enforcement authority to *Congress*. Relying on that section, the Supreme Court in *Katzenbach v. Morgan*, 384 U.S. 641 (1966), affirmed *Congress's* authority to secure constitutional rights.

dent were no longer constrained by any constitutional limitations, just because federal judges withdrew from enforcing state powers and certain types of economic liberties as absences of federal regulatory authority. According to the standards of the Constitution itself, Congress and the president continued to lack authority to exceed the scope of their delegated powers or to abridge retained rights or reserved powers. The fourteenth amendment likewise continued to impose restrictions on the states, whether or not judges enforced those restrictions. As a result, it became increasingly problematic to assume that constitutional restraints on legislative and executive actions were coextensive with judicially enforced limitations. Other types of limitations—including those provided by principles and structures of legislative and executive representation and popular accountability—assumed greater importance as judges removed themselves from being intermediaries between the Constitution, elected officials, and the people at large.

More specifically, it would be coherent for persons to argue that particular rights and powers, including economic choices, were beyond the legitimate reach of collective determination even if judges would not enforce those prerogatives. A state could continue to insist that some of its reserved powers corresponded to categorical absences of federal regulatory authority. Individuals and groups could likewise continue to argue that some of the people's economic rights and powers were beyond the legitimate reach of federal or state regulation. But those making such arguments would be compelled to rely primarily on structures of legislative and executive representation, rather than judicial processes, to vindicate their claims.[43] Through self-restraint and in response to popular checks, the federal government has in fact upheld a large measure of state autonomy. Both governments have continued to treat a wide range of economic choices as reserved to individuals and groups, acting separately.

It is also important to recognize that judges did not take a position that there were *no* judicially enforceable constitutional limitations. In a contemporaneous opinion, *United States v. Carolene Products*, Harlan Fiske Stone articulated a framework for judicial enforcement of rights other than economic liberties.[44] In addition, he and others emphasized the im-

---

[43] As indicated above, the Supreme Court has acted more recently to protect reserved powers in *New York v. United States* (1992) and *United States v. Lopez* (1995). But these exceptions confirm the general pattern and underscore the need to account for limits on federal and state powers in addition to the limits enforced by judges. In this connection, it is noteworthy that since the 1930s there has continued to be far-reaching *constitutional* debate *throughout the polity* over relationships among economic rights and federal and state governmental powers.

[44] See 304 U.S. 144 (1938), at 152–53 n. 4. Footnote 4 identifies three categories of cases in which a presumption of constitutional validity might not operate: (1) "when legislation appears on its face to be within a specific prohibition of the Constitution, such as those of

portance of judges' scrutinizing the functioning of political processes, particularly electoral processes. Among other things, judges would seek to guard the people's foundational rights and powers of political participation. By exercising these prerogatives, the people at large would presumably be able to secure other constitutional rights and powers *through* government.

PRIVACY AND ITS LIMITATIONS

Judges have not, moreover, confined themselves to guarding structures and processes of political participation. To be sure, courts have played important roles protecting the people's ability to act *through* representative structures. But even in the wake of *Lochner*'s repudiation, judges have sought to enforce other types of limits on government.

Several rationales have been offered. According to some, judges may scrutinize governmental interference with enumerated but not unenumerated rights—or may enforce "fundamental" rights but not "ordinary" liberties. Others have emphasized overlapping distinctions between the review of governmental "processes" or "means" and enforcing "substantive" limits or reviewing governmental "ends." The idea of constitutional rights as spheres of individual autonomy has persisted, as has commitment to principles of limited government. Combinations and permutations of such positions, along with competing conceptions of egalitarian ideals and other norms, have provided perspectives for interpreting enumerated rights and more open-ended provisions such as those contained in the ninth and fourteenth amendments.

There have been problems with leading approaches. Delegations of powers and enumerations of rights have substantive as well as procedural components. The constitutional text includes categorical along with qualified prohibitions. For these reasons, the fourteenth amendment's due process clause has been a peculiar vehicle for enforcing the Bill of Rights against the states. Judicial reliance on that clause has also been plagued by comparisons to *Lochner*. There have been corresponding problems associated with judicial review of national actions.

---

the first ten amendments"; (2) cases involving "legislation which restricts those political processes which can ordinarily be expected to bring about repeal of undesirable legislation"; and (3) "statutes directed at particular religious, or national, or racial minorities" or reflecting "prejudice against discrete and insular minorities" (citations omitted). See Walter F. Murphy, James E. Fleming, and Sotirios A. Barber, *American Constitutional Interpretation*, 2d ed. (Mineola, N.Y.: Foundation Press, 1995), at 618–21, for an overview of the footnote's history and bibliographic references. In *Democracy and Distrust* (Cambridge: Harvard University Press, 1980), John Hart Ely developed what he claimed were the central ideas of the footnote.

Cases involving rights of sexual and reproductive autonomy highlight some of the enduring tensions. Various arguments converged to support the Court's holding in *Griswold v. Connecticut*: a state could not legitimately prohibit use by married couples of medically safe contraception.[45] In addition to standing on solid normative foundations, *Griswold* has proven to be politically durable.[46] But these virtues have also been stumbling blocks. Efforts to articulate a general "right of privacy" or to enforce it in other contexts have met substantial opposition. The issues of constitutional theory and practice are complex.

Beyond Enforcing Enumerated Rights

The holding in *Griswold* gains support from enumerations of rights, overlapping conceptions of constitutional privacy, and configurations of political power. Although the Court went beyond enforcing enumerated rights, the majority opinion relies heavily on express prohibitions in the constitutional text. Following interpretive conventions, Justice William O. Douglas treated the fourteenth amendment's due process clause as pivotal and interpreted its open-ended provisions with reference to specific prohibitions in the Bill of Rights. On this score, the first, third, fourth, and fifth amendments served important functions.[47]

Justice Douglas was correct to acknowledge, however, that the Court was doing more than enforcing enumerated rights. It was enforcing an unenumerated "right of privacy."[48] The three concurring opinions sought to reinforce this position, while the dissenters criticized this move.[49]

---

[45] A director of Planned Parenthood and one of its physicians were convicted under an accessory statute for aiding in the use of contraception. In addition to invoking their own rights, they asserted those of the married couples they served. See *Griswold*, 381 U.S. 479 (1965).

[46] Subsequent developments have, therefore, confirmed Madison's expectation that one of the political effects of a bill of rights would be its effects on public opinion. Unenumerated along with enumerated rights have been incorporated into political rhetoric within society at large. The rhetoric of rights of privacy has doubtless influenced governmental and extragovernmental choices—actions by the people *through* government and independently, in public and private.

[47] Ely, for example, suggested in *Democracy and Distrust*, at 221 n. 4, that the Court's decision could be defended even from an "interpretivist" perspective. But for an argument that *Griswold* was inconsistent with principles of popular sovereignty, see Peter de Marneffe, "Popular Sovereignty and the *Griswold* Problematic," 13 Law and Phil. 97 (1994).

[48] For a thoughtful treatment of the Court's need to depart from interpretive conventions, see Charles L. Black Jr., "The Unfinished Business of the Warren Court," 46 Wash. L. Rev. 3 (1970).

[49] Justices Goldberg, Harlan, and White wrote separate concurrences; and Justices Black and Stewart each wrote dissents. Chief Justice Earl Warren and Justice Brennan joined Justice Goldberg's concurrence, each of which also joined Justice Douglas's majority opinion;

The idea of a "right of privacy" is multifaceted. It evokes images of boundaries between "private" (including intimate) places and others that are open to the "public." It gains support from distinctions between "private" decisions or choices, typically made by individuals for "personal" reasons, and those made by "public" actors for common or public reasons. There are further distinctions between "private" and "public" institutions. Religious organizations and news media exemplify the former category, government the latter.[50]

Considerations of spacial, decisional, and institutional privacy overlapped to support the holding in *Griswold*. At issue was the use of contraceptives by married persons in intimate settings. Such persons could typically invoke rights associated with private property such as those given by trespass laws and the fourth amendment. Individuals were claiming the right to make personal decisions on matters primarily affecting themselves. Professionals sought to give medical advice in conjunction with doing their jobs within the commercial, or "private," sector. Marriage is also prototypically a "private" institution that has functioned somewhat autonomously from "public" institutions.

The idea of a "right of privacy" also complemented principles of limited government. There was no pressing "public interest."[51] Thus one could reasonably conceive of decisions and activities involving contraception as falling outside spheres of governmental authority. It would be appropriate to invoke the concept of normative "boundaries."

In his majority opinion, Justice Douglas treated the right of privacy primarily as a limit on the government's choice of "means." This approach complemented the structure of the fourteenth amendment's due process clause and interpretive conventions associated with its judicial enforcement. Justice Douglas presumed that the state had a legitimate purpose but had chosen impermissible means to obtain it.[52]

In his concurrence, Justice Arthur Goldberg analyzed more thoroughly relationships among the rights and powers at issue. He also argued that

---

Justices Harlan and White concurred in the majority's judgment but not its opinion; and each dissenter joined the other's dissent.

[50] See generally Randy E. Barnett, "Foreword: Four Senses of the Public-Private Law Distinction," 9 Harv. J. L. and Pub. Pol'y 267 (1986); "Symposium on the Public/Private Distinction," 130 U. Pa. L. Rev. 1289–1440 (1982); Jennifer Nedelsky, "Reconceiving Autonomy: Sources, Thoughts, and Possibilities," 1 Yale J. L. and Fem. 7 (1989).

[51] There was no immediate health threat to individuals using contraception or to the public more generally. Nor, apparently, were there any strong interests in sustaining the state's population. The justices considered interests in preventing illicit sex but argued those interests could be achieved other ways. I deal with this issue below in connection with analyzing the justices' treatment of relationships between a "right of privacy" and pertinent governmental powers.

[52] See *Griswold*, 381 U.S. at 485.

the Connecticut law was unconstitutional according to prevalent tests of legislative means and ends. He indicated that because "fundamental personal liberties" were involved, the statute could be upheld "only upon [the State's] showing a subordinating interest which is compelling." Thus he questioned whether the Connecticut statute was necessary to achieve what he claimed was a legitimate objective: discouraging extramarital sexual relations. He suggested that this objective could have been accomplished by using other means that did not "sweep unnecessarily broadly, reaching far beyond the evil sought to be dealt with and intruding upon the privacy of all married couples." He claimed the state could have "safeguard[ed] marital fidelity" with "a more discriminately tailored statute" that did not "invade the area of protected freedoms."[53]

According to this line of reasoning, like Douglas's, the right of privacy protected spheres of marital activity by constraining the state's choice of means to exercise its reserved powers. The right of privacy "trumped" the means used by the state to exercise its powers, though not the powers themselves. These arguments were, therefore, consistent with broad conceptions of state authority.

Significantly, Goldberg also emphasized limitations on legislative ends. He suggested that the state's efforts to justify the statute were "dubious" because it was not even a rational means of discouraging extramarital affairs.[54] In sum, he implied that the statute was a pretextual exercise of power in the sense that it had an unarticulated, impermissible purpose.

He compared the Connecticut law to a hypothetical "decree that all husbands and wives must be sterilized after two children have been born to them."[55] He claimed that such a decree "would be at complete variance with our constitutional concepts," because, "if upon a showing of a slender basis of rationality, a law outlawing voluntary birth control by

[53] Ibid., at 497–98 (Goldberg, J., concurring) (quoting in part *NAACP v. Alabama*, 377 U.S. 288 [1964], at 307). Goldberg referred, as an example of such a "more discriminately tailored statute," to the state's existing laws that directly forbade adultery and fornication. He asserted that the constitutionality of these statutes was "beyond doubt." Thus he asserted that "the Court's holding . . . in no way interfere[d] with a State's proper regulation of sexual promiscuity or misconduct." *Griswold*, 381 U.S. at 498–99).

[54] Ibid., at 498.

[55] Goldberg identified a possibility that is not merely speculative. China and other nations have laws that limit or penalize childbirth. In addition, some persons convicted of rape and other violent crimes in America are sterilized and subjected to behavior-altering drugs as punishment. See *Buck v. Bell*, 274 U.S. 200 (1927) (the Supreme Court upheld a Virginia law that allowed sterilization of "mental defectives"); but see also *Skinner v. Oklahoma*, 316 U.S. 535 (1942) (invalidated a statute requiring sterilization for "habitual criminals" based on the equal protection clause; the statute exempted from its coverage certain classes of "white-collar" crimes). See generally Mary L. Dudziak, "Oliver Wendell Holmes as a Eugenic Reformer: Rhetoric in the Writing of Constitutional Law," 71 Iowa L. Rev. 833 (1986).

married persons is valid, then, by the same reasoning, a law requiring compulsory birth control also would seem to be valid."[56] He implied, in other words, that controlling family size was not a legitimate governmental purpose.[57]

In addition, Goldberg linked his criticism of governmental ends to his analysis of the right of privacy in ways that called into question prevalent dichotomies between interpreting powers and enforcing rights. Rather than treating the right of privacy as a limitation on means alone, he treated it as a sphere of activity over which government had no coercive authority. For example, he cited Louis Brandeis's dissent in *Olmstead v. United States* for the proposition that the right of privacy is "the right to be left alone."[58] Goldberg also cited *Meyer v. Nebraska*, *Pierce v. Society of Sisters*, and *Prince v. Massachusetts* for the proposition that the Constitution guaranteed a "private realm of family life which the state cannot enter."[59] He suggested that the state had no authority to disrupt "the traditional relation of the family—a relation as old and as fundamental as our entire civilization."[60] Finally, he denied that state governments had power "to experiment with the fundamental liberties of citizens."[61] He asserted: "I cannot agree that the Constitution grants such power either to the States or to the Federal Government."[62] These passages reflect a

[56] *Griswold*, 381 U.S. at 497. Compare Justice George Sutherland's opinion for the Court in *Adkins v. Children's Hospital*, 261 U.S. 525 (1923), at 560 ("The power to fix high wages connotes, by like course of reasoning, the power to fix low wages"); and Justice Stephen Johnson Field's dissent in *Munn v. Illinois*, 94 U.S. 113 (1877), at 140 ("If this be sound law, if there be no protection, either in the principles upon which our republican government is founded, or in the prohibitions of the Constitution against such invasion of private rights, all property and all business in the State are held at the mercy of a majority of its Legislature"). In each instance, the justice was concerned with questions of power, not merely the propriety of means chosen to exercise it.

[57] Goldberg continued: "In my view, . . . both types of law would unjustifiably intrude upon rights of marital privacy which are constitutionally protected" (*Griswold*, 381 U.S. at 497). Thus he implied that a state might under some circumstances limit family size, but he did not elaborate on what might constitute such circumstances. See also ibid., at 496, where he implied that a "subordinating state interest" might qualify as such a legitimate basis for overriding the rights at issue. He apparently thought that if the state had such an interest, a law to achieve it would not have as its primary objective limiting family size, but would impose such limitations as a means of achieving the compelling (or "subordinating") interest.

[58] Ibid., at 494, quoting *Olmstead v. United States*, 277 U.S. 438 (1928), at 478 (Brandeis, J., dissenting).

[59] *Griswold*, 381 U.S. at 495, citing *Meyer v. Nebraska*, 362 U.S. 390 (1923), and *Pierce v. Society of Sisters*, 262 U.S. 510 (1925), and quoting *Prince v. Massachusetts*, 321 U.S. 158 (1944), at 166.

[60] *Griswold*, 381 U.S. at 496.

[61] Ibid, quoting *Pointer v. Texas*, 380 U.S. 400 (1965), at 413 (Goldberg, J., concurring).

[62] *Griswold*, 381 U.S. at 496.

premise that state powers, like federal powers, are intrinsically limited: neither government has authority to infringe rights retained by the people.

It is noteworthy that Goldberg treated the relevant rights and powers as dichotomous rather than overlapping. He suggested that the people had retained private rights as individuals rather than given to government authority to restrict their exercise. (There were problems, however, with his suggestion that the United States Constitution "grants" powers to the states.) At the same time, he presumed that federal courts did have authority to *secure* such rights from abridgment by state officials.

Spheres of Autonomy Revisited

David A. J. Richards has argued that the "enduring principle" underlying *Griswold* was a commitment to "moral independence."[63] His analysis of rights and powers as mutually limiting normative spheres is instructive.

According to Richards, constitutional guarantees "define substantive spheres of moral self-government."[64] He argued, moreover, that the idea of "essential moral spheres" includes the right of intimate association in marriage. Especially because "the wall separating the political or the religious from intimate personal life has quite collapsed," he observed, "the moral resources of private life may require as much protection as politics or religion against oppressive, majoritarian orthodoxy."[65] His use of the metaphor of a "wall" evokes images of normative boundaries between constitutional rights and powers. In this respect, his arguments parallel parts of Goldberg's concurrence.

But Richards has not adhered to the implications of treating rights and powers as separated by a "wall." Instead, he argued that a state could, with proper justification, "intrude[] into an essential sphere of moral independence—a sphere protected by both enumerated and unenumerated rights." He suggested that a state could satisfy this burden by proving that a particular exercise of power was "of indispensable necessity in protecting the general goods of life, liberty, and property." He compared the burden required for a state to infringe rights of intimacy with that required to abridge the right of conscience: "The state may . . . justify even abridging a fundamental right like the right of conscience if necessary to protect life, liberty, and property, because the just role of the republican state is to insure the general conditions of life and security."

[63] See David A. J. Richards, "Constitutional Legitimacy and Constitutional Privacy," 61 NYU L. Rev. 800 (1986), at 832–48.

[64] Ibid., at 843.

[65] Ibid., at 845 (citations omitted).

Similarly, he implied that a state could, under some circumstances, legitimately abridge rights of intimacy such as those at issue in *Griswold* in order to promote the general welfare. In his view, the problem with the Connecticut statute was that it did not satisfy this burden of justification.[66]

Thus Richards treated the right of privacy as a "liberty" that was subject to "reasonable" governmental regulations—i.e., those consistent with the requirements of "due process." Justice Brian Walsh of the Irish Supreme Court articulated a similar view of the right to use contraceptives. In *McGee v. Attorney General and Revenue Commissioners*,[67] the court invalidated a law that prohibited importation of contraceptives. As had justices of the United States Supreme Court, the Irish judges based their decision in part on an unenumerated right of privacy.[68] As had Justice Goldberg, Justice Walsh argued that there was not sufficient justification for the ban. But the Irish judge suggested that under different circumstances, the government could ban the importation of contraceptives "where the public good requires it, as for example a dangerous fall in population threatening the life or essential welfare of the State."[69] He likewise indicated that "state intervention" might be justified if the use of contraceptives by married couples were demonstrated to have "an adverse effect on public morality."

Although Goldberg did not preclude a similar conclusion in the American context, parts of his opinion suggest a more absolute conception of the right of privacy. In places, he indicated that Connecticut would have no authority, under any circumstances, to regulate or interfere with some persons' decisions to obtain and use medically safe contraceptives. Those portions of his opinion support conceiving of married couples' right to use contraceptives in the privacy of their homes as a fundamental "privilege" or "immunity." The government had no authority to abridge this right, period.

[66] See ibid., at 845–47. Richards explained: "Far from harming a general public good, contraceptive use in marriage enables married couples to better control their reproductive aims consistent with other personal and ethical aims, including the expression of marital sexuality as an end in itself, an expression of natural affection and mutual love."

[67] [1974] I.R. 284, in Walter F. Murphy and Joseph Tanenhaus, *Comparative Constitutional Law: Cases and Commentaries* (New York: St. Martin's, 1977), at 398–403.

[68] The Irish Constitution gave the Irish judges greater textual warrant for their decision than the United States Constitution gave the American judges. Among other things, article 41 provided: "The State recognizes the Family as the natural primary and functional unit group of Society, and as a moral institution possessing inalienable and imprescriptible rights, antedating and superior to all positive law. . . . The State pledges itself to guard with special care the institution of Marriage, on which the Family is founded, and to protect it against attack." See Murphy and Tanenhaus, *Comparative Constitutional Law*, app. 6, at 739–40. Not surprisingly, Justice Walsh relied on these provisions in *McGee*.

[69] Walsh did not concede, however, that the government would have authority to compel couples to have children, even under these more extreme circumstances.

According to this reading of Goldberg's concurrence, he was implying that rights of privacy have protected spheres of autonomy that have been more categorical in character than Richards would claim. Portions of Goldberg's opinion support a conclusion that the Connecticut legislature had no authority to prohibit certain forms of contraception even if doing so was necessary to accomplish a substantial collective interest and even if a majority of the legislature thought the conduct at issue was immoral. Goldberg implied, in short, that some decisions about contraception were reserved to the people as individuals and couples. It would be up to them to respond appropriately to any public exigencies. Couples might at some time have a moral duty to refrain from using contraceptives, but not a legal duty.

The Constitution has drawn boundaries primarily between the permissible and impermissible rather than simply between the moral and immoral.[70] Thus it has presupposed a degree of separation between constitutional law and some issues of morality. Other examples of separations between law and morality include the Constitution's original compromise over slavery, the first amendment's guarantees of religious liberty and the freedom of speech, and the fourth amendment's prohibition of unreasonable searches and seizures. The federal government could not legitimately prevent importation of slaves at least until 1808 even if slavery was immoral; individuals have had a constitutional right to hold religious beliefs that have not accorded with prevailing norms; the first amendment has not made moral considerations determinative of whether persons could engage in the protected speech; and the fourth amendment has shielded some types of immoral as well as moral uses of private property.

As these examples suggest, one reason the Constitution has separated law from some issues of morality has been to finesse controversy. On the assumption that political cooperation and the integrity of the community have not depended on resolving all moral controversies, and based on widely shared commitments to individual liberty and concomitant aspects of personal autonomy, some divisive moral issues have been relegated to "private" realms. Legal toleration has not implied lack of importance but allocation of responsibility.

John Rawls has examined similar issues. He has emphasized the importance of consensus as one of the principal bases for political cooperation in constitutional democracies such as the United States. In American political culture, this consensus has ironically embraced principles of tolera-

[70] The Constitution does not, of course, always draw such a boundary. For example, the eighth amendment seemingly incorporates moral principles into constitutional law. Even in that case, however, it is not clear that the Constitution *directly* incorporates moral principles—i.e., without any mediation by principles of legal interpretation and the like. Prohibitions on murder also reflect moral commitments that are embedded in legal norms.

tion on matters that have not been essential to social cooperation or the moral integrity of society as a whole.[71] These dual components of political cooperation, consensus on a range of issues but toleration on others, have been reflected in America's legal institutions. These principles have also provided standards for interpreting, criticizing, and advocating changes in legal and other political institutions.[72]

The first amendment's provisions concerning religious liberty epitomize this sort of separation between law and highly contested issues of morality. As Rawls has explained, principles of religious toleration in constitutional democracies have not presupposed that religion has been either unimportant or irrelevant to politics. On the contrary, religious toleration has protected the liberty of individuals to develop and actualize ultimate beliefs in an environment that purportedly has not been tainted by improper legal coercion.

But religion has not been entirely separated from politics. Religious beliefs have directly and indirectly shaped many persons' moral judgments. These judgments, in turn, have provided foundations for shared political commitments. Rawls's arguments support using coercion, under appropriate circumstances, to enforce laws that have flowed from these shared commitments. Personal convictions alone, however, would not justify governmental coercion.

The issues involved in *Griswold* overlapped and paralleled religious divisions of this sort. Many persons' religious beliefs have shaped their positions on matters of sexuality, and reproductive choices have fallen in other ways outside realms of public agreement. Sexuality, like religious faith, has been central to personal autonomy, and social cooperation has not depended on fully consistent religious commitments or entirely congruous attitudes toward sexuality. Thus decisions involving these matters

[71] See John Rawls, "Justice as Fairness: Political Not Metaphysical," 14 Phil. and Pub. Aff. 223 (1985); Rawls, *Political Liberalism* (New York: Columbia University Press, 1993); Rawls, *A Theory of Justice* (Cambridge: Harvard University Press, 1971). By citing Rawls on this issue, I am not committed to his conception of the content of an overlapping political consensus in America—i.e., his principles of justice. Nor am I committed to endorsing his use of the device of a "veil of ignorance" to arrive at principles of justice. Likewise, I am not committed to the conception of persons that underlies his theory. Finally, I am not committed to an individualistic conception of rights or principles of justice.

[72] Just as I am not committed to endorsing Rawls's theory of justice, I am not committed to using that moral theory as a basis for interpreting, criticizing, or advocating change in America's governing laws—which include, of course, the United States Constitution. I am assuming, however, that there are political communities within America with shared moral commitments that are capable of contributing to political and legal analysis in the ways suggested. I am also considering implications of Rawls's moral theory that he did not emphasize: its implications for legal analysis. In this respect, my project overlaps Ronald Dworkin's. See, e.g., Ronald Dworkin, *Taking Rights Seriously* (Cambridge: Harvard University Press, 1978), esp. chs. 5–7; Dworkin, *Law's Empire* (Cambridge: Harvard University Press, 1986).

may reasonably be relegated to spheres of private choice, at least to the extent that choices made within those spheres do not threaten moral commitments and activities properly reflected in laws and regulated by them.

Moreover, the Constitution has gone further in some cases and placed prerogatives off limits even from decisions based on consensus or supposed collective interests. The first amendment has prohibited governmental enforcement of religious orthodoxy and has shielded individuals who have adopted religious views that have gone against prevailing conceptions of the public welfare. For example, the Constitution has arguably protected the choice of particular religious sects to encourage practices that have led to low economic productivity or high consumption. There have been limits on such independence, but these limits have not diminished the significance of choices within protected normative spheres.

It is not clear whether various components of the right of privacy have had such privileged status. *Griswold* held that couples could legally use contraceptives in some circumstances. These choices have had moral dimensions, and thus the decision affirmed a type of moral "independence," or autonomy. In other words, the decision enforced a degree of separation between some people's opinions of morality and the law. Justice Goldberg's opinion implies a strong conception of that right, but other justices in the majority apparently thought it was more qualified and could have been defeated by certain types of public interests.

It was not necessary to resolve this issue in *Griswold*. But it would become more important in other contexts. In *Roe v. Wade*, for example, considerations of reproductive privacy would be pitted against arguments that government could and should protect the lives of fetuses and promote respect for life. Claims of public interest have also supported governmental restrictions on economic choices. There have been strong pressures to conceive of the rights involved as limited in scope or as subject to governmental preemption.

In other contexts, it would also be more important to confront questions about *who* may provide security for rights of privacy. *Griswold* followed *Lochner, Hammer*, and a solid line of other precedents that rest on an assumption that *judges* could legitimately secure private rights from abridgment by other governmental officials. It would be logically coherent to argue that the people have held some such rights without arguing that *judges* have had exclusive or primary authority for their enforcement.[73] Public opinion, electoral checks, executive vetoes, legislative self-

---

[73] Justice Hugo Black suggested such a possibility in *Griswold* by claiming that the ninth amendment undercut rather than supported enforcement by federal judges of unenumerated rights as limitations on the states. Raoul Berger developed such an argument more fully in "The Ninth Amendment," 66 Cornell L. Rev. 1 (1980). Both claimed that the ninth amend-

restraint, and national legislation might provide security for private rights independently of their judicial enforcement. These other checks take on particular importance in light of evidence regarding the limited effects of judicial decisions.[74]

Griswold does not provide fertile ground for examining this issue, because the decision did not provoke substantial political opposition. Subsequent developments have reinforced rather than challenged the holding. Governmental officials and private actors have not mobilized to place in jeopardy the use of contraceptives by married couples.

In contrast, *Roe v. Wade* thrust the right of privacy to the top of the political agenda. Opponents of that decision and its progeny have organized "pro-life" media campaigns and political demonstrations, supported federal and state laws prohibiting or restricting abortions or funding for them, favored appointment of federal and state judges sympathetic with restrictions on abortion, advocated constitutional amendments to protect the unborn, and otherwise sought to influence "private" choices and governmental actions. In opposition, other persons have organized "pro-choice" media campaigns and political demonstrations, sponsored federal and state legislation to guarantee rights of choice and funding for abortions, supported federal and state judges committed to rights of choice, and advocated constitutional amendments and interpretations of them that would ensure the availability of legal abortions.

Controversy over abortion has precipitated constitutional crises comparable in some respects to those surrounding the New Deal. Although the nation's economic and political functioning have not been on the verge of collapse, separate and collective prerogatives have again been opposed on issues of high political salience. Rather than being divided on matters of economic power, the people and their representatives have been divided on whose public and private moralities the Constitution has sanctioned and how it has done so. The legal system has been stretched to

---

ment had originally denied federal power for the benefit of the states (not just the people). Going further, they argued that the Supreme Court in *Griswold*, by exercising *federal* power to invalidate a *state* law, turned the amendment's meaning on its head. Although Black and Berger denied that an unenumerated right of privacy had the status of a "constitutional right" (either originally or based on the fourteenth amendment), many of their arguments concerning the scope of federal judicial power would still hold even if they conceded that the ninth and fourteenth amendments have guarded "constitutional" rights even as the Constitution has withheld from federal judges authority for their enforcement. But for criticism of Berger's failure to distinguish judicial *enforcement* authority from federal *regulatory* authority, see Simeon C. R. McIntosh, "On Reading the Ninth Amendment: A Reply to Raoul Berger," 28 Howard L. J. 913 (1985).

[74] See generally Gerald N. Rosenberg, *The Hollow Hope: Can Courts Bring About Social Change?* (Chicago: University of Chicago Press, 1991) (though it seems to me that Rosenberg overstates the limited impact of judicial decisions).

its limits by defiance of laws—both by those obtaining illegal abortions and by those using violence (even murder) to interfere with legal abortions. It would be wrong to think judges have been making all the important constitutional decisions.

Limitations of Law

Those advocating legal restrictions on abortion may rely on several important differences between contraception and abortion. First, abortions are not intimate in some ways that sexual activity is. Abortions are typically performed by physicians in hospitals or clinics; thus the persons involved, the types of activities, and the places are significantly different from couples' having sexual intercourse in private places. Second, the bases for claiming decisional autonomy are weaker, because in most cases the pregnant woman has chosen to engage in sexual activity and has had the option of using contraceptives. As a result, it is less clear that guaranteeing a right to obtain abortions is necessary for women (or both partners) to have sexual autonomy.[75] Third, at some point after conception (whenever that event takes place), a morally significant being—the fetus—exists. This fact makes it difficult to argue that some or all abortions affect only the persons deciding to obtain or perform them. Beginning at some stage of pregnancy, individuals and communities have moral responsibilities to care for the fetus and treat it as a valuable form of human life. (Even pro-choice advocates typically concede that late-term abortions may be restricted or prohibited for reasons going beyond the need to ensure the health of the woman carrying the fetus.) Fourth, many abortions have involved unwed women whose pregnancies have gone against rather than reinforced traditional institutions and values. Restricting abortions might be a reasonable means of influencing people's sexual practices.

Nevertheless, proponents of a right to obtain abortions, at least during the early stages of pregnancy, have frequently treated that right as analogous to the one announced in *Griswold*. It has been common to emphasize the decisional components of a more general right of privacy, based on a premise that persons primarily affected by certain matters, not the people's elected representatives, have a right to make decisions relating to those matters. Because a woman's pregnancy concerns her more than the public at large, she should be able to decide whether to continue or abort that pregnancy. According to this line of reasoning, there are rights of

---

[75] This distinction does not apply to cases of rape and incest, but in those cases there is more involved than considerations of decisional autonomy.

legal independence involving abortion that are similar to those involving use of contraceptives. The operative metaphor in many cases, whether explicitly or implicitly, is of normative boundaries that separate individual from collective prerogatives.[76]

Contraception and abortion are also closely related insofar as each permits severing sexuality from reproduction. Each therefore expands opportunities for sexual freedom, family planning, and related choices of lifestyle. Proliferation of contraceptives has made it possible for women to pursue educational and career paths without forgoing sexual intimacy. This wider range of opportunities includes many personal matters other than sexuality itself: matters reserved to individuals rather than entrusted to governmental officials. (Whether to pursue higher education, what to study, whether to work, where to work, where to live, and how to spend one's earnings are prototypical examples of "personal" choices, or "private" matters, in this sense of being reserved to individuals rather than entrusted to collective determination.) Thus sexual self-determination is not only an important form of personal autonomy, it is also instrumental to realizing other forms of autonomy. In this respect, using contraceptives and obtaining abortions are largely indistinguishable: each frees sexuality from constraints otherwise associated with it and creates corresponding opportunities.

Increasing opportunities have not, of course, settled moral choices that have accompanied those opportunities. A variety of considerations may inform analysis of when, if ever, it is morally permissible for a woman to obtain an abortion. Does it matter whether the woman is married, the couple has used contraception, or she (or they) can afford an abortion or the expenses of raising a child? Chances of physical or mental disability (to the woman or the fetus) may be relevant, as might the availability of adoption. Some persons regard abortions as morally permissible during the early stages of pregnancy in cases of rape and incest even if not in other circumstances. Changes in technology have added further complication, making abortions safer at later stages but also moving up fetal viability. New drugs have blurred the line between contraception and abortion.

Many analyses of whether women have a constitutional right to obtain abortions have focused on issues like these, apparently based on assumptions that constitutional and moral boundaries have been coextensive.[77]

---

[76] See, e.g., Susan R. Estrich and Kathleen M. Sullivan, "Abortion Politics: Writing for an Audience of One," 138 U. Pa. L. Rev. 119 (1989); Suzanna Sherry, "Women's Virtue," 63 Tul. L. Rev. 1591 (1989). As explained below, not all persons have advocated conceiving of abortion-related rights as entirely "negative" in the sense of precluding governmental power to *secure* rights of choice.

[77] For analysis of moral issues relating to abortion, see, e.g., Marshall Cohen, Thomas Nagel, and Thomas Scanlon, eds., *The Rights and Wrongs of Abortion* (Princeton: Prince-

Generality is a virtue of law, and thus interpreters have appropriately searched for general conclusions. But because moral issues relating to abortion have been complex and multidimensional, they have resisted generalization and have been difficult to govern through law.

The complexity of moral issues has had important consequences for constitutional analysis. Insofar as the Constitution has guaranteed a right to act morally, it would seem to have precluded laws that have abridged moral choice through overgeneralization. Constitutional standards of generality may have required entrusting to individuals a right to make some choices even if not all of the resulting decisions have been morally commendable. Moreover, governmental functioning apparently has not depended on whether women have obtained abortions, even assuming some such choices—obtaining and/or not obtaining abortions—have been immoral. Absent governmental regulation, individuals should be capable of making a wide range of choices—including important choices with moral dimensions—within the context of families, communities, and "private" institutions.

Many would not concede, however, that the Constitution has reserved moral choice in this manner or that abortion should not be restricted or regulated through generally applicable laws. The Constitution's separating law from morality might have cut in more than one direction. In addition to protecting a range of possibly immoral choices, the Constitution may have allowed legislation that has gone against principles of morality. Not all unjust laws have been unconstitutional.

Neither proponents nor opponents of abortion rights would typically acknowledge, however, that their position would entail or sanction immoral action. Disagreement instead has centered on who has had constitutional authority to make the important and difficult choices at issue. Some persons have urged, in essence, that the Constitution has reserved some or all of these choices to the women involved, perhaps because they could best take into account all the appropriate circumstances. Other persons have argued that the Constitution has allowed governmental officials to preclude individual choice as necessary and proper to promote collective ends or protect individual rights (including the fetus's right to life).

The Eye of the Storm

The Supreme Court's decisions on rights of abortion reveal some of these tensions. Although there has been some coherence, the justices have been

ton University Press, 1974) (reprint of essays by John Finnis, Judith Jarvis Thomson, Michael Tooley, and Roger Wertheimer that originally appeared in *Philosophy and Public Affairs*).

deeply divided. As this book goes to print, a majority of the Court has not fully repudiated *Roe v. Wade*,[78] but various majorities have qualified major parts of this watershed precedent. Some justices have voted consistently either to follow or to reverse applicable precedents, but other members of the Court have repudiated their earlier positions. Alignments among the justices have been unstable, and those voting together for various results have given conflicting reasons for doing so. Instead of moving closer together, the justices seem to have moved further apart.

As with many important judicial opinions, *Roe v. Wade* set the terms of much subsequent debate but left many issues unresolved. In his majority opinion, Justice Harry Blackmun linked the right of women to have abortions to other rights involving marital and sexual autonomy. But he also identified public interests that had not been present in earlier cases involving claims of constitutional privacy.

Blackmun claimed that state governments had authority to promote at least two "interests" that intersected with abortion rights: protecting maternal health and prenatal life. He was unclear, however, how he conceived of relationships between state authority to promote these interests and the right of women to obtain abortions in at least some circumstances. His lack of clarity on this issue invited dispute over the character of the right enforced, including whether it might be consistent in other circumstances with restrictions on its exercise short of criminal prohibition.

Portions of his opinion suggest he was assuming that women have had the same right to abort throughout their pregnancies even as he was arguing that governmental interests or rights of fetuses could limit or override a woman's exercise of her right to abort during the second and third trimesters. Under this conceptualization, governmental powers and the rights they secured could in some circumstances "trump," or override, a woman's right to have an abortion. If Blackmun assumed that the relevant rights and powers could conflict, he apparently thought one set of prerogatives could prevail over another.

According to this reading of Blackmun's opinion in *Roe*, the majority decision depended on the justices' weighing the strength or priority of the respective prerogatives and not merely on the justices' locating normative boundaries. If so, the justices must have presumed that *their* weighing of the relevant prerogatives carried greater authority than the state legislature's. The justices did not, after all, assume constitutionality or defer to the outcome of legislative processes within Texas.

But other portions of Blackmun's opinion suggest a significantly different type of judicial inquiry based on a more complementary view of rela-

---

[78] 410 U.S. 113 (1973).

tionships among the rights and powers at issue. The majority may well have been assuming that women had no right to make choices that a state could legitimately restrict or prohibit. According to this scheme, women have not had the same right at different stages of their pregnancies. Under this alternative conceptualization, the relevant inquiry in *Roe* was where the boundaries between prerogatives were located rather than which had priority.

These two paradigms, including variations of each, could have significantly differing practical implications. According to the former assumptions, individual rights and governmental powers have been capable of conflicting, and thus finding either has not been determinative of constitutional validity. Finding a legitimate governmental interest has not established validity, nor has interference with exercising a constitutional right implied invalidity. If there has been both a governmental interest and interference with a constitutional right, judges must have decided which had priority or deferred to others' (e.g., legislators') judgment on this issue. The Constitution might have provided standards for resolving the conflict or left the issue legally indeterminate. On the other hand, if some of the governmental powers and rights at issue have been mutually exclusive, it would be logically incoherent to find a legitimate conflict. Either government has had the power at issue or there has been a right of individual choice, not both.

Although much of *Roe* suggests the former paradigm, the decision did not foreclose the latter. Moreover, even if Blackmun had articulated more clearly how he conceived of the rights and powers involved and how they related to one another in the context of *Roe*, his opinion alone could not have settled divisions within constitutional theory and practice on issues of abortion.

Questions of Influence and Entitlement

Various institutions of federal and state government, acting within a complicated matrix of social pressures, have given the justices plenty of opportunities to reconsider the character and scope of abortion-related rights. In subsequent opinions, moreover, justices have dealt explicitly with an issue overlapping but conceptually distinct from those identified by Blackmun in *Roe*: whether institutions of federal or state government have constitutional authority to influence how women exercise protected rights of choice. In addressing this issue, some of the justices have continued to rely on distinctions between public and private choices even as they have suggested connections among such choices and have treated boundaries between them as somewhat permeable. These opinions also raise further questions about how to conceive of the rights at issue—as corresponding to categorical absences of governmental authority or as capable of otherwise limiting exercises of collective power.

In *Maher v. Roe*,[79] for example, a majority of the justices upheld a Connecticut regulation that prohibited Medicaid funding for most abortions but allowed funding for childbirth. Justice Lewis Powell, writing for the majority, asserted that prior decisions did not preclude the state from making "a value judgment favoring childbirth over abortion, and . . . implement[ing] that judgment by the allocation of public funds." He claimed that the state's decision not to fund abortions "place[d] no obstacles—absolute or otherwise—in the pregnant woman's path to an abortion." He recognized, however, that the state's policy of funding childbirth but not abortions might influence women's choices.[80] Later decisions, most notably *Harris v. McRae*[81] and *Webster v. Reproductive Health Services*,[82] have extended this line of reasoning to uphold federal restrictions on using Medicaid funds and state restrictions on using public funds, employees, or facilities to perform or assist abortions except as necessary to save women's lives.[83]

These decisions, along with earlier majority opinions, reflect a premise that the right of women to obtain abortions has been a limitation on governmental authority rather than a source of affirmative governmental responsibilities. The later opinions are clearer, however, in not treating the right to abort (whatever its scope) as completely beyond the legitimate reach of federal and state coercive power. While a majority of the justices have affirmed the right of women to obtain abortions under some circumstances, the judges have also held that governmental institutions could seek to influence how women exercised that right.

According to this line of reasoning, the Constitution has not obliged governmental institutions to be neutral on how women exercise their limited rights of choice. Nor have such institutions been obliged to ensure

---

[79] 432 U.S. 464 (1977). Dissenters in prior cases had already articulated a similarly qualified view of the right to obtain an abortion, but *Maher* marked the beginning of a majority of the Court's upholding laws or other governmental policies that favored childbirth over abortion.

[80] *Maher*, 432 U.S. at 474. Justice Powell distinguished decisions in which the Court had invalidated more direct interferences with obtaining abortions. See, e.g., *Doe v. Bolton*, 410 U.S. 179 (1973); *Planned Parenthood v. Danforth*, 428 U.S. 52 (1976); *Bellotti v. Baird*, 443 U.S. 622 (1979); *Akron v. Akron Center for Reproductive Health*, 462 U.S. 416 (1983); *Thornburgh v. American College of Obstetricians and Gynecologists*, 476 U.S. 747 (1986).

[81] 448 U.S. 297 (1980).

[82] 492 U.S. 490 (1989).

[83] See also *Rust v. Sullivan*, 500 U.S. 173 (1991) (upheld the Title X "Gag Rule" then in effect; it restricted federal funding for facilities that performed abortions or provided counseling on abortions).

that women have the means of exercising those rights. On the contrary, the Constitution has allowed governmental institutions to make resources (such as financial assistance) available to women who carry their pregnancies to term but not to those who abort. Institutions of federal and state government may use their spending and regulatory powers to discourage constitutionally protected abortions—i.e., abortions insulated from criminal prohibition.

But not all the justices have agreed on these matters. Justice William J. Brennan Jr., dissenting in *Maher*, criticized the majority's willingness to sanction some forms of governmental involvement with women's choices while ruling out other forms of interference. He argued that "*Roe v. Wade* and cases following it [held] that an area of privacy invulnerable to the State's intrusion surrounds the decision of a pregnant woman whether or not to carry her pregnancy to term." He claimed, in other words, that the Constitution established a broader constitutional immunity than a majority of the justices were willing to enforce. In his view, withholding funding for abortions but not for childbirth was a form of "coercion" that "inhibited" or "impinge[d] upon" a fundamental right. Thus he denied that a state had authority to interfere in any manner with women's freedom of choice at least during the first trimester of pregnancy. But he suggested that the states did have authority to provide funding for abortions and had a responsibility to do so if they provided funding for other medical procedures.[84]

Justice Brennan likewise argued in *Harris v. McRae* that Congress had no authority "to impose the political majority's judgment of the morally acceptable and socially desirable preference on a sensitive and intimate decision that the Constitution entrusts to the individual." Once again, he argued that a denial of funding for abortions, in this case by the federal government, "not only was designed to inhibit, but does in fact inhibit the woman's freedom to choose abortion over childbirth."[85] In sum, he treated a woman's right to choose as a normative boundary that has precluded not only preemption through law but also governmental interference with the woman's exercise of that right.

It is noteworthy that Justice Brennan argued in *Maher* and *Harris* that

---

[84] See *Maher*, 432 U.S. at 483–90 (Brennan, J., dissenting) (Justice Brennan, who would have required a "compelling interest" to justify the state's interference with a woman's choice to obtain an abortion, was joined in his dissent by Justices Thurgood Marshall and Harry Blackmun).

[85] *Harris*, 448 U.S. at 332 (Brennan, J., dissenting) (Justice Brennan was again joined in his dissent by Justices Thurgood Marshall and Harry Blackmun). (The issue in *Harris* was the constitutionality of the "Hyde Amendment," which limited the use of federal funds for abortions to those that were medically necessary.) See also Justice Marshall's argument in *Harris*, dissenting at 345, that the issues of equal protection were more acute in that case than in *Maher*.

a right of privacy similarly limited exercises of federal and state power. In *Maher*, although he addressed only the issue of whether the state had a "compelling" reason to restrict abortions during the first trimester, he apparently thought the state had *no* legitimate reason for interfering with a woman's decision to abort her pregnancy during that stage.[86] He likewise suggested in *Harris* that Congress had no authority to enact the Hyde Amendment, even in reliance on spending powers, because that law interfered with a fundamental right. Contrasting the majority's argument that institutions of federal and state government could legitimately promote respect for potential life by withholding funding for abortions, even during the first trimester, he apparently thought this objective was not a legitimate basis for making the spending distinctions in either case.

Part of the disagreement between the majority and Justice Brennan and other dissenters concerned whether promoting respect for life and fostering a certain type of community were sufficient bases for exercising governmental power. In addition, beneath the surface were questions concerning the status of fetuses as "persons," whether fetuses had rights, and if so how the state could secure those rights. The majority held that federal and state officials had legitimate reasons for encouraging childbirth rather than abortion and thus could fund the former but not the latter.[87] Justice Brennan, on the other hand, took a position that the purposes and effects of the governmental choices under consideration in *Maher* and *Harris* were impermissible: to influence how women exercised their constitutional rights. He suggested that if a woman had a constitutional right to choose whether to continue or abort her pregnancy, then governmental institutions had no power to use machinery of law to pressure her to

---

[86] See *Maher*, 432 U.S. at 489–90 (Brennan, J., dissenting). Compare Justice Blackmun's argument that the viability-testing provision at issue in *Webster* did not serve any legitimate state interest, and thus did not even pass the least restrictive "rational basis standard" of review used by the Court to assess the constitutionality of economic legislation (*Webster*, 492 U.S. at 543) (Blackmun, J., dissenting). See also ibid., at 547 n. 7, comparing the issues in *Webster* to those in *Griswold*, where the Court held there was no legitimate state interest in regulating the use of medically safe contraceptives.

[87] The justices did not analyze whether that commitment was capable of overriding rights of privacy, because (as indicated) the majority did not think that there was any normative conflict between women's rights and the exercises of governmental power at issue in *Maher* and *Harris*. Similarly, the justices brushed over the issue of whether it was coherent for judges, legislators, or others to affirm or recognize a right to choose abortion while also taking or endorsing a position, implemented through the machinery of law, against the exercise of that right. This sort of practical tension between a legal right and laws relating to their exercise is peculiar even if it is not logically incoherent. More typically, interpreters ascribe value to the exercise of constitutional rights and for that reason favor governmental choices protecting or promoting conditions necessary for the exercise of those rights. The majority opinions, therefore, reflect the justices' qualified commitment to a right to obtain abortions, along with limited conceptions of the scope and priority of any such right.

exercise that right one way or the other. He apparently thought that withholding funding, but not providing it, would unduly influence women's choices.[88]

Interpretive Plurality

More recent cases have not settled these issues or others involving abortion. On the contrary, changes in the Court's composition, the types of restrictions and policies under review, and other factors have exacerbated divisions among the justices. In *Planned Parenthood v. Casey*,[89] for example, there were five different opinions, each of which dealt with the validity of various provisions in a Pennsylvania statute. The judges were divided not only on which provisions were constitutional but also on how to decide these issues.

Justices Sandra Day O'Connor, Anthony Kennedy, and David Souter announced the Court's decision. The judges' opinions converged to uphold the Pennsylvania statute's definition of "medical emergencies" and its informed consent, parental consent, and recordkeeping requirements but to invalidate its spousal notification provisions. Justices Stevens and Blackmun joined in parts of the joint opinion but not others: Justice John Paul Stevens would have invalidated the informed consent requirements along with the spousal notifications provisions, and he would have upheld the parental consent provisions but for different reasons; Justice Blackmun would have invalidated all the challenged provisions. Chief Justice William Rehnquist, joined by Justices White, Scalia, and Thomas, argued that all the provisions were valid. Justice Anthony Scalia, joined by the Chief Justice and Justices Byron White and Clarence Thomas, likewise would have upheld all the provisions but by using significantly different reasoning.

Not surprisingly, the opinions in *Casey* present various conceptions of the rights and powers involved and relationships among them. Parts of the joint opinion suggest that the right to abort, whatever its reach, has been unqualified. Justices O'Connor, Kennedy, and Souter placed their analysis of abortion rights within the context of claims that "there is a

[88] Justice Brennan did not reach the question of whether governmental institutions could take a position against abortion other than through law—for example, through media campaigns. The cases did not present that question. The issue in *Maher* and *Harris*, after all, was the constitutionality of legally authoritative allocations of resources. Brennan did not argue, however, that governmental institutions had no legitimate powers relating to abortion; instead, he claimed that institutions of federal and state government could legitimately provide funding for abortions.

[89] 112 S. Ct. 2791 (1992).

realm of personal liberty which the government may not enter." The joint opinion implies in places that government has had no power to interfere with a range of choices involving abortion.[90]

But these same judges also argued that "not every law which makes a right more difficult to exercise is, *ipso facto*, an infringement of that right." According to some parts of the joint opinion, the validity of the provisions under review hinged on whether they placed an "undue burden" on the right to have an abortion or placed a "substantial obstacle" in the path of women seeking to exercise that right. Moreover, these three justices upheld "restrictions" on women's choice, even during the first trimester. The restrictions were allegedly "reasonable" as means of securing interests in potential life. Rather than treating a woman's right to abort as completely immune from governmental regulation, the joint opinion allowed the state to regulate directly the exercise of that right.

Justice Stevens treated the right to abort as more absolute in character, at least in the sense that its exercise under some conditions was beyond the reach of some forms of governmental authority. He criticized the joint opinion's departure from *Roe*'s trimester framework and argued that restrictions on abortion during the first trimester were not permissible. Although he conceded that states had legitimate interests in protecting potential life and could express a preference for childbirth over abortion, he denied that a state could "influence" women's decisions. He suggested, moreover, that a state could restrict abortions before fetal viability only if the restriction was reasonably necessary to protect maternal health. Yet he claimed that certain types of informational requirements were permissible as long as they enhanced the deliberative quality of decisions rather than interfered with them. In short, Stevens distinguished permissible from impermissible types of regulations based on whether they interfered with constitutionally protected choices. In other words, he conceived of women's rights of choice as corresponding to absences of some forms of governmental power.

Justice Blackmun defended even more vigorously the trimester framework he had announced in *Roe*. Although he conceded that a state had "legitimate" interests in protecting maternal health and potential life from the beginning of pregnancy, he insisted that the appropriate standard for reviewing restrictions on the right of privacy, including the right to abort, was "strict scrutiny." He adhered to his arguments in *Roe* that states only had "compelling" interests in protecting maternal health and potential life from approximately the end of the first trimester and from

[90] Ibid., at 2805. See also ibid., at 2807 (citing *Prince v. Massachusetts*, 321 U.S. 158 (1944), for the proposition that the fourteenth amendment protects "a realm of family life which the state cannot enter"). Compare also *Casey*, 112 S. Ct. at 2816–17, where the joint opinion used the rhetoric of drawing "lines."

the point of fetal viability, respectively. He was explicit, moreover, in claiming that constitutional validity hinged on a "balance" of "interests." He treated a woman's right to choose abortions until the point of fetal viability as weighty enough to preclude all interferences with the woman's exercise of that right except under circumstances in which a state had a "compelling" reason to do so. He claimed that none of the Pennsylvania provisions under review satisfied this burden.

Chief Justice Rehnquist, in contrast, adhered to his position that a "rational basis" test was appropriate for reviewing state actions that restricted choices involving abortion. He would have followed earlier opinions that treated "a woman's interest in having an abortion [as] a form of liberty protected by the Due Process Clause" of the fourteenth amendment. But he denied that this right was "fundamental." In addition, he claimed that all the challenged provisions in the Pennsylvania statute were constitutionally permissible because they were "rationally related" to the accomplishment of "legitimate" state interests. Rehnquist, like Blackmun, apparently assumed that the relevant rights and powers (each based on "interests") were conflicting. But the Chief Justice, unlike the author of *Roe*, claimed that the balance in each case tipped in the state legislature's favor.

Justice Scalia's approach was significantly different. He avoided the rhetoric of "balancing" by denying that the fourteenth amendment's reference to "liberty" embraced a woman's decision to have an abortion. He grouped abortion with homosexual sodomy, polygamy, adult incest, and suicide as "forms of conduct" that "have long been criminalized in America" and were "*not* entitled to constitutional protection." In short, he did not think women had any "right" to abort based on the fourteenth amendment, whether alone or in conjunction with the ninth. Thus he did not have to confront whether any such right corresponded to an absence of some forms of governmental authority or could "trump" otherwise valid laws.

Exercising Constitutional Powers

The applicable judicial precedents underscore a need to move beyond widespread preoccupation with the United States Constitution's *judicial* interpretation and enforcement. Constitutional adjudication has facilitated resolution of disputes, brought others to the surface, and in the process established authoritative legal precedents and provoked further debate within the polity. In addition, judges' opinions in constitutional cases provide access to competing interpretive positions, many of which have remained viable. But judicial precedents do not contain exhaustive accounts of authoritative and politically significant constitutional decision-making.

Cases involving claims of reproductive autonomy direct attention toward exercises of power by the legislative and executive branches of government at the federal and state levels, along with choices made by the people at large. The constitutional landscape is more a function of political contexts surrounding adjudication than of the decisions themselves. Judges have not been alone in purporting to act on behalf of "the people." In addition, "the people" have been acting independently of government and will doubtless continue to do so.

State legislatures have been making pivotal decisions: enacting laws to secure rights of choice, restrict abortion, and otherwise affect choices involving abortion. Some such decisions have gone against applicable judicial precedents and provoked their reconsideration. Others have operated within the confines of such decisions.

State executives have also played important roles. For example, state governors have sponsored bills restricting or guaranteeing access to abortions. They have held and exercised the veto power. Prosecutors have decided whether and how to enforce legislation. Some such decisions have involved laws enacted to deal with broader issues than abortion. Demands have been placed upon state courts.

The national legislative and executive branches have likewise been involved in shaping norms and practices relating to abortion. Presidents have issued executive orders providing or restricting funding for abortions and precluding or allowing counseling on abortion. Congress has alternatively attempted to guarantee access to abortions and sought to impose restrictions on choice. The Department of Justice has sued to enforce civil right statutes and other laws to protect or block abortions. Various institutions of national government, acting in numerous capacities, have limited and secured "constitutional" rights in ways that the Supreme Court alone could not have done.

Of equal importance, the people at large have made constitutionally authoritative decisions relating to abortion. Through voting, for example, the people have chosen representatives and influenced the course of official law. By serving on juries and the like, citizens have also participated in the administration of justice. The media and political rallies, along with other forms of popular political activity, have powerfully influenced governmental actions and private choices.

It is crucial not to overlook the obvious: popular efforts and governmental decisions have been directed at individual choices. An overarching objective has been to influence whether *individuals* obtain or perform abortions. "Private" choices are definitive both insofar as they gain support from government and to the extent they have gone against imperatives of official law.

One may conceive of the choices at each stage as assertions of "constitutional" power. Those who act through representative structures affect how governmental officials act on behalf of "the people" in their various collective capacities. By exercising rights of speech and the like, citizens uphold prerogatives of "the people" at large. By making personal choices, individuals guard fundamental limits of American constitutionalism. The law of the land has emerged from complex configurations of persons' exercising power in these diverse ways.

CONVERGENCE AND DIVERGENCE

The text of the United States Constitution does not provide definitive criteria for resolving controversies involving restrictions on economic, sexual, or reproductive choices. The pertinent delegations and reservations of power are open-ended, as are the restrictions contained in the Bill of Rights, the fourteenth amendment, and other parts of the Constitution. Applying these provisions requires more than literalism or formal analysis.

Instead of searching for "right answers" in all contexts, it is helpful in some to identify convergences and divergences among competing positions. Various threads of American constitutionalism have not always been mutually reinforcing. Often they have pulled strongly against one another.

Efforts by governmental officials to limit or reinforce popular choices have touched on basic goods: private property, commerce, employment, individual autonomy, democratic legitimacy, national uniformity, community, equality, moral and religious convictions, education, respect for life, intimacy, marriage, friendship, toleration. Constitutional coherence has been greatest when conceptions of these goods and how to achieve them have overlapped. It has been weakest when they have led in different directions.

Judges have played important roles resolving disputes and will doubtless continue to do so. But they have not fully defined the constitutional terrain. Other governmental officials have made "constitutional" decisions by purporting to act in various capacities on behalf of "the people." Individuals and groups, acting independently of government and through representative structures, have also made constitutionally authoritative choices. In addition, citizens have upheld constitutional norms by exercising their "private" rights.

It would be a mistake to treat the law of the Constitution as having been settled through prior practices. Allocations of commercial power among institutions of federal and state government have remained open issues, as have relationships between governmental regulations and the functioning of "private" markets. The spread of sexually transmitted diseases has made it necessary and appropriate to revisit constitutional principles relating to contraception. Historical divisions on governmental practices relating to abortion have already become obsolete through changes in medical technology and other developments. Rather than being isolated from such changes, the Constitution has been reshaped by responses to them.

Constitutional coherence depends on complementarity among the disparate norms and practices of American constitutionalism. Responsibility for such coherence rests upon the people at large and those holding reigns of power within institutions of federal, state, and local government. Responsibility for constitutional breakdown, to the extent it continues, will also be widely shared.

CHAPTER 8

Interpretive Autonomy Revisited

> [I]n case of a deliberate, palpable and dangerous exercise
> of other powers not granted by the said compact, the
> states who are parties thereto have the right, and are in
> duty bound, to interpose for arresting the pro[gress] of
> the evil, and for maintaining within their respective
> limits, the authorities, rights and liberties appertaining
> to them.[1]

SINCE THE Constitution went into effect, there have been numerous examples of states asserting their independence and defying national power. Most prominently, efforts by states from the South to secede from the Union precipitated the Civil War. Northern states had also asserted their autonomy in opposing the use of federal power to expand or protect slavery. In the 1930s states refused to follow judicial precedents invalidating commercial regulations. More recently, state officials actively defied federal efforts to eliminate racial segregation. States continue to assert their autonomy by seeking to restrict abortions and by otherwise opposing applicable federal laws and judicial precedents. One may readily imagine state officials challenging future national policies regarding immigration, welfare, health care, the environment, or other matters.

In evaluating the legitimacy of such efforts to oppose assertions of central governmental power, principles of national supremacy have obvious relevance. Marshall's opinion in *McCulloch v. Maryland* remains persuasive: principles of legal supremacy give priority to norms established by federal officials when they are acting within delegated authority and consistently with other limits on national powers. But this rationale only extends to actions authorized by the Constitution. Thus it directs attention toward a more fundamental question: Who may decide whether federal officials are acting within constitutional boundaries?

Early controversy over national efforts to restrict political expression brought these problems of interpretive authority to the surface in a context unfavorable to claims of national interpretive supremacy. In 1798 a predominantly Federalist Congress enacted four laws, known popularly as the Alien and Sedition Acts. Two of the laws were especially controver-

---

[1] Virginia Resolutions, December 21, 1798, in *Papers of James Madison* 17:189.

sial: the Alien Friends Law ("An Act concerning Aliens"), which allowed the president to order deportation of aliens; and the Sedition Law, which made seditious libel a criminal offense. The latter was directed primarily toward Republican critics of the Federalist administration.[2]

The legislatures of two states, Kentucky and Virginia, passed resolutions formally declaring the federal enactments unconstitutional because not authorized by the Constitution. In contrast, federal judges (most of whom were Federalist) treated the laws as valid and enforced them against Republican critics of the Federalist administration. A majority of the other states also sided with Congress.[3]

There was intense disagreement not only about *whether* the Alien and Sedition Acts were valid but also about *who* had authority to decide on their validity. These issues are conceptually distinct. One may reasonably argue, for example, that the Sedition Act was unconstitutional without endorsing the dissenting states' claims of interpretive authority. Today it is common to regard federal judges, not institutions of state government, as preeminent constitutional interpreters.

Especially in light of these interpretive conventions, the Virginia and Kentucky Resolutions warrant close examination. These assertions of state interpretive authority were radical when written, in the sense that they dealt with fundamental problems of American constitutionalism. Over the past two centuries, these documents have become radical in new ways: they identify features of the constitutional design that have become increasingly obscured by current ways of thinking.

It would be a mistake to dismiss variations of early arguments for state interpretive autonomy as completely obsolete. On the contrary, they continue to offer insights into vital components of constitutional self-governance. They deserve affirmation and emulation, not repudiation.

THREE FORMS OF PROTEST

The Alien and Sedition Acts resulted from and exacerbated divisions between the Federalist and Republican parties that had formed during the Republic's early years. John Adams, a leading Federalist, defeated Thomas Jefferson, a leading Republican, in the presidential election of

---

[2] Except where otherwise specified, this chapter refers to the Alien Friends Act and the Sedition Law as "the Alien and Sedition Acts." James Morton Smith, *Freedom's Fetters: The Alien and Sedition Laws and American Civil Liberties* (Ithaca, N.Y.: Cornell University Press, 1956), reprints these acts and gives an account of the historical circumstances surrounding their adoption and enforcement, along with similar information on the Naturalization Act and the Alien Enemies Law of 1798.

[3] I review below the Alien and Sedition Acts, their enforcement, and responses to them.

1796. Jefferson became vice president pursuant to electoral rules that were in effect at the time.

Congress enacted the controversial laws of 1798 to deal with overlapping matters of domestic and foreign policy. War with France loomed, and Federalists characterized the Republicans as unruly demagogues who were sympathetic with the French and movements underlying the 1798 French Revolution. The Alien Friends Act gave the president authority to order deportation of such aliens "as he shall judge dangerous to the peace and safety of the United States, or shall have reasonable grounds to suspect are concerned in any treasonable or secret machinations against the government thereof." The Sedition Act made it a crime "to write, print, utter or publish . . . any false, scandalous and malicious writing or writings against the government of the United States, or either house of the Congress of the United States, or the President of the United States."[4]

Jefferson was in a peculiar predicament. He opposed the laws and their enforcement, but he was not in a good position to challenge federal authority openly. The vice president thus turned to one of the "external" checks contemplated by the authors of The Federalist Papers: state legislatures.[5] He secretly drafted a set of resolutions for adoption by the North Carolina legislature, which he sought to use as a vehicle for voicing opposition to the Alien and Sedition Acts.

Jefferson's messenger, Wilson Cary Nicholas, apparently gave the draft to John Breckinridge of Kentucky for consideration by that state's legislature instead of North Carolina's. The Kentucky legislature approved some but not all of the resolutions in Jefferson's draft. (The draft, though written for adoption by North Carolina's legislature, is now generally identified as Jefferson's *draft* of the *Kentucky* Resolutions.) As approved, the Kentucky Resolutions of 1798 took a more modest position than Jefferson's draft on the state legislature's powers of protest.

The same year, 1798, Virginia's legislature approved resolutions that

---

[4] See Smith, *Freedom's Fetters*, app. at 438–42. For historical analyses of the Alien and Sedition Acts and their enforcement, see also Walter Berns, "Freedom of the Press and the Alien and Sedition Laws: A Reappraisal," 1970 Sup. Ct. Rev. 109 (1970); Adrienne Koch and Harry Ammon, "The Virginia and Kentucky Resolutions: An Episode in Jefferson's and Madison's Defense of Civil Liberties," 4 Wm. and Mary Q. (3d ser.) 145 (1948); John C. Miller, *Crisis in Freedom: The Alien and Sedition Acts* (Boston: Little, Brown, 1951); Stephen B. Presser, *The Original Misunderstanding: The English, the Americans, and the Dialectic of Federalist Jurisprudence* (Chapel Hill: Carolina Academic Press, 1991), chs.7 and 8; Nathan Schachner, *Thomas Jefferson: A Biography* (New York: Appleton-Century-Crofts, 1951), vol. 2, ch. 43; Ethelbert D. Warfield, *The Kentucky Resolutions of 1798: An Historical Study* (New York: Putnam, 1894).

[5] John C. Calhoun adopted a similar strategy to oppose tariffs when he was vice president under Andrew Jackson. See William W. Freehling, *Prelude to Civil War* (New York: Harper and Row, 1966), at 154–73.

had been drafted by Madison, who had joined Jefferson in opposing the Federalists. (Ironically, Madison had been allied with the Federalists in debates over the Constitution's ratification.) In addition, the following year, 1799, the Kentucky legislature endorsed a variation of the stronger claims of state authority that had been in Jefferson's draft but deleted from the resolutions approved by that state's legislature in 1798. These various drafts, along with responses to them and subsequent analyses, identify at least three forms of state protest against federal governmental actions: nullification, reversal, and interposition. I deal with each in turn.[6]

Nullification

In his draft of the Kentucky Resolutions, Jefferson claimed that the states had authority to nullify acts of Congress, at least for some purposes and in some contexts, whether or not the Supreme Court concurred that the acts were unconstitutional. He distinguished "cases of an abuse of the delegated powers" from cases in which "powers are assumed which have not been delegated." Apparently referring to federal electoral processes, he claimed that a "change by the people" was the "constitutional remedy" for the former abuse. But his resolutions declared that if the federal government usurped powers other than those delegated to it by the Constitution, "a nullification of the act [was] the rightful remedy."[7]

Jefferson's position on interpretive authority, therefore, paralleled his conception of constitutional boundaries. He characterized the Constitution as a "compact" among "the several States composing the United States of America." He claimed that the states "constituted a General Government for special purposes" and "delegated to that government certain definite powers." Accordingly, he argued that "whensoever the General Government assumes undelegated powers, its acts are unauthoritative, void, and of no force."[8]

Jefferson ran together his analysis of the states' and the people's pre-

[6] Jefferson wrote two drafts of the resolutions, both of which are reprinted in Paul L. Ford, ed., *Writings of Thomas Jefferson* 7:289–309, along with a facsimile of the resolutions approved by the Kentucky legislature in 1798. The Kentucky Resolutions of 1799, as approved, are reprinted in Jonathan Elliot, ed., *Debates in the Several State Conventions, on the Adoption of the Federal Constitution, as Recommended by that General Convention at Philadelphia, in 1787*, 2d ed. (Philadelphia: Lippincott, 1888), vol. 4, at 544–45. The Virginia Resolutions, which were almost identical to a draft prepared by Madison, are reprinted in *Papers of James Madison* 17:188–90.

[7] Jefferson's draft of the Kentucky Resolutions (November 1798), in Ford, ed., *Writings of Thomas Jefferson* 7:301.

[8] Ibid., at 289–91.

rogatives. Part of this imprecision may be attributed to the fact that his principal objective was to articulate bounds of federal power rather than to distinguish the people's rights from state powers. He placed the people and the states on the same side of the boundary that most concerned him. In addition, he assumed that institutions of state government were accountable to the states' citizens, had primary responsibility to secure rights over which the federal government had no power, and were authorized to voice the people's collective determinations.[9]

Jefferson argued that unless the states had authority to "nullify" the federal government's assumptions of undelegated power, the states and their residents "would be under the dominion, absolute and unlimited, of whosoever might exercise this right of judgment for them." He asserted that Congress could not have this authority because it was "not a party, but merely a creature of the compact." Similarly, he characterized federal courts as part of "the government created by the compact." He claimed that no part of this government could be "the exclusive or final judge of the extent of powers delegated to itself; since that would have made its

[9] For example, Jefferson argued in reliance on the tenth amendment that because "no power over the freedom of religion, freedom of speech, or freedom of the press [was] delegated to the United States by the Constitution, nor prohibited by it to the States, all lawful powers respecting the same of right remain, and were reserved to the States or the people." Similarly, he cited the first amendment and claimed that because "libels, falsehood, and defamation, equally with heresy and false religion, are withheld from the cognizance of federal tribunals," the states and the people "retain to themselves the right of judging how far the licentiousness of speech and of the press may be abridged without lessening their useful freedom, and how far those abuses which cannot be separated from their use should be tolerated, rather than the use be destroyed." He elaborated on his reference to "themselves" in the context of discussing powers over religion. He referred to the people of the states, acting through their legislatures and/or limiting them, and declared that "*they* guarded against all abridgment by the United States of the freedom of religious opinions and exercises, and retained to *themselves* the right of protecting the same, as this State, by a law passed on the general demand of its citizens, had already protected them from all human restraint or interference" (ibid., at 294–95; emphasis added). Cf. Koch and Ammon, "The Virginia and Kentucky Resolutions" (underscored linkages among state prerogatives and those of the people at large).

But see Leonard W. Levy, *Emergence of a Free Press* (New York: Oxford University Press, 1985), for an argument that the main concern of those opposed to the Alien and Sedition Acts, at least initially, was to resist encroachment on state prerogatives rather than retained rights. Walter Berns, in "Freedom of the Press and the Alien and Sedition Laws," placed even greater emphasis on issues of federalism. (Although Berns linked Jefferson's position on state independence to his arguments concerning the nature of the federal compact, these arguments were conceptually distinct. Jefferson's claim of limited federal powers did not depend on an assumption that the federal government had no powers that could preempt separate determinations by states and the people—i.e., in cases of the federal government's acting within delegated authority. In addition, issues of state authority and the people's rights overlapped more than Berns conceded.) See also Wayne D. Moore, "Taking a Stand for Speech," 9 Mag. Hist. 19 (1995).

discretion, and not the Constitution, the measure of its powers." On the other hand, he argued that the states alone were "parties to the compact." In the absence of a "common judge," he submitted, the states were "solely authorized to judge in the last resort of the power exercised under [the Constitution]."[10]

Jefferson equivocated on whether *each* state had authority to nullify as *ultra vires* actions by the federal government or whether the states could only do so *collectively*. Suggesting the former but referring to the states plurally, he argued: "[E]*very* State has a natural right in cases not within the compact, (*casus non foederis*,) to nullify of *their* own authority all assumptions of power by others within *their* limits."[11] The draft provided that it would "nevertheless" be communicated from one state to its "co-States" out of "regard and respect." Furthermore, the resolutions sought the other states' "concur[rence] in declaring these acts void, and of no force." Jefferson attached importance to collective action by the states but anticipated that each state could legitimately "take measures on its own for providing that neither of these acts, nor any others of the General Government not plainly and intentionally authorized by the Constitution, shall be exercised within their respective territories."[12]

Although Madison later argued that Jefferson had not claimed that a single state could unilaterally nullify a congressional enactment,[13] his draft of the Kentucky Resolutions leaves little doubt that he was taking a position that the states collectively had authority to take such an action.[14] Furthermore, at a time when the Union depended heavily on cooperation by state governments for enforcing federal laws, Jefferson apparently contemplated disregard by state officials of the Alien and Sedition Acts.[15] In

---

[10] Ford, ed., *Writings of Thomas Jefferson* 7:291–92 and 301–302.

[11] Ibid., vol. 7, at 301 (emphasis added). As explained below, this provision was deleted by the Kentucky legislature in 1798 but then affirmed in 1799.

[12] Ibid., at 301 and 306.

[13] James Madison, Letter to ——— Townsend, October 18, 1831, in *Letters and Other Writings of James Madison* (Philadelphia: Lippincott, 1865), vol. 4, at 198–200.

[14] See Koch and Ammon, "The Virginia and Kentucky Resolutions"; Schachner, *Thomas Jefferson*.

[15] It is not clear whether Jefferson also approved more direct forms of interference with the laws' enforcement such as releasing prisoners from jails. (Compare later controversies over extradition or rendition of slaves or other persons charged with breaking fugitive stave laws.) According to Warfield, there was not a single prosecution in Kentucky under the Alien and Sedition Acts, and "[t]he situation in Virginia, though different, was never serious enough to lead to any thing like organized resistance. Indeed it is now impossible to know how far and in just what form resistance was contemplated by these Resolutions" (Warfield, *The Kentucky Resolutions*, at 110). See also Jefferson's letter to Madison of August 23, 1799, in which Jefferson affirmed the importance of the principles involved, considered possible forms of resistance, and indicated that he wished to preserve as many options as possible—to be able "hereafter [to] do, what we might now rightfully do." The letter is

sum, he sanctioned independent action by the states based in part on the legislature's interpretation of its reserved prerogatives.

Reversal and Other Options

As indicated above, the Kentucky legislature adopted two versions of Jefferson's draft. The initial version, the Kentucky Resolutions of 1798, made two significant changes to Jefferson's draft. First, the Resolutions of 1798 did not claim that the states had authority, either separately or collectively, to nullify congressional enactments. The legislature eventually embraced Jefferson's position, however, in a second set of resolutions that were adopted in 1799. I discuss this reversal more thoroughly below.

Second, the Kentucky Resolutions of 1798, as approved, were submitted to the state's senators and representatives in Congress, and other states were requested to "unite with this commonwealth in requesting the[] repeal at the next session of Congress" of the "unconstitutional and obnoxious acts." (Jefferson's draft had not been addressed to Congress. He claimed it was only proper for the states to communicate with one another, "they alone being parties to the compact.") Whereas Jefferson had presumed that the states could nullify unconstitutional laws on their own authority, the Kentucky legislature initially placed greater reliance on established federal structures such as repeal by Congress or a declaration of unconstitutionality by the United States Supreme Court.

The Resolutions of 1798 were a type of communication, or petition. They functioned, among other things, to communicate the state's purported determination that the Alien and Sedition Acts were unconstitutional. The Resolutions did not, however, claim to oblige the state's representatives in Congress to vote for repeal of the acts.[16] Instead, the state

---

reprinted in Ford, ed., *Writings of Thomas Jefferson* 7:389–92. For analyses of patterns of federal enforcement of the Alien and Sedition Acts, see Frank M. Anderson, "The Enforcement of the Alien and Sedition Laws," *Annual Report of the American Historical Association for 1912* (Washington, D.C., 1914), at 115–26; Smith, *Freedom's Fetters*, chs. 9–17, esp. ch. 15 (on enforcement of the Sedition Act in Virginia).

[16] See debates in the First Congress over whether to add to the first amendment's precursor a declaration that the people had a right "to instruct their Representatives." See *Annals of Congress* (Gales and Seaton ed., 1834), vol. 1 (August 15, 1789), at 733. This proposal sparked more controversy, measured by the volume of discussion reported in the *Annals*, than any other single provision. The *Senate Journal* for September 3, 1789 (volume 1, at 117) indicates that a similar motion was made and rejected in the Senate on September 3, 1789, but there are no records of the Senate's debates or other proceedings on this matter. These proposals had broad importance: whether constituents had a constitutional right or power, through instructions, to preempt or otherwise constrain choices by governmental officials—including official positions on issues of constitutional interpretation.

legislature "enjoined" the state's senators and congressmen to "use their best endeavors" to procure a repeal of the "unconstitutional and obnoxious acts."

The Kentucky Resolutions of 1798 were nevertheless significant, because they asserted the state's *interpretive* independence. The Resolutions did not presuppose that Congress or the Supreme Court had preclusive interpretive authority on issues of constitutional meaning. Instead, the Resolutions included a provision from Jefferson's draft that asserted each state's authority to "judge for itself" both whether the federal government had exceeded its legitimate powers and how to remedy any such infraction.

Under the circumstances, the Kentucky legislators apparently thought the most appropriate remedy was congressional repeal rather than formal state nullification.[17] The legislators sought to influence all the state's representatives: those selected by the state legislature and those elected by the people directly. The legislature acted on its own behalf by enjoining the state's senators to represent the legislature's considered position and acted on behalf of the people of the state in taking a similar position vis-à-vis members of the House of Representatives. Madison and Hamilton had contemplated both possibilities in *The Federalist*: state legislatures' acting as representatives on behalf of the states as such and on behalf of their citizens.[18]

The Kentucky legislature's position was partially vindicated. Although Congress did not repeal any of the acts, the Alien Friends Act and the Sedition Act expired according to their terms in 1800 and 1801, respectively. The immediate crisis with France passed; and after the Republicans' electoral successes in 1800, the Federalists had no interest in renewing the Sedition Act. The Naturalization Act and the Alien Enemies Act remained in effect, but they had not been the main objects of Republican opposition.

[17] For accounts of changes to Jefferson's draft, the introduction of revised resolutions, and their adoption by the Kentucky legislature, see Edward Channing, "Kentucky Resolutions of 1798," 20 Am. Hist. Rev. 333 (1915); Koch and Ammon, "The Virginia and Kentucky Resolutions," at 156–58; Schachner, *Thomas Jefferson*, at 615–16; and Berns, "Freedom of the Press and the Alien and Sedition Laws," at 127–28. From the sources I have reviewed, there appears to be no conclusive evidence that Breckinridge made the changes to Jefferson's draft, although Schachner and Berns reasonably assumed that he had a major role in making such changes. Moreover, Schachner's work refers to evidence that Breckinridge thought "the several States" had authority to nullify the Alien and Sedition Acts "[i]f, upon representations of the States from whom they derive their powers, [Congress] should nevertheless attempt to enforce [the acts]." The idea of exhausting constitutional means would have been attractive to members of the Kentucky legislature, whether or not at the behest of Breckinridge.

[18] See, e.g., Madison's arguments in *The Federalist*, nos. 44, 45, 46, and 51; and Hamilton's arguments in *The Federalist*, nos. 26, 28, 32, 33, and 60. See also chs. 3 and 5, above.

Before the two objectionable acts expired, however, a majority of the other states criticized the Kentucky Resolutions of 1798 and Madison's "Virginia Resolutions." At issue were the states' powers of protest, not just the validity of the acts in question. Thus it is important to consider whether the Resolutions of 1798 had any intrinsic effects, independent of subsequent action or inaction by other states or by federal officials.

The Kentucky Resolutions of 1798 were unclear on what formal effect, if any, the state's declaration of unconstitutionality purported to have. Was it only (though significantly) a public utterance, or type of petition, designed to influence Kentucky's costates and their federal representatives? Or did it also authorize state officials to ignore the laws or interfere more actively with their enforcement? Did the declaration authorize the state's residents to disobey the laws? Did it have any other legal effects, short of formal nullification? For all practical purposes, did it even nullify the acts, or suspend their enforceability within the state, notwithstanding the omission of an explicit claim to do so?

The Kentucky legislature finessed these questions in 1798 by relying directly on Jefferson's idea that the Alien and Sedition Acts were "not law" and thus were "altogether void, and of no force." This position rested on a premise that the Constitution had meaning independent of any person's or institution's interpretations of it. If the acts of Congress were not enacted in pursuance of the Constitution, they were not valid, measured by the criteria set forth in the constitutional text itself.

According to this line of reasoning, the Alien and Sedition Acts were void and unenforceable even if the state legislature did not formally nullify them and Congress did not repeal them. In 1798 the state officials were apparently unsure of whether they had authority to nullify the acts, and for practical reasons the legislators favored repeal. But they did not make their declaration of unconstitutionality dependent on any such future actions. Furthermore, the legislators evidently thought the state had justification, whether based on the Kentucky Resolutions or otherwise, to oppose enforcement of the laws within the state's borders.

This position raised but did not resolve important practical dilemmas. Assuming the Alien and Sedition Acts were unconstitutional and thus void and unenforceable even absent their formal nullification, what was the "supreme law of the land" in this context? How could persons ascertain the requirements of "supreme law" for purposes of guiding their behavior if the Constitution's meaning transcended any particular person's or institution's interpretations of the law? Did each person have constitutional authority to act based on his or her analyses of constitutional meanings and their implications in particular circumstances? Alternatively, did the Constitution give governmental officials some sort of final authority to resolve interpretive disputes at least pending formal reconsideration of such decisions or change in the law? What recourse did states and their residents have if federal officials used institutions of collective power to enforce what may have been an unconstitutional law?

Other states' responses to the Kentucky and Virginia Resolutions of 1798 and Madison's defense of the latter resolutions against the other states' criticisms shed light on these issues. These materials also provide criteria for evaluating some of the differences between Jefferson's draft and the Kentucky Resolutions of 1798 (or, what amounts to much the same thing, differences between the Kentucky Resolutions of 1798 and 1799). Moreover, the Virginia Resolutions and Madison's defense of them presented intermediate positions on several issues of constitutional resistance, thus providing a third model that is worth considering along with the stronger and weaker versions of the Kentucky Resolutions.

Interposition

Madison expressed to Jefferson some important concerns about whether state legislatures had authority to nullify federal legislation. Madison questioned his friend and mentor:

> Have you ever considered thoroughly the distinction between the power of the *State* & that of *the Legislature*, on questions relating to the federal pact? On the supposition that the former is clearly the ultimate Judge of infractions, it does not follow that the latter is the legitimate organ especially as a Convention was the organ by which the compact was made.

Madison sought to guard against this criticism in his draft of resolutions for adoption by the Virginia legislature:

> This was a reason of great weight for using general expressions that would leave to other States a choice of all the modes possible of concurring in the substance, and would shield the Genl Assembly [of Virginia] agst the charge of Usurpation in the very act of protesting agst the usurpations of Congress.

The Virginia Resolutions appealed to "the like disposition of the other States, in confidence that they will concur with this Commonwealth in declaring, as it does hereby declare, that the [Alien and Sedition] acts are unconstitutional."[19]

Madison drafted the Virginia Resolutions for adoption by the state's

---

[19] See James Madison, Letter to Thomas Jefferson, December 29, 1798, in *Papers of James Madison* 17:191–92 (emphasis in original); Virginia Resolutions (December 21, 1798), in ibid., at 188 and 190. The Virginia Resolutions provided that a copy of the document be transmitted to "the Executive authority of each of the other States, with a request that the same may be communicated to the Legislature thereof." Jefferson's draft of the Kentucky Resolutions treated this issue similarly. It provided for transmission of the resolutions by a conference committee to "the legislatures of the several States" but also invited

legislature rather than a state convention. He presumed, as had Jefferson, that state legislatures could speak on behalf of the respective states. But in place of Jefferson's claims of state authority to "nullify" the federal laws, Madison used the rhetoric of "interposition." The resolutions "interposed" the state's authority, expressed by its legislature, between the people of the state, on the one hand, and the federal government, on the other. In this manner, he apparently sought to ground the legislature's opposition to the Alien and Sedition Acts more solidly in the authority of the people of the state.

Although he left open the possibility that the states might have had collective nullifying authority, he concentrated on less extraordinary measures. The Virginia Resolutions had four main components. First, the legislature "declare[d]" the Alien and Sedition Acts "unconstitutional." Apparently at Jefferson's urging, a draft of the resolutions also declared the acts "not law, but utterly null, void and of no force or effect." The legislature struck those words, making the final resolutions silent on whether the federal laws continued in effect or were void based on constitutional standards alone.[20]

Second, the Virginia Resolutions declared that the state would take "necessary and proper" measures to "maintain[] unimpaired the authorities, rights, and liberties reserved to the States respectively, or to the people." The legislature called for "universal alarm" and urged that it would be "reproachful inconsistency and criminal degeneracy, if an indifference were now shown to the most palpable violations" of rights so anxiously secured by constitutional amendment.[21] The resolutions were

---

the "co-States" (not their legislatures) to concur in Kentucky's declaration of unconstitutionality. See Ford, ed., *Writings of Thomas Jefferson* 7:300, 301–302, and 305–306.

[20] See *Papers of James Madison* 17:185–88, 190, and 191 n. 2. According to this source, the words had not been in Madison's original draft but were added by Wilson Cary Nicholas, at Jefferson's request, before John Taylor introduced the resolutions into the Virginia General Assembly. This position, suggested by Koch and Ammon, "The Virginia and Kentucky Resolutions," at 159–60, is based largely on a letter from Jefferson to Nicholas, dated November 29, 1798, which is reprinted in Ford, ed., *Writings of Thomas Jefferson* 7:312–13. Jefferson urged that "instead of the invitation to cooperate in the annulment of the acts," it would be better to make the resolutions "an invitation 'to concur with this commonwealth in declaring, as it does hereby declare, that the said acts are, and were *ab initio*, null, void and of no force, or effect.'" But Gaillard Hunt, ed., in *The Writings of James Madison* 6:326–27 n. 1, claimed that the draft, "as Madison prepared it," declared the acts "unconstitutional, *null, void and of no effect*." According to Hunt, "the words in italics [were] struck out as unnecessary repetition" (ibid). The available evidence is inconclusive.

[21] *Papers of James Madison* 17:189–90. Madison was referring, of course, to the first amendment. His draft emphasized that the Alien and Sedition Acts were "levelled against the right of freely examining public characters and measures, and of free communication among the people thereon, which has ever been justly deemed the only effectual guardian of every other right."

silent, however, on what measures state officials had authority to take in protecting those rights. The document again asserted the state's interpretive independence and implied that those officials had no obligation to enforce the Alien and Sedition Acts but did not address whether any such person had authority to interfere with federal enforcement.

Third, the legislature appealed to other states to join Virginia in declaring the Alien and Sedition Acts unconstitutional and in protecting reserved prerogatives of the states and the people. The legislature pledged its "mutual friendship" in maintaining "a scrupulous fidelity to [the] Constitution" and appealed to "the like dispositions of the other States." Among other things, these passages reflect Madison's commitment to joint as well as separate action.

Finally, unlike Jefferson's resolutions but like those adopted by the Kentucky legislature in 1798, copies of the Virginia Resolutions were transmitted to "each of the Senators and Representatives representing this State in the Congress of the United States." Like a majority of the Kentucky legislators in 1798, Madison sought formal change through established institutions of federal government. His aspirations, like those of the Kentucky legislators, were realized in some form through the Republican Party's rise to power and the demise of the Alien and Sedition Acts.

In the shorter term, however, concurrence and reversal were not forthcoming. On the contrary, a majority of costates criticized the Kentucky and Virginia legislatures' claims of interpretive independence. Madison was asked to defend the Virginia Resolutions against the other states' criticisms, which he did by drafting a "Report on the Virginia Resolutions." Before studying that report, it is helpful to review the charges to which Madison was responding and some of the dilemmas he faced.

REJOINDERS

Other States Respond

Ten of the existing sixteen states' legislatures formally or informally rejected the Kentucky and Virginia Resolutions of 1798.[22] Seven states responded directly by returning formal resolutions. Five of these states' legislatures asserted that federal courts held the prerogative that Jefferson had claimed the states held: authority to invalidate federal legislation as unconstitutional.[23] The legislatures' positions on this issue were remark-

[22] The formal responses are reprinted in Elliot, ed., *Debates* 4:532–39. Other responses are described and reprinted in Frank M. Anderson, "Contemporary Opinion of the Virginia and Kentucky Resolutions," 4 Am. Hist. Rev. 45–63 and 225–52 (1899–1900).

[23] The General Assembly of Rhode Island claimed that the United States Supreme Court had ultimate authority to decide on "the constitutionality of any act or law of the Congress of the United States." The Massachusetts legislature was less direct but clearly implied that

ably confident, considering that the controversy over the Alien and Sedition Acts preceded *Marbury v. Madison*.[24] Two other states' legislatures affirmed principles of federal supremacy more generally by asserting that the Virginia Resolutions unjustifiably interfered with the "constituted authorities" of the United States.[25] Three states rejected the resolutions without returning formal protests,[26] and four states were silent.[27]

It is not surprising that a majority of the states sided with the federal government. Representative structures made that result likely. Although Congress had means of rising above (or sinking below) majority sentiment, the national legislature was also designed to be responsive to its constituents. Furthermore, executive and judicial officials were not isolated from pressures or sentiments that presumably had led to passage of the Alien and Sedition Acts. Each state had interests in backing the federal government's enforcement of laws benefiting them, and federal structures provided no formal means for dissenting states to go against collective determinations. Instead, the concept of national supremacy weighed against particular states' impeding the enactment and enforcement of laws that were backed by at least a majority of the states' legislatures (and presumably the people at large).

Hence the feature that made the concept of national supremacy most

---

the Supreme Court had ultimate authority to decide on the constitutionality of federal legislation. The New York legislature indicated that states were bound by decisions of federal courts and denied that state legislatures had authority "to supervise the acts of the general government." The New Hampshire legislature claimed that the duty to decide on the constitutionality of "laws of the general government . . . is properly and exclusively confided in the judicial department" of that government. Finally, the Vermont legislature asserted that power "to decide on the constitutionality of laws made by the general government [was] exclusively vested in the judiciary courts of the Union."

[24] *Marbury* was decided in 1803. But see *Calder v. Bull*, 3 U.S. (Dall.) 386 (1798), in which the Supreme Court assumed authority to review the constitutionality of state legislation. See also James B. Thayer, "The Origin and Scope of the American Doctrine of Constitutional Law," 7 Harv. L. Rev. 129 (1893); Edward S. Corwin, "The Establishment of Judicial Review," 9 Mich. L. Rev. 102–25 and 283–316 (1910).

[25] The General Assembly of Delaware tersely characterized the resolutions of 1798 as "a very unjustifiable interference with the general government and constituted authorities of the United States, and of a dangerous tendency." The General Assembly of Connecticut expressed its approval of the constitutionality of the Alien and Sedition Acts and declared that they had been enacted by "the constituted authorities." Elliot, ed., *Debates* 4:532, 538.

[26] The legislatures of Maryland, New Jersey, and Pennsylvania took actions that opposed the Kentucky and Virginia Resolutions but did not return formal responses. See Anderson, "Contemporary Opinion of the Virginia and Kentucky Resolutions," at 46–52 and app.

[27] The four silent states were from the South: North Carolina, South Carolina, Georgia, and Tennessee. See ibid., at 235–36, for a summary of the meager evidence of proceedings in such states with respect to the Kentucky and Virginia Resolutions. Anderson reasonably speculated that some southern legislators may have been uncertain what remedies were appropriate even if such persons were sympathetic with the Kentucky and Virginia legislatures' opposition to the Alien and Sedition Acts.

attractive, the principle of subordinating separate to collective prerogatives, also posed the greatest threat to principles of limited government. There was a danger that those entrusted with instruments of collective power would use them to enforce compliance with decisions on matters that were reserved by the Constitution for separate determination. These principles applied to rights and powers reserved to the people separately, not just powers of the states. In each case, it was problematic to rely on institutions that held collective power to define the scope of their authority and limitations on its exercise.

It made sense, therefore, for the dissenting states not to make their opposition to the Alien and Sedition Acts contingent on other states' concurrence. Accordingly, the Virginia and Kentucky legislatures asserted that the acts were unconstitutional *even if* a majority of the states supported them. If the laws *were* unconstitutional, and if a majority of the states *did* favor them, there would have been a failure of constitutionalism, and dissenting states would have been in a perilous predicament.

The two dissenting states' legislatures argued, in essence, that there had been a form of constitutional breakdown but tempered opposition to federal representational processes with recognition of the need to give such structures a chance to correct themselves. The Kentucky and Virginia legislatures primarily emphasized an established means of constitutional correction: repeal by Congress. But these two legislatures also asserted that interim or alternative measures were necessary to protect the people's rights within the states' borders.[28] The Resolutions apparently sanctioned disregard of the Alien and Sedition Acts by state citizens and public officials. Perhaps the legislators also sought to reinforce opposition, in practice, to enforcement of the laws by federal officials.

The Republican Party's electoral victories in 1800 did not negate the importance of the Kentucky and Virginia legislatures' efforts to oppose the objectionable acts' enforcement even prior to their expiration. These forms of resistance were comparable to individuals' disobeying laws prior to their repeal or judicial declarations of unconstitutionality. In many cases, disregard of laws has been a predicate to judicial review, stimulated political discourse, or otherwise influenced legislative reconsideration.[29]

---

[28] The Kentucky Resolutions of 1798, like Jefferson's draft, placed less emphasis on the possibility of correction by the federal judiciary, but neither set of resolutions ruled out that possibility. As indicated in the text, judicial review is best viewed as an alternative means of constitutional correction. It has important advantages over ordinary legislative processes: its interim character (it does not depend on elections), and the fact that it operates through ordinary constitutional forms (adjudication) rather than extraordinary forms (such as constitutional amendment). The principal disadvantage of judicial review, of course, is that it permits legislators to escape responsibility for repealing unconstitutional acts.

[29] Cf. Robert M. Cover's argument, in "Foreword: *Nomos* and Narrative," 97 Harv. L. Rev. 4 (1983), at 46–47, that those who disregard laws as unconstitutional do not neces-

INTERPRETIVE AUTONOMY REVISITED 253

Similar forms of resistance by institutions of state government have also been warranted under appropriate circumstances. In each case, later reversals have affirmed rather than mooted challenges on constitutional grounds.[30]

Kentucky Embraces Nullification

Jefferson's draft was solidly grounded to the extent it asserted the states' interpretive independence. But the draft was on more tenuous ground insofar as it went further and claimed to have greater formal significance than the resolutions actually approved by the Kentucky and Virginia legislatures in 1798. Jefferson's version of the Kentucky Resolutions claimed to do within the state what several of the states assumed judicial review could do within the nation: formally invalidate, or annul, acts of legislation on constitutional grounds prior to legislative repeal or expiration.

Both methods would have utilized established constitutional forms: state legislatures or federal courts. Both would have been means of vindicating individual rights and other constitutional prerogatives that were vulnerable to majoritarian infringement. There was textual support for each position: the tenth amendment and articles III and VI of the original text.[31] But these two means of nullification presupposed radically different conceptions of the proper methods for correcting constitutional mistakes at the federal level.

The Kentucky legislature eventually embraced Jefferson's claim that the states had authority to nullify the Alien and Sedition Acts. After a majority of the states rejected Kentucky's and Virginia's overtures, the Kentucky legislature adopted a second set of resolutions in 1799 that included provisions on nullification comparable to those in Jefferson's original draft but deleted from the Kentucky Resolutions of 1798. In 1799 the Kentucky legislature resolved:

---

sarily regard their actions as forms of "civil disobedience." Such actions may be defended as consistent with the higher law standards of the Constitution itself. To treat such actions as forms of "civil disobedience" privileges official interpretations that may be erroneous.

[30] Claims of constitutional prerogative to resist enforcement of laws do not necessarily depend, however, on any particular governmental officials' subsequently endorsing such positions. The example of Frederick Douglass, as examined in ch. 2, is analogous. One may affirm Douglass's radical antislavery interpretive positions and regard them as constitutionally authoritative, even though they never received official endorsement by the Supreme Court or other federal institutions. It took a Civil War and formal amendments, not just reinterpretations of existing norms, before antislavery constitutionalism received official prominence.

[31] The constitutional text does not, however, explicitly delegate the power of judicial review.

That the several states who formed [the Constitution], being sovereign and independent, have the unquestionable right to judge of the infraction; and, *That a nullification, by those sovereignties, of all unauthorized acts done under color of that instrument, is the rightful remedy.*[32]

These resolutions reflect a significantly stronger conception of state authority than the Resolutions of 1798.

As with Jefferson's draft, it is not clear whether the Kentucky legislators were claiming in 1799 that they had authority to nullify the Alien and Sedition Acts unilaterally or whether the legislators presupposed only that the states collectively had such authority. The Kentucky legislature expressed its unwillingness to "surrender its opinion to a majority of its sister states" on this "momentous" issue. In any event, the legislators apparently concluded that they had exhausted all other appropriate interim remedies and no longer looked to statutory repeal or constitutional amendment as likely means of redress. They vowed to "oppose, in a constitutional manner, every attempt, at what quarter soever offered, to violate [the federal] compact."[33]

The state legislature's assertion of authority to disregard decisions by federal officials was in tension with principles of constitutional representation. The Constitution's authority purported to flow from the people of the United States as a collectivity and/or from the states' acting collectively, not only from the states separately or their legislatures. The Constitution, in turn, has entrusted a range of governing authority to institutions that have purportedly represented the whole people and all the states. Principles of legal supremacy have required the subordination of separately held prerogatives to laws made by such institutions. It would have been anomalous if state officials, acting on behalf of a state, could legitimately preempt decisions made by federal officials on behalf of the entire United States. Similar principles have applied to relationships between assertions of individual rights or powers and exercises of federal or state governmental powers.

The Constitution has not, however, given federal officials authority to preempt all separate determinations. On the contrary, it has delegated limited federal powers and reserved some rights and powers to be exercised separately by individuals, groups, and the states as such. Along with arguing that the Alien and Sedition Acts were invalid as *ultra vires*, the Virginia and Kentucky legislatures exercised forms of speech, petitioning, and other means of influencing federal actions. These two legislatures

---

[32] See Elliot, ed., *Debates* 4:545 (emphasis in original). Compare Jefferson's draft, in Ford, ed., *Writings of Thomas Jefferson* 7:301.
[33] Elliot, ed., *Debates* 4:545.

presumed that the Constitution reserved these prerogatives to the respective states rather than precluded their separate exercise.

The Virginia and Kentucky Resolutions did more than assert *the states'* powers of political expression. The two legislatures also claimed to be protecting similar prerogatives of *the people* from abridgment by federal officials. According to the Resolutions, the Alien and Sedition Acts imposed impermissible restraints on citizens' rights of free speech, the press, and the like. Other rights and powers were beneath the surface but no less significant: voting prerogatives of the people and state legislatures, along with their respective powers to initiate constitutional change through formal amendments.

It is noteworthy that the Constitution has not expressly reserved to the states or their legislatures the authority to act on behalf of the states' residents by the forms of speech, petitioning, and influence that the Kentucky and Virginia Resolutions exemplify. This omission did not imply, however, that the states had no such authority. On the contrary, the tenth amendment's reference to the states' reserved powers, like the ninth and tenth amendments' references to unenumerated rights and powers of the people, reinforced the legislatures' positions.

Because the tenth amendment is open-ended, it no more settled questions concerning the states' powers of protest than it settled arguments over the constitutional validity of the acts themselves. These two issues were, of course, distinct: the validity of the Alien and Sedition Acts and the validity of the Kentucky and Virginia legislatures' responses to the federal enactments. Problems of interpretive authority were equally relevant at both levels. The controversy over the Alien and Sedition Acts not only raised questions about who had authority to decide on the acts' validity; it also raised questions about who had authority to decide on the scope of the states' powers of protest.

Madison Reports Again

In a lengthy "Report on the Virginia Resolutions," which the Virginia General Assembly approved early in 1800, Madison defended the Virginia Resolutions of 1798 against the other states' criticisms.[34] Among other things, the report revisited the issue of a collective nullifying author-

---

[34] Madison's "Report on the Virginia Resolutions," January 7, 1800, is reprinted in *Papers of James Madison* 17:307–51. The Virginia legislature adopted the Report substantially as drafted by Madison, and thus it is not necessary to distinguish his draft from the final version.

ity. It also analyzed more thoroughly the constitutional significance of state legislatures' separate determinations.

In the course of defending the state legislature's approval of the Virginia Resolutions, Madison relied on distinctions among the states, their legislatures, and the people thereof. He observed that the term "states" had several meanings:

> It is indeed true that the term "states" is sometimes used in a vague sense, and sometimes in different senses, according to the subject to which it is applied. Thus it sometimes means the separate sections of territory occupied by the political societies within each; sometimes the particular governments established by those political societies; sometimes those societies as organized into those particular governments; and lastly, it means the people composing those political societies, in their highest sovereign capacity.[35]

He claimed that "all will at least concur" that the "states," in the last sense, were parties to the Constitution because it was submitted to the people of the states and they ratified it in their highest sovereign capacity.[36]

Madison extended this line of reasoning, with its emphasis on the states' foundational political powers, by arguing explicitly what he had only suggested before. He argued that the states, as sovereign entities, had authority to overrule usurpations of power by federal officials. Echoing Jefferson's position in his draft of the Kentucky Resolutions, Madison asserted that the Constitution, like other compacts, was governed by the "plain principle, founded in common sense, illustrated by common practice, and essential to the nature of compacts, that where resort can be had to no tribunal superior to the authority of the parties, the parties themselves must be the rightful judges, in the last resort, whether the bargain made has been pursued or violated." Because "the states [were] parties to the constitutional compact, and in their sovereign capacity," Madison reasoned, "there can be no tribunal, above their authority, to decide, in the last resort, whether the compact made by them be violated." Thus he concluded that the states "must themselves decide, in the last resort, such questions as may be of sufficient magnitude to require their interposition."[37]

Accordingly, Madison denied that the United States Supreme Court was, as several of the state legislatures had claimed, "the sole expositor of the Constitution in the last resort." Again echoing Jefferson's position, Madison explained that "this resort must necessarily be deemed the last

[35] *Papers of James Madison* 17:308–309.
[36] Ibid., at 309.
[37] Ibid., at 309–10.

in relation to the authorities of the other departments of the government; not in relation to the rights of the parties to the constitutional compact, from which the judicial, as well as the other departments, hold their delegated trusts." Even the judiciary might "exercise or sanction dangerous powers beyond the grant of the Constitution." For this reason, "the ultimate right of the parties to the Constitution, to judge whether the compact has been dangerously violated, must extend to violations by one delegated authority as well as by another—by the judiciary as well as by the executive, or the legislature."[38]

Later in the Report, however, Madison equivocated on the status of the Virginia legislature's declaration of unconstitutionality. In these later passages, he emphasized the states' powers to act as intermediaries and their powers of communication rather than their powers to judge authoritatively the validity of federal actions. On the other hand, several passages indicate that he was taking a position that the states collectively had some sort of nullifying power, even if they did not have that authority separately.

In analyzing the states' powers of "interposition," Madison referred to expectations during the founding period that state legislatures would act as intermediaries between the people and the federal government. He alluded to criticisms of the proposed Constitution and pointed out that in response to such criticisms, "the appeal was emphatically made to the intermediate existence of the state governments between the people and [the general] government." More specifically, he observed that state governments had been expected to "descry the first symptoms of usurpation" and to "sound the alarm to the public." It is not clear whether Madison was endorsing the potential role of state legislatures as protectors of the people's rights simply (though profoundly) because there had been a historical understanding on this issue or because he thought it was a good argument, independently of historical expectations. In any event, he linked the states' action to historical expectations.[39]

Madison's "Report on the Virginia Resolutions" thus complemented earlier arguments (by Madison and others) that state legislatures could legitimately act on behalf of the states' citizens by opposing unconstitutional federal legislation at least some ways and for some purposes. At a high level of generality, Madison's arguments were thus solidly grounded. The important question, however, was more specifically whether the Vir-

---

[38] Ibid., at 311. Madison also explained that interposition by the states was warranted in those "great and extraordinary cases, in which all the forms of the Constitution may prove ineffectual against infractions dangerous to the essential rights of the parties" (ibid). Compare his anticipation in *The Federalist*, no. 51, of the need for checks on the federal government by the states.

[39] *Papers of James Madison* 17:349–50.

ginia Resolutions used valid means in pursuance of a legitimate end under
the particular circumstances. That question, in turn, depended on what
the Resolutions purported to do.

In places, Madison attributed limited significance to the Resolutions.
His Report indicated that declarations of unconstitutionality by one or
more states, whether expressed by their legislatures or otherwise, were
merely "expressions of opinion, unaccompanied with any other effect
than what they may produce on opinion, by exciting reflection." Such
declarations "may lead to a change in the legislative expression of the
general will; possibly to a change in the opinion of the judiciary." Madison repeatedly denied that such a declaration would either nullify the
Alien and Sedition Acts or adjudicate their validity. He emphasized his
point by way of contrast in assuming that "[e]xpositions of the judiciary,
on the other hand, are carried into immediate effect by force."[40]

He compared communications among state governments to communications among the people themselves:

> [A] free communication among the states, where the Constitution imposes
> no restraint, is as allowable among the state governments as among other
> public bodies or private citizens. This consideration derives a weight that
> cannot be denied to it, from the relation of the state legislatures to the federal
> legislature as the immediate constituents of one of its branches.[41]

Madison emphasized how state legislatures were distinctively positioned
to act in dual capacities as representatives and as constituents. He argued
that state legislatures were responsible for fostering communication
among their constituents and also needed to communicate among themselves both to ensure their proper representation in the Senate and as
predicates to other collective actions.[42]

Madison did not, therefore, view state legislative interposition merely
as an exercise of the state's will. He also suggested that such an action
could appeal to others' judgment as it might relate to further formal action. He had explained in the 44th *Federalist* that state legislatures could
seek congressional repeal of unconstitutional legislation by replacing
their senators and exerting their "local influence" over elections to the

---

[40] Ibid., at 348.

[41] Ibid.

[42] Madison suggested that communication among states was necessary in connection
with their (1) conveying views to their representatives in the Senate, (2) originating constitutional amendments, (3) deciding whether to admit new states, and (4) entering into contracts with one another (see ibid). The seventeenth amendment's ratification in 1913 did not
preclude state officials from representing the people in the ways that Madison defended. If
anything, the resulting changes in constitutional structures increased the importance of institutions' acting as intermediaries between the people and the federal government.

House of Representatives.[43] He later extended this reasoning and suggested that state officials might have petitioned Congress to propose an explanatory amendment or applied for a constitutional convention to overrule the Alien and Sedition Acts.[44] These remarks indicate that he thought the success of the Virginia Resolutions would depend largely on their effects on constitutional choices by members of Congress, the federal judiciary, and state legislators.

Madison was unclear, however, on whether he was assuming that the Resolutions were significant only as predicates to other actions or also because they had some sort of intrinsic normative effect. He presumed that "if the other states had concurred in making a like declaration, supported, too, by the numerous applications flowing immediately from the people, it can scarcely be doubted that these simple means would have been as sufficient as they are unexceptionable."[45] He did not give his views on what the consequences of such concurrence would have been.

There are at least three ways of reading this passage. First, he might have been claiming that applications (or "petitions") from among the people at large would have annulled the Alien and Sedition Acts even if the state legislatures' declarations of unconstitutionality had not had that effect. Second, he might have thought the concurrence of other state legislatures would have effectively nullified the laws, at least if there was evidence that a preponderance of the people supported the states against the federal government. Third, he might have thought that public opinion would eventually prevail in dictating the choices made by federal representatives even if petitions or resolutions from state legislatures and/or the people at large had not themselves had any intrinsic normative consequences. According to this last reading, the appropriate measure of the resolutions' success would be their effects on public opinion rather than whether they had annulled the federal laws.

The first reading, that the people's separate petitions might nullify the acts, would have been inconsistent with other positions that Madison had articulated. He would not have considered separate actions by the people at large to be any more effective than separate resolutions by state legislatures. As he had explained to the First Congress, separate bodies of the people could not overturn actions by representatives of the whole people.[46]

[43] See *The Federalist*, no. 44.

[44] *Papers of James Madison* 17:349. See also Madison's "Notes On Nullification," 1835–36, in Hunt, ed., *Writings of James Madison* 9:573–607.

[45] *Papers of James Madison* 17:349.

[46] In debates over whether the First Congress should add to the first amendment's precursor a provision guaranteeing a right of the people to instruct their representatives, Madison argued that sovereignty in America was held by the whole American people rather than

The second reading, that collective state action might nullify the acts, would have best complemented the text of the Virginia Resolutions, Madison's comments to Jefferson, and earlier passages in the "Report on the Virginia Resolutions." These materials presupposed that concurrent actions by at least a majority of the states, acting together on behalf of the people of the respective states and/or the people of the United States in their combined sovereign capacity, would have had normative consequences transcending actions by the states separately and even might have superseded actions by the federal government. Madison did not, however, fully explore that possibility in his Report because the issue had become moot by then. Between 1798 and 1800 a majority of the states had declined to concur in the Kentucky and Virginia declarations of unconstitutionality.[47]

Nevertheless, it is significant that Madison apparently would have attributed greater authority to joint actions by united states than to actions by the federal government, at least under some circumstances, even if the states had acted outside forms established by the Constitution. Such a concurrent action, claiming to be grounded in the sovereign authority of the American people (whether of the states combined or of the United States as such), would have represented an exercise of power comparable to judicial review but surpassing it in scale. Like judicial review, this determination would not have purported to change constitutional standards. Instead, it allegedly would have reaffirmed existing constitutional norms. The vehicle for making that affirmation, however, would have been state legislatures rather than federal courts. Given the states' roles in ratifying

"detached bodies" of them. He reportedly observed that "the inhabitants of any district" do not "speak the voice of the people; so far from it, their ideas may contradict the sense of the whole people." He indicated that "the people [could] change the constitution if they please[d]," but he claimed that "while the constitution exists, they must conform themselves to its dictates." His position, in other words, was that part of "the people" could not legitimately "contravene an act established by the whole people." He concluded, therefore, that it was "not true" that "the people have a right to instruct their representatives in such a sense as that the delegates are obliged to conform to those instructions." *Annals* 1:738–39 (August 15, 1789).

[47] In his later comments on the Virginia Resolutions, Madison wrote: "It is sometimes asked in what mode the States could interpose in their collective character as parties to the Constitution against usurped power. It was not necessary for the object and reasoning of the resolutions and report, that the mode should be pointed out. It was sufficient to show that the authority to interpose existed, and was a resort beyond that of the Supreme Court of the United States, or any authority derived from the Constitution. The authority being plenary, the mode was of its own choice; and it is obvious that, if employed by the States as co-parties to and creators of the Constitution, it might either so explain the Constitution or so amend it as to provide a more satisfactory mode within the Constitution itself for guarding it against constructive or other violations." Madison, "Notes On Nullification," in Hunt, ed., *Writings of James Madison* 9:592.

and amending the Constitution and their direct and indirect representation in the federal government, the constitutional and political dimensions of such a determination could not have been easily dismissed.

It was unlikely such a combined action would take place unless there was a wide gulf between governmental actions and predominant dispositions among the people at large. At the time of the Constitution's framing, however, many persons appear to have been concerned about precisely that type of possibility. Furthermore, it is conceivable that much of the public at large might have supported combined efforts of several states against the federal government during the Republic's early years if the latter government had egregiously violated foundational principles of American constitutionalism (as the dissenting states understood them). Jefferson and Madison treated the Alien and Sedition Acts as if they might precipitate a constitutional crisis of this seriousness and magnitude.

The third reading of Madison's remarks, looking to the Resolutions' effects on public opinion, would have complemented the idea of a collective nullifying authority and would have been more practically relevant under the circumstances. Madison recognized that elected officials were ordinarily responsive to constituents' demands. Furthermore, public sentiment within much of the nation presumably supported rather than opposed the Alien and Sedition Acts.[48] Madison's awareness of the power of public opinion in a republic such as the United States alerted him to the dangerous tendencies of national sentiment.

In addition to setting a dangerous precedent for the improper working of governmental institutions, the Alien and Sedition Acts tested popular commitment to principles of representative government. The crisis might have been a turning point on whether the public at large would sanction or oppose exercises of federal power beyond constitutional boundaries. The people's acquiescence in such a transgression would have provided a foundation for future encroachments on rights.[49] That prospect would have deeply troubled Madison.

Much of what we know of Madison's thinking relates to his hope that constitutional structures would elevate government above transient sentiments and allow representatives to make and enforce laws in accordance with the first principles set forth in the Constitution itself. Congress's passage of the Alien and Sedition Acts and the federal judiciary's enforcement of the laws went against these aspirations. Rather than rising above public sentiments, the federal government had led the people away from

---

[48] See Anderson, "Contemporary Opinion of the Virginia and Kentucky Resolutions."

[49] In a letter to Stephens Thompson Mason dated October 11, 1798, Jefferson warned that public acquiescence in the Alien and Sedition Acts would set a dangerous precedent. The letter is reprinted in Ford, ed., *Writings of Thomas Jefferson* 7:282–83.

foundational principles. This crisis thus highlighted the need for additional precautions against abuses of power. The Bill of Rights had been one such "ancillary precaution," but that "legal check" had failed even in the hands of the federal judiciary.[50] Thus Madison turned to another major check on federal power: state governments.

In addition to having regulatory powers of their own, these governments were uniquely situated to influence public opinion. State officials could also serve one of the same crucial functions that federal structures had been designed to achieve: to recall public opinion to fundamental principles and to encourage the people and their representatives to rise above passing factionalism. Madison was probably aware that his efforts to enlist state legislatures as vehicles for shaping public opinion went against the people's momentary inclinations and those of their federal representatives. But he expressed a conviction that the viability of constitutional government would depend on the success of efforts by him and others of like mind.

PROBLEMS OF CONTINUING VIABILITY

Constitutional developments since the late eighteenth century have brought to the surface at least three sets of issues involving claims of state interpretive autonomy. First, is the idea of dispersed interpretive authority consistent with commitment to the rule of law? Second, is that idea consistent with the Constitution's premise that its authority flows from "the people of the United States"? Third, have constitutional changes made obsolete the idea of state officials exercising powers inconsistently with federal positions?

A full examination of these issues is beyond the scope of this work. But some treatment of them is necessary to evaluate the contemporary relevance of the Kentucky and Virginia Resolutions and Madison's defense of the latter. Even if it is not possible to resolve finally problems that are wonderfully open-ended, there are good reasons for suggesting directions for further analysis.

Commitment to the Rule of Law

There are at least three ways to deal with controversies involving efforts by state officials and/or the people of a state to act inconsistently with

---

[50] The quotes are from Jefferson's Letter to Madison, March 15, 1789; and from Madison's remarks to the House of Representative on June 8, 1789. See ch. 3.

federal positions. First, one may assume that as a matter of constitutional logic, the Constitution necessarily means what one or more authoritative institutions of federal government declare it to mean. Jefferson, Madison, and the other authors of the Kentucky and Virginia Resolutions rejected such a skeptical conception of constitutional meaning. They presumed that the Constitution's meaning was independent not only of their positions but also of interpretations by one or more federal officials. Many persons today would likewise deny that the Constitution's meaning is properly reducible to interpretations of it by any particular institution or set of institutions, including the Supreme Court and/or other federal officials.[51]

A second possibility is that the Constitution does not presuppose skepticism regarding its own meaning but does give legal finality for some purposes to certain types of governmental decisions, such as decisions by courts of last resort, *even when those decisions do not measure up to standards of the Constitution itself.* Writing in the mid-1830s, Madison took such a position in the context of criticizing the South Carolina legislature's claim of a unilateral nullifying authority. In an apparent retreat from his position in the Virginia Resolutions and his defense of them, Madison argued that it would be incoherent for a state to claim a *constitutional* right to disobey "the constitutional authority":

> It remains, however, for the nullifying expositors to specify the right & mode of interposition which the resolution meant to assign to the States *individually.* . . .
>
> They cannot say that the right meant was a *Constl* right to resist the Constitutional authy; for that is a contradiction in terms, as much as a legal right to resist a law.[52]

Variations of this argument remain viable. The Supreme Court has treated its own decisions as parts of the "supreme law" that others have been bound to obey; and commentators have defended that approach as an essential component of the rule of law.[53]

[51] Arguments for judicial review, as articulated by Alexander Hamilton in the 78th *Federalist* and as asserted by John Marshall in *Marbury v. Madison,* have traditionally rested on an assumption that the Constitution's meaning transcends judicial interpretations. For more recent analyses of this issue from various perspectives, see Sotirios A. Barber, *On What the Constitution Means* (Baltimore: Johns Hopkins University Press, 1984); William F. Harris II, *The Interpretable Constitution* (Baltimore: Johns Hopkins University Press, 1993); Edwin Meese III, "The Law of the Constitution," 61 Tul. L. Rev. 979 (1987).

[52] Madison, "Notes On Nullification," in *Papers of James Madison,* vol. 89 (Library of Congress, manuscript collection) (emphasis in original). (Hunt's version incorrectly shows "construction" instead of "contradiction.")

[53] See, e.g., *Cooper v. Aaron,* 358 U.S. 1 (1958) (cited *Marbury* for the proposition that "the federal judiciary is supreme in the exposition of the law of the Constitution" and

But Madison's reference to "the constitutional authority" raises serious questions about what institution, if any, has had final interpretive authority for purposes of resolving contests among institutions of federal government—whether or not the decisions of that "constitutional authority" have been final for other purposes. Andrew Jackson, Abraham Lincoln, Franklin Roosevelt, Frederick Douglass, and others have joined Jefferson and the early Madison in denying that the Supreme Court's interpretive precedents have precluded presidents and members of Congress from independently interpreting the scope of their delegated powers and limitations on their exercise. These persons treated conflicts among institutions of the federal government as integral components of a constitutional design that depended on mutually checking exercises of overlapping powers—including interpretive powers.[54]

Accordingly, interpretive disputes may be viewed as signs of constitutional vitality, not just failure. Commitment to the rule of law, understood as compliance with the Constitution's own imperatives, undercuts rather than supports interpretive autonomy. In practice, moreover, it seems that the rule of law has been promoted by the Constitution's being flexible enough to allow different persons, at least at the federal level, to act based on diverging interpretive positions. In short, constitutional government has arguably presupposed rather than preempted interpretive disagreement among federal officials.[55]

The Kentucky and Virginia Resolutions support an analogous concep-

---

claimed that "the interpretation of the Fourteenth Amendment in the Brown Case is the supreme law of the land," binding upon state officials); *United States v. Nixon*, 418 U.S. 683 (1974) (the judges presumed that they—not the president—had ultimate authority to determine the scope of executive privilege). See also the articles by Burt Neuborne, Rex E. Lee, and Ramsey Clark in "Perspectives on the Authoritativeness of Supreme Court Decisions," 61 Tul. L. Rev. 976–1095 (1987). For a more general defense of treating decisions by particular governmental institutions as legally preclusive (at least for some purposes), see H. L. A. Hart, *The Concept of Law* (Oxford: Oxford University Press, 1961).

[54] See nn. 58–59, below, and accompanying text. See also Louis Fisher, *Constitutional Dialogues* (Princeton: Princeton University Press, 1988); Sanford Levinson, *Constitutional Faith* (Princeton: Princeton University Press, 1988); Stephen Macedo, *Liberal Virtues: Citizenship, Virtue, and Community in Liberal Constitutionalism* (New York: Oxford University Press, 1990), esp. ch. 4; Walter F. Murphy, "Who Shall Interpret?" 48 Rev. Pol. 401 (1986); Michael Stokes Paulsen, "The Most Dangerous Branch: Executive Power to Say What the Law Is," 83 Georgetown L. J. 217 (1994), along with the essays by Christopher L. Eisgruber and Sanford Levinson and the reply by Paulsen which follow; and the articles by Mark Tushnet, Robert Nagel, and Sanford Levinson in "Perspectives on the Authoritativeness of Supreme Court Decisions," 61 Tul. L. Rev. 976–1095 (1987).

[55] There are doubtless limits, in practice, to the Constitution's ability to accommodate interpretive disagreement—limits that were crossed around the time of the Civil War. The important point for present purposes is that the Constitution can accommodate *some* interpretive disagreement.

tion of relationships between federal and state interpretive powers. These documents, in various forms, reflect an assumption that the states had authority to interpret and exercise *their* powers even in opposition to authoritative decisions by one or more federal officials. This position offers an alternative to those identified above: skepticism about the independence of constitutional meanings from particular interpretations, or assuming that federal decisions have preempted opposing actions even when the decisions have been inconsistent with constitutional norms.

Notwithstanding Madison's later claim, it is not inconsistent to argue that states have had constitutional authority to oppose assertions of federal power in some circumstances. But there is an important qualification: constitutional logic supports a conclusion that state officials have only had authority to exercise *their* powers, not others'. The Constitution presumably has not sanctioned interpretive conflicts arising from *state officials'* purporting to exercise *federal* powers.[56] There are good reasons for concluding, though, that states have had authority to interpret and exercise *their* powers independently—with reference to the Constitution itself and not in subordination to applicable federal precedents—even if the result has been conflicts, in practice, between state and federal actions.

This approach treats interpretive and other powers as symmetrical. As John Marshall argued in *Marbury v. Madison*, judges may interpret the Constitution independently for purposes of deciding cases over which they have jurisdiction.[57] Likewise, presidents have had the power claimed by Andrew Jackson: authority to decide for themselves on the validity of acts of Congress, at least for purposes of deciding whether to veto them,

---

[56] There may be special circumstances under which *state* judges or other officials may have authority to invalidate federal actions that are alleged to be unconstitutional, based on the standards of the *federal* Constitution, through the exercise of *state* powers. Sec. 25 of the Judiciary Act of 1789 apparently contemplated state *judges'* deciding on the validity of federal treaties, statutes, and other exercises of federal power. The Judiciary Act, like its contemporary equivalent, also presumed that article III gave the Supreme Court authority to review these decisions, among others. Not surprisingly, states have opposed the Supreme Court's exercise of this appellate power. See generally Charles Warren, "Legislative and Judicial Attacks on the Supreme Court of the United States—A History of the Twenty-Fifth Section of the Judiciary Act," 47 Am. L. Rev. 1–34 and 161–89 (1913).

[57] Marshall's primary objective in *Marbury* was to deny claims of legislative interpretive supremacy, a position inconsistent with judges' reviewing the validity of legislative acts. It is less clear that Marshall sought to assert judicial interpretive supremacy. Ironically, his premise that other officials might, in practice, act inconsistently with constitutional norms also applies to judges. Thus his claim that judges had authority to interpret the Constitution (particularly its delegation of judicial powers) independently of Congress supports, by analogy, arguments by other officials that they have a constitutional obligation to order their actions with reference to the Constitution even if doing so entails disregarding judicial positions.

even when the result has been exercising presidential power inconsistently with legislative and judicial interpretive precedents.[58] Similar principles support Abraham Lincoln's argument that Congress and the people at large have had interpretive powers corresponding to their respective constitutional prerogatives: the Constitution has given Congress authority to interpret its legislative powers, and the people at large have had authority to interpret the Constitution independently of governmental officials for purposes of deciding how to exercise their rights and powers of political expression, voting, and the like.[59] Although the Constitution has obligated the states and their representatives to respect the authority of other persons to exercise their powers, the states (typically through representatives) have also been able to decide for themselves how to exercise their own.

Such an approach has not automatically settled all disputes over constitutional issues or precluded interpretive mistakes. On the contrary, efforts by state officials to oppose federal actions have presumably heightened some political conflicts. Some persons have used force, not just reasoning, to back up their positions.[60]

These considerations do not indicate that diffused or multifaceted conceptions of interpretive authority have necessarily been flawed or that variations of such positions are now unacceptable. Principles of constitutional fidelity call for conviction to the imperatives of supreme law.[61] Sometimes those imperatives may require persons to oppose others' actions. Being willing to vindicate constitutional norms by acting consistently with them, even in the face of opposition, is a sign of constitutional commitment that deserves commendation, not repudiation.[62] (A large

[58] See Andrew Jackson, "Veto of the Bank Bill," July 10, 1832, in James D. Richardson, ed., *A Compilation of the Messages and Papers of the Presidents* (Washington, D.C.: Bureau of National Literature and Art, 1908), vol. 2, at 576–91.

[59] See the portion of Lincoln's speech at Springfield, Illinois, on July 17, 1858, that is quoted in ch. 2, n. 45. Cf. Frederick Douglass's assumption of popular interpretive autonomy in his speech on July 5, 1852, as quoted in the headnote to ch. 2.

[60] One of the goals of the Federalists was to create a central government with enough coercive power to be able to overcome opposition from among the states, not just to be able to enforce laws against individuals. On this score, the Federalists' vision has largely been achieved. Federal military, fiscal, regulatory, and enforcement powers are capable of imposing serious restraints on state actions. It is less clear that the states have had adequate means, in practice, of protecting their separately reserved powers.

[61] The Civil War is a reminder of the extremes to which individuals and public officials may go when seeking to preserve or establish their normative visions. Constitutional disputes are typically resolved in a more orderly manner, though not necessarily without the use of force. See generally Cover, "The Bonds of Constitutional Interpretation,"20 Ga. L. Rev. 815 (1986), for analysis of coercive dimensions of legal decision making.

[62] The Constitution imposes constraints on how governmental officials may seek to vindicate constitutional norms; and there are corresponding legal limitations on the means

measure of tentativeness in the exercise of political power is also appropriate, particularly for those acting in opposition to others' normative claims.)

Extending principles of interpretive autonomy to embrace the states' independently interpreting and exercising their reserved powers depends, of course, on an assumption that the Constitution has continued to reserve some powers to the states, acting separately. In addition, there remain questions about whether affirming state interpretive autonomy is consistent with principles of popular sovereignty.

Limited, Delegated Powers

The Kentucky and Virginia Resolutions based arguments for state autonomy, including diffused interpretive powers, on a premise that the Constitution was a "compact" among sovereign states. That premise was controversial even in its time. But the basic principles underlying these arguments remain viable: federal officials depend on affirmative delegations of power, and those delegations are limited in scope.

In an essay published in 1985, H. Jefferson Powell criticized the Kentucky and Virginia Resolutions for ignoring arguments during the founding period that the Constitution would not constitute a "compact." As Powell explained, James Wilson and others had argued that "this system is not a compact or contract; the system itself tells you what it is; it is an ordinance and establishment of the people."[63] According to Powell, "the [Kentucky and Virginia] Resolutions simply ignored the recent and well-known debates over the Constitution's character, as well as the absence within its text of references to a compact or to the states as sovereign contracting parties." Powell also contrasted Jeffersonian positions on the Constitution's character with arguments by John Marshall and others who subsequently emphasized principles of national supremacy.[64]

---

available to individuals. For example, governmental officials are obliged to respect principles of due process, and individuals are likewise obliged to respect laws against harming persons, property, and the like. Adding further complication, various actions have differing effects in supporting or undercutting respect for legal institutions and the Constitution itself.

[63] H. Jefferson Powell, "The Original Understanding of Original Intent," 98 Harv. L. Rev. 885 (1985), at 930, citing James Wilson's remarks at the Pennsylvania Ratifying Convention on December 11, 1787, as reported by Thomas Lloyd. This account is reprinted in *Documentary History of Ratification* 2:556.

[64] See Powell, "Original Understanding of Original Intent," at 930 and 942–48. Although this article focused on historical conceptions of the Constitution's "intent," rather than configurations of interpretive authority, Powell has dealt with the latter issue in a subsequent article whose conclusions largely complement and reinforce the thrust of this chapter (and the central theses of this book more generally). See H. Jefferson Powell, "The Principles

It is important not to overstate the differences between Jefferson's and Madison's reliance on the idea of a constitutional "compact" and Wilson's repudiation of contractual analogies during the founding period. As explained in chapter 4, Wilson argued that the proposed Constitution would form neither a compact among state governments nor a contract between the people and governmental institutions. Instead, he relied on the preamble and emphasized the constitutional design's dependence on the people's foundational political authority, including the people's authority to recall at any time powers previously delegated by them to state governmental institutions. He likewise argued that the people would continue to hold all sovereign powers after the proposed Constitution's ratification.

For good reasons, Wilson avoided the rhetoric of "compacts." But his analysis may be coherently recast as flowing from assumptions that "the people" formed "compacts" among themselves, both as members of states and as members of the United States, and in those capacities delegated governmental powers to institutions at both levels.[65] Whether individuals and states were bound by a particular federal action thus hinged,

---

of '98: An Essay in Historical Retrieval," 80 Va. L. Rev. 689 (1994). I am not persuaded by Powell's claim that "[t]he principles of '98, formulated and proclaimed by statesmen and legislators, reduced American constitutionalism to the constitutional law *enforced by courts*" (ibid., at 731; emphasis added). In his intricate argument Powell acknowledges, however, that "Jefferson in particular intended no such result," and he explored ways that the resolutions also reflected commitments to interpretive plurality and could have supported different "line[s] of development" from those he attributes to "the principles of '98" (ibid., at 732 and 736 ff.).

[65] In *Chisholm v. Georgia*, 2 U.S. (2 Dall.) 419, 471 (1793), Chief Justice John Jay characterized the Constitution as a "compact" among "the people": "Every state constitution is a compact made by and between the citizens of a state to govern themselves in a certain manner; and the constitution of the United States is likewise a compact made by the people of the United States to govern themselves as to general objects, in a certain matter." (Jay was a leading *Federalist* from *New York*.) Madison's position, as articulated in a letter to N. P. Trist dated February 15, 1830, was similar: "Although the old idea of a compact between the Government and the people be justly exploded, the idea of a compact among those who are parties to a Government is a fundamental principle of free Government. The original compact is the one implied or presumed, but nowhere reduced to writing, by which a people agree to form one society. The next is a compact, here for the first time reduced to writing, by which the people in their social state agree to a Government over them. These two compacts may be considered as blended in the Constitution of the U.S., which recognizes a union or society of States, and makes it the basis of the Government formed by the parties to it" (Hunt, ed., *Writings of James Madison* 9:355n). President Andrew Jackson, in his Nullification Proclamation dated December 10, 1832, presupposed that the Constitution formed a compact even as he repudiated claims of state nullifying authority. The Proclamation is reprinted in William W. Freehling, ed., *The Nullification Era: A Documentary Record* (New York: Harper and Row, 1967), at 153–63. See especially ibid., at 159 (Jackson relied on, rather than repudiated, a premise that the Constitution "was formed by a compact").

in his view, on whether power to perform that action had been "surrendered" (even if only tentatively) by them through the Constitution's adoption.

Thus there was substantial overlap among Wilson's arguments and those presented in the Kentucky and Virginia Resolutions. Each depended on an assumption that the Constitution delegated limited powers to institutions of federal government. Each claimed that the Constitution also reserved powers to the respective states and contemplated their exercising these powers separately. Each assumed that the states would be bound by federal actions within the scope of delegated powers but not outside them.

Wilson placed greater emphasis on the authority of "the people," joined as members of a national political community and not just as members of states. Thus he identified important problems with arguments that the Constitution was fundamentally a compact among states. He emphasized how the people at large, not just the states as such, were constituents.

Even so, many of Wilson's arguments were consistent with affirming some forms of state interpretive autonomy. He argued that "the people" had divided governmental powers among federal *and state* institutions. There was no need to assume that the people, acting through the federal Constitution and state constitutions, had withheld all interpretive powers from the latter institutions. On the contrary, his claim that the people divided governmental powers could support arguments that they also gave the respective institutions adequate means of exercising those powers. Rather than leading to a conclusion that state officials should have treated federal officials as ultimate interpreters, the concept of popular sovereignty could accommodate arguments that state officials should have subordinated their exercises of power to the superior will of the people, as expressed in the Constitution itself.

Subsequent Developments

Other efforts by states to assert interpretive independence have received even wider condemnation than the Virginia and Kentucky Resolutions. Invoking the Resolutions of 1798 and 1799 as precedents, John C. Calhoun developed arguments for state nullification during controversy over tariffs in the 1820s and 1830s.[66] According to William W. Freehling, the

---

[66] See Calhoun's draft of the South Carolina "Exposition," December 1828, in Richard K. Cralle, ed., *The Works of John C. Calhoun* (New York: Appleton, 1883), vol. 6, at 1–59; Calhoun, "Address on the Relations of the States and Federal Government," Fort Hill, July 26, 1831, in ibid., at 59–94; Freehling, *Prelude to Civil War*.

political reaction "smashed nullification forever."[67] But states from the North and South invoked similar principles to argue for secession during the antebellum period. Walter F. Murphy suggested that "the Civil War effectively invalidated" claims of "nullification or confederational departmentalism" in the forms advocated by Jefferson, Calhoun, and states of the South in their acts of secession.[68] But several southern state legislatures purported to formally nullify the Supreme Court's 1954 and 1955 decisions in *Brown v. Board of Education*.[69] Institutions of state government backed up these claims in practice by resisting federal efforts to desegregate schools.

Madison repeatedly denied that the Resolutions of 1798 supported claims during the nullification era of unilateral nullifying authority or arguments that there was a *constitutional* right to secede from the Union. He distinguished "constitutional" rights from "a natural right to resist intolerable oppression." He suggested that the latter "was a right not less admitted by all than the collective right of the States as parties to the Constitution the nondenial of which was urged as proof that it could not be meant by the Resolution."[70]

His distinctions between "natural" and "constitutional" rights (or powers) and between unilateral and collective prerogatives were valid. But the ninth and tenth amendments make the first distinction problematic.[71] More importantly, the latter amendment supports arguments that the states may legitimately exercise their reserved powers autonomously. Although Madison denied that the states could legitimately nullify federal laws or secede from the Union, he did not repudiate the central premises of the Virginia and Kentucky Resolutions: that the respective states had authority to exercise independently their separately held powers, and those powers included declaring positions on the validity of federal laws.

It may be possible to reach general conclusions about whether the Constitution has reserved (or now reserves) state powers of nullification and/or secession. It seems more reasonable, however, to approach these issues on a case-by-case basis and in a way that may account for the plural character of constitutional meaning and authority. Particular claims of constitutional authority deserve serious consideration. Whether they deserve affirmation as components of the law of the Constitution would

---

[67] Freehling, ed., *The Nullification Era*, at xvi. According to Freehling, nullification was smashed by President Andrew Jackson's Nullification Proclamation and by Congress's approval of the Force Bill of 1833. See also Freehling, *Prelude to Civil War*, ch. 8.

[68] Murphy, "Who Shall Interpret?" at 460 n. 28.

[69] See 1 *Race Relations Law Reporter* 437–47 (1956).

[70] Madison, "Notes On Nullification" (1835–36), in Hunt, ed., *Writings of James Madison* 9:592–93.

[71] For analysis of this issue as it relates to powers of constitutional change, see ch. 3.

appear to depend, among other things, on the extent to which they resonate with broader interpretive commitments.

For this reason, it would be impossible in a work of this scope to evaluate exhaustively the coherence of Calhoun's thesis or similar assertions of state power in other contexts. It is possible, however, to underscore serious problems with *general* claims of nullifying authority. It would be anomalous to endorse state nullification of federal laws as an enduring component of constitutional structures, even if it might be appropriate under some circumstances.[72]

Calhoun's position would, in effect, privilege interpretations of the Constitution by particular states. Once a particular state (through a convention) purported to nullify a federal law, it would be unenforceable unless approved by three-fourths of the states (through conventions or legislatures). Although such a scheme might be effective to protect the states' separately held prerogatives, it would allow systematic inversion of the Constitution's commitment to principles of collective determination. A single state would be able to veto the functioning of the ordinary lawmaking procedures established by the Constitution.

It is coherent for a state to claim authority to interpret and exercise *its* powers independently. But it would be anomalous to conceive of that authority as enabling state officials to preclude federal officials from independently interpreting and exercising *their* powers. For similar reasons, it would be anomalous to conceive of the states' reserved powers as including authority to nullify judicial precedents like *Brown v. Board of Education*.

More modest *declarations* of invalidity, along the models of the Virginia and Kentucky Resolutions of 1798, are less problematic. It is more plausible to regard such assertions of *interpretive authority* as among reserved powers. By themselves, such claims do not conflict with principles of collective determination that appear to be logical corollaries of affirming the authority of the Constitution itself.

Affirming the validity of state interpretive powers does not necessarily entail endorsing the positions taken. Though typically overlapping in practice, these issues are conceptually severable. One may reasonably

---

[72] If a federal law targeted a particular state and its residents, if there were strong arguments that the law interfered with reserved powers and retained rights, and if the law rested on a weak claim of federal authority, then it might be reasonable for a state to interpose its authority and declare the law void. The state might, for example, treat the law as a pretextual exercise of federal power not falling within delegated authority (rather than as an abuse of delegated authority). In effect, the state would be asserting authority to displace a *claim* of federal power. Arguments that the state should rely on national representative structures would be weak if there were egregious discrimination (e.g., an enactment that unreasonably singled out the state or its residents for severe treatment).

conclude that a South Carolina convention had authority in 1828 to declare federal tariffs invalid. One might likewise conclude that southern legislatures had authority in the 1950s to express criticism of *Brown v. Board of Education*. But one might still disagree with the positions taken by these representative institutions. Concluding that the states have had (and continue to have) reserved powers of constitutional expression does not require accepting the views expressed, any more than affirming an individual's rights of free speech entails agreeing with everything the person says.

As a result, it is important to distinguish the viability of positions taken in particular contexts from the viability of arguments that the tenth amendment embraces interpretive autonomy. It may no longer be reasonable to argue that Congress lacks authority to pass protective tariffs. (The argument was anomalous even in the nineteenth century.) There are substantial obstacles to arguing that states have authority to secede from the Union or to maintain segregated schools. But there are good reasons to conclude that states have had authority to *express* these views. Similar principles will presumably validate efforts by state officials to articulate constitutional norms in future controversies—even if the positions taken are unpopular.

Constitutional developments have doubtless made it increasingly difficult to defend the narrow views of federal authority and the expansive conceptions of state power presented in the Virginia and Kentucky Resolutions and successors to them. Over the past two centuries, the Constitution has withdrawn some powers from the states, placed additional limitations on powers not withdrawn, and delegated new powers to Congress and other federal institutions. Constitutional norms have been impacted by numerous events, both gradually and suddenly.

These changes have not, however, made obsolete the concepts of limited federal authority and separately reserved state powers. Not even the sweeping prohibitions of the fourteenth amendment have made these ideas obsolete. On the contrary, that amendment expressly delegates authority to Congress and presupposes the existence of state powers to be limited.

In addition, the fourteenth amendment preserves the idea of state citizenship. Section 1 identifies persons born or naturalized in the United States as "citizens of the United States *and of the State wherein they reside.*" The amendment supports rather than undercuts arguments that "the people" remain constituted in part as members of states (not only a nation) and may continue to act through institutions of state government (not just the federal government).

It is possible to conceive of federal laws that would arguably exceed delegated authority and encroach on powers reserved to the respective states. Congress might enact a law to prohibit states from making abortions illegal at any stage of pregnancy. A president might order states to provide medical benefits to resident illegal aliens. The Supreme Court might order one state to accept nuclear waste from another. In each case, a state could reasonably declare the federal actions invalid through legislation or a convention. Other states might formally express their support for the federal actions.[73]

As long as the Constitution preserves the states as autonomous political units that have distinguishable reserved powers, the idea of corresponding interpretive prerogatives remains coherent. The constitutional design continues to allow state officials and the people of the respective states to play important roles not only in ratifying formal amendments but also in exercising other rights and powers in ways that shape political discourse.[74] It would be anomalous, indeed, to claim that state action is a prerequisite to formally amending the constitutional text but does not count for purposes of ascertaining the meaning of that text.[75] It is more coherent to attribute to the states important roles not only in changing the constitutional text but also in sustaining and otherwise recreating fundamental law through interpretive dialogue.

There are also good reasons for affirming rather than undercutting commitment to constitutional ideals even in the face of their popular denial or official disregard. Although the states acting separately may pose serious threats to principles of American constitutionalism, cutting off the states' contributions to interpretive dialogue would threaten more directly the Constitution itself. Commitment by state officials to constitutional norms, like affirmation of the Constitution's meaning and authority by members of the people at large, deserves commendation rather than repudiation. There are reasons for concern, not celebration, should state officials and the people of the states lose the capacity to interpret and exercise

---

[73] It would also be possible to defend a federal law guaranteeing rights of abortion, for example, by relying on sections 1 and 5 of the fourteenth amendment. One could reasonably rely on these provisions, along with Congress's powers regarding naturalization and commercial regulation, to support the laws pertaining to resident aliens and nuclear waste. In each case, it would be important to distinguish declarations of constitutional positions from assertions of authority to nullify federal laws.

[74] It is important to pay attention to how a variety of state officials, not just legislators, may act on behalf of the people of a state. This issue is especially important since there is increasing diversity among the people of the respective states (which is also a more inclusive category, as a matter of federal constitutional law, than during the founding period).

[75] As explained in ch. 3, however, not all persons regard state participation as a necessary condition for amending the text.

their powers independently of federal officials.[76] Constitutional theory and practice should, therefore, be expanded to embrace the core principles of state interpretive autonomy that are common to the Kentucky and Virginia Resolutions.

[76] Even if one is only (or primarily) concerned about the ability of the people to sustain principles of American constitutionalism, there are reasons for paying attention to the roles of states in fostering popular political participation. See generally "Symposium: The Republican Civic Tradition," 97 Yale L. J. 1493–1723 (1988); "Symposium: Roads Not Taken: Undercurrents to Republican Thinking in Modern Constitutional Theory," 84 Nw. Univ. L. Rev. 1–249 (1989); Sheldon S. Wolin, "The People's Two Bodies," 1 *Democracy* 9 (1981).

We the People: Reflections

> I want to suggest that in the American political tradition, the people has had two "bodies," with each standing for a different conception of collective identity, of power, and of the terms of power.[1]

THIS BOOK does not reach univocal conclusions about the character or identity of those upon whose authority the U.S. Constitution purports to rest: "the people of the United States." Nor does it resolve questions about how their "rights" and "powers" fit within the normative order—including how they relate to federal and state governmental powers and other representative structures. On the contrary, my analysis leads in many directions. Interpretive precedents underscore the open-ended character of American constitutionalism, offering a range of options rather than full closure.

Federalists and Anti-Federalists presented opposing conceptions of "the people" and sought to reinforce different forms of political activity. Madison and other members of the founding generation relied on competing models of representation. Various parts of the constitutional text have accommodated contradictory approaches to analyzing constitutional structures. The normative visions of Federalists and Republicans were at odds, as were those of Douglass and Taney. Exercises of state power have opposed and supported claims of individual rights, and assertions of national power have likewise served both functions. Federal and state officials have at times acted consistently with one another, at times inconsistently.

At issue have been fundamental matters of constitutional design: the composition of basic categories of constitutional discourse and the mapping of relationships among them. What roles have the constitutional text of 1787 and its formal amendments played in justifying power and placing limits on its exercise? How have "rights" and "powers" enumerated in the text intersected with one another and with other "rights" and "powers" not so enumerated? How have "the people" and their representatives acted to authorize and re-authorize constitutional norms? How

---

[1] Sheldon S. Wolin, "The People's Two Bodies," 1 *Democracy* 9 (1981), at 11.

have "the people" acted otherwise—separately and collectively, through government and independently, to reinforce existing parts of the Constitution and bring about change?

A number of patterns have emerged, several of which are diagramed in chapter 4. Those figures portray distinctive conceptions of constitutional structures which find support in sources from the founding period and subsequent interpretive precedents. The competing positions are based, among other things, on premises regarding relationships among federal powers, state powers, and the people's rights and powers—including prerogatives of constitutional change. These norms have been viewed as distinct or overlapping, complementary or in tension, hierarchically or coordinately arranged. Governmental structures have been conceived as distinct from retained and reserved prerogatives or as vehicles through which constituents may act.

The competing models and corresponding interpretive precedents both underscore shared features of political rhetoric and locate areas of constitutional disputation. Not surprisingly, those claiming fidelity to the U.S. Constitution have relied on similar categories of normative discourse. But superficial resemblances have not signified interpretive hegemony. On the contrary, persons using similar terms and professing commitment to the same objects of interpretation—features of the existing Constitution— have committed themselves to radically different constitutional visions.

Issues of normative theory and practical politics have been intertwined. Whether on the surface of political rhetoric or beneath it, premises about relationships among various categories of constitutional "rights" and "powers" have been central components of constitutional reasoning. Explicitly or implicitly, they have supported distinctive positions in debates over the Constitution's ratification and initial amending and in subsequent controversies involving slavery, rights of citizenship, banking, commercial regulation, limits on political expression, restrictions on sexual and reproductive autonomy, and other efforts to defend or oppose assertions of collective power.

The stakes have been high. It has mattered a great deal, for example, whether interpreters have conceived of "the people" as holding rights and powers separately as individuals or collectively as members of a nation or states. Presumptions that the Constitution has enabled "the people" to exercise constitutional power primarily through representative institutions have supported significantly different conceptions of constitutional structures from premises that governmental powers and popular rights have been mutually exclusive and reciprocally limiting. Efforts to create and sustain communities held together by common interests and complementary aspirations have competed with features of American constitutionalism that have promoted diversity and reinforced plurality. Those who have endorsed the idea that popular rights have gained security from assertions of collective power have defended governmental actions finding little support among those who have presumed that the combined results of exercising constitutional prerogatives are zero-sum.

Greater attentiveness to these matters of constitutional design may serve a number of purposes. Among other things, bringing underlying conceptions of constitutional structures to the surface may facilitate identifying interpretive options, analyzing convergences and divergences among competing positions, seeking common ground or isolating disagreement, reconsidering problems of constitutional continuity and change, exploring features of the constitutional terrain that have largely escaped careful scrutiny, and otherwise rethinking the character of constitutional politics in the United States. The potential for fresh insights into norms and practices of American constitutionalism is vast indeed.

Some may draw on these insights to gain or reinforce particular conceptions of constitutional meaning and authority. The constitutional order doubtless sanctions such argumentation in various contexts. Adjudication, for example, depends on dichotomous analysis. Legislators and executive officials must decide whether or not to enact or enforce particular legislation. Through voting, speech, and other forms of public commitment, the people at large may likewise take positions on issues of constitutional structure and corresponding matters of practical politics.

Throughout this book, however, I have resisted a conclusion that the Constitution has embraced only one set of relational premises, a particular conception of constitutional structures, or corresponding interpretive conclusions. I have argued instead that the Constitution has reinforced interpretive plurality and been enriched by it. The result has been layers of intersecting constitutional meaning and authority, not flat terrain.

According to this view, mapping the constitutional order and being aware of one's location within it does not merely require dichotomous analysis—such as a search for "right answers" to interpretive problems. It also requires identifying competing positions, exploring intersections among them, and locating them within broader theoretical perspectives. Even as the people and those purporting to act on their behalf have variously chosen among interpretive commitments, they have constructed and sustained a constitutional universe that demands a more inclusive vision. While the constitutional text has constrained political deliberations, it has left unresolved fundamental problems of constitutional meaning and authority. Historic choices have thus preserved interpretive options at the very moments they have purported to foreclose them.

The last figure in chapter 4 preliminarily maps these features of the constitutional order. The four quadrants of that figure correspond to four distinct relational paradigms, including variations of those depicted by figures 1, 2, and 3. Accordingly, figure 4 draws upon and complements the first three figures and facilitates analyzing intersections among the competing relational paradigms. The use of two axes forming four primary quadrants directs attention to ways that alternative conceptions of constitutional structures such as those portrayed by the first three figures have been mutually reinforcing in some respects but have diverged in others. In addition, by portraying the competing models as within a single scheme, the figure implies that American constitutionalism as a whole has embraced disputation rather than a single paradigm of normative structures.

The interpretive precedents examined throughout this book provide additional examples of these competing interpretive positions and offer further contexts for exploring intersections among them. In *McCulloch*, for example, Marshall treated federal and state powers as hierarchically arranged and potentially overlapping. Maryland's counsel, in contrast, emphasized boundaries between federal and state powers and conceived of the powers at issue as arranged coordinately. Precedents involving economic, sexual, and reproductive autonomy exemplify variations of these models and suggest reconceptualization across time to account for normative change.

Mapping the constitutional terrain requires accounting for areas of overlap as well as divergence. Insofar as they have supported complementary positions in various contexts, competing interpretive frameworks have been mutually reinforcing. But they have also supported opposing positions and thus reflected disjunctions or fissures within the constitutional terrain. By being attentive to areas of tension as well as overlap, one may account for the plural character of constitutional discourse and gradations of constitutional meaning and authority.

I

Figure 5 seeks to account more fully for these types of intersections among competing conceptions of constitutional structures. Like the figures in chapter 4, the new figure aspires to represent schematically, in summary fashion, complex dimensions of American constitutionalism that are examined throughout this book. For analytic purposes, deliberate simplification is necessary.

The figure shows two sets of structural premises, designated "unitary" and "pluralistic."[2] Each model has six components that complement one another. The corresponding positions from the two models are arrayed in oppositional pairs, with polar positions near the perimeter of a circle.

---

[2] I use the terms *unitary*, *pluralistic*, and *nationalistic* for the descriptive purposes explained in the text and not to suggest linkages between my analysis and theories of state unification (as in Europe), studies of American interest group pluralism, debates about the

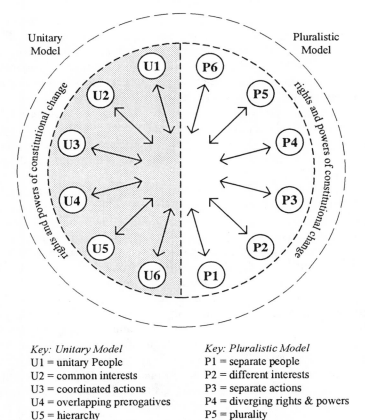

Fig. 5. Dimensions of the Constitutional Order

Key: Unitary Model
U1 = unitary People
U2 = common interests
U3 = coordinated actions
U4 = overlapping prerogatives
U5 = hierarchy
U6 = downplaying of
       participatory citizenship

Key: Pluralistic Model
P1 = separate people
P2 = different interests
P3 = separate actions
P4 = diverging rights & powers
P5 = plurality
P6 = virtues of active,
       critical citizenship

The surrounding rights and powers of constitutional change may be conceived as vehicles for amending parts of the existing order and as bridges to more fundamental constitutional re-formation.[3]

---

roles of ethnic groups in American political culture, or other specialized usages of these terms.

[3] Since the figure attempts to portray multiple dimensions using two, readers may find it helpful to conceive of the figure as portraying concentric three-dimensional spheres, not merely variations of a two-dimensional circle. Although an adequate metaphor to represent six dimensions of constitutional discourse (or seven, counting constitutional continuity and change) is lacking, the ideas of multifaceted crystals and architectural structures may be helpful in some respects.

The figure can accommodate analysis of the two primary forms of constitutional structures in the United States: national (or "federal") and state. In the first instance, the scheme represents the primary design of the United States Constitution. But since that Constitution incorporates states into its design, accounting for the entire constitutional order requires second-order analysis of features of state constitutionalism. The U.S. Constitution joins these issues by presuming the existence of states, guaranteeing their "republican" character, and placing limitations on their activities. Yet there remain good reasons to distinguish the main features of constitutional forms established and maintained at the macro and micro levels.

At the macro level, for example, the unitary model posits a consolidated, national people (or "the People"). Accordingly, when dealing with macro structures, I also refer to this model as "nationalistic." The pluralistic model, in contrast, posits separate people, with distinct constitutional identities. Moving to the micro level, those people may be conceived on a unitary model as joined into respective states; or according to a pluralistic model as having separate constitutional identities as individuals and members of various organizations.

Figure 5 does not presume that particular features of constitutionalism in the United States have been located near one boundary or another, at the macro or micro levels. Nor does the figure presume that the competing positions are mutually exclusive. Finally, for reasons just given, it does not presume that commitments at the macro and micro levels coincide. On the contrary, the scheme is designed to enable mapping of mixed or hybrid approaches in each of these respects.

For example, the third dimension deals with the legitimacy of coordinated or separate actions. Approaching this issue at the macro level, persons have emphasized national powers or realms of autonomous choice. But in many such contexts, individuals have not presumed that the Constitution has authorized *only* national power or affirmed *only* separate practices. More typically, controversy has centered on whether the Constitution has supported or undercut a particular assertion of national power. Disagreement on this issue has often reinforced rather than undercut an underlying premise that the Constitution has authorized some coordinated actions (for the whole) but not others, thereby precluding some but not all separate choices. Variations of such a position may be mapped on figure 5 at locations between U3 and P3.

Intermediate or mixed positions are likewise possible on the other dimensions. The figure can accommodate arguments, for example, that the Constitution both forms a unitary People for limited purposes and recognizes the separate constitutional identities of states, private associations, and individuals. One may conceive of the People as having common interests in some respects, divided interests in others. The Constitution arguably both provides for forms of coordinated action on behalf of the whole People and protects normative spheres within which parts of the whole may act separately. Representative structures are vehicles through which constituents may exercise and secure some of their reserved powers and retained rights through coordinated actions; these structures also presuppose the exercise of separately held rights and powers. Some constitutional norms are arranged hierarchically, others coordinately. The Constitution depends on some forms of active, critical citizenship and displaces others. Particular constitutional commitments reflect combinations and permutations of positions like these.

Issues of federalism and instrumental rationality make for interesting mixes. For example, Anti-Federalists emphasized the advantages of common interests and endorsed representative structures at the state level while criticizing federal structures in part because of the diversity of interests within the nation. Thus the Constitution's critics endorsed elements of a unitary model at the state level but repudiated corresponding features at the federal level. Madison, in contrast, argued ironically that the common welfare and rights of individuals would be more secure in a diverse republic than in smaller, more homogeneous polities. One may characterize his arguments as instrumentally pluralistic at the national level but as flowing from deep unitary commitments. Accordingly, it makes sense to allow for layers of commitments and asymmetrical as well as symmetrical positions at various levels.

Considered separately, the predominant features of each scheme are mutually reinforcing. At the national level, unitary premises regarding a single People complement premises of common (though perhaps dispersed) interests and other shared ends. On this model, it makes sense to conceive of constitutional structures as vehicles through which the People and their representatives may ascertain those interests and promote them through coordinated actions. Popular elections, conventions, and legislatures are examples of such structures. Depending on the characteristics of the People and the purposes for which they or their representatives seek to act, it makes sense to assign voting rules within a range including unanimity, super-majoritarianism, and simple-majoritarianism. Parts of the U.S. Constitution reflect variations of each.

According to unitary schemes, moreover, governmental powers and the People's rights and powers are largely complementary and overlapping. Public officials act on behalf of the People to secure shared rights, common interests, collective goods, and the like. But despite general complementarity among the basic elements of the constitutional order, some hierarchical structures are appropriate to preclude assertions of separate interests from interfering with actions by or on behalf of the whole. For similar reasons, there may be good reasons to minimize opportunities for widespread political participation by the People at large (particularly in a *national* scheme). Nevertheless, a primary objective is coordinated action, which may be incompatible with some forms of pluralistic decision-making. (On the other hand, some forms of popular political activity may be necessary to promote or maintain favorable public opinion.)

Pluralistic approaches at the national level, in contrast, emphasize the distinct identities of states, other associations, and individuals who compose the polity. According to this model, the states and their respective citizens have diverging interests, making coordinated actions at the national level difficult and inappropriate (at least in most instances). These premises support arguments that constitutional structures should guard separate actions, conceived as assertions of distinct constitutional rights and powers. A basic objective is to protect conditions under which pluralistic decision-making is possible.

Pluralists may be willing, however, to endorse some mechanisms for coordinated action. This model can recognize the possible benefits, for example, of economies of scale. Yet the primary objective of macro structures, for those committed to pluralistic decision-making, is to secure separate rather than collective ends.

Thus pluralists are likely to oppose assertions of national power that promote some constituents' interests at the expense of others'—which is an acute possibility if one presumes that members of the polity have radically diverging interests. According to this scheme, most governmental powers and residual prerogatives are arrayed across normative boundaries and are exercised in a zero-sum manner. Expansions of collective power entail narrowing of autonomous choice, and vice versa.

If one assumes from a pluralistic perspective that desirable constitutional structures are in place (probably as a result of some sort of compromise among contending parties), it makes sense to construct obstacles to changing those structures. More generally, those committed to protecting spheres of autonomous choice have reasons to oppose expansion of national power and corresponding diminution of retained or reserved prerogatives. In this respect, limits on formally amending the constitutional text have central importance: super-majoritarian or unanimity voting requirements, possibilities of popular conventions, and the like. But barriers to formally amending the constitutional text may be insufficient. Parceling out political power, providing for legislative vetoes, and similar devices may play mutually reinforcing roles in making it more difficult for representatives to exceed the bounds of their authority and encroach on realms of autonomous choice. Instead of entrusting constitutional interpretive authority to a particular representative institution (especially unelected judges), it makes sense on this scheme to favor dispersal of such authority.

An active, critical citizenry and autonomous institutions of state government may also play important roles within a pluralistic regime. Among other things, the people at large and state officials representing them may reinforce limits on centralized power. Precisely because their interests diverge in many respects, the people of the states have good reasons to unite in guarding their respective zones of autonomy. But even when they cannot unite for that purpose, the Constitution affirms separately held prerogatives. Their vitality may well depend in part on independent exercises of state governmental power and pluralistic forms of popular political activity which oppose impermissible assertions of national power.

II

These models are useful for summarizing the precedents examined throughout this book and for exploring intersections among competing interpretive approaches. Several such precedents deal primarily with macro structures. Others provide contexts for highlighting intersections among macro and micro versions of the unitary and pluralistic models.

I have already suggested how these models facilitate comparing Federalist and Anti-Federalist positions. Most simply, the Federalists defended unitary structures at the national level, while Anti-Federalists expressed pluralistic commitments. But despite important differences among the competing positions, they also overlapped insofar as leading Anti-Federalists endorsed variations of a unitary model at the state level and prominent Federalists embraced many of the features of a pluralistic model even at the national level. These affinities may help to account for the eventual willingness of many Anti-Federalists to endorse constitutional forms, especially following the ratification of the Bill of Rights. The respective positions intersected, moreover, in ways that formed a Constitution able to accommodate variations of Federalist and Anti-Federalist *interpretive* frameworks.

Not surprisingly, they resurfaced following ratification. John Marshall, a prominent Federalist, predictably endorsed nationalistic arguments. He presumed the existence of a unitary People and emphasized common interests, the need for coordinated actions, the benefits of representative structures, and principles of legal hierarchy. But he, like those who opposed the establishment and functioning of a national bank, presumed that the Constitution also had significant pluralistic components. In

McCulloch, for example, he referred to spheres of state power and rights of individuals, suggesting that norms within each category were among residual prerogatives. In sum, he presumed that the constitutional order in the United States was partly unitary, partly pluralistic.

Stone likewise invoked forms of unitary, nationalistic reasoning in *Darby*. The Chief Justice upheld a national scheme of coordinated commercial regulation and treated the pertinent rights and powers as overlapping and mutually reinforcing. Congress, the president, federal courts, and other national officials acted in concert to reinforce state commercial powers and individual liberties. In this respect, *Darby* complemented *Parrish*, which in turn affirmed features of a unitary model at the state level. Yet Stone, like Marshall, did not deny that the Constitution also had substantial pluralistic components.

The Kentucky and Virginia Resolutions, in contrast, were predominantly pluralistic in emphasis. The various drafts presumed that "the people" were joined as members of states, not into a single national community. According to this scheme, the states remained sovereign even with respect to powers delegated to federal institutions. The resolutions of 1798 and 1799 emphasized separate prerogatives—of states and of individuals. The two state legislatures asserted interpretive powers which may be conceived as flowing from principles of sovereignty and/or as devices for protecting reserved powers more generally.

But Jefferson, in his draft of the Kentucky Resolutions, implied that the U.S. Constitution did not impose a pluralistic model on the states with respect to rights of political expression. On the contrary, he suggested that although Congress could not legitimately restrict the exercise of these rights, the states could. Madison, in contrast, implied in his defense of the Virginia Resolutions that a pluralistic model of political expression applied at the state level. Although he was not clear on the source of such a limitation, he presumed that institutions of state government could not legitimately abridge popular rights of speech or the press. Thus his arguments in this context reflect pluralistic commitments at the macro and micro levels.[4]

The majority opinion in *Hammer* is likewise pluralistic. The decision itself enforced limits on federal authority. In addition, as explained in chapter 7, Justice Day appears to have presumed that there were corre-

---

[4] Jefferson's position on this issue is summarized in ch. 8, esp. at n. 9 and in the accompanying text. Madison's position is articulated most fully in his "Report on the Virginia Resolutions," where he argued that rights of political expression were corollaries of principles of popular sovereignty, distinguished "American constitutions" from "the British government," and claimed that rights of free speech were uniformly protected at the state level. See *Papers of James Madison* 17:336–38. See also Moore, "Taking a Stand for Speech," 9 Mag. Hist. 19 (1995).

sponding limits on state powers. Although he articulated a sweeping conception of the states' police powers and thus endorsed features of a unitary model at the state level, the Court's decision reinforced *Lochner* in blocking a wide range of commercial regulation. *Hammer* and *Lochner* together reflect an overarching commitment to guarding realms of pluralistic economic decision-making.

The majority opinions in *Griswold* and *Roe* parallel *Lochner* insofar as they reflect commitments to guarding spheres of individual autonomy through judicial decision-making. None of these opinions relies explicitly on the idea of a unitary, nationalistic People. The opinions do, however, assert national judicial power and purport to guarantee a range of individual choices nationally. In addition, a majority of the justices in these cases presumed that federal judicial powers and rights of individual autonomy were mutually reinforcing but treated some governmental powers and private rights as potentially diverging. In sum, the judges endorsed forms of pluralistic decision-making at the individual level and denied opposing authority at the state level.

The dissenting opinions in these cases, by contrast, affirmed state autonomy and denied the validity of opposing assertions of national power, fitting squarely in these respects within a macro pluralistic model. Yet the dissenting judges repudiated full extension to the state level of pluralistic models of individual rights. On the contrary, the dissenters affirmed state authority to restrict economic, sexual, and reproductive choices.

Taney's opinion in *Dred Scott* and Curtis's dissent also reflect pluralistic commitments. Both affirmed state authority regarding slavery, and both presumed that federal judges had important roles to play in maintaining constitutional boundaries. Their approaches diverged insofar as Taney sought to reinforce the powers of slave states and rights of slave ownership, whereas Curtis sought to guard the autonomy of free states and the rights of some black persons. But despite these important differences, their approaches converged to affirm large measures of state autonomy regarding slavery or its abolition.

Frederick Douglass asserted forms of constitutional pluralism by exercising rights and powers of citizenship—including interpretive prerogatives—in opposition to official positions. But his overarching commitment was to abolishing slavery through national action. Thus he relied on pluralistic premises to support some forms of autonomy but not others: rights of blacks as citizens but not claims of property rights by slave owners or assertions of state power to maintain slavery. Competing with his pluralistic conception of interpretive authority, moreover, he advocated a unitary conception of "the people," emphasized collective goods, endorsed national representational structures, and treated federal powers as superior to those of the states. He was not the first or last constitutional interpreter to endorse a complex blend of pluralistic and unitary relational premises.

Those mapping constitutional politics in the United States should embrace these interpretive precedents—along with others that exemplify additional attributes of American constitutionalism—within a more general theory of constitutional structures. These precedents have been complementary in some respects but at odds in others. They have variously reinforced and eroded features of the normative terrain, moved with predominant currents and against them, promoted stability and brought about change. They call attention to recurring dimensions of the constitutional design and more ephemeral attributes. Together, they underscore the Constitution's rich texture.

Separately and through their intersections, moreover, these sources may be conceived as representing various dimensions of "the people" and their constitutional "rights" and "powers." Each demonstrates how the Constitution has channeled and reinforced choices by "the people" and those purporting to act on their behalf, thereby mediating a range of contributions to constitutional discourse. In each case, those presuming to be subject to constitutional authority may be understood as having authored or re-authorized constitutional norms, maintaining continuity and bringing about change. There are good reasons to regard these dynamic and interrelated features of American constitutionalism as configured into a whole constituting the identities and actions of "the people of the United States."

Yet the character of the whole, its relations to the parts, and the ways they intersect with norms and practices beyond the existing order, are open to dispute. These issues must remain radically open-ended if the concept of popular sovereignty is not to be entirely a fiction. For it to be made real in practice, those composing the polity must be capable of being authors of constitutional norms, not only subjects.

It matters a great deal, of course, what choices the people and their representatives make. One may evaluate particular decisions based on their consistency with historic attributes of American constitutionalism, other contemporaneous choices, moral standards such as those articulated in the preamble, and similar criteria. It would be good to move toward making these types of evaluations instead of perpetuating myths of constitutional determinacy or abandoning any pretense of constitutional restraint.

Postscript

AS THIS BOOK went to press, the Supreme Court invalidated an effort by the state of Arkansas to limit the terms of its representatives in Congress. Justice Stevens in his opinion for the majority and Justice Thomas in his dissent invoked "first principles" to support their respective positions. The case underscores the importance of rethinking issues of constitutional character and structure with reference to principles of popular sovereignty.

At a general election in 1992, the people of Arkansas approved an amendment to the state's constitution. Among other things, it made members of Congress ineligible for inclusion on an election ballot if they had served three or more terms in the House or two or more terms in the Senate. Twenty-three other states had adopted similar term limits for members of Congress.[1]

In arguing that such limits were unconstitutional, Justice Stevens relied heavily on nationalistic rhetoric. For example, he asserted that the Constitution "creates a uniform national body representing the interests of a single people." He argued, moreover, that "[i]n the National Government, representatives owe primary allegiance not to the people of a State, but to the people of the Nation." He claimed that "[a]llowing individual States to adopt their own qualifications for congressional service would be inconsistent with the Framers' vision of a uniform National Legislature representing the people of the United States." In addition, he criticized pluralistic arguments that the tenth amendment reserved such a power to the respective states. In his view, the Constitution could not have "reserved" to the states a power they did not have before the Constitution went into effect.[2]

Justice Thomas, in contrast, opposed nationalistic reasoning and presented an expansive conception of reserved powers. He argued that "[t]he ultimate source of the Constitution's authority is the consent of the people of each individual State, not the consent of the undifferentiated people of the Nation as a whole." He claimed that "[t]he Constitution simply does not recognize any mechanism for action by the undifferentiated people of the Nation." He relied on the tenth amendment and the idea of normative boundaries both to emphasize the limited scope of delegated powers and to reinforce claims of state autonomy (characterized as

---

[1] See *U.S. Term Limits, Inc. v. Thornton*, 115 S. Ct. 1842 (1995).
[2] See 115 S. Ct. at 1845, 1853–56, and 1864. See also ibid., at 1871 and passim.

falling within a "residuum of power"). Denying that members of Congress represent the people of the nation as a whole, he claimed that they represent "distinct entities." Stressing connections between the people of a state and their state legislators, he took a position that "the selection of the Representatives and Senators from each State has been left entirely to the people of that State or to their state legislature." The term limits at issue were, according to Thomas, "the act of the people of Arkansas, adopted at a direct election and inserted into the state constitution." In this connection, he presumed that a simple majority of the voters in a general election expressed the will of "the people" of the state.[3]

Stevens's and Thomas's opinions are remarkable examples of what I describe in the conclusion as "unitary" and "pluralistic" models of reasoning. The two opinions are at opposite poles on each of the six dimensions portrayed by figure 5. These relational premises are, moreover, on the surface of constitutional rhetoric, transparently supporting opposite interpretive conclusions.

There are problems with these opinions. Both contain questionable historical analysis. Each begs important theoretical issues. Neither takes advantage of alternative interpretive frameworks that reinforce the respective conclusions. But the thrust of this book is that neither falls outside the bounds of reasonable argumentation.

An article published by the New York Times immediately after the Court's decision suggested otherwise. Linda Greenhouse quoted Professor Paul Gewirtz of Yale Law School for the following proposition: "Some of what Justice Thomas thinks of as first principles were actually the first principles of those who opposed ratification of the Constitution." According to Greenhouse, "it is only a slight exaggeration to say that the dissent brought the Court a single vote shy of reinstalling the Articles of Confederation." She suggested, in short, that Thomas's dissent was outside the bounds of the existing constitutional order.[4]

Thomas did not, however, advocate a return to the scheme established by the Articles of Confederation. He did not repudiate national institutions like Congress, the presidency, and federal courts. He did not deny the authority of the constitutional text of 1787 and its formal amendment. Just the opposite, he asserted powers authorized by the existing Constitution and professed commitment to its maintenance.

At issue is a fundamental distinction between alternative constitutional orders and alternative conceptions of the existing order. Thomas—as with Stevens—expressed interpretive commitments that may well ap-

---

[3] Ibid., at 1875–82 and passim (Thomas, J., dissenting).

[4] Linda Greenhouse, "Focus on Federal Power: Split Over Term Limits Shows the Depth [of the] High Court's Division on 'First Principles,' " New York Times, May 24, 1995, at A1, col. 2, and A19, col. 4. I am indebted to William F. Harris II for calling to my attention this article and several issues it raises.

proach the margins of what the existing order can reasonably accommodate. But he did not repudiate the Constitution itself.

By relying on a pluralistic conception of "the people," emphasizing limits on federal authority and presenting an expansive conception of reserved powers, Thomas endorsed variations of Anti-Federalist *interpretive* commitments—not their arguments against original ratification of the Constitution. In this respect, he acted consistently with norms of constitutional decision-making that have embraced pluralistic along with unitary conceptions of constitutional structures. One of the primary objectives of this book has been to trace this mixed lineage and to oppose arguments that the Constitution is merely a Federalist creation.

In light of that mixed lineage, it is inappropriate to treat Thomas's opinion—any more than Stevens's—as out of bounds. Once the Court accepted jurisdiction, it was committed to ruling in favor of one party or the other and thus to deciding that the Arkansas provision limiting congressional terms was either valid or invalid. In addition, it makes sense to regard the Court's decision as authoritative for purposes of resolving the particular case and setting a precedent to constrain future deliberations. But there is no need to presume that the Constitution's meaning is properly reducible to the Court's decision or to confine oneself to dichotomous rhetoric in evaluating constitutional norms more generally.

The case is thus instructive on both dimensions of constitutional texture emphasized throughout this book. Constitutional norms are richly textured in the sense that they are capable of supporting a range of positions in contexts of political argumentation and analysis. In addition, they emerge from interpretive plurality, not univocality.

In dealing with constitutional issues surrounding term limits, it is necessary to account for voices in addition to those of the majority and dissenting justices in *Thornton*. The people of the states and those purporting to act on their behalf have made constitutionally authoritative decisions. Members of Congress and presidents have taken positions on the constitutional issues at stake. New federal or state legislation, judicial reconsideration, or constitutional amendments are conceivable. Important choices remain open to the people at large—as they vote, exercise rights of speech, and the like.

Constitutional norms involving structures of congressional representation have emerged from complex configurations of choices made by the people at large and governing officials. These choices will, of course, constrain future deliberations. Yet it would be a mistake to treat the constitutional issues surrounding term limits as now settled. The existing constitutional order allows room for further deliberation and debate on these issues and others raising profound questions of constitutional architectonics.

Index